AIDS, Women, and the Next Generation

AIDS, Women, and the Next Generation

Towards a Morally Acceptable Public Policy for HIV Testing of Pregnant Women and Newborns

Edited by

RUTH R. FADEN
School of Hygiene and Public Health
Johns Hopkins University

GAIL GELLER
School of Hygiene and Public Health
Johns Hopkins University

MADISON POWERS
Georgetown University

New York   Oxford
OXFORD UNIVERSITY PRESS
1991

Oxford University Press

Oxford   New York   Toronto
Delhi   Bombay   Calcutta   Madras   Karachi
Petaling Jaya   Singapore   Hong Kong   Tokyo
Nairobi   Dar es Salaam   Cape Town
Melbourne   Auckland

and associated companies in
Berlin   Ibadan

Published by Oxford University Press, Inc.,
200 Madison Avenue, New York, New York 10016

Oxford is a registered trademark of Oxford University Press

Library of Congress Cataloging-in-Publication Data
AIDS, women, and the next generation : towards a morally acceptable
public policy for HIV testing of pregnant women and newborns
edited by Ruth R. Faden, Gail Geller, Madison Powers.
p. cm.   Includes bibliographical references.
ISBN 0-19-506572-7
1. AIDS (Disease) in pregnancy—Diagnosis—Government policy—United States.
2. AIDS (Disease) in infants—Diagnosis—Government policy—United States.
I. Faden, Ruth R.   II. Geller, Gail.   III. Powers, Madison.
[DNLM: 1. Acquired Immunodeficiency Syndrome—diagnosis.
2. Acquired Immunodeficiency Syndrome—in pregnancy.
3. Health Policy—United States—legislation.
4. Infant, Newborn, Diseases—diagnosis.
5. Prenatal Diagnosis—United States—legislation.
WD 308 A28877]   RG580.A44A35   1991
362.1'969792'00973—dc20
DNLM/DLC   90-14328

9 8 7 6 5 4 3 2 1

Printed in the United States of America
on acid-free paper

To Our Mothers

PREFACE

Among the many tragic dimensions of the HIV epidemic as it moves into the 1990s is the growing number of infected women, infants, and children. Women now constitute approximately 10 percent of the AIDS cases thus far reported to the Center for Disease Control (CDC). Most of these women are of reproductive age. Although the number of women and children infected with HIV is unknown, the U.S. Public Health Service has projected approximately 3,000 cases of pediatric AIDS by the end of 1991. In most of these cases, infants will have acquired the infection through vertical transmission from their mothers.

As the public health impact of HIV infection in women and children has increased, so has interest in screening pregnant women and newborns for evidence of HIV infection. Currently, however, knowing that a pregnant woman is seropositive does not guarantee that her fetus is or will be affected. HIV testing of the newborn reveals only the presence or absence of maternal antibodies and thus establishes whether mothers are infected, not whether infants themselves are infected. It is currently estimated that in the United States about 30 percent of HIV-positive mothers transmit HIV to their newborn infants.

Whether among pregnant women or newborns, HIV infection disproportionately affects disadvantaged women and children of color, adding yet another layer of complexity to the policy problems surrounding screening. Currently, the CDC reports that the majority of clinical cases of AIDS in women occur in African-American (52 percent) and Hispanic (19 percent) women. The mode of transmission in most of these cases is intravenous drug use or sexual intercourse with an intravenous drug user.

Screening of pregnant women and newborns raises profound moral, legal, and policy issues. Whether there exists now, or ever will exist, compelling justification for state-mandated HIV screening of pregnant women or newborns remains one of the most controversial aspects of the policy problem. However, even if state-mandated screening is never instituted, many serious policy issues remain for the institutions and clinicians who provide prenatal and newborn care. These include whether HIV antibody testing should be added to the current panel of routine screening tests performed on most pregnant women and newborns without express informed consent, and whether HIV testing should be routinely performed on or offered to all women and infants, or only those who belong to high-risk groups.

This book provides a comprehensive analysis of the complex medical, public health, legal, ethical, and social issues raised by HIV screening and testing of pregnant women and newborns. We use the terms "screening" and "testing" advisedly here. "Screening" generally is reserved for the public health context in which interventions that can detect disease or the risk of disease are employed in populations, and "testing" generally denotes the use of such interventions with specific individuals in clinical encounters. In practice, this distinction often is hard to draw.

Authored by an interdisciplinary group of scholars in the fields of epidemiology, infectious disease, pediatrics, obstetrics, health policy, law, moral philosophy, and religious studies, the book analyzes alternative policy options for both the private and public sectors of health care, addressing head on the most controversial dimensions of the public policy problem. Plausible medical advances are anticipated in analyses of specific issues and policies. Programs of public policy are presented for the future, including, for example, the possibility that a prenatal intervention could prevent transmission of HIV infection to the fetus.

A grant from the American Foundation for AIDS Research (AmFAR) has made possible an unusual process for creating this edited volume of original contributions. All the contributors to this volume have been meeting as the Working Group since May 1988. Meetings have involved general discussion of HIV testing among pregnant women and newborns, debate about policy options, and the conducting of small, interdisciplinary "writing groups" for the purpose of critiquing chapter drafts.

The Working Group also conducted a pilot study of pregnant women's knowledge of and attitudes toward HIV antibody testing, and convened focus groups of pregnant women from an economically disadvantaged inner-city community. These focus groups provided a forum for Working Group members to discuss issues about HIV testing with women who would be among those most directly affected by a screening policy. Results of the pilot study and the focus groups were consistent in suggesting that the majority of women were eager to do what was best for their babies, would continue with their pregnancies even if there was a significant risk that their babies would die at an early age, and were quite ignorant about the limits of medical confidentiality and the social risks specific to HIV infection of breaching that confidentiality. That these women generally favored HIV testing in pregnancy is explained partly by these findings.

Finally, the Working Group presented earlier versions of its proposed policy at two public conferences and one invitational conference. Reactions from advocates for women of color, as well as from public health officials in city and state governments, were specifically sought.

The book provides a unique contribution to the debate about perinatal HIV screening and testing by focusing as much on pregnant women as on newborns. Throughout our discussions, we have attempted to pay equal attention to the interests of women and infants, and to recognize that in most cases these interests are aligned and not opposed. This perspective is apparent in many of the chapters and reflects several concerns.

First is the historical context in which the medical decisions of women, especially pregnant women, have been viewed. Women throughout the centuries have been counseled, persuaded, or compelled to refrain from various activities, submit to treatment regimens, and make sacrifices for the putative benefit of their babies. The medical decisions of pregnant women have been among the most likely to be determined and shaped by social and political interests lying beyond their own judgments of the best interests of themselves and their families.

It is our view that all too often public policy questions surrounding women's reproductive and child welfare decision making reflect an unjustifiable adversarial framing of the relationship between women and their fetuses and children. As Jay Katz has observed, many supposed maternal–child conflicts actually are conflicts between the mother and others who presume to be better able to judge what course of action is in the infant's best interest. As we argue in Chapter 14, we think that a defensible public policy should be guided by a presumption that women will act responsibly to protect and promote the best interests of their children. We believe that a public health policy of screening pregnant women and newborns should reflect this reality, not the exceptional case where the identity of interests between mother and infant breaks down.

Second, in part because of this history of societal willingness to interfere with maternal decision making, we are concerned about the development of public health policies that view women primarily as an instrument for the realization of the common good. The issue is not what can be done to women to reduce vertical transmission rates, but how women and their families can be provided with the information, medical services, and social resources necessary to make truly meaningful health-care decisions. Indeed, HIV infection among women and children highlights an important and tragic aspect of our nation's health care policy. Historically, the health-care needs of women and children, especially minority women and children, have been among the least well served in our country. As questions of access to health-care services dominate the 1990s, more and more attention must be given to the unmet needs of those who are largely left out of account in the design of the health-care delivery system. Although this volume does not speak directly to these larger issues of distributive justice and the allocation of health-care resources, the relevance of such questions becomes apparent to anyone who examines the circumstances of women who must make decisions for themselves and for their families without adequate social and economic resources to assist them.

Third, and finally, the discussion of HIV infection among women as well as children highlights the need for a greater appreciation of the moral relevance of differences in ethnicity, class, gender, and sexual practices in the formulation of public health policy. Although this project does *not* consider the situation for women and children outside the United States, where there may be substantial variation in the patterns of socioeconomic and prevalence distribution of HIV disease, it does pay close attention to the population of women and children most affected in this country.

This volume consists of 14 chapters. Chapter 1 serves as an introduction to the volume and provides it with a conceptual structure. In this chapter, Ruth Faden, Nancy Kass, and Madison Powers present a taxonomy of screening programs; describe public health, legal, and ethical frameworks for evaluating policy alternatives for HIV screening and testing; and put forward a conceptual analysis of various types of programs that far extends the traditional mandatory–voluntary dichotomy.

Chapters 2 through 13 are divided into three parts. Chapters 2 through 5 make up the part on public health and medical issues.

In Chapter 2, John Modlin and Alfred Saah highlight important gaps in epidemiologic and medical research on HIV infection in women and children in their discussion of the demographics and risk factors of HIV infection in these groups, anticipated sensitivity and specificity of HIV antibody testing among pregnant women and newborns, pathogenesis and natural history of perinatal transmission of HIV, and clinical management and manifestations of HIV-infected infants.

Chapter 3 puts the problem of HIV screening of pregnant women and newborns into historical perspective by reviewing the American experience with other screening programs in these populations. Although there are clear lessons to be learned from the past. Katherine Acuff and Ruth Faden argue that screening for HIV infection is relevantly different from all previous screening programs. Chapter 4 examines the medical implications of HIV infection during pregnancy. John Repke and Timothy Johnson conclude that, at least at present, pregnancy does not appear to have a significant impact on the course of HIV infection, and, with the exception of the risk of vertical transmission, HIV infection does not appear to adversely affect pregnancy outcomes. Chapter 5 analyzes the risks and benefits of HIV screening of pregnant women and newborns from a pediatric perspective. Nancy Hutton and Lawrence Wissow focus on the impact of screening on the child and his or her family, focusing on the complex social effects.

Legal issues arising from HIV screening of pregnant women and newborns are discussed in Chapters 6 to 9. In Chapter 6, Katherine Acuff examines whether

HIV screening can be implemented under existing legislation in each state and reviews current professional practice guidelines and hospital practices by which pregnant women and newborns are screened for other conditions. In Chapter 7, Anita Allen argues that state-mandated nonvoluntary HIV screening programs for pregnant women raise profound constitutional issues, and nonvoluntary screening programs implemented by private health care providers are subject to numerous legal challenges based on rights guaranteed by statute, common law, and state constitutions. In Chapter 8, Patricia King discusses a physician's legal obligations to discuss HIV testing with pregnant women and evaluates the legal liability of physicians for failure to advise a pregnant woman about her reproductive and personal health risks. In Chapter 9, Madison Powers examines existing and proposed laws for the protection against breaches of medical confidentiality and argues that the numerous exceptions to legal duties of confidentiality, the financial and emotional impediments to enforcement of those duties, and the lack of uniformity among the state laws underscore the need for more stringent confidentiality protections and comprehensive antidiscrimination laws.

Chapters 10 through 13 examine ethical and social issues. Chapter 10 focuses on HIV screening of newborns. Ruth Faden and Judith Areen consider both legal and ethical issues in arguing against a policy of mandatory newborn screening. In Chapter 11, LeRoy Walters presents a careful discussion of the ethical issues raised by prenatal HIV screening, including an examination of the complex question of fetal interests.

In Chapter 12, Gail Geller and Nancy Kass highlight the implications of various kinds of screening programs for obtaining valid informed consent, including the difficulty of decision making under conditions of uncertainty about fetal outcome and the potential for coercion and manipulation.

In Chapter 13, Nancy Kass describes the components of education and counseling appropriate for reproductive decision making after HIV testing and argues for nondirective counseling of HIV-positive women regarding abortion, delay of childbearing, and sterilization.

Chapter 14, which has been jointly written by all the contributors to this volume, presents a detailed, 10-point program of policy recommendations for both pregnant women and newborns. Potential objections to these recommendations are discussed and refuted. The volume concludes with our analysis of how these policy recommendations should change with advances in diagnostic technologies and medical management, including the prospect that in the future it will be possible to reduce or prevent vertical transmission by medical interventions during pregnancy.

Baltimore   R.R.F.
November 1990   G.G.
                                                                     M.P.

ACKNOWLEDGMENTS

This volume would not have been possible without assistance from various sources. We are indebted to the American Foundation for AIDS Research for its support of this project. We will be forever grateful to Frank Polk for his initial advice and support and his dedication to the field of AIDS research. Stephen Teret assisted us in conceptualizing the project and obtaining the support to make it possible.

The views presented have benefited considerably from constructive and critical comments by numerous colleagues. We are particularly grateful to Mark Barnes, Patrick Chaulk, Curtis Decker, Dazon Dixon, Iris Garcia, Sam Grosclose, George Halpin, Laura Hardesty, Lynne Mofenson, Audrey Rogers, Patricia Tyson, and Neil Williams for their comments on earlier versions of our policy proposal. We also thank the Forum on Bioethics of the American Public Health Association and Andrew Sorenson and the Hopkins AIDS Conference for the chance to present our views at their public meetings and benefit from the reactions of the audience. Robin Weiss and Leslie Hardy of the Institute of Medicine Committee on Prenatal and Neonatal HIV Screening welcomed us at their conference and provided us with the opportunity to assess our views against new information.

Those who participated in our interview study of pregnant women at the Hopkins obstetrics clinic also deserve special mention. Many thanks to Ginny Bradford, Andrea Gielen, Nancy Kass, Chris Lindquist, and Patricia O'Campo. The receptionists and nurses at the clinic were invaluable in identifying and helping us gain access to respondents. And, of course, the study and indeed this project never would have been possible without the women attending the clinic, who willingly and openly shared their beliefs and attitudes about HIV infection and HIV testing.

Superb assistance was provided through our university offices. We could not have done without our research assistants, Elizabeth Emmett and Wilhelmine Miller, and the excellent administrative support provided by Adria Carey, Moheba Hanif, Irene McDonald, and Gwen Thomas.

CONTENTS

CONTRIBUTORS

Katherine L. Acuff, J.D., M.P.H.
Program in Law, Ethics and Health
The Johns Hopkins University, School of Hygiene and Public Health
Baltimore, Maryland   21205

Anita L. Allen, J.D., Ph.D.
Georgetown University Law Center
Washington, D.C.   20001

Judith Areen, J.D.
Dean, Georgetown University Law Center
Washington, D.C.   20001

Ruth R. Faden, Ph.D., M.P.H.
Director, Program in Law, Ethics and Health
The Johns Hopkins University, School of Hygiene and Public Health
Baltimore, Maryland   21205
Kennedy Institute of Ethics,
Georgetown University
Washington, D.C.   20057

Gail Geller, Sc.D.
Program in Law, Ethics and Health
The Johns Hopkins University, School of Hygiene and Public Health
Baltimore, Maryland   21205

Nancy Hutton, M.D.
Department of Pediatrics
The Johns Hopkins University, School of Medicine
Baltimore, Maryland   21205

Timothy R. B. Johnson, M.D.
Director, Division of Maternal and Fetal Medicine
The Johns Hopkins University, School of Medicine
Baltimore, Maryland   21205

Nancy E. Kass, Sc.D.
Program in Law, Ethics and Health
The Johns Hopkins University, School of Hygiene and Public Health
Baltimore, Maryland   21205

Kennedy Institute of Ethics, Georgetown University
Washington, D.C.   20057

Patricia A. King, J.D.
Georgetown University Law Center
Washington, D.C.   20001

John Modlin, M.D.
Pediatric Infectious Disease and Pediatric AIDS Clinic
The Johns Hopkins University, School of Medicine
Baltimore, Maryland   21205

Madison Powers, J.D. D.Phil.
Department of Philosophy
Kennedy Institute of Ethics, Georgetown University
Washington, D.C.   20057

John T. Repke, M.D.
Medical Director of Obstetrics Clinic
The Johns Hopkins Hospital
Medical Director, Maternal and Infant Family Planning Project
The Johns Hopkins Hospital
Maternity Center East Medical Director
The Johns Hopkins Hospital Adolescent Program
Baltimore, Maryland   21205

Alfred Saah, M.D., M.P.H.
Director, Infectious Disease Program
The Johns Hopkins University, School of Hygiene and Public Health
Baltimore, Maryland   21205

LeRoy Walters, Ph.D.
Director, Center for Bioethics
Kennedy Institute of Ethics, Georgetown University
Washington, D.C.   20057

Lawrence S. Wissow, M.D., M.P.H.
Director, Child Advocacy Program
The Johns Hopkins University, School of Medicine
Baltimore, Maryland   21205

I

INTRODUCTION

1

Warrants for Screening Programs: Public Health, Legal, and Ethical Frameworks

RUTH R. FADEN, NANCY E. KASS, AND MADISON POWERS

The purpose of this chapter is to examine the legal, ethical, and public health warrants for compulsory and voluntary public health programs, thereby laying a common groundwork for the rest of the chapters. The chapter is divided into two parts. First, we examine the traditional distinction between compulsory and voluntary programs and argue for expanded distinctions concerning the levels of compulsoriness in public health programs. We then sketch the structure of the public health, legal, and ethical frameworks against which the justification for each of these types of programs can be evaluated.[1] Although examples will be drawn from many areas of public health and medicine, particular attention will be paid to programs of most direct relevance to screening and testing for the human immunodeficiency virus (HIV) among pregnant women and newborns.

Before proceeding with our analysis, however, it is necessary to lay out the scope of our inquiry. Conventionally, the phrase "public health program" is used to refer to a systematic, coordinated effort to achieve a specified public health goal for a defined community or population. Although voluntary agencies in the private sector do sponsor public health programs, such programs are most commonly mounted by government agencies, and it is with respect to programs initiated by government that issues of compulsoriness generally emerge. While in this volume we are concerned primarily with government-sponsored public health programs, we also consider certain health-related programs or policies of private institutions, such as workplaces, hospitals, and educational institutions. These programs often are similar to public programs in terms of the interventions used, although in certain instances they are created to serve different goals. An example of a relevant private sector practice is the policy of many industries requiring prospective employees to be screened for selected health conditions. We also are concerned with certain activities undertaken by individual clinicians that, although not under the authority of any institutional policies, are practiced so uniformly that they take on many dimensions of a program. Frequently in this chapter we use the term "program" to represent all these varied activities—

3

public health programs, institutional policies, and routinized professional practices. Where appropriate, the specific context and type of activity are identified.

Types of Screening Programs

When a screening program is designed, it is necessary to decide how participation in the program is to be determined. Conventionally, this decision is viewed as a choice between two options: participation in the program is to be either compulsory or voluntary.[2] Often, however, it is difficult to categorize programs simply as one or the other; some elements of the program make participation appear voluntary, while others seem to include some level of compulsion. As a step toward better organizing this issue for the purpose of analysis, we propose dividing programs into five, rather than two, categories: (1) completely mandatory programs; (2) conditionally mandatory programs; (3) "routine without notification" programs; (4) "routine with notification" programs; and (5) voluntary programs. It should be emphasized that these categories are not mutually exclusive or exhaustive. Some programs may contain elements of several categories, while others are difficult to classify even with the expanded number of categories. In addition, it should be emphasized that although for government programs these categories may approximate a continuum of legal compulsoriness, they do not necessarily represent a continuum either of autonomous choice on the part of participants or of protection of the public's health, issues to which we will return shortly.

The most stringent level of testing in terms of legal compulsoriness is a *completely mandatory* program, in which, typically, a government agency requires citizens to undergo an intervention, with sanctions imposed on those who do not comply. A historic example of a completely mandatory program is a vaccination program established during an epidemic of smallpox in Massachusetts at the beginning of this century:

> The Board of Health of a city or town if, in its opinion, it is necessary for the public health or safety shall require and enforce the vaccination and revaccination of all the inhabitants thereof and shall provide them with the means of free vaccination. Whoever, being over twenty-one years of age and not under guardianship, refuses or neglects to comply with such requirement shall forfeit five dollars.[3]

The compulsory nature of the program was challenged by a citizen who did not want to be vaccinated.[4] He, moreover, challenged the logic of the law based on its sanction, which merely provided a penalty for violation, in contrast to British vaccination laws of the nineteenth century, which permitted the state to use force to vaccinate citizens who refused to comply. The program was upheld by the courts, however, on the grounds that "under the pressure of great dangers," others must be protected; it was believed that the public health benefits of

vaccination could not be achieved unless the program was completely compulsory and (presumably) that fines constituted a sufficient sanction to ensure compliance.

Such a "preference for social control over individual autonomy" was characteristic of policies at the turn of the century.[5] Even at that time, however, medical
evidence still was necessary to support restrictive measures.

Chapter 3 reviews the history of prenatal and neonatal screening programs in
the United States, including several examples of completely mandatory programs. In 1938, for example, New York and Rhode Island enacted laws requiring
prenatal blood tests for syphilis for all pregnant women. Eventually, every other
state adopted comparable legislation.[6] More recently, certain states have enacted
newborn screening programs on a completely mandatory basis. In some states
the type of testing is specified, whereas in others the legislation provides the
broader directive of, for example, screening for "inborn errors of metabolism"
but specifies that the health department or a particular official will determine
which tests will be included. In five states, screening is mandatory, with no
exceptions.[7] In an additional 31 states, a screening test may be refused on
religious grounds only.[8] Examples of sanctions for violating the law include a
fine of "not less than twenty-five nor more than fifty dollars"[9] or being "guilty
of a misdemeanor."[10]

In a *conditionally mandatory* program, either government or an institution in
the private sector makes access to a designated service or opportunity contingent
on participating in the program. These could be rules either established by
government (such as having to be screened for syphilis in order to obtain a
marriage license, having to be screened for the antibody to HIV in order to join
the military, or having to undergo a vision test in order to apply for a driver's
license) or privately authorized (such as having to undergo a preemployment
physical examination in order to work for numerous industries or having to
undergo a general health screening for certain health or life insurance policies).
In each of these instances, the individual has the right not to participate in the
activities or services offered by the institution; however, if he or she wants access
to that institution, participation in the program is mandatory for eligibility. A
program is not conditionally mandatory, according to this definition, if it is
required only for those who fall within some classification, such as a demographic or risk group. Such programs are fully mandatory for a targeted or select group
of persons. For example, a program of screening only some newborns would be
targeted but fully mandatory; but a targeted program would be conditionally
mandatory if, for example, HIV testing was made a condition for further medical
treatment.

In a *routine without notification* program, the intervention is routinely and
automatically implemented unless an individual expressly asks that it not be
done. However, participants are not notified about the intervention or their right
to refuse. Thus as a practical matter, refusals rarely occur. (Typically, this is how

the prenatal panel of screening tests operates: a series of screening tests are conducted automatically for all pregnant women. Women usually are not told which tests are being done or informed that they do not have to undergo each test.) For example, 31 states have laws permitting parents to refuse on religious grounds testing of newborns for phenylketonuria (PKU) and related conditions. Seven states permit parents to refuse testing on any grounds.[11] However, in most instances, there is no obligation in law to inform parents about the testing and the conditions for refusal.

In a *routine with notification* program, participants are informed of the intervention and their right to refuse before the intervention is implemented. This approach has been proposed for newborn testing for PKU but rarely has been adopted.[12]

In a *voluntary* program, the intervention is not implemented without the authorization of participants. In some instances, written informed consent is solicited; in others, authorization or consent is considered to be implied in that participants must ask for or seek out the program. Current examples of voluntary screening programs are programs that screen for the antibody to HIV or those that offer mammograms for screening of breast cancer.

At first, it might appear that these five categories of programs—completely mandatory, conditionally mandatory, routine without notification, routine with notification, and voluntary—represent a rank ordering, with completely mandatory programs being the most restrictive and voluntary programs being the least restrictive in terms of their impact on autonomous choice. However, depending on the circumstances, conditionally mandatory programs can be as restrictive of choice as completely mandatory ones. The penalties imposed for failing to comply with some completely mandatory programs may be easier to resist than the consequences of forgoing a conditionally mandatory program. For example, in communities where jobs are scarce and needs are great, individuals may have no choice but to submit to preemployment testing. Similarly, routine programs that do not require prior notification may be equally restrictive of choice if the target individuals are unaware that the interventions are being implemented and thus have no opportunity to choose to refuse. Even routine programs with notification requirements and completely voluntary programs provide no guarantees that participation reflects autonomous choice. Questions of manipulation, understanding, and adequacy of information necessarily remain. Clearly, issues of compulsoriness understood narrowly in terms of legal mandates must be distinguished from the impact of a specific program on issues of choice. Any serious analysis of the legal and ethical acceptability of a program must examine not only its formal structure with respect to the presence or absence of legal or institutional sanctions or controls but also the context in which the program is to be conducted.

For many of the same reasons, these five categories cannot be taken as a rank ordering of programs with respect to their impact on the pubic's health. In many instances, conditionally mandatory and routine without notification programs may be as effective as or more effective than completely mandatory programs in achieving public health goals, at least in terms of the number of people successfully screened.

Also, as noted previously, programs sometimes contain elements of several categories. Combinations of elements often result in hybrid programs that are in some respects contradictory and may be difficult to characterize in terms of issues of choice. For example, childhood immunization programs are not performed without the signed, informed consent of parents. At the same time, however, proof of immunization must be provided in order to enroll in elementary school, and school attendance (with certain exceptions, such as home schooling) is compelled by law in all jurisdictions. How, then, would one classify a childhood immunization program in terms of level of compulsoriness?

Public Health Framework

Public health is concerned with the prevention and reduction of morbidity and mortality. At the core of a public health framework for evaluating screening programs is a single criterion—the program's harm-to-benefit ratio, where harms and benefits are understood in terms of impact on a community's morbidity and mortality.[13] Although not sufficient in itself, it is always necessary to use the public health framework in assessing the acceptability of a screening program. An acceptable ratio of benefits to harms is, at minimum, a threshold consideration, and, as we shall see, both the legal and ethical frameworks incorporate a public health assessment of harms and benefits in their analyses. No screening program can be justified either legally or morally without first satisfying public health criteria.

Specific criteria have been proposed for different types of public health programs that permit a more careful evaluation of harm-to-benefit considerations. For example, key criteria for determining whether to implement a vaccination program include the prevalence of the disease in the community, the costs of developing a vaccine and implementing a program, the efficacy and safety of the vaccine, and the morbidity and mortality associated with uncontrolled disease.[14]

Screening programs first were implemented in the late nineteenth century for the purpose of detecting contagious diseases in schoolchildren.[15] Screening of workers began in the early twentieth century. By the 1930s, insurance companies, public services, the military, and employers were involved in screening for disease.[16]

In contrast to other types of medical care, screening typically is not initiated by the individual patient. This distinction has prompted some health professionals to argue that there is an even greater responsibility to ensure that benefit will accrue to the patient in screening than in other medical interventions. For example, in 1971 Cochrane and Holland wrote:

> We believe there is an ethical difference between everyday medical practice and screening. If a patient asks a medical practitioner for help, the doctor does the best he can. He is not responsible for defects in medical knowledge. If, however, the practitioner initiates the screening procedures he is in a very different situation. He should, in our view, have conclusive evidence that screening can alter the natural history of disease in a significant proportion of those screened.[17]

Moreover, there is uniform agreement that screening is valuable only when it is part of a larger health program that includes, at minimum, treatment and follow-up for the condition detected by the screening.

Consistently, screening programs have as their goal the reduction of morbidity or mortality in either the general population or a specific population. Screening programs can be justified only if they effect a positive outcome that would not have occurred without the screening. Whitby has written that before implementing a screening program one must ask:

> Have suitably controlled investigations been carried out to show that the natural history of the disease is favorably influenced by the screening procedures, with their consequent possibility of early institution of treatment, as compared with allowing patients to present with the illness when symptoms demand attention?[18]

The degree to which a screening program can be successful in reducing morbidity and mortality depends on the prevalence of the condition in the population to be screened, the validity and reliability of the screening tool, the availability of a treatment or intervention for the condition, and the follow-up plans for those detected to be positive. Numerous authors have translated these considerations into more specific criteria.[19] Wilson and Jungner's framework is typical. They identify nine specific requirements for the establishment of a screening program:

1. The condition for which the screening is done should be an important health problem.
2. There should be an accepted treatment for patients detected.
3. Facilities for diagnosis and treatment should be available.
4. There should be a recognizable latent or early symptomatic stage so that detection can prove beneficial.
5. There should be a suitable screening test.
6. The test should be acceptable to the population.
7. The natural history of the condition should be adequately understood.
8. There should be agreement as to who will treat the patients.
9. The cost of case finding, diagnosis, and treatment should be economically balanced in relation to possible expenditure on medical care as a whole.

Chapters 2, 4, and 5 examine the extent to which HIV screening programs for pregnant women and newborns satisfy these criteria. Only after a given type of screening program has been thoroughly examined in terms of the degree to which it satisfies the public health criteria is it appropriate to examine the legal and ethical justifications for accepting or rejecting that program as a public policy choice.

Legal Framework

Elements of the legal system

Although public health criteria provide a threshold test for acceptability, screening programs also must conform to the requirements of the U.S. Constitution and, in many instances, to state constitutional, common law, and statutory provisions. Legislators framing new laws or judges deciding individual cases must balance other important interests, such as the civil liberties of persons to be tested, against public health goals.

The U.S. Constitution and the constitutions of individual states guarantee legal protection for a variety of individual interests. These include the following: protection against undue infringement of personal liberty; protection of the individual's right to privacy against the unwanted disclosure of sensitive personal information; protection of the right of privacy that guarantees the freedom to make certain medical decisions without undue interference in the physician–patient relationship; protections against unfair and discriminatory treatment under the law; and protection against unreasonable searches and seizures.

The acceptability of screening programs also must be tested against standards of professional conduct set forth in statutes and court decisions. For example, a well-developed body of judge-made law, or "common law," in each state sets forth criteria for defining medical malpractice and other legal duties and responsibilities of health care providers. Similarly, statutes enacted by the U.S. Congress and, more often, by state legislatures set forth requirements for maintaining patient confidentiality, obtaining informed consent for medical procedures, and regulating the practice of medicine and the delivery of health care.

Courts may have several occasions to evaluate the legality of screening programs. First, judges may be called upon to assess the legality of screening programs implemented by statute or administrative regulation adopted by a governmental body such as the U.S. Congress, a state legislature, a local council or city commission, or a department of government with legislative authority to promulgate rules and regulations. Legislation and administrative regulations adopted at all levels of government must conform to federal constitutional requirements; state and local ordinances or regulations, in addition, must conform to state constitutional provisions and, in some instances, to more comprehensive federal statutory and regulatory schemes.

Second, the screening practices of public hospitals, clinics, and other government-sponsored institutions may be subject to constitutional and other legal challenges even though the practices are not implemented pursuant to a specific statute or government regulation. If, for example, a publicly funded clinic for sexually transmitted diseases adopts screening practices that violate the constitutional rights of its patients, these practices may be subject to judicial scrutiny even though no specific law is being challenged. Health policies implemented by public agencies or other government-sponsored institutions without statutory mandate must comply with existing statutes and common law requirements as well.

Moreover, the conduct of private health care institutions may be subject to legal challenge, for example, when their practices violate laws protecting statutory or common law rights of informed consent and confidentiality. In addition, courts extend the application of certain constitutional duties to the actions of the private sector when the public and private spheres are sufficiently intertwined that private action may entail a significant degree of state action or involvement. Substantial financial or regulatory involvement by the government in the activities of private institutions may subject private institutions to constitutional duties and standards of conduct required of their counterparts in the public sector.[20]

For the most part, challenges to laws and regulations or to practices of the government or the private sector arise at the state level, and constitutional challenges arise primarily as a result of laws passed by the various states. The reason for the emphasis upon individual states is apparent. Although Congress has expanded the exercise of its power to enact legislation related to public health, the primary responsibility for the protection of the health, welfare, and safety of the public remains with the states. And indeed, the acquired immunodeficiency syndrome (AIDS) epidemic has precipitated a flood of state legislation designed to direct both private and public responses to the disease. In addition, most of the constitutional issues raised involve mandatory and conditionally mandatory screening programs because of their obvious potential for interference with constitutionally protected liberties. Hence, much of our focus is upon public health policy as reflected in state laws regulating both private and public health care institutions, even though many of the issues we discuss originate in policies adopted by public institutions without express statutory authorization or in policies adopted by private institutions.

Legislating health policy: constitutional challenges

Historically, courts have shown considerable reluctance to question the public health rationale for a variety of measures, including compulsory testing, vaccination, denial of access to public facilities such as schools and hospitals, and even isolation or quarantine.[21] In particular, they have been reluctant to second-guess the wisdom of public health officials or to substitute their own judgments for those of democratically elected legislators in striking the proper balance between public health and other interests. The historic trend has been to protect public health by compromising some individual civil liberties.

More recent developments in constitutional theory suggest that these older cases do not offer sufficient guidance for predicting how courts will rule on legislation specific to HIV infection and AIDS.[22] Constitutional developments of the past two decades have made the decisional process more sensitive to the importance of competing constitutionally protected interests. There is little agreement, however, even among members of the Supreme Court, regarding the degree of scrutiny that ought to be given to presumptively valid legislative purposes, the standards by which competing interests are to be weighed, and the extent to which the courts legitimately may interfere with legislative judgments regarding the appropriate means of realizing legitimate governmental objectives.[23] The upshot is that there is considerable uncertainty regarding the precedential value of cases decided during earlier periods of health crisis. Despite this general uncertainty, any substantially nonvoluntary screening program raises serious constitutional issues that must be resolved if such programs are to be found acceptable.

Constitutional issues in screening programs
We can conveniently divide the constitutional issues raised by the judicial review of screening programs into two categories: (1) objections to compulsory testing as an infringement of certain fundamental constitutionally protected liberties, and (2) objections based upon the identities of the persons tested or the composition of the group of persons singled out for testing.[24]

Cases that pose serious constitutional issues by virtue of the impact of compulsory testing on individual liberty include those that infringe upon the right to refuse treatment, which is protected by the rights of bodily integrity and privacy. For example, one kind of privacy right that might be affected by screening programs involving pregnant women is the right to protection from interference with the decision of whether or not to terminate a pregnancy. Constitutional issues of this sort are of special relevance when the screening programs involve a significant degree of nonvoluntariness. Screening programs that have a significant impact upon fundamental liberties must be narrowly tailored to meet the government's legitimate objectives without interfering unduly with the individual's constitutionally protected rights.

Cases in which objections are based upon either the identities of the persons or the composition of the group screened are of two kinds. In the first instance, targeted mandatory screening, resulting in different treatment for particular groups of persons, may raise a question of denial of the equal protection of the laws guaranteed by the Fourteenth Amendment. Targeted screening programs are legally problematic if the proposed classification affects interests that courts have declared to be fundamental or if such programs disproportionately affect members of a "suspect class"—that is, ones who already are subject to the devastating potential of invidious discrimination on the basis of arbitrary personal characteristics such as race.

A second objection is based upon the overinclusiveness of the group screened. It involves potential infringement of the right of protection against arbitrary searches and seizures guaranteed by the Fourth Amendment. These problems arise in the context of mass screening programs involving a significant degree of nonvoluntariness, including conditionally mandatory screening programs or programs that are routine without notice (and opportunity for refusal). Potential Fourth Amendment objections are based upon the claim that HIV screening without a particular suspicion or a special reason for testing a specific person may constitute an unreasonable search and seizure, which is constitutionally prohibited.

Summary of the legal framework

Government-sanctioned screening programs must first satisfy certain constitutional requirements. Targeted screening must avoid problems of denial of equal protection inherent in focusing upon particular groups for testing. In addition, mass, nonvoluntary screening without a particular basis for suspicion of infectiousness may run afoul of Fourth Amendment prohibitions against unreasonable searches and seizures. Moreover, the means to achieve otherwise acceptable governmental objectives must be narrowly tailored to avoid interference with the exercise of other important liberties, such as those subsumed under the right of privacy.

Even if screening programs meet all the relevant constitutional criteria (including any additional protections guaranteed by state constitutions), both public- and private-sector programs, without new statutory authority, may not comply with existing statutory and common law requirements concerning informed consent and confidentiality, statutory or common law duties to treat, and standards of professional negligence or malpractice. The need for conformity to existing legal requirements applies to programs that are voluntary or routine with notification, as well as to programs that are less voluntary in nature.

Ethical Framework

Just as the application of public health criteria may yield a recommendation that conflicts with legally recognized interests, there may be moral considerations that conflict with public health objectives. Public health interests may conflict with values other than those given attention within an existing legal framework.

As a consequence, interests based on moral considerations *not* protected by the laws also must be balanced against public health interests.

Central to this framework of ethical analysis is the notion that moral deliberation and justification ordinarily rest on principles, rules, and rights understood as abstract action guides.[25] These action guides, the choice and analysis of which are inherently controversial, together with questions of their relationship both to one another and to a theory of human virtues, constitute the heart of modern ethical theory.

Although it is neither possible nor necessary to outline a full ethical theory in this chapter, three moral principles relevant to our subject need to be addressed and briefly analyzed: beneficence, respect for autonomy, and justice. These broad principles, which provide the basis for most analyses in biomedical ethics, are sufficiently comprehensive to provide an analytic framework in which many moral problems surrounding policies of participation in public health programs may be understood and evaluated.

Beneficence

The principle most closely associated with the public health framework we have discussed is beneficence, which focuses upon considerations of human welfare or well-being. This principle asserts a duty to confer benefits and actively to prevent and remove harms, but equally important is the duty to balance possible benefits against possible harms of an action.[26] The benefit sought through public health measures is the welfare of the community. In clinical health care and in therapeutic research, the goal is the welfare of the individual patient. These welfare objectives provide the context and justification for both public health and medicine: in both instances, interventions are aimed at the promotion of health by the prevention, amelioration, or treatment of disease, clearly considered to be beneficial goals.

The principle of beneficence includes the following four elements, all linked through the common theme of promoting the welfare of others:

1. One ought not to inflict evil or harm.
2. One ought to prevent evil or harm.
3. One ought to remove evil or harm.
4. One ought to do or promote good.[27]

Many philosophers have held that the fourth element may not, strictly speaking, be a duty; and some have claimed that these elements should be hierarchically arranged so that the first takes precedence over the second, the second over the third, and the third over the fourth.

There is a definite appeal to this hierarchical ordering internal to the principle of beneficence. In particular, good philosophical reasons exist for separating passive nonmaleficence (a so-called negative duty to avoid doing harm, as expressed in element 1) and active beneficence (a so-called positive duty to afford assistance, as expressed in elements 2–4). Much of ordinary moral discourse and many philosophical systems suggest that the negative duty not to injure others is more compelling than the positive duty to benefit others.[28]

Despite the attractiveness of this hierarchical ordering rule, it is not firmly sanctioned by either morality or ethical theory. The duty expressed in element 1 may not *always* outweigh those expressed in elements 2–4. For example, the harm inflicted in element 1 may be negligible or trivial, while the harm to be prevented in element 2 may be substantial. For instance, preventing a person from contracting a deadly disease by vaccination often justifies the inflicted harms of being vaccinated. One of the motivations for separating the duties of nonmaleficence and beneficence is that they themselves conflict when one must *either* avoid harm *or* provide aid. In such cases, one needs a decision rule to prefer one alternative to another. But if the weights of the two principles can vary depending upon the circumstances, as they often do, there can be no mechanical decision rule asserting that one principle always must outweigh the other.

In concrete cases, the conceptual distinctions among elements 1–4 often break down. For example, when the state provides HIV antibody testing for citizens, it can be argued that the state not only is providing a benefit (element 4) but, at least in some cases, also is preventing and removing the harms of illness and death (elements 2 and 3). Similarly, to avoid running down a child playing in the street—that is, to refrain from doing harm (element 1)—requires positive steps of braking, turning, warning, and the like.[29]

Such problems lead us to unify the moral demands that we should benefit and not injure others under a single principle of beneficence, taking care to distinguish, as necessary, between strong and weak requirements of this principle. The strength of these requirements corresponds only in some cases to the ordering of elements 1–4. In its general form, then, the principle of beneficence requires us to abstain from intentionally injuring others and to further the important and legitimate interests of others, largely by preventing or removing possible harms.

There are several problems with the principle so understood. For example, to what extent does the principle require the benefactor to assume personal risk or to suffer harm? Although it is widely agreed that we are obligated to act beneficently only if we can do so with minimal personal risk or inconvenience, are there no circumstances or role relationships in which we are obligated to act beneficently even in the face of significant personal risk? The problem is especially vexing to the extent that the principle of beneficence includes element 4. The duty to promote good potentially demands severe sacrifice and extreme generosity in moral life—for example, giving a kidney for transplantation or donating bone marrow. Many have objected to making such acts matters of moral duty.[30] Nonetheless, are not parents morally bound to sacrifice time and financial resources for their children? And if so, are pregnant women and parents similarly morally bound to assume the risks associated with HIV testing if testing would benefit their children?

A related problem is determining in any given instance to whom duties of beneficence are owed. Whose interests count, and whose count the most? The principle of beneficence should not, as a *principle,* be restricted to single parties even in special contexts, such as the patient–physician or citizen–state relationship. Thus the principle itself leaves open the question of to whom one's beneficence should be directed. For example, in prenatal HIV screening programs, there may be duties of beneficence to numerous third parties (fetuses, future generations, other children, health care workers, sexual partners, etc.), even if the interests of pregnant women are the primary reason for the program. But third parties may not always have interests that should count or that should count as much.

Both the class of beneficiaries and the scope of acts required by the duty of beneficence are undecided issues, and perhaps undecidable ones. Fortunately, our arguments do not depend on their full resolution. That we are morally obligated on *some* occasions to assist others is hardly a matter of moral controversy. Beneficent acts are demanded by the roles involved in fiduciary relationships between parents and children, health care professionals and patients, public health officials and citizens, lawyers and clients, brokers and customers, and so on.

We will treat the basic roles and concepts that give substance to the principle of beneficence in public health and medicine as follows: the positive benefit that the health professional is obligated to seek is the alleviation of disease, disability, and injury if there is a reasonable hope of cure or improvement. The harms to be prevented, removed, or minimized are the pain, suffering, and disability of injury and disease. In addition, the health professional is enjoined from *doing* harm, such as when interventions inflict unnecessary pain and suffering. In public health, these duties of beneficence are owed to the community, although the interests of individuals as distinct from those of the community are morally relevant. For example, prenatal HIV screening programs have been defended on the ground that they will provide useful prevalence data.[31] Here the positive benefit sought by the public health program is new knowledge that is expected to contribute to the resolution of the AIDS epidemic. By contrast, in clinical medical care, duties of beneficence are owed first and foremost to the patient, although here again, wider community interests, as well as the interests of third parties, can count.

Those engaged in both public health and medical practice appreciate that risks of harm presented by interventions constantly must be weighted against possible benefits for patients, communities, or the public interest. The physician who professes to "do no harm" is not pledging never to cause harm but to strive to create a positive balance of benefits over inflicted harms. Such a balancing principle is essential to any sound moral system: beneficence assumes an obligation to weigh and balance benefits against harms, benefits against alternative benefits, and harms against alternative harms.

Public health officials, health care professionals, and lay persons often disagree over how to balance the various factors, and there may be no objective evidence that dictates one course rather than another. A classic example in public health is the swine flu immunization program, in which the official public health community's judgment of the relative risks and benefits of immunization differed sharply from that of the general public. In clinical contexts, this balancing of harms and benefits also can present situations in which health care professionals and patients differ in their assessments of the professional's obligations. For example, when a pregnant woman refuses a physician's recommendation of fetal surgery, she may be basing her decision on the benefit to a third person. Alternatively, the refusal may be exclusively self-regarding. At the same time, whereas some health care professionals will accept the patient's refusal as valid, others who believe that the patient will benefit from the medical intervention may seek to perform it without the consent of the patient.[32]

This problem of whether to override the decision of patients in order to benefit them or prevent harm to them is one dimension of the problem of medical paternalism, in which a parent-like decision by a professional overrides an autonomous decision of a patient. Of greater relevance to screening programs are the paternalistic justifications that may be found at the level of public policy, where programs are made mandatory on the belief that significant numbers of individuals who would benefit from the testing would refuse it if it were not required.

More typically, however, the dilemmas raised in the public policy area are less ones of balancing harms and benefits to the same individual, as is true in instances of medical paternalism, than they are of balancing harms to the individual with benefits to the *public*. Such is the classic dilemma raised by public health measures proposed in response to contagious diseases.

Respect for autonomy

Respect for autonomy is the moral principle most frequently mentioned in defense of voluntary screening programs. In this context, it is a principle deeply rooted in the liberal Western tradition emphasizing the importance of individual freedom and choice, both for political life and for personal development. Perhaps no single definition of autonomy can be given for all contexts in which the term is used;[33] nonetheless, we can appreciate its rough contours in the familiar claim that it is characteristic of persons and, indeed, seems to be a distinctively human ability, to value "choosing one's own course through life, making something out of it according to one's own lights,"[34] and "to be (part) author of one's own life."[35] In moral philosophy, personal autonomy has come to refer to personal self-governance: personal rule of the self by adequate understanding while remaining free from controlling interference by others and from personal limitations that prevent choice. "Autonomy," so understood, has been analyzed loosely in terms of external nonconstraint and the presence of critical internal capacities integral to self-governance.[36]

However, it is one thing to be autonomous and another to be *respected* as autonomous. The moral demand that we respect the autonomy of persons recognizes the importance of the principle that persons should be free to choose and act without controlling constraints imposed by others. The principle provides the justification for the right to make autonomous decisions. This, in turn, takes the form of specific autonomy-related rights and obligations, such as the right of patients to refuse medical interventions and the obligation of providers to solicit informed consent before implementing such interventions. Many criticisms of the moral acceptability of screening programs focus on their failure to respect autonomy, ranging from manipulative underdisclosure of pertinent information in voluntary programs to not permitting refusals of testing in completely mandatory programs. To respect an agent as autonomous is to recognize with due appreciation that person's capacities and perspective, including his or her right to hold certain views, to make certain choices, and to take certain actions based on personal values and beliefs. Such respect historically has been connected to the idea that persons possess an intrinsic value independent of special circumstances that confer value. As expressed in Kantian philosophy, autonomous persons are ends in themselves, capable of determining their own destiny, and are not to be treated merely as means to the ends of others.[37] The burden of moral justification, then, must rest on those who would restrict a person's exercise of autonomy.

Although the importance of the principle of respect for autonomy in moral life is well established, many issues about the proper scope and limits of the principle remain unsettled. Of particular relevance to policies for HIV antibody testing are questions concerning the restrictions society may rightfully place on autonomous choices when these choices conflict with other values. If choices might endanger the public health, potentially harm a fetus, or involve a scarce resource for which an individual cannot pay, it may be justifiable to disregard the obligation to respect autonomy and restrict the exercise of autonomy severely, perhaps by state intervention. If restriction is in order, the justification rests on a competing moral principle such as beneficence or justice. (This issue of *balancing* the demands of conflicting moral principles will be addressed later in this section.)

Many issues also surround the *scope* of the principle of respect for autonomy. A key issue here is whether the duty to respect the privacy of others is derived from the principle of respect for autonomy or from an independent principle. We take the view that a broad moral framework adequate for the analysis of participation in public health programs does not need to postulate a right to privacy in addition to a principle of respect for autonomy because the latter alone will suffice as a basic principle. This is not to suggest, however, that the *meaning* of "privacy" can be reduced to the meaning of "autonomy."[38] As we saw earlier in this chapter, the legal right to privacy also has roots in respect for autonomy, expressed in the law as respect for individual choice and self-determination.

For our purposes, one of the key issues concerning the principle of respect for autonomy is how to determine when an action is autonomous. This is particularly important for completely voluntary programs, where the goal is to have individuals make autonomous choices as to whether or not they wish to be tested. This is discussed in detail in Chapter 12.

Justice

Every civilized society is a cooperative venture structured by moral, legal, and cultural principles that define the terms of social cooperation. Beneficence and respect for autonomy are principles in this fabric of social order, and our discussion of these principles recognizes the possibility that these values may compete and that the circumstances of social cooperation may be such that not everything of value is capable of simultaneous realization. Principles of justice, however, view the competition of values from a somewhat different perspective. In the most general sense, a person has been treated in accordance with the principle of justice if treated according to what is fair, due, or owed. In many instances, questions of justice are questions about the proper distributions of benefits and burdens. In these cases, judgments of what is due, fair, or owed are essentially comparative. They are concerned with the comparative treatment of members of a group when benefit and burdens are distributed, when members cooperate or compete, or when we are concerned with claims of members against other members of the group independent of the claims that derive from duties of beneficence or duties to respect autonomy. For example, if equal political rights are due all citizens, then justice is done when those rights are accorded to all. Similarly, any denial of a good, service, or piece of information to which a person has a right or entitlement is an injustice. It is also an injustice to place an undue burden on the exercise of a right—for example, to make a piece of information owed to a person unreasonably difficult to obtain.

Many appeals to "justice" present a confused picture because they are not appeals to a *distinctive principle* of justice that is independent of other principles, such as beneficence or respect for autonomy. These appeals to "what is just" use the term "just" in a broad and nonspecific sense to refer to that which is generally *justified* or, in the circumstances, morally *right*. Claims of justice tend to emerge in literature on informed consent when it is believed that someone's legal or moral rights have been violated. Sometimes these claims also confuse conduct that is unjust with action that is unjustified. For example, completely mandatory programs can be denounced as *unjustly* denying individuals the right to decide for themselves whether they wish to be tested. Yet if the argument were to be developed, it would likely turn out that the controlling moral principle in such a judgment was less one of justice per se than an unjustified interference with or lack of respect for autonomy. (The argument, of course, could involve an appeal to both principles.)

Many complaints of "injustice" against public health programs can be linked to alleged violations of the principle of respect for autonomy or the principle of beneficence. However, in the context of public health programs, not all issues of justice can be accounted for entirely by appeal to other principles. Whether only high-risk pregnant women, in contrast to all pregnant women or all individuals, may be the target of HIV antibody screening programs is a classic example of a justice-based problem. This question turns on the just distribution of the burden of risks associated with responding to the AIDS epidemic and thus is *centrally* a problem about justice rather than beneficence or respect for autonomy. The issue is whether the disproportionate burden that would result from targeted screening (a consideration of justice) can be warranted, even if the public welfare is enhanced by the practice (a consideration of beneficence in the form of public utility) and even if high-risk women are capable of giving, and *do* give, voluntary informed consent (a consideration of autonomy). The point of many analyses of public interventions involving vulnerable persons is whether autonomous consent is sufficient to *override reservations based on justice* about targeting such persons for programs in the first place.

Balancing moral principles

Controversial problems about moral principles such as respect for autonomy, beneficence, and justice inevitably arise over how much these principles demand and how to handle situations of conflict among them. Whatever the prominence of these principles, we must acknowledge that if they conflict—as they do on occasion—a serious weighting or priority problem is created. Novels and dramas often depict these moral principles in their baldest forms of conflict: a person steals in order to preserve a life, lies in order to protect a sworn secret, or breaks a duty to keep confidentiality in order to protect a person endangered by its maintenance. Under such conditions, it must be decided which (if any) moral consideration has priority—a problem known in ethical theory as how to "weigh and balance moral principles."[39] Many problems about policies governing program participation take this form. Primarily they involve whether to override the obligation to respect the autonomy of individuals, as when programs are made completely mandatory.

W. D. Ross is one philosopher widely known for his attempt to handle this problem of conflict.[40] Ross provides a list of several valid moral principles, including principles similar to the three we have examined. According to him, we must determine the most stringent duty in *any* circumstance of conflict, while others have suggested that we determine which duty is most stringent by finding the "greatest balance" of right over wrong in each particular context. This metaphor of weights moving up and down on a balance scale is vivid but crude and potentially misleading. Ross sought to give as much precision to his ideas as possible through a fundamental distinction between *prima facie* duties and *actual* duties. "Prima facie duty" refers to a duty always to be acted upon unless it conflicts on a particular occasion with an equal or stronger duty. A prima facie duty is always right and binding, all other things being equal. Although a firm duty, it is conditional on not being overridden or outweighed by competing moral demands. One's actual duty, then, is determined by the balance of the respective weights of the competing prima facie duties.

Consider the following example: a 73-year-old man was mortally ill in a hospital and required a mechanical respirator. Although he had been judged competent, his request to have the respirator disconnected was refused. He then disconnected it himself, only to have the hospital staff reconnect it. The matter wound up in court.[41] The patient contended that the hospital and his physicians had an obligation to allow him to make his own choice, even though this choice entailed his death. His physicians and legal representatives of the state of Florida argued that they had a duty to preserve life and to prevent suicide. Here the duty to preserve life was in direct conflict with the duty to respect the autonomous decision of another person. Both were prima facie duties. A Florida court then had to decide the *actual* duty of the hospital and physicians. In a complicated balancing of the conflicting obligations, the court concluded that the patient's choice should be overriding because considerations of autonomy *here* (though not *everywhere*) were weightier. The court reasoned that "the cost to the individual" of refusing to recognize his choice in a circumstance of terminal illness could not be overridden by the duty to preserve life.

Partially as a result of Ross's arguments, moral philosophers have generally come to regard both duties and rights not as absolute trumps but as strong prima facie moral demands that may be validly overridden in circumstances where stringent opposing demands are presented by a competing moral principle.[42] To call lying prima facie wrong means that if an act involves lying it *is* wrong, *unless* some weightier moral consideration prevails in the circumstances. Moral principles and statements of rights thus have far greater moral importance than mere rules of thumb, which do not have the same force of standing obligations.

As Ross admits, neither he nor any other moral philosopher has been able to present a system of rules that is free of conflicts and exceptions. He argues that the nature of the moral life simply makes an exception-free hierarchy of rules and principles impossible. Contemporary moral philosophy has proved incapable of providing a solution to this problem of weighing and balancing that substantially improves on Ross's approach. The metaphor of "weight" has not proved amenable to precise analysis, and no one has claimed to be able to arrange all moral principles in a hierarchical order that avoids conflicts.

Ross's thesis also applies to circumstances in which a single principle directs us to two equally attractive alternatives, only one of which can be pursued. For example, the principle of beneficence, when applied to policies for program participation, could require both disclosure *and* nondisclosure of the risks of testing; both options could lead to equally *beneficial,* albeit *different,* outcomes. Whether the conflict is of this sort or between two different principles, there may not be a *single* right action in some circumstances, because two or more morally acceptable actions may be unavoidable in conflict and prove to be of equal weight in the circumstances.

In subsequent analyses, the principle of respect for autonomy often will emerge as the most important principle with regard to HIV antibody screening and testing of pregnant women. However, we assume throughout this volume that respect for autonomy is but a prima facie principle, and that it therefore has the same, *but only the same,* prima facie claim to override as other valid moral principles of comparable significance, such as beneficence or justice. Neither respect for autonomy nor any other moral principle has an absolute standing that allows it on every occasion to override conflicting moral claims. Our analysis presupposes, as an inherent feature of the moral life, a pluralism of moral principles, none of which outweighs the others in abstraction from particular circumstances or falls neatly into an exceptionless hierarchy.[43] Therefore, we hold that the moral principles of beneficence and justice (as well as role-specific responsibilities such as providing optimal professional care) can have sufficient weight under *some* conditions to override respect for autonomy.

The moral view underlying this claim is not meant to diminish the standing of autonomy. Autonomy gives us respect, moral entitlement, and protection against invasion by others. Few matters of morals could be more important. But we should step back and ask, as Daniel Callahan has put it, "what it would be like to live in a community for which autonomy was the central value . . . [and] sole goal."[44] There is a historical and cultural oddity about giving a standing of overriding importance to the autonomous individual. Moral communities—indeed, morality itself—is founded at least as much on the other principles we have mentioned, and usually in a context of strong commitment to the public welfare.

Callahan has argued that making autonomy *the* moral value rather than *a* moral value, having it outweigh every other moral value, buys autonomy at too high a price, and we would agree. However, we would be well advised not to depress the value of autonomy relative to that of the other principles in our framework. Autonomy, almost certainly, has been the most important value discovered in medical and research ethics in the past two decades. The pertinent point is that autonomy be neither overvalued nor undervalued, since both evaluations have presented serious problems.

This analysis of plural prima facie *duties* applies to *rights* as well. It often has been assumed, perhaps stemming from political statements about fundamental human rights, that certain rights are absolute trumps.[45] However, decisive arguments against this thesis can be mounted. For example, it is sometimes proclaimed that the right to life is absolute, irrespective of competing claims or social conditions. The dubious validity of this thesis is evidenced by common moral judgments allowing capital punishment, killing in war, and killing in self-defense. Many writers in ethics concur with the view of the nature of rights that argues that we have an *exercisable right* not to have our life taken only if there is not a *sufficient moral justification* to override the right. The right to life—like the right to make an autonomous decision, the right to give an informed consent, or a parent's right to decide for a child—is legitimately exercisable and creates actual duties on the part of others if and only if the right has an overriding status in the situation. Rights such as the right to informed consent, the right to die, and the right to lifesaving medical technology thus must compete with other rights in many situations, producing protracted controversy and a need to balance with great discretion the claims of competing rights.

Numerous authors in biomedical ethics believe that if a person is acting autonomously and is the bearer of an autonomy right, then his or her choices morally ought *never* to be overridden by considerations of beneficence. This is not our assumption. Although the burden of moral proof generally falls on those who seek to intervene in another's choice, as the need to protect persons from harm becomes more compelling and increases the "weight" of moral considerations of beneficence in these circumstances, it becomes more likely that these considerations will validly override the demand to respect autonomy. Similarly, because some autonomy rights are less significant than others, the demands to protect these rights are less weighty in the face of conflicting demands.

In the context of public health programs, the most widely accepted justification for failing to respect autonomy by making program participation mandatory is the "harm principle."[46] This principle argues that restrictions of autonomous action are justified if the exercise of such action would result in direct and imminent harm (or a reasonable risk of such harm) to the health or well-being of others. In effect, the harm principle evokes the first element of the principle of beneficence as justification for overriding obligations grounded in the principle of respect for autonomy. This direct harm argument has been the underpinning of the vast majority of mandatory public health policies, from the earliest compulsory immunization programs to current restrictions on smoking in public places.

Recently, a variant on the harm principle also has been invoked. Instead of requiring the prevention of direct harm to the health or well-being of others, it has been argued that harm to shared communal resources, often in the form of economic harm, may be sufficient to override the obligation to respect autonomy. This argument has loomed large in the motorcycle helmet law debate, where it has been argued that the financial costs to society from head trauma associated with motorcycle accident injuries, as well as costs in the form of utilization of emergency room resources, are sufficient cause to justify mandatory helmet laws.

As noted previously, paternalistic arguments also have been used to justify public health policies that fail to respect autonomous choice. Here again, the principle of beneficence is invoked, but in instances of paternalism the person who is to be benefitted is also the person whose autonomy is to be restricted.

We have stated that the principle of beneficence can be defended in terms of a duty to prevent direct harm to the health or well-being of others, to prevent harm to a community because of the effect on shared resources, or to prevent harm to the individual patient or subject involved in a clinical or research encounter. As we will see later in this volume, all three of these justifications for invoking the principle of beneficence can be used to argue in favor of completely mandatory prenatal and neonatal HIV antibody screening, although not necessarily persuasively. As noted earlier, issues of justice arise more with the question of who should be screened than with the question of whether programs should be completely mandatory. The only exception to this concerns what we have called "conditionally mandatory" programs. Questions of justice can arise if such programs identify particular classes of persons who then must assume burdens or forego benefits that others must not.

Conclusion

It must be remembered that the decision of whether to implement a screening program requires a balancing of the goals of the three frameworks described. In an important respect, the public health framework is the most fundamental. No screening program can be justified without satisfying at least some public health criteria, and, as has been noted, both the legal and ethical frameworks incorporate a public health interest into their analyses when defining harms and benefits.

It should be noted that in referring to a public health framework, a narrow definition of public health goals was used, based on the criteria enumerated earlier, rather than a broad definition that might also incorporate the goals of law and ethics. Although, for certain purposes, we endorse the broader definitions of public health, such as the World Health Organization (WHO) definition, the narrower conception draws a useful contrast that will serve important analytic goals in later chapters.

It is our belief that how completely the public health criteria must be satisfied depends on the degree to which the specific type of program proposed compromises other criteria. When a program poses a conflict between public health interests and other interests, greater fulfillment of the public health criteria is necessary in order to justify public health interests taking precedence. For this reason, analyses of the five types of programs must include the *degree* to which they satisfy public health criteria, understanding that the more programs challenge legal and ethical mandates, the greater will be the requirement that the public health criteria be satisfied.

Notes

1. Parts of the discussion of ethics are adapted liberally from Ruth R. Faden and Tom L. Beauchamp, *A History and Theory of Informed Consent* (New York: Oxford University Press, 1986), chap. 1.
2. See Ronald Bayer, Carol Levine, and Susan M. Wolf, "HIV Antibody Screening: An Ethical Framework for Evaluating Proposed Programs," *Journal of the American Medical Association* 256 (1986): 1768–1774, and James F. Childress, "An Ethical Framework for Assessing Policies to Screen for Antibodies to HIV," *AIDS and Public Policy* 2 (1987): 28–31.
3. Revised Laws of the Commonwealth of Massachusetts, ch. 75, sec. 137, cited in *Landmark Briefs and Arguments of the Supreme Court of the United States: Constitutional Law,* ed. Philip B. Kurland and Gerhard Casper (Arlington, Va.: University Publications of America, 1984), 15: 987.
4. *Jacobson v. Massachusetts,* 197 U.S. 11 (1905).
5. See Larry Gostin, "Traditional Public Health Strategies," in *AIDS and the Law: A Guide for the Public,* ed. Harlon Dalton and Scott Burris (New Haven, Conn.: Yale University Press, 1987), 47–65.
6. Allan M. Brandt, *No Magic Bullet: A Social History of Venereal Disease in the United States Since 1880* (New York: Oxford University Press, 1985), 149–150.
7. For a detailed description of existing state laws and statutes, see Chapter 6.
8. Lori B. Andrews, *State Laws and Regulations Governing Newborn Screening* (Chicago: American Bar Foundation, 1985), 1.
9. West Virginia Code, sec. 16-22-4 (1985).
10. Michigan Compiled Laws, sec. 333.5431 (1987).
11. Alaska, Arizona, Florida, Louisiana, Nevada, New Hampshire, and New Mexico. See Lori B. Andrews, *Legal Liability and Quality Assurance in Newborn Screening* (Chicago: American Bar Foundation, 1985), 4.
12. Ruth R. Faden, Neil A. Holtzman, and A. Judith Chwalow, "Parental Rights, Child Welfare, and Public Health: The Case for PKU Screening," *American Journal of Public Health* 72 (1982): 1396–1400.
13. This is not to say that costs are not relevant as well. Though the primary focus of a public health perspective is the reduction or prevention of morbidity and mortality, the overall benefits and harms themselves frequently are portrayed in monetary terms; in other instances, alternative public health programs are often compared on the basis of cost effectiveness.
14. See, for example, Institute of Medicine, *New Vaccine Development: Establishing Priorities* (Washington, D. C.: National Academy Press, 1985).

15. Stanley Joel Reiser, "The Emergence of the Concept of Screening for Disease," *Milbank Memorial Fund Quarterly* 56 (1978): 403–425.
16. Robert W. Buck, "The Physical Examination of Groups," *New England Journal of Medicine* 221 (1939): 883–887.
17. A. L. Cochrane and W. W. Holland, "Validation of Screening Procedures," *British Medical Bulletin* 27 (1971): 3–8.
18. L. G. Whitby, "Screening for Disease: Definitions and Criteria," *Lancet* (1974): 819.
19. J. M. G. Wilson and F. Jungner, "Principles and Practice of Screening for Disease," *Public Health Papers*, no. 34 (Geneva: WHO, 1968); W. W. Holland, "Screening for Disease: Taking Stock," *Lancet* 2 (1974): 1494–1497; Whitby, "Screening for Disease," Cochrane and Holland, "Validation of Screening Procedures."
20. See *Jackson* v. *Metropolitan Edison Co.*, 419 U.S. 345 (1974); *Moose Lodge No. 107* v. *Irvis*, 407 U.S. 163 (1972); and *Flagg Bros.* v. *Brooks*, 436 U.S. 149 (1978).
21. See Larry Gostin and William J. Curran, "Legal Control Measures for AIDS: Reporting Requirements, Surveillance, Quarantine, and Regulation of Public Meeting Places," *American Journal of Public Health* 77 (1987): 214, citing *Jacobson* v. *Massachusetts*, 197 U.S. 11, 28 (1905) (upheld mandatory smallpox vaccination, concluding that "a community has the right to protect itself against an epidemic or disease which threatens the safety of its members"); *Jew Ho* v. *Williamson*, 103 F. 10 (N.D. Cal. 1900) (upheld quarantine); *Buck* v. *Bell*, 274 U.S. 200 (1927) (upheld compulsory sterilization of mentally impaired women); and *Reynalds* v. *McNichols*, 448 F.2d 1378 (10th Cir. 1973) (upheld an ordinance requiring compulsory detention and examination of prostitutes for venereal disease).
22. For comments suggesting that recent developments in constitutional law reflect a substantial shift away from the previous deference shown to public health objectives and regulations, see, for example, Debra Jones Merritt, "Communicable Disease and Constitutional Law: Controlling AIDS," *New York University Law Review* 61 (1986): 739–799, and Gostin and Curran, "Legal Control Measures for AIDS."
23. See, for example, *Plyler* v. *Doe*, 457 U.S. 202, 216–218 (1982); *San Antonio Independent School District* v. *Rodriguez*, 411 U.S. 1 (1973); and R. Rotunda, J. Nowak, and J. Young, *Treatise on Constitutional Law* (St. Paul: West, 1986), 2: sec. 18.5
24. Citations to the relevant constitutional provisions and court decisions on which this discussion is based are found primarily in Chapter 7 of this volume.
25. The authors acknowledge that, in contemporary moral theory it is highly controversial whether morality is fundamentally a matter of rules or principles. Critics of the modern emphasis upon moral principles argue that this focus ignores important aspects of morality that do not reduce to a set of principles. They argue, for example, that the exercise of moral judgment may often be a matter of skill or good judgment in particular cases, rather than an ability to subsume all practical decisions under general rules or principles. Although at least one of the present authors agrees somewhat with this criticism, our position does not depend upon any particular resolution of this question at its most fundamental level. It is enough for our purposes to claim that a substantial part of moral deliberation, especially in the area of public choice and the development of public policy, does appropriately rely upon the appeal to general moral principles, even if these principles are viewed as no more than intermediate generalizations halfway between our judgments in particular cases and what we take to be the foundation of morality.
26. Tom L. Beauchamp and James F. Childress, *Principles of Bioethics*, 3rd ed. (New York: Oxford University Press, 1989), 148–149.

27. Ibid., 148.
28. For example, Philippa Foot, *Virtues and Vices* (Oxford: Basil Blackwell, 1978), 27–29.
29. See, for example, Bart Gruzalski, "Killing by Letting Die," *Mind* 90 (1981): 91–98.
30. Compare Marcus Singer, *Generalization in Ethics* (New York: Knopf, 1960), 186–189, and Peter Singer, *Practical Ethics* (Cambridge: Cambridge University Press, 1979), 168.
31. See, for example, K. Krasinski, W. Borkowsky, D. Bebenroth et al., "Failure of Voluntary Testing for HIV to Identify Infected Parturient Women in a High Risk Population," *New England Journal of Medicine* 318 (1988): 185.
32. Veronika E. B. Kolder, Janet Gallagher, and Michael T. Parsons, "Court-Ordered Obstetrical Interventions," *New England Journal of Medicine* 316 (1987): 1192–1196.
33. See, for example, Gerald Dworkin, *The Theory and Practice of Autonomy* (Cambridge: Cambridge University Press, 1988), 4–20.
34. James Griffin, *Well-Being: Its Meaning, Measurement, and Moral Importance* (Oxford: Oxford University Press, 1986), 67.
35. Joseph Raz, *The Morality of Freedom* (Oxford: Oxford University Press, 1986), 154–157, 368–373.
36. Of course, autonomy is a matter of degree; no one can expect to lead his or her life free from all external constraints. Nor must a workable conception of autonomy require an unlimited range of options. See, for example, Gerald Dworkin, "Is More Choice Better Than Less Choice?" in Dworkin, *Theory and Practice of Autonomy*, 62–81.
37. I. Kant, *Foundations of the Metaphysics of Morals*, trans. Lewis White Beck (Indianapolis: Liberal Arts Library, 1959), AK section 429.
38. For a discussion of the conceptual difficulties involved in understanding the notion of privacy, see Chapter 9 of this volume.
39. See Christopher Gowans, ed., *Moral Dilemmas* (New York: Oxford University Press, 1987).
40. W. D. Ross, "Prima Facie Duties," reprinted from his *The Right and the Good*, in Gowans, ed., *Moral Dilemmas*, 83–100.
41. *Satz v. Perlmutter*, 362 So. 2d 160 (Fl. Dis. Ct. App. 1978).
42. But see Alan Donagan, "Consistency in Rationalist Moral Systems," in Gowans, ed., *Moral Dilemmas*, 271–290.
43. Compare Thomas Nagel, who argues that it is absurd to think that there is a "single scale on which these apparently disparate considerations can be measured, added, and balanced" ("The Fragmentation of Value," in Nagel, *Mortal Questions* [Cambridge: Cambridge University Press, 1979], 131). See also Isaac Levi, *Hard Choices* (Cambridge: Cambridge University Press, 1986), 83–107.
44. Daniel Callahan, "Autonomy: A Moral Good, Not a Moral Obsession," *Hastings Center Report* 14 (1984): 40–42.
45. For example, Ronald Dworkin, "Rights as Trumps," in *Theories of Rights*, ed. Jeremy Waldron (Oxford: Oxford University Press, 1984). 153–167.
46. The classic expression of the harm principle appears in J. S. Mill's *On Liberty:* "That the only purpose for which power can be rightfully exercised over any member of a civilized community, against his will, is to prevent harm to others. His own good, either physical or moral, is not a sufficient warrant." Compare H. L. A. Hart, *Law, Liberty and Morality* (Oxford: Oxford University Press, 1963).

II

PUBLIC HEALTH AND MEDICAL ISSUES

2

Public Health and Clinical Aspects of HIV Infection and Disease in Women and Children in the United States

JOHN MODLIN AND ALFRED SAAH

In this chapter we describe the epidemiology and clinical features of HIV infection in women and children in the United States. The first part begins with a brief description of the present-day epidemic in women and children, including geographic and demographic distributions of infection and risk factors for infection. The second part describes various modes of serologic diagnosis of HIV infection in adults and infants. Considerable detail is provided because so much of any screening process rests on appropriate interpretation of a reliable test. The third part describes the clinical picture of HIV infection in women and its natural history in adults. The fourth part discusses the natural history and what little is known of the pathogenesis of HIV vertical transmission. The fifth and sixth parts discuss clinical disease and clinical management of HIV-infected infants. As in the second part, the discussion of clinical disease in the fifth part is extremely detailed and is provided for those involved in patient care. Some readers may wish to skip subsections of these parts. Chapter 5 provides some of the same information in less detail.

This chapter cites data from Johns Hopkins Hospital, many of which are unpublished. We have firm reason to believe that the data from our institution are comparable in most respects to data from other medical centers serving inner-city populations in communities with significant HIV infection in women and children.

Epidemiology of HIV Infection and AIDS in Women and Children

Morbidity data

As of September 1990, 152,126 cases of AIDS were reported to the Centers for Disease Control (CDC), including 3,854 cases in women and 2,627 cases in children under 13 years old.[1] These data are based on the clinical definition of AIDS devised for surveillance purposes by public health authorities.[2] This clinical definition has gone through several iterations with the development of

HIV-specific diagnostic assays and new data about the natural history of the disease. Currently, the same clinical definition is used for both women and men. The case definition for AIDS in young children is made more complex by the obligatory passive transfer of maternal antibodies to the newborn infant. Maternal antibodies may persist at detectable concentrations in the uninfected infant into the second year of life. The CDC has adopted 15 months as the maximum age at which maternal HIV antibody may be detected.[3] However, data from the European Collaborative Study suggest that maternal antibodies may persist in the uninfected infant until 18 months of age.[4]

In many jurisdictions, only AIDS cases are reportable to the local or state public health authority. Adults and children known to be infected with HIV are not reported unless they meet the surveillance definition for AIDS. It is currently estimated that 20 percent of HIV-infected adults have AIDS as defined by the CDC criteria. The number of identified HIV infections among children is estimated to be two to three times the number of AIDS cases.

Demographic data

HIV is now estimated to have infected between 1 million and 1.5 million persons in the United States.[5] The majority of cases are reported from New York, New Jersey, California, and Florida, but the incidence of AIDS is now rising rapidly in other areas, particularly urban areas where intravenous drug use is prevalent. In the Baltimore Standard Metropolitan Statistical Area (SMSA), there were approximately 1,744 reported AIDS cases as of September 28, 1990, including 261 (15 percent) who are women and 48 (3 percent) children who are less than 13 years of age.[6] We estimate that more than 90 percent of HIV-infected women and children in the Baltimore area are referred to either Johns Hopkins Hospital or the University of Maryland Hospital for either primary or specialty care. As of November 1, 1990, the Johns Hopkins experience included 20 children with AIDS (11 living), 31 others with symptomatic HIV infection, and 5 with asymptomatic HIV infection. In addition, the infection status of 30 infants remains indeterminant because of young age, and 74 children born to HIV-infected mothers have become antibody negative.

TABLE 2.1.   Estimated Number of HIV-
Exposed and HIV-Infected Children Born to
IVDU Women in Baltimore Annually

IVDU total (est.)	30,000
Women (25%)	7,500
HIV seropositive (25%)	1,875
Fertility (10%/year)	187
Elected abortions (20%)	37
Live births	150
HIV-infected infants (35%)	52

TABLE 2.2.   AIDS in Women by Risk Group and Race/Ethnicity
Through May 1990, United States

	White, Not Hispanic	Black, Not Hispanic	Hispanic
IVDU	1,084	2,932	1,000
Heterosexual contact	698	1,562	668
IVDU associated	357	892	561
Blood products and other	888	557	230
Total	2,670	5,051	1,898
Percent IVDU associated	54	76	82

The U.S. Public Health Service (USPHS) has projected that a total of 270,000 cases of AIDS will occur in the United States by the end of 1991, including 3,000 pediatric cases.[7] At Johns Hopkins, we have projected a cumulative incidence of 900 adult patients with AIDS and 100 children with symptomatic HIV infection during the same time period. These projections are based on both extrapolations from the USPHS figures and on estimates of the prevalence of intravenous drug use within the Baltimore SMSA (Table 2.1).

HIV infection in women and vertical transmission of HIV are primarily associated with intravenous drug use (IVDU).[8] Consequently, it primarily affects the disadvantaged and is concentrated in African-American and Hispanic populations. Both of these populations are overrepresented in the number of patients with AIDS when compared proportionally with their population size. Of the 12,607 women with AIDS in the United States reported through May 1990, 9,085 (72 percent) are African-American or Hispanic. Of those who are African-American or Hispanic, 76 percent and 82 percent, respectively, are associated with IVDU (Table 2.2). Vertically transmitted AIDS, predictably, has a similar pattern. Of 1,914 vertically acquired AIDS cases, 1,609 (84 percent) were African-American or Hispanic, and of these, 73 percent were IVDU associated. Sixty-nine percent of white children with vertically acquired AIDS were IVDU associated as well (Table 2.3).

TABLE 2.3.   Perinatally Acquired AIDS in Children (<13 Years Old) by Maternal Risk Group and Race/Ethnicity Through September 1989, United States

	White, Not Hispanic	African-American, Not Hispanic	Hispanic
Mother IVDU	104	453	211
Sex with IVDU	44	143	117
Other	68	294	56
Total	216	890	384
Percent IVDU associated	69	70	85

Diagnosis of HIV Infection[9]

The EIA screening test

The EIA (enzyme immunoassay) is the most widely used serologic test for antibodies to HIV in serum or plasma. It is used for clinical diagnosis, to screen blood and blood products,[10] for epidemiologic studies,[11] and to test individuals who believe that they may be infected with HIV.[12] As of May 1990, seven EIA assays from six manufacturers were licensed by the U.S. Food and Drug Administration (FDA) to screen blood products (Abbott Laboratories; Cellular Products, Inc.; ElectroNucleonics, Inc.; Genetic Systems; Organon Teknika, Inc.; and Ortho Diagnostic Systems, Inc.).

Like other serologic tests, the EIA indicates the occurrence of past infection. However, individuals with confirmed positive test results are presumed to be currently infected and capable of transmitting infection through blood or sexual contact. The EIA cannot predict which asymptomatic infected individuals will develop AIDS. There are indications that the EIA antibody level decreases as disease progresses,[13] but individual variation is too great to be useful for prognostic purposes.

The EIA uses disrupted virus grown in tissue culture. Each test kit has a somewhat different method of determining the threshold value above which a positive reaction is defined. This cutoff value for each kit has been selected to optimize its sensitivity and specificity.

The EIA is designed to be sensitive because its primary purpose has been to prevent contaminated blood from being used for transfusion.[14] In practice, the test sera are screened initially as single specimens. If the test result is positive, duplicate tests (two wells) are repeated from the same serum specimen. If one of the two tests is positive, the serum specimen is considered reactive by EIA; hence the term "repeatedly reactive" is often used in place of "positive." If both repeat tests are negative, the serum specimen is reported to be negative by EIA. Therefore, for an individual to be reactive by EIA, at least two of three tests with the same serum specimen should have reacted positively.

Since the test well also contains antigens from the cell lines (i.e., H9 or CEM) used to grow HIV and other reagents that may cause a nonspecific reaction, the EIA test result will appear to be positive with some truly negative sera.[15] Therefore, it is necessary to confirm all repeatedly reactive specimens using another, more virus-specific test, usually the Western blot (see below).

The prevalence of antibody-positive individuals in a given population determines the types of false results that are produced.[16] For instance, if the EIA identifies approximately 0.1 percent of donated blood as repeatedly reactive and the Western blot confirms HIV infection in 0.01 percent, or 1 per 10,000, then for every 10 million individuals in the general U.S. population who are screened, approximately 10,000 (0.1 percent) will be repeatedly reactive by EIA, but only 1,000 (0.01 percent) will be confirmed by Western blot. Therefore, in the general population where antibody prevalence is very low, a repeatedly reactive EIA has poor predictive value. However, in a high-risk population, where the prevalence of HIV infection is as high as 10 to 70 percent, a positive EIA is almost always confirmed by Western blot, thus giving a very high positive predictive value (Table 2.4); confirmation by Western blot is nonetheless necessary.

In pregnant women, the false-positive problem of screening in low-prevalence populations is compounded by the increased nonspecific reactivity in this population. Pregnant women become sensitized to human antigens and produce antibodies that react with antigens from cell lines used to cultivate HIV or, because of increased antibody "stickiness," to antigens of all types. Very little has been published on this topic in HIV testing, but it has been well recognized that pregnant or multiparous women often produce artifactual results in serologic assays. Such nonspecific reactivity adds to the burden of confirming repeatedly reactive enzyme-linked immunosorbent assay (ELISA) results and frequently results in indeterminate Western blot patterns. However, it is likely that such nondiagnostic test results in very-low-prevalence areas are, in fact, negative (see Chapter 14).

Second-generation EIA assays use synthetic or recombinant peptides instead of native virus as antigen to test for antibody. Many synthetic core and envelope antigens are being tested to identify HIV antibody-positive serums. Such research not only identifies potential antigens that may prove useful as diagnostic reagents, but also helps to identify the regions of the various antigens that appear most immunogenic.[17] The latter has great importance in the search for an effective vaccine.

TABLE 2.4. Positive Predictive Value When Screening in Low- or High-Prevalence Populations, Assuming 100% Sensitivity and 99.9% Specificity in a Population of 10 Million

Test Result	Infection	
	Present	Absent
Low-prevalence population (0.01%)		
Positive	1,000	9,000
Negative	0	9,990,000
Positive predictive value	1,000/10,000 = 10%	
High-prevalence population (10%)		
Positive	1,000,000	9,000
Negative	0	8,991,000
Positive predictive value	1,000,000/1,009,000 = 99%	

A recombinant HIV-1 envelop product (CBre3) manufactured by Cambridge BioSciences was licensed by the FDA in December 1988 as a rapid screening test. The test is a latex agglutination assay; it is licensed to screen blood donors when EIA testing is impractical or infeasible; reactivity in this assay requires confirmation before results are reported to the person being tested.

The Western blot

In the Western blot, the serologic test is performed with purified virus antigens that have been separated by electrophoresis. With this technique, one can deter-

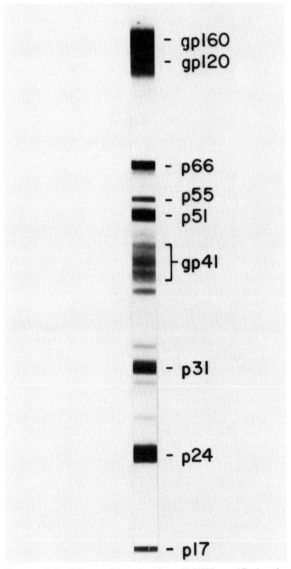

FIGURE 2.1   Western blot showing all HIV-specific bands.

TABLE 2.5. Criteria for Interpreting a Positive Western Blot

Name of Organization	Interpretive Criteria
FDA	p24 and p31 and either gp41 or gp120/gp160
American Red Cross	One band from each gene product: GAG—p17 or p24 or p55 POL—p31 or p51 or p66 ENV—gp41 or gp120/gp160
Consortium for Retrovirus Serology Standardization	p24 or p31 and either gp41 or gp120/gp160
CDC and Association of State and Territorial Public Health Laboratory Directors	Any two bands of p24, gp41, or gp120/gp160

mine whether the antibody that reacts in the EIA is specific for HIV antigens or whether it cross-reacts with nonviral components of the EIA system. The antigens in the Western blot are HIV proteins or glycoproteins of varying molecular weight. They are designated as "p" for protein and "gp" for glycoprotein, with a number that indicates their molecular weight in thousands of daltons (kd). Therefore, a band designated gp41 is a glycoprotein of molecular weight 41,000 daltons. The Western blot is usually interpreted with the naked eye. When bands are weakly reactive, the interpretation is highly subjective. The Western blots manufactured by Ortho Diagnostic Systems/Biotech Research Laboratories and Bio Rad are licensed by the FDA at this writing.

Figure 2.1 shows a Western blot with a characteristic positive band pattern. Like the EIA, the Western blot measures IgG antibodies. HIV has three structural genes that are called GAG for the core antigens (p17, p24, p55), POL for polymerase (p31, p51, p66), and ENV for envelope (gp41, gp120/gp160). Important bands include p24 (a core protein of the virus) and gp41, gp120, and gp160 (envelope glycoproteins of the virus). Most laboratories are unwilling to interpret a blot as positive if it does not demonstrate reactivity to at least two bands that include one or more envelope antigens. The diagnostic specificity of the Western blot may improve if reactivity to endonuclease (p31) or reverse transcriptase (p51, p66) is considered in defining a positive blot.

Attempts are being made to establish a national standard for Western blot interpretation.[18] A recent report published by the CDC[19] recommends that any two bands of the following three should be considered diagnostic: p24, gp41, or gp120/gp160. Other criteria exist that have varying degrees of sensitivity and specificity (Table 2.5). We prefer the criteria used by the American Red Cross, which make all virus-specific bands eligible for reading. In this way, Western blot preparations from a variety of sources can be used with less worry that particular bands react differently.

Reactivity to core antigens exclusively may represent early infection with HIV or another retrovirus, or may represent a poorly understood cross-reaction. Another serum specimen should be obtained from the patient in 4 to 6 months and the Western blot repeated. If the patient is truly infected with HIV, this interval should allow antienvelope antibody to become detectable. The Western blot should be interpreted cautiously; in equivocally reactive specimens, testing the uninfected cell line against the patient's serum may prove helpful but frequently fails to identify the source of nonspecific reactivity. The radioimmunoprecipitation assay may be helpful when the Western blot is equivocal. In general, however, when the Western blot band pattern does not progress over this time period in an individual with no risk behavior, the patient is highly likely to be uninfected with HIV-1.

The radioimmunoprecipitation assay (RIPA)

The RIPA is a research tool[20] that is expensive, requires radioisotopes and expertise for interpretation, and is labor intensive. The assay reacts serum with an HIV-infected cell lysate as substrate for immunoprecipitation and subsequent electrophoresis. The cell lysate is rich in relatively undenatured HIV envelope antigens and therefore is useful in defining antigenic differences among various human and simian immunodeficiency viruses.[21] The RIPA appears to be more sensitive than the Western blot for the higher molecular weight envelope antigens (gp120 and gp160).

The indirect immunofluorescence assay (IFA)

The IFA is an effective confirmatory test in experienced hands.[22] In fact, the California State Health Department Laboratory and other state health department laboratories are using the IFA as their confirmatory test. With this test, serum reacts with HIV-infected tissue culture cells. Antibodies to HIV attach to many sites within the infected cells, and the attached antibodies are detected with fluorescein-labeled goat antihuman globulin and read under a fluorescent microscope. Positive specimens are usually identified easily because of the bright fluorescence in a given proportion of cells. The IFA has not been widely used because of the high level of experience required for interpretation and the need for uninfected cells to absorb nonspecifically reactive serums. Refinements of the IFA also have been reported.[23]

Uses of serologic tests

Serologic testing for HIV is generally used for screening blood donors or for diagnosis. The use of these tests as a screening device for the blood supply requires notifying the person to be screened that the testing will be done and that if positive results are confirmed, counseling and medical referral will be provided.

When the purpose of serologic testing is diagnosis, the use and meaning of the EIA and Western blot tests should be discussed with the person considering the test during history taking and subsequent evaluation. The results of such testing should be a part of the patient's medical record, but confidentiality is important. In research protocols, confidentiality is doubly important because many subjects may be infected with HIV but are healthy and their participation in research may not benefit them directly. Although clinicians may wish to perform HIV testing under a coding scheme if anonymity is requested, such a scheme may produce devastating errors in a hospital laboratory setting where names and patient numbers are used. Such procedures ensure a higher degree of confidentiality but are more appropriate in an HIV counseling and testing site (formerly known as "alternate test sites") than in a hospital laboratory. A positive result gives the physician the responsibility to counsel the patient.

The HIV counseling and testing sites provided through state health departments allow interested persons to determine their serologic HIV status anonymously and without attempting to donate blood. At these sites, counseling is provided both before and after testing, regardless of the test result. Those going to a counseling and testing site either belong to a high-risk group or think that they may have been exposed. These individuals should be counseled on methods to reduce their risk of infection if they are seronegative, and those who test positive need to know the practical implications (see below).

In the clinical setting, an HIV-positive result is useful in that it may lead the physician to take an aggressive approach to the patient's infection and to include an AIDS-related condition in the differential diagnosis should the patient become ill. Individuals who are identified as positive also require careful counseling.[24]

Interpretation of test results

If the EIA is negative, a Western blot is usually not done. Blood from EIA-negative individuals who do not belong to any risk groups may be used for transfusion. Individuals from high-risk groups should be notified that a negative EIA test does not carry the same degree of confidence as in low-risk individuals because of the greater likelihood of pre-antibody infection in high-risk groups. If the EIA is repeatedly reactive and is confirmed by Western blot or IFA, then the individual is infected with HIV even if he or she lives in a low-prevalence community and claims to have no risk factors. If the Western blot and/or IFA is equivocal, infection status with HIV is unknown and the Western blot should be repeated on a new specimen obtained in 4 to 6 months.

If the serologic test results do not fit the clinical situation, repeating the EIA and the Western blot with a freshly obtained blood specimen is recommended. Furthermore, routinely repeating the testing procedure with a fresh blood specimen is recommended whenever seropositive individuals from low-prevalence populations are identified. Because of the reproductive issues at stake, including the possibility that a pregnant woman falsely identified as HIV positive may elect to terminate her pregnancy, we also recommend that prenatal screening programs routinely repeat the testing procedure, even in high-prevalence populations. This practice safeguards against laboratory and/or clerical errors that produce inaccurate results.

Diagnosis of HIV infection in infants

Because passively acquired maternal antibody may persist in the uninfected infant of an HIV-seropositive mother,[25] serologic tests are not considered diagnostic of HIV infection until the infant reaches 15 months of age. The diagnosis of HIV infection for younger HIV-seropositive infants generally depends on either the identification of an AIDS-defining illness or the presence of signs or symptoms suggestive of HIV infection.[26] To date, no laboratory test has proved to be both sensitive and specific for the diagnosis of HIV infection in this age group. A positive HIV culture or p24 antigen assay is diagnostic of infection, but these tests may be falsely negative, particularly for infected infants less than 6 months of age. In addition, HIV culture is extremely expensive to perform and is usually available only in selected research facilities. Another research technique, the polymerase chain reaction (PCR), has the potential to detect a single copy of the viral genome in virtually any specimen. Although extremely sensitive, PCR has not become widely applicable because of existing methodological problems.

Children with infection proven by HIV isolation or p24 antigenemia have had negative EIA tests with or without negative Western blot tests;[27] some of these children are asymptomatic.[28] As many as 10 percent of infants with HIV infection may be antibody negative.[29]

Natural History of HIV Infection in Women

As noted in Table 2.3, close to half the women with AIDS are IVDUs, and many others are sexual contacts of men with AIDS risk factors (mostly IVDU). The proportion of AIDS cases in women due to heterosexual transmission is thought to be increasing. The overall prevalence of HIV infection among women in the general population can only be roughly estimated from current data. Nationwide, the HIV seroprevalence rate in female military recruits is 0.04 percent, adjusted for age and race.[30]

It is estimated that 79 percent of women with AIDS in the Unites States are in the childbearing age range.[31] The prevalence of HIV infection among parturient women nationally is not known. Anonymous testing of newborn sera obtained during state-mandated neonatal screening in Massachusetts produced a statewide seroprevalence of 0.21 percent, but the distribution, as expected, was not uniform. Neonates delivered in inner-city hospitals had a seroprevalence rate of 0.80 percent compared with 0.09 percent among neonates born in suburban and rural hospitals.[32] In some hospitals in high-incidence areas such as New York City, Newark, and Baltimore, the prevalence among parturient women is as high as 3 to 5 percent.[33]

The efficiency of HIV transmission is greater for male-to-female sex than for female-to-male sex.[34] There is reason to believe that the prognosis is probably better for women who acquire HIV infection sexually than for women who acquire infection through IVDU, but this has not been documented.

Unfortunately, at this writing there are virtually no published, prospective data on the natural history of HIV infection in women or IVDUs. The best available data on the natural history of HIV infection in adults come from cohort studies of homosexual males[35] and of male hemophilia patients,[36] groups in which the risk of HIV infection is documented and the probable dates of exposure can be estimated. Current cross-sectional prevalence information indicates that 15–20 percent of seropositive homosexual men have AIDS, 40–50 percent have AIDS-related complex (ARC), and 30–50 percent remain asymptomatic.[37] In this population the risk of developing AIDS does not appear to diminish with time. Currently, the median time from infection to the development of AIDS in homosexual men is estimated to be 8–11 years[38] or longer.[39] Although the prevalence of AIDS and other symptomatic HIV infections is higher among HIV-seropositive homosexual men than among seropositive hemophilia patients, there is little difference in the risk of developing AIDS when the data are adjusted for duration of HIV infection.[40]

It seems that male IVDUs who develop an AIDS-defining illness have a median survival of 8–10 months. It is not known if the prognosis is different for female IVDUs, but it is suspected to be approximately the same for both sexes. Survival is brief when compared with that of homosexual men, which may be due to access to health care, health care–seeking behavior, or the known serious medical complications of nonsterile intravenous injections.

As with the natural history, the literature to date on the clinical management of HIV infection is necessarily based almost exclusively on reports involving male patients, most of whom contracted the infection through homosexual sex or blood transfusions. The current standard of care for HIV infection in adults has not been based on women because of the relatively small number of female cases in any one medical center and the complicating issues of intravenous drug addiction or underprivileged social status. Therefore, we are unable to review that subject here. However, a few issues of particular relevance to this volume deserve comment.

First, although in general it seems reasonable to assume that proper medical management for women with HIV infection is the same as proper medical management for men, it is likely that women with HIV infection will develop somewhat different manifestations or symptoms as the disease progresses. For example, some physicians are reporting abnormal gynecological symptoms in women who are HIV-positive, including cervical cancer, human papillomavirus infection, and pelvic inflammatory disease.[41] It is likely that as the clinical experience with HIV-infected women grows and more is learned about how HIV infection affects women, treatment regimens for women will be modified accordingly.

Second, it is currently a standard of care to recommend zidovudine (AZT) for HIV-infected adults with a CD4 cell count of 500 or less and prophylaxis for *Pneumocystis carinii* pneumonia (PCP) for persons whose CD4 cell count is 200 or less. In a 24-month follow-up study, zidovudine has been shown to delay the onset of symptoms in asymptomatic, HIV-infected individuals for about 6 months and to improve symptoms in those who already have them.[42] Data presented at the Sixth International Conference on AIDS suggest that the benefits of zidovudine early in the course of infection may be greater than previously expected.[43] Prophylaxis for PCP has been demonstrated to reduce the risk of this life-threatening illness. However, the effect of PCP prophylaxis on long-term survival relative to all the other improvements in diagnosis and treatment is unknown. As discussed in Chapter 4, despite the likely benefit to HIV-positive persons of both these interventions, their use in HIV-positive women who are pregnant is controversial.

The third issue is the relationship between pregnancy and HIV infection, a topic discussed in detail in Chapter 4. Although women at all stages of HIV infection have given birth to infected infants, in the United States most women have been asymptomatic at the time of delivery. There is no firm evidence that pregnancy adversely affects the natural history of HIV infection in women (see Chapter 4 for elaboration). Women who use drugs are more likely to give birth to low-birth-weight babies and more likely to suffer perinatal complications. A study from Montefiore Hospital in New York indicates that asymptomatic HIV infection confers no additional risk of adverse pregnancy outcome; that is, it has no effect on gestational age, birth weight, APGAR score, or perinatal complication rate.[44]

Pathophysiology and Natural History of Vertical HIV Transmission

Pathogenesis of vertical HIV transmission

Approximately 80 percent of reported AIDS cases in children (<13 years old) are transmitted before or during birth from mothers with known or suspected HIV infection. Now that the risk of HIV infection from transfused blood or blood products is extraordinarily low, it is probable that virtually all newly acquired pediatric HIV infections will occur via vertical transmission.

The mechanism and timing by which HIV is transmitted from an infected mother to her newborn infant are not well understood. There is evidence that some infants are infected in utero via transplacental passage of HIV early in gestation. HIV has been recovered in cell culture from the tissues of fetuses aborted between 12 and 20 weeks of gestation.[45] The virus has also been detected by in situ cDNA hybridization in the peripheral blood mononuclear cells (PBMC) of a 1-day-old infant,[46] as well as by polymeras chain reaction (PCR) in several infants within a few days of birth.[47]

The role of intrapartum (i.e., perinatal) transmission of HIV remains an important but mostly unexplored issue. The majority of infants of HIV-seropositive women escape infection in utero. It is entirely plausible, if not likely, that some of these infants are infected at the time of delivery as a result of contact with maternal blood or genital tract secretions. If the intrapartum route proves to be an important mechanism for vertically acquired HIV infection, it is possible that the postnatal natural history of HIV infection will be different for infants infected perinatally compared with infants infected in utero. New data indicate that maternal antibody to certain portions of the virus envelope may protect the neonate from infection.[48]

There are also implications for possible prevention of vertical HIV transmission or for altering the course of intrapartum acquired infection. It is possible that an antiviral agent such as zidovudine or soluble CD4, or HIV immune globulin administered to either the mother or the infant in the perinatal period, could prevent neonatal infection in the same way that intrapartum hepatitis B infection can be prevented.[49] Alternatively, antiviral therapy initiated at birth might favorably alter the natural history of HIV infection acquired at birth.

There are several reported cases of postnatal HIV infection in infants who appear to have acquired the infection via breast-feeding from their postnatally infected mothers.[50] HIV has been isolated from the breast milk of healthy seropositive women,[51] and a prospective French study suggested an increased risk of infection among breast-fed infants of seropositive women; however, the number of infants at risk was small.[52] In contrast, several large studies have not demonstrated an increased risk among infants born to HIV seropositive mothers who have been breast-fed.[53] The level of infectivity of breast milk has yet to be established. As noted above, one group has reported the successful culture of HIV from cell-free extracts of breast milk,[54] but other investigators have repeatedly failed to culture virus from breast milk samples obtained from seropositive mothers.[55] With the exception of breast-feeding, it is unlikely that infants are at risk of HIV infection from postnatal maternal exposure.

Natural history of vertically transmitted HIV infection

Prospectively obtained data from several sources suggest that the risk of infection among infants born to HIV-seropositive women in Western countries ranges from 7 to 33 percent.[56] These studies have all selected for prospective analysis infants born to seropositive women. The consensus of the larger studies indicates an overall vertical transmission rate of 30 percent. Some studies have included only offspring of women who were known to be seropositive during their pregnancies;

others have also included some infants identified as seropositive during the first 3 months of life because of the presumption that all such infants acquired their antibodies passively from an infected mother. These studies also have benefitted from more uniform application of explicit definitions of HIV infection in infants, such as those published by the CDC.

In some instances, analysis of the outcome was confined to those infants who were 15–18 months of age or older (an age at which the continuing presence of antibody is almost certainly a reflection of endogenous infection) or who had died earlier, meeting the clinical criteria for CDC-defined AIDS. In most of the cohorts examined, there continued to exist a group of patients whose infection status was indeterminate. These were infants who manifested symptoms and clinical signs compatible with HIV infection but who had seroreverted and lacked other virologic evidence of infection. In the French collaborative study, approximately 20 percent of the infants had died of their underlying disease by 1 year of age, and in the Zairian study the mortality rate among infants of seropositive mothers at 1 year was 21 percent compared with 3.8 percent in a matched group of controls.[57]

The great majority of pregnant women observed so far in developed countries either were asymptomatic or had only mild symptoms of HIV infection.[58] In Zaire, where many of the mothers have advanced disease, a vertical transmission rate of 73 percent was observed in one hospital.[59] Thus it is likely that the risk of vertical transmission will vary among different populations and that the clinical status of maternal HIV infection during gestation may be an important variable.

Other maternal factors that influence the risk of vertical transmission have not been clearly defined. Preliminary observations suggest that preterm delivery,[60] increased maternal age,[61] low maternal anti-gp120 antibody titer,[62] and elevated maternal serum IgA concentration[63] are each associated with an increased risk of neonatal infection. The presence of sexually transmitted infections (other than HIV) and the presence of chorioamnionitis are potential cofactors that are currently under study in several domestic and international studies.

The duration of the HIV epidemic has been too brief to allow accurate characterization of the natural history of vertically acquired infection. Early data from centers that have had large numbers of cases are illuminating,[64] but infants with the worst outcomes are likely to be overrepresented in these data bases because of the relatively short duration of observation. In December 1987, the nine pediatric centers participating in the initial Phase II zidovudine trial pooled information on the 250 untreated, HIV-infected infants collectively followed at the participating institutions. Even though these data are subject to the limitations noted above, this is the most reliable data base currently available because of the relatively large number of affected infants included in the analysis.

Virtually all HIV-infected infants appear normal at birth. However, 60 percent of prospectively followed infected infants will develop clinical signs of HIV infection within the first 12 months of life, and 75 percent will have symptoms by 2 years of age. The median age of presentation with clinical signs or symptoms is 9–10 months. However, the range is very wide; some infants present within the first 2 months of life, while others live for more than 7 years without symptoms.

By 18 months of age, 25 percent of the ACTG cohort of HIV-infected children developed an AIDS-defining illness, such as opportunistic infection, lymphoid interstitial pneumonia (LIP), recurrent bacterial infection, or neurologic disease. By 43 months of age, 50 percent experienced such an event. The median survival from onset of symptoms is about 28 months. Infants presenting with PCP or other opportunistic infections in the first year of life have a very poor prognosis, with a median survival of less than 6 months after diagnosis. There may be two different survival distribution curves for vertically acquired infection—one with early onset of symptoms in the first months of life and a poor prognosis, and a second with later onset and a natural history closer to that of adults with HIV infection.[65]

Clinical Manifestations of HIV-Infected Infants and Children

The CDC classification scheme is listed in Table 2.6. The major categories, P0, P1, and P2, refer to indeterminate infection, asymptomatic infection, and symptomatic infection, respectively.[66] The P0 category comprises those asymptomatic infants vertically exposed to HIV who remain seropositive at less than 15 months of age. As indicated above, approximately 30 percent of these infants are suspected of being infected. Because the annual incidence of HIV-seropositive

TABLE 2.6. CDC Classification of HIV-Infected Infants

P0   Indeterminate infection in perinatally exposed children with HIV antibody <15 months of age

P1   Asymptomatic infection
   A.   Normal immune function
   B.   Abnormal immune function
   C.   Immune function not tested

P2   Symptomatic infection
   A.   Nonspecific disease
   B.   Progressive neurologic disease
   C.   Lymphoid interstitial pneumonia (LIP)
   D.   Secondary infectious diseases
      D-1: opportunistic infections
      D-2: recurrent serious bacterial infections
      D-3: other infections (oral candidiasis >2 months, severe or recurrent herpes virus infections)
   E.   Secondary malignancies
   F.   Other HIV-related diseases (hepatitis, Cardiomyopathy, nephritis, hematologic Disease, rash)

deliveries is increasing rapidly, infants with a P0 status make up about one-third of the total population of HIV-infected and HIV-exposed children who are now followed at Johns Hopkins Hospital (Figure 2.2). P1 (asymptomatically infected) status is uncommon because most infants develop symptoms within the first 2 years of life. The few P1 infants identified by the Johns Hopkins Pediatric AIDS Service had HIV isolated from their blood during the first 6 months of life; all of these infants developed symptomatic disease within a few months.

The P2 (symptomatically infected) category contains several important subgroups (Table 2.6). About two-thirds of our current P2 clinical population belong to subgroup P2A. This classification generally corresponds to the clinical entity known as "AIDS-related complex (ARC)," but the P2A designation is generally replacing this older term in clinical parlance. Children with P2A disease have one or more nonspecific manifestations of HIV infection, including generalized adenopathy, growth failure, hepatomegaly, splenomegaly, persistent oral candidiasis, or recurrent infections of the middle ear, respiratory tract, or gastrointestinal tract (Table 2.7). Persistent salivary gland enlargement is a more specific manifestation of P2A HIV infection found in about 20 percent of patients. The remaining one-third of the children with symptomatic HIV infection have class P2B, P2C, or P2D disease. Unlike P2A disease, cases that meet the criteria for each of these classes are reportable as AIDS.

Children with neurologic manifestations of HIV infection who do not have opportunistic infections fit the P2B classification. While a static or progressive encephalopathy ultimately occurs in 30–60 percent of HIV-infected children,[67] isolated central nervous system (CNS) disease is relatively uncommon; that is, most children with neurologic involvement also have other serious manifestations of HIV infection. Reported CNS abnormalities include acquired microcephaly, loss of developmental milestones, intellectual deterioration, motor defi-

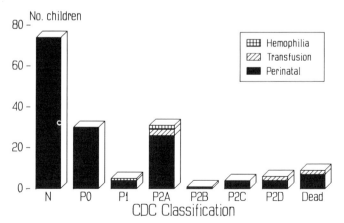

FIGURE 2.2   Clinical status of HIV-infected and HIV-exposed children at Johns Hopkins.

TABLE 2.7.   Early, Nonspecific
Manifestations of HIV Infection

Lymphadenopathy	90%
Hepatomegaly	86%
Splenomegaly	69%
Failure to thrive	62%
Oral candidiasis	48%
Recurrent or chronic otitis media	45%
Chronic diarrhea	17%

cits with weakness, pyramidal tract signs, spastic quadriparesis, dysphagia, dysarthria, ataxia, seizures, and myoclonus.[68]

Lymphocytic interstitial pneumonitis (LIP) is an AIDS-defining pulmonary complication that is unique to pediatric HIV infection. LIP in the absence of opportunistic infection is classified according to the CDC criteria as P2C disease. It is extremely common in HIV-infected children who survive the first year of life, occurring in at least half of such children.[69] LIP develops slowly and insidiously, with tachypnea, cough, and progressive hypoxia, but little or no fever. It is associated with other manifestations of HIV infection including generalized adenopathy, salivary gland enlargement, splenomegaly, clubbing, hypergammaglobulinemia, and increased lactic dehydrogenase enzyme concentrations.

The occurrence of opportunistic infections (CDC class P2D-1) reflects the most severe degree of underlying immunodeficiency and represents the most life-threatening events in HIV-infected children. The more common pathogens that cause opportunistic infections in HIV-infected children are listed in Table 2.8. PCP is the most common opportunistic infections and one of the most serious. It is seen most frequently in the first year of life, occasionally as the initial clinical

TABLE 2.8.   Opportunistic Infections in HIV-
Infected Infants

PCP	30–65%
LIP	40–50%
Disseminated cytomegalovirus infection	15–25%
Candida esophagitis	15–25%
Mycobacterium avium-intracellulare	5–10%
Disseminated cryptococcal infection	5–10%
Other	
Disseminated herpes simplex virus	
CNS toxoplasmosis	
Cryptosporidium enteritis	
Giardiasis	
Disseminated histoplasmosis	
Disseminated strongyloidosis	

manifestation of perinatal HIV infection. Even when successfully managed, the occurrence of PCP indicates a poor long-term prognosis.

While systemic and deep-seated bacterial infections may occur in normal children, particularly in those less than 2 years of age, recurrent bacterial infections are indicative of underlying immunodeficiency. HIV-infected children who develop more than one serious bacterial infection are classified as P2D-2. These infections are most often due to encapsulated organisms such as *Streptococcus pneumoniae* or *Hemophilus influenzae,* which cause bacteremia, meningitis, pneumonia, and other serious infections. Staphylococcal infections of the skin, malignant otitis externa, gram-negative pneumonia, and severe *Salmonella* infections are other bacterial infections that occur in HIV-infected children.

Measles and varicella are prominent among the other agents (P2D-3) associated with serious infections in pediatric AIDS patients. Like other children with deficiencies of cell-mediated immunity, HIV-infected children are at risk for severe, fatal measles virus infections.[70] HIV-infected children who are unvaccinated but exposed should receive immune serum globulin or intravenous immune globulin as prophylaxis, although the efficacy of these immunobiologicals is not known. Since live, attenuated measles vaccine virus does not represent an appreciable risk, it is recommended for all HIV-infected children regardless of the status of their underlying disease.[71] Viral pneumonia is the most threatening visceral complication of varicella, but encephalitis, myocarditis, hepatitis, and serious secondary bacterial infections may occur as well. Some reports indicate the presence of a unique, atypical form of varicella in HIV-infected children and adults consisting of persistent or recurrent lesions that are keratotic and non-vesicular.[72] Since the risk of varicella-zoster virus infection is considered to be substantial, the use of varicella-zoster immune globulin is indicated following exposure of an HIV-infected child to either varicella or zoster.

HIV-related malignancies (P2E) are considerably less common in children than in adults. A report from Newark suggests that B-cell lymphomas occur in as many as 3 percent of HIV-infected children.[73] These are principally CNS tumors, but they have also been seen in the gastrointestinal (GI) tract and liver. Kaposi's sarcoma, a common malignancy seen in homosexual males with AIDS, is rare in children; only two or three cases have been reported.[74]

In addition to opportunistic infections and neoplasms, HIV infection is associated with abnormalities in multiple organs including the brain, GI tract, heart, liver, and kidneys. GI and cardiac involvement have proven to be prominent and especially difficult to manage in our population at Johns Hopkins Hospital.

While opportunistic infections of the GI tract are common in adult AIDS patients, they are uncommon in children.[75] A nonspecific gastroenteritis has been much more common than documented infections in the GI tract. Persistent or intermittent diarrhea, gastroesophageal reflux, malabsorption, malnutrition, and growth failure have been the most troublesome features of this syndrome in

our patients and those of others.[76] Many children require various types of nutritional supplementation. The cause of the nonspecific gastroenteritis is not known, although many suspect that it is secondary to direct involvement of the GI tract with HIV. HIV has been detected in the GI tract by in situ hybridization in cells thought to be macrophages.[77]

Echocardiogram or electrocardiogram (ECG) abnormalities can be demonstrated in 30–64 percent of pediatric patients with HIV infection.[78] A smaller number manifest symptomatic heart disease, mostly acute or chronic congestive heart failure (CHF). The prevalence of clinical CHF was $7/38$ (18 percent) among children with P2 disease in one study.[79] A variety of arrhythmias are reported, and sudden deaths have also been observed.

Persistent hepatitis unrelated to cytomegalovirus or other opportunistic pathogens has been seen in 10 percent of HIV-infected children in Miami; it has been the presenting illness in some.[80] Renal disease is also seen in HIV-infected children, mostly among those with advanced underlying disease.[81]

Management of the HIV-Infected Child

A complete review of the management of the HIV-infected child is beyond the scope of this chapter. However, there are several unique or important aspects of management that are worthy of brief mention. Because these children usually come from extremely disadvantaged backgrounds, attention to housing, transportation, and basic child care and supervision often occupies an inordinate amount of the medical caregiver's time and effort. The provision of adequate nutrition to HIV-infected children, particularly those with advanced disease, is also challenging. We have found the services of both a social worker and a nutritionist to be invaluable.

Special attention is given to the routine immunizations received by HIV-infected children because they are considered to be at high risk from the vaccine-preventable diseases, because they may have a poor or absent immune response to certain vaccines, and because of the theoretical risk of adverse reactions from live virus vaccines such as oral polio and measles vaccines. Routine immunization with diphtheria-tetanus-pertussis (DTP) vaccine bears no increased risk of reactions to the vaccine, but the immune response to all three antigens varies inversely with the severity of the underlying immune deficit.[82] Because live, attenuated oral poliovirus vaccine (OPV) carries a theoretical risk of vaccine-associated paralytic disease, and because the vaccine virus may be transmitted to close contacts who may also be immunodeficient, use of the inactivated poliomyelitis vaccine is recommended.[83] In fact, OPV has been given to hundreds of truly infected or HIV-positive mothers, without evidence of neurologic disease in either recipients or contacts of vaccinees.[84] Similarly, live measles vaccine (usually given with mumps vaccine and rubella vaccine as trivalent MMR) has been administered to more than 300 HIV-infected children without incident.[85] Because these vaccine viruses are not communicable to contacts, and because the risk of severe disease with natural measles infection is high, MMR is highly recommended for all HIV-infected children regardless of the severity of their underlying disease. Because of the considerable risk of disease with encapsulated bacteria, both *H. influenzae* type B polysaccharide conjugate vaccine and pneumococcal vaccine are highly recommended for all HIV-infected children.[86] The only vaccine that is contraindicated in HIV infected persons is bacille Calmette Guérin (BCG). The World Health Organization recommends withholding BCG from infants and children with symptomatic HIV infection.[87]

The opportunistic infections that complicate HIV infection present a special diagnostic and therapeutic challenge to the clinician caring for children with AIDS. Because of the large number of patients affected, there is considerable experience with the diagnosis and treatment of the more common opportunistic infections in adults, such as PCP, Kaposi's sarcoma, cytomegalovirus infections, *M. avium-intracellulare* infections, cryptococcosis, and toxoplasmosis. The pediatric experience with each of these pathogens is limited, and our approach to the management of these infections is based on the clinical experience and controlled trials reported in adult patients.

On the basis of uncontrolled observations,[88] some physicians advocate prophylactic administration of intravenous immune globulin (IVIG) in a dose of 300 mg/kg every 2 weeks. It is claimed that IVIG controls unrestricted B-cell activation, improves the humoral antibody response to protein antigens, restores suppressor T-cell function, prevents recurrent bacterial infections, and prolongs survival. At Johns Hopkins, we have not embraced IVIG therapy because of its immense cost and uncertain benefit. We are awaiting the results of controlled pediatric trials of IVIG under way in Europe and the NIH ACTG.

Most pediatrics AIDS experts consider the future of therapy of human HIV infection to lie with a growing number of antiviral and immunomodulating agents. Zidovudine was the first promising drug to achieve widespread clinical testing in both adults and children, and this agent is now the only licensed anti-HIV drug available in the United States. Zidovudine is a specific inhibitor of the viral reverse transcriptase.[89] It is well absorbed orally and penetrates the cerebrospinal fluid. Controlled trials of oral zidovudine have demonstrated efficacy in adults with AIDS,[90] adults with mild to moderate symptoms of HIV infection, and asymptomatic adults with fewer than 500 CD4+ lymphocytes. Another nucleoside analogue, dideoxyinosine (ddI), is undergoing extensive clinical investigation in both adults and children. A variety of other drugs such as soluble CD4 and a variety of immunomodulating agents are in the early stages of investigation.[91] In addition, combinations of antiviral agents (i.e., zidovudine, ddI) and other types of drugs (interferon, soluble CD4) are under active investigation for in vitro synergy against HIV.[92]

Zidovudine has been the only antiretroviral agent to be extensively tested in HIV-infected children. Based on successful Phase I[93] and Phase II studies, zidovudine recently has been approved by the FDA for use in symptomatic, HIV-infected children older than 6 months. The pharmacokinetics of zidovudine in these children appear to be similar to those in adults.[94] The major side effects are anemia and leukopenia.[95] The efficacy of zidovudine has not been assessed in children in randomized, controlled clinical trials, but there is strong evidence of neurologic improvement in children given the drug by continuous infusion.[96] In our experience, children who have received oral zidovudine for long periods have improved growth, and appear to have fewer hospitalizations and serious infections.

Phase I studies to assess the pharmacokinetics and safety of zidovudine in newborn infants and in third-trimester pregnant women are now under way. Based on the results of these small studies, a placebo-controlled trial of prophylactic zidovudine beginning prior to birth is being initiated by the NIH ACTG to determine whether early administration will prevent vertical transmission of HIV infection.

Prevention

Efforts at active prevention of HIV infection have, naturally, focused on the development of vaccines. A number of candidate vaccine antigens have reached various stages of development (Table 2.9). Studies of these vaccines are now under way.[97] Recently published data indicate that a whole virus vaccine prepared from simian immunodeficiency virus (SIV) protects rhesus monkeys from a low-dose virus challenge. This information is encouraging because of the similarity between SIV disease in nonhuman primates and HIV disease in humans. If a safe, effective HIV vaccine were developed, then it would probably be

TABLE 2.9.   Candidate Vaccines

Type	Antigen	Source
Subunit	ENV	Virus
Recombinant	ENV	*Escherichia coli* Yeast Mammalian cells Insect cells
Viral vectors	ENV	Vaccinia Adenovirus Herpes simplex virus
Synthetic peptides	ENV Core	
Anti-idiotype	ENV	Monoclonal antibody
Inactivated	All	Whole virus

developed for universal administration to all infants early in life. However, discovery of such a vaccine is unlikely to occur in the near future.

Because more than 90 percent of vertically transmitted pediatric HIV infections are related to IVDU, any real hope of preventing childhood HIV infection in the near future must be based on efforts to reduce infection among women who are active IVDUs and their male sexual partners. It has been suggested that voluntary HIV testing, controlled free distribution of sterile needles, and methadone maintenance programs are the most appropriate and most effective vehicles for reaching IVDUs with educational messages and programs designed to alter their high-risk behavior. This may be the only effective approach to preventing HIV infection in future generations of children and stemming the tide of this terrible epidemic.

Notes

1. Centers for Disease Control (CDC), "HIV/AIDS Surveillance Report," October 1990.
2. CDC, "Revision of the Case Definition of Acquired Immunodeficiency Syndrome for National Reporting—United States," *Morbidity and Mortality Weekly Report* 34 (1985): 373–375.
3. In 1985, this definition was revised to include the presence of lymphocytic interstitial pneumonia (LIP), a clinicopathologic entity that was considered unique among children with AIDS. With the development of HIV-specific diagnostic assays, the pediatric criteria were revised again in September 1987. The current criteria include the occurrence of isolated LIP, neurologic disease, and more than one episode of bacterial sepsis as AIDS-defining conditions in the presence of HIV antibody, HIV antigen, or a positive HIV culture. Children with clinical evidence of the acquired immunodeficiency continue to be reportable regardless of the results of any specific HIV diagnostic tests (CDC, "Revision of the CDC Surveillance Case Definition for Acquired Immunodeficiency Syndrome," *Morbidity and Mortality Weekly Report* 36 [1987]: 1S–15S).
4. European Collaborative Study, "Mother-to-Child Transmission of HIV Infection," *Lancet* 2 (1988): 1039–1042.
5. Coolfont Planning Conference, "A Public Health Service Plan for the Prevention and Control of AIDS and the AIDS Virus," *Public Health Report* 101 (1986): 341–348.
6. Baltimore City Health Department, "AIDS Surveillance Report," September 28, 1990.
7. Coolfont Planning Conference, "Public Health Service Plan for Prevention and Control of AIDS and the AIDS Virus."
8. Mary E. Guinan and Ann Hardy, "Epidemiology of AIDS in Women in the United States: 1981 Through 1986," *Journal of the American Medical Association* 257 (1987): 2039–2042.
9. Alfred J. Saah, *Diagnosis of Human Immunodeficiency Virus (HIV) Infection.* Monographs for Physicians and Other Health Care Workers. Norbert Rapoza (Chicago: Council on Scientific Affairs, American Medical Association, 1989), pp. 127–134.
10. John C. Petricciani, "Licensed Tests for Antibody to Human T-Lymphotropic Virus

Type III: Sensitivity and Specificity," *Annals of Internal Medicine* 103 (1985): 726–729.

11. B. Frank Polk, Robin Fox, Ron Brookmeyer et al., "Predictors of the Acquired Immunodeficiency Syndrome Developing in a Cohort of Seropositive Homosexual Men," *New England Journal of Medicine* 316 (1987): 61–66; David K. Henderson, Alfred J. Saah, Barbara J. Zak et al., "Risk of Nosocomial Infection with Human T-Cell Lymphotropic Virus Type III/Lymphadenopathy-Associated Virus in a Large Cohort of Intensively Exposed Health Care Workers," *Annals of Internal Medicine* 104 (1986): 644–647; Eugene McCray, "Occupational Risk of the Acquired Immunodeficiency Syndrome Among Health Care Workers," *New England Journal of Medicine* 314 (1986): 1127–1132; CDC, "Human T-Lymphotrophic Virus Type III/Lymphoadenopathy-Associated Virus Antibody Prevalence in U.S. Military Recruit Applicants," *Morbidity and Mortality Weekly Report* 35 (1986): 1–78; Jerome E. Groopman, Francis W. Chen, James A. Hope et al., "Serological Characterization of HTLV-III Infection in AIDS and Related Disorders," *Journal of Infectious Diseases* 153 (1986): 736–737.

12. CDC, "Human T-Lymphotroic Virus Type III/Lymphadenopathy Associated Virus Antibody Testing at Alternate Sites," *Morbidity and Mortality Weekly Report* 35 (1986): 284–287.

13. Polk et al., "Predictors of the Acquired Immunodeficiency Syndrome"; Robert J. Biggar, Mads Melbye, Peter Ebbesen et al., "Variation in Human T Lymphotropic Virus III (HTLV-III) Antibodies in Homosexual Men: Decline Before Onset of Illness Related to Acquired Immune Deficiency Syndrome (AIDS)," *British Medical Journal* 291 (1985): 997–998; G. G. Frosner, V. Erfle, W. Mellest et al., "Diagnostic Significance of Quantitative Determination of HIV Antibody Specific for Envelope and Core Proteins" (letter), *Lancet* 1 (1987): 159–160.

14. Petricciani, "Licensed Tests for Antibody."

15. C. L. Mendenhall, G. A. Roselle, C. J. Grossman et al., "False Positive Tests for HTLV-III Antibodies in Alcoholic Patients with Hepatitis" (letter), *New England Journal of Medicine* 314 (1986): 921–922; P. Kuhl, S. Seidl, and G. Holzberger, "HLA Dr4 Antibodies Cause Positive HTLV-III Antibody ELISA Results," *Lancet* 1 (1985): 222–223.

16. B. E. Statland, P. Winkel, M. D. Burke et al., "Quantitative Approaches Used in Evaluating Laboratory Measurements and Other Clinical Data," in *Clinical Diagnosis and Management by Laboratory Methods,* 16th ed., ed. J. B. Henry (Philadelphia: Saunders, 1979), 529–530; Michael J. Barry, Albert G. Mulley, and Daniel E. Singer, "Screening for HTLV-III Antibodies: The Relation Between Prevalence and Positive Predictive Value and Its Social Consequences" (letter), *Journal of the American Medical Association* 253 (1985): 3395; James R. Carlson, Martin L. Bryant, Steven H. Hinrichs et al., "AIDS Serology Testing in Low and High-Risk Groups," *Journal of the American Medical Association* 253 (1985): 3405–3408.

17. S. D. Putney, T. J. Matthews, W. G. Robey et al., "HTLV-III/LAV: Neutralizing Antibodies to an *E. coli*-Produced Fragment of the Virus Envelope," *Science* 234 (1986): 1392–1395; D. S. Burke, B. L. Brandt, R. R. Redfield et al., "Diagnosis of Human Immunodeficiency Virus Infection by Immunoassay Using a Molecularly Cloned and Expressed Virus Envelope Polypeptide: Comparison to Western Blot on 2707 Consecutive Serum Samples," *Annals of Internal Medicine* 106 (1987): 671–676.

18. Consortium for Retrovirus Serology Standardization, "Serological Diagnosis of

Human Immunodeficiency Virus Infection by Western Blot Testing," *Journal of the American Medical Association* 260 (1988): 674–679; S. G. Sandler, R. Y. Dodd, and C. T. Fang, "Diagnostic Tests for HIV Infection: Serology," in *AIDS: Etiology, Treatment, and Prevention,* 2nd ed., ed. V. T. DeVita, S. Hellman, and S. A. Rosenberg (Philadelphia: Lippincott, 1988), 121–126.

19. CDC, "Interpretation and Use of the Western Blot Assay for Serodiagnosis of Human Immunodeficiency Virus Type 1 Infections," *Morbidity and Mortality Weekly Report* 38 (Suppl. 7) (1989): 1–7.

20. F. Barin, M. F. McLane, J. S. Allan et al., "Virus Envelope Protein of HTLV-III Represents Major Target Antigen for Antibodies in AIDS Patients," *Science* 22 (1985): 1094–1096.

21. P. J. Kanki, F. Barin, M. Souleyman et al., "New Human T-Lymphotropic Retrovirus Related to Simian T-Lymphotropic Virus Type III (STLV-IIIAGM)," *Science* 232 (1986): 238–243.

22. J. A. Levy and J. Shimabukuro, "Recovery of AIDS-Associated Retroviruses from Patients with AIDS or AIDS-Related Conditions and from Clinically Healthy Individuals," *Journal of Infectious Diseases* 152 (1985): 734–738; D. Gallo, J. L. Diggs, G. R. Shell et al., "Comparison of Detection of Antibody to the Acquired Immunodeficiency Syndrome Virus by Enzyme Immunoassay, Immunofluorescence and Western Blot Methods," *Journal of Clinical Microbiology* 23 (1986): 1049–1051.

23. R. S. Blumberg, E. G. Sandstrom, T. J. Paradis et al., "Detection of Human T-Cell Lymphotropic Virus Type III-Related Antigens and Anti-Human T-Cell Lymphotropic Virus Type III Antibodies by Anticomplementary Immunofluorescence," *Journal of Clinical Microbiology* 23 (1986): 1072–1077.

24. Institute of Medicine, National Academy of Sciences, *Confronting AIDS* (Washington, D.C.: National Academy Press, 1988); Coolfont Planning Conference, "Public Health Service Plan for the prevention and Control of AIDS and the AIDS Virus"; American Medical Association Council on Scientific Affairs: "Status Report on the Acquired Immunodeficiency Syndrome: Human T-Cell Lymphotropic Virus Type III Testing," *Journal of the American Medical Association* 254 (1985): 1342–1345; CDC, "Provisional Public Health Service Inter-Agency Recommendations for Screening Donated Blood and Plasma for Antibody to the Virus Causing Acquired Immunodeficiency Syndrome," *Morbidity and Mortality Weekly Report* 34 (1985): 1–5.

25. European Collaborative Study, "Mother-to-Child Transmission."

26. CDC, "Classification System for Human Immunodeficiency Virus (HIV) Infection in Children Under 13 Years of Age," *Morbidity and Mortality Weekly Report* 36 (1987): 225–235.

27. European Collaborative Study, "Mother-to-Child Transmission"; S. Pahwa, M. Kaplan, S. Fikrig et al., "Spectrum of Human T-Cell Lymphotropic Virus Type III Infection in Children: Recognition of Symptomatic, Asymptomatic, and Seronegative Patients," *Journal of the American Medical Association* 255 (1986): 2299–2305; K. Martin, B. Z. Katz, and G. Miller, "AIDS and Antibodies to Human Immunodeficiency Virus (HIV) in Children and Their Families," *Journal of Infectious Diseases* 155 (1987): 54–63; R. Pahwa, R. A. Good, and S. Pahwa, "Prematurity, Hypogammaglobulinemia, and Neuropathology with Human Immunodeficiency Virus (HIV) Infection," *Proceedings of the National Academy of Sciences of the United States of America* 84 (1987): 3826–3830; M. V. Ragni, A. H. Urbach, S. Taylor et al., "Isolation of Human Immunodeficiency Virus and Detection of HIV

DNA Sequences in the Brain of an ELISA Antibody-Negative Child with Acquired Immunodeficiency Syndrome and Progressive Encephalopathy," *Journal of Pediatrics* 110 (1987): 892–894; L. R. Krilov, N. Kamani, R. M. Hendry et al., "Longitudinal Serologic Evaluation of an Infant with Acquired Immunodeficiency Syndrome," *Pediatric Infectious Disease Journal* 6 (1987): 1066–1067; W. Borkowsky, K. Krasinski, D. Paul et al., "Human-Immunodeficiency-Virus Infections in Infants Negative for Anti-HIV by Enzyme-Linked Immunoassay," *Lancet* 1 (1987): 1168–1171; K. H. Pyu, H. D. Ochs, R. J. Wedgwood et al., "Seronegativity and Paediatric AIDS," *Lancet* 1 (1987): 1152–1153.

28. European Collaborative Study, "Mother-to-Child Transmission."

29. Borkowsky et al., "Human-Immunodeficiency-Virus Infections."

30. CDC, "Human Immunodeficiency Virus Infection in the United States: A Review of Current Knowledge," *Morbidity and Mortality Weekly Report* 36 (Suppl. S-6) (1987): 6–7.

31. Guinan and Hardy, "Epidemiology of AIDS."

32. Rodney Hoff, Victor P. Berardi, Barbara J. Weiblen et al., "Seroprevalence of Human Immunodeficiency Virus Among Childbearing Women," *New England Journal of Medicine* 318 (1988): 525–530.

33. CDC, "Quarterly Report to the Domestic Policy Council on the Prevalence and Rate of Spread of HIV and AIDS in the United States," *Morbidity and Mortality Weekly Report* 37 (1988): 223–226.

34. Guinan and Hardy, "Epidemiology of AIDS."

35. A. R. Lifson, G. W. Rutherford, and H. W. Jaffe, "The Natural History of Human Immunodeficiency Virus Infection," *Journal of Infectious Diseases* 158 (1988): 1360–1367; N. A. Hessol, G. W. Gutherford, A. R. Lifson et al., "The Natural History of HIV Infection in a Cohort of Homosexual and Bisexual Men: A Decade of Follow-Up" (presented at the Fourth International AIDS Conference, Stockholm, June 1988), A. Muñoz, M. C. Wang, S. Bass et al., "Estimation of the AIDS-Free Times After HIV-1 Seroconversion" (presented at the Fourth International AIDS Conference, Stockholm, June 1988); K.-J. Lui, W. W. Darrow, and G. W. Rutherford, "A Model-Based Estimate of the Mean Incubation Period for AIDS in Homosexual Men," *Science* 248 (1988): 1333–1335; G. F. Lemp, N. A. Hessol, G. W. Rutherford, et al., "Projections of AIDS Morbidity and Mortality in San Francisco Using Epidemic Models" (presented at the Fourth International AIDS Conference, Stockholm, June 1988); Janine Jason, Kung-Jong Lui, M. V. Ragni et al., "Risk of Developing AIDS in HIV-Infected Cohorts of Hemophilic and Homosexual Men," *Journal of the American Medical Association* 261 (1989): 725–781; A. Muñoz, personal communication.

36. Lifson et al., "Natural History"; Jason et al., "Risk of Developing AIDS."

37. Hessol et al., "Natural History"; Muñoz et al., "Estimation of the AIDS-Free Times"; Lui et al., "Model-Based Estimate."

38. Ibid.

39. A. Muñoz, personal communication.

40. Jason et al., "Risk of Developing AIDS."

41. This is taken from Margaret McCarthy, Women's Action Committee of the AIDS Coalition to Unleash Power, "Calls for HIV Antibody Testing in Women of Reproductive Age Ignore the Realities of Women's Lives" May, 1990.

42. Paul A. Volberding, Stephen W. Lagakos, Matthew A. Koch et al., "Zidovudine in Asymptomatic Human Immunodeficiency Virus Infection," *New England Journal of Medicine* 322 (1990): 941–949.

43. Margaret Fischl, "Controversies in Early Therapy of HIV Disease" (presented at the Sixth International Conference on AIDS, San Francisco, June 21, 1990).
44. Peter A. Selwyn, Ellie E. Schoenbaum, Katherine Davenny et al., "Prospective Study of Human Immunodeficiency Virus Infection and Pregnancy Outcomes in Intravenous drug Users," *Journal of the American Medical Association* 261 (1989): 1289–1294.
45. S. Sprecher, G. Soumenkoff, F. Puissant et al., "Vertical Transmission of HIV in 15-Week Fetus," *Lancet* 2 (1986): 288–289; J. M. Kashkin, J. Shliozberg, W. D. Lyman et al., "Detection of Human Immunodeficiency Virus (HIV) in Human Fetal Tissues," *Pediatric Research* 23 (part 2) (1988): 355A; E. Jovaisas, M. A. Koch, A. Schafer et al., "LAV/HTLV-III in 20 Week Fetus" (letter), *Lancet* 2 (1985): 1129; H. Di Maria, C. Courpotin, C. Rouzioux et al., "Transplacental Transmission of Human Immunodeficiency Virus," *Lancet* 2 (1986): 215–216.
46. D. G. Harnish, O. Hammerberg, I. R. Walker et al., "Early Detection of HIV Infection in a Newborn," *New England Journal of Medicine* 316 (1987): 272–273.
47. F. Laure, V. Courgnaud, C. Rouzioux et al., "Detection of HIV1 DNA in Infants and Children by Means of the Polymerase Chain Reaction," *Lancet* 2 (1988): 538–541; S. Wolinsky, D. Mack, R. Yogev et al., "Direct Detection of HIV Infection in Pediatric Patients and Their Mothers by the Polymerase Chain Reaction (PCR)," *Proceedings of the 4th International Conference on AIDS, Stockholm, June 1988,* book 2, p. 87.
48. Yair Devash, Theresa A. Calvelli, David G. Wood et al., "Vertical Transmission of Human Immunodeficiency Virus Is Correlated with the Absence of High-Affinity/Avidity Maternal Antibodies to the gp120 Principal Neutralizing Domain, *Proceedings of the National Academy of Sciences* 87 (1990): 3445–3449.
49. C. S. Crumpacker, "Hepatitis," in *Infectious Diseases of the Fetus and Newborn Infant,* 2nd ed. ed. J. S. Remington and J. O. Klein (Philadelphia: Saunders, 1983), 591–618.
50. For a complete review see M. J. Oxtoby, "Human Immunodeficiency Virus and Other Viruses in Human Milk: Placing the Issues in Broader Perspective," *Pediatric Infectious Disease Journal* 7 (1988): 825–835.
51. L. Thiry, S. Sprecher-Goldberger, T. Jonckheer et al., "Isolation of AIDS Virus from Cell-Free Breast Milk of Three Healthy Virus Carriers," *Lancet* 1 (1985): 881–892.
52. Stéphane Blanche, Christine Rouzioux, Marie-Luce G. Moscato et al., "A Prospective Study of Infants Born to Women Seropositive for Human Immunodeficiency Virus Type 1," *New England Journal of Medicine* 320 (1989): 1643–1648.
53. Neal Halsey, personal communication; J. M. Mann, H. Frances, F. Davachi et al., "Risk Factors for Human Immunodeficiency Virus Seropositivity Among Children 1–24 Months Old in Kinshasa, Zaire," *Lancet* 2 (1986): 654–657; J. Q. Mok, C. Giaquinto, A. De Rossi et al., "Infants Born to Mothers Seropositive for Human Immunodeficiency Virus," *Lancet* 1 (1987): 1164–1168; M. Stanback, J. W. Pape, R. Verdier et al., "Breastfeeding and HIV Transmission in Haitian Children," *Proceedings of the 4th International Conference on AIDS, Stockholm, June 1988,* book 1, p. 340.
54. Thiry et al., "Isolation of AIDS Virus."
55. Neal Halsey and N. Tafari, "Round Table: Breast Feeding, Vaccination, and Child Care in Developing Countries" (discussion at the Fourth International AIDS Conference, Stockholm, June 1988).
56. European Collaborative Study, "Mother-to-Child Transmission"; Blanche et al.,

"Prospective Study"; Italian Multicentre Study, "Epidemiology, Clinical Features and Prognostic Factors of Paediatric HIV Infection," *Lancet* 2 (1988): 1043–1046; P. A. Thomas and the New York City Perinatal HIV Transmission Collaborative Study Group, "Early Predictors and Rate of Perinatal HIV Disease," *Proceedings of the 5th International Conference on AIDS, Montreal, June 1989*, p. 524; J. J. Goedert, H. Mendez, A. Willoughby et al., "High Perinatal HIV Rates with Prematurity or Low Anti-gp120," *Proceedings of the 5th International Conference on AIDS, Montreal, June 1989*, p. 524; W. Andiman, J. Simpson, L. Dember et al., "Prospective Studies of a Cohort of 50 Infants Born to Human Immunodeficiency Virus (HIV) Seropositive Mothers," *Proceedings of the 4th International Conference on AIDS, Stockholm, June 1988*, book 2, p. 294; Nancy Hutton, A. Butz, M. Joyner et al., unpublished data; J. J. Goedert, H. Mendez, J. E. Drummond et al., "Mother-to-Infant Transmission of Human Immunodeficiency Virus Type 1: Association with Prematurity or Low Anti-gp120," *Lancet* 2 (1989): 1351–1354; G. B. Scott, C. Hutto, C. Mitchell et al., "Maternal Risk Factors for Perinatal Transmission of Human Immunodeficiency Virus-1 (HIV-1)," *Proceedings of the 5th International Conference on AIDS, Montreal, June 1989*, p. 524; J. Y. O. Mok, R. A. Hague, P. L. Yap et al., "Vertical Transmission of HIV: A Prospective Study," *Archives of Disease in Childhood* (1989) 64: 1140–45.

57. Blanche et al. "Prospective Study"; Robert W. Ryder, Wato Nsa, Susan E. Hassig et al., "Perinatal Transmission of the Human Immunodeficiency Virus Type 1 to Infants of Seropositive Women in Zaire," *New England Journal of Medicine* 320 (1989): 1637–1642.

58. European Collaborative Study, "Mother-to-Child Transmission"; Italian Multicentre Study, "Epidemiology"; Thomas and the New York City HIV Transmission Collaborative Study Group, "Early Predictors"; Goedert et al., "High Perinatal HIV Rates"; Andiman et al., "Prospective Studies"; Hutton et al., unpublished data.

59. Robert Ryder, Wato Nsa, F. Behets et al., "Perinatal HIV Transmission in Two African Hospitals: One Year Follow-Up," *Proceedings of the 4th International Conference on AIDS, Stockholm, June 1988*, book 1, p. 291.

60. Goedert et al., "Mother-to-Infant Transmission."

61. Hutto et al., "Maternal Risk Factors."

62. Goedert et al., "Mother-to-Infant Transmission"; P. Rossi, V. Moschese, P. A. Broliden et al., "Presence of Maternal Antibodies to Human Immunodeficiency Virus 1 Envelope Glycoprotein gp120 Epitopes Correlates with the Uninfected Status of Children Born to Seropositive Mothers," *Proceedings of the National Academy of Sciences* 86 (1989): 8055–8058.

63. Gwendolyn B. Scott, Cecilia Hutto, Robert Makuch et al., "Survival in Children with Perinatally Acquired Human Immunodeficiency Virus Type 1 Infection," *New England Journal of Medicine* 321 (1989): 1791–1796.

64. K. Krasinski, W. Borkowsky, and R. S. Holzman "Prognosis of Human Immunodeficiency Virus Infection in Children and Adolescents," *Pediatric Infectious Disease Journal* 8 (1989): 216–220.

65. E. J. Abrams, "Longitudinal Study of Infants Born to Women at Risk for AIDS," *Proceedings of the 4th International Conference on AIDS, Stockholm, June 1988*, book 1, p. 442.

66. CDC, "Human Immunodeficiency Virus Infection."

67. Pahwa et al., "Spectrum of Human T-Cell Lymphotropic Virus Type III Infection."

68. L. G. Epstein, L. R. Sharer, J. M. Oleske et al., "Neurologic Manifestations of

Human Immunodeficiency Virus Infection in Children," *Pediatrics* 78 (1986): 678–687; Anita L. Belman, Monica H. Ultmann, Dikran Horoupian et al., "Neurological Complications in Infants and Children with Acquired Immunodeficiency Syndrome," *Annals of Neurology* 18 (1985): 560–566; A. L. Belman, G. Diamond, D. Dickson et al., "Pediatric Acquired Immunodeficiency Syndrome: Neurologic Syndromes," *American Journal of Diseases of Children* 142 (1988): 29–35.

69. A. Rubinstein, R. Morecki, B. Silverman et al., "Pulmonary Disease in Children with Acquired Immune Deficiency Syndrome and AIDS-Related Complex," *Journal of Pediatrics* 108 (1986): 498–503; V. V. Joshi and J. M. Oleske, "Pulmonary Lesions in Children with the Acquired Immunodeficiency Syndrome: A Reappraisal Based on Data in Additional Cases and Follow-Up Study of Previously Reported Cases," *Human Pathology* 17 (1986): 641–642.

70. CDC, "Measles in HIV-Infected-Children, United States," *Morbidity and Mortality Weekly Report* 37 (1988): 183–186; L. E. Markowitz, F. W. Chandler, E. O. Roldan et al., "Fatal Measles Pneumonia without Rash in a Child with AIDS," *Journal of Infectious Disease* 158 (1988): 480–483; M. Mvula, R. Ryder, M. Oxtoby et al., "Measles and Measles Immunization in African Children with Human Immunodeficiency Virus" (presented at the Fourth International AIDS Conference, Stockholm, June 1988).

71. M. McLaughlin, P. Thomas, I. Onorato et al., "Live Virus Vaccines in Human Immunodeficiency Virus-Infected Children: A Retrospective Survey," *Pediatrics* 82 (1988): 229–233; I. M. Onorato, L. E. Markowitz, and M. J. Oxtoby, "Childhood Immunization, Vaccine-Preventable Diseases and Infection with Human Immunodeficiency Virus," *Pediatric Infectious Disease Journal* 7 (1988): 588–595.

72. Savita Pawha, Karen Biron, Wilma Lim et al., "Continuous Varicella-Zoster Infection Associated with Acyclovir Resistance in a Child with AIDS," *Journal of the American Medical Association* 260 (1988): 2879–2882.

73. L. G. Epstein, F. J. DiCarlo, V. V. Joshi et al., "Primary Lymphoma of the Central Nervous System in Children with Acquired Immunodeficiency Syndrome," *Pediatrics* 82 (1988): 355–363.

74. B. E. Buck, G. B. Scott, M. Valdes-Dapena et al., "Kaposi Sarcoma in Two Infants with Acquired Immune Deficiency Syndrome," *Journal of Pediatrics* 103 (1983): 911–913.

75. V. D. Rodgers and M. F. Kagnoff, "Gastrointestinal Manifestations of the Acquired Immunodeficiency Syndrome," *Western Journal of Medicine* 146 (1987): 57–67.

76. J. Perman, John Modlin, Nancy Hutton et al., unpublished data; L. C. McLoughlin, K. S. Nord, V. V. Joshi et al., "Severe Gastrointestinal Involvement in Children with the Acquired Immunodeficiency Syndrome," *Journal of Pediatric Gastroenterology and Nutrition* 6 (1987): 517–524.

77. J. A. Nelson, C. A. Wiley, C. Reynolds-Kohler et al., "Human Immunodeficiency Virus Detected in Bowel Epithelium from Patients with Gastrointestinal Symptoms," *Lancet* 1 (1988): 259–262; C. H. Fox, D. Kotler, A. Tierney et al., "Detection of HIV-1 RNA in the Lamina Propria of Patients with AIDS and Gastrointestinal Disease," *Journal of Infectious Diseases* 159 (1989): 467–471.

78. Henry J. Issenberg, Morris Charytan, and Arye Rubinstein, "Cardiac Involvement in Children with Acquired Immunodeficiency Syndrome" (abstract), *American Heart Journal* 110 (1985): 710; S. Lipshultz, S. Chanock, S. Sanders et al., "Cardiac Manifestations of Pediatric HIV Infection" (presented at the Fourth International AIDS Conference, Stockholm, June 1988).

79. Julian M. Stewart, Aditya Kaul, Donald S. Gromisch, et al., "Congestive Heart Failure in Children with HIV Infection," *Circulation* 76 (1987): 515.
80. Gwendolyn B. Scott, Billy E. Buck, Joni G. Leterman et al., "Acquired Immunodeficiency Syndrome in Infants," *New England Journal of Medicine* 310 (1984): 76–81.
81. T. K. S. Rao, E. A. Friedman, A. D. Nicastri et al., "The Types of Renal Disease in the Acquired Immunodeficiency Syndrome," *New England Journal of Medicine* 316 (1987): 1062–1068; E. Connor, S. Gupta, V. Joshi et al., "Acquired Immunodeficiency Syndrome-Associated Renal Disease," *Journal of Pediatrics* 113 (1988): 39–44.
82. H. Mendez, S. Fikrig, A. de Forest et al., "Response to Childhood Immunizations in Children with Human Immunodeficiency Virus (HIV) Infection" (presented to the Society for Pediatric Research, Washington, D.C., May 1988).
83. CDC, "Immunization of Children Infected with Human Immunodeficiency Virus—Supplemenary ACIP Statement," *Morbidity and Mortality Weekly Report* 37 (1988): 181–183.
84. McLaughlin et al., "Live Virus Vaccines"; Onorato et al., "Childhood Immunization."
85. Ibid.
86. CDC, "Immunization of Children."
87. F. M. la Force, "Expanded Programme on Immunization: Immunization Policy in Countries with Endemic and Epidemic Human Immunodeficiency Virus (HIV) Infection," World Health Organization EPI background paper, WHO/EPI, Geneva, 1986.
88. U. B. Schaad, A. Gianella-Borradori, B. Perret et al., "Intravenous Immunoglobulin in Symptomatic Pediatric Human Immunodeficiency Virus Infection," *European Journal of Pediatrics* 147 (1988): 300–303.
89. M. Vogt and M. S. Hirsch, "Prospects for the Prevention and Therapy of Infections with the Human Immunodeficiency Virus," *Review of Infectious Diseases* 8 (1986): 991–1000; M. S. Hirsch, "Azidothymidine," *Journal of Infectious Disease* 157 (1988): 7–431.
90. Margaret A. Fischl, Douglas D. Richman, Michael H. Grieco et al., "The Efficacy of Azidothymidine (AZT) in the Treatment of Patients with AIDS and AIDS-Related Complex," *New England Journal of Medicine* 317 (1987): 185–191.
91. Vogt and Hirsch, "Prospects"; Volberding et al., "Zidovudine"; Robert Yarchoan and Samuel Broder, "Development of Antiretroviral Therapy for the Acquired Immunodeficiency Syndrome and Related Disorders," *New England Journal of Medicine* 316 (1987): 557–564.
92. Kevan L. Hartshorn, Markus W. Vogt, Ting-Chao Chou et al., "Synergistic Inhibition of Human Immunodeficiency Virus in Vitro by Azidothymidine and Recombinant Alpha A Interferon," *Antimicrobial Agents and Chemotherapy* 31 (1987): 168–172; Marcus W. Vogt, Amy G. Durno, Ting-Chao Chou et al., "Synergistic Interaction of 2′,3′-Dideoxycytidine and Recombinant Interferon Alpha A on Replication of Human Immunodeficiency Virus Type 1," *Journal of Infectious Disease* 158 (1988): 378–385; V. A. Johnson, M. A. Barlow, Ting-Chao Chou et al., "Synergistic Inhibition of Human Immunodeficiency Virus Type 1 (HIV-1) Replication in Vitro by Recombinant soluble CD4 and 3′-Azido-3′-Deoxythymidine," *Journal of Infectious Disease* 159 (1989): 837–844.
93. Pediatric Zidovudine Study Group, "Safety and Tolerance of Zidovudine (ZDV, Retrovir) during a Phase I Study in Children" (presented to the Society for Pediatric

Research, Washington, D.C., May 1988); F. M. Balis, P. A. Pizzo, J. Eddy et al., "Pharmacokinetics of Zidovudine Administered Intravenously and Orally in Children with Human Immunodeficiency Virus Infection," *Journal of Pediatrics* 114 (1989): 880–884; F. M. Balis, P. A. Pizzo, R. F. Murphy et al., "The Pharmacokinetics of Zidovudine Administered by Continuous Infusion in Children," *Annals of Internal Medicine* 110 (1989): 279–285; P. A. Pizzo, J. Eddy, J. Falloon et al., "Effect of Continuous Intravenous Infusion of zidovudine (AZT) in Children with Symptomatic HIV Infection," *New England Journal of Medicine* 319 (1988): 889–896.

94. Balis et al., "Pharmacokinetics of Zidovudine Administered by Continuous Infusion in Children."

95. Pediatric Zidovudine Study Group, "Safety and Tolerance."

96. Pizzo ct al., "Continuous Intravenous Infusion."

97. A. S. Fauci, R. C. Gallo, S. Koenig et al., "Development and Evaluation of a Vaccine for Human Immunodeficiency Virus (HIV) Infection," *Annals of Internal Medicine* 110 (1989): 373–385.

3

A History of Prenatal and Newborn Screening Programs: Lessons for the Future

KATHERINE L. ACUFF AND RUTH R. FADEN

The screening of all pregnant women and newborns for the presence of HIV infection has been advocated as a means of controlling the spread of AIDS.[1] As noted throughout this volume, however, such screening is not without a great deal of medical, legal, and ethical controversy. HIV screening of pregnant women and newborns is also not without precedent. The purpose of this chapter is to place present policy controversies surrounding HIV screening in the context of the histories of other prominent prenatal and neonatal screening programs.

"Screening" has been defined as

> a search in a healthy population for a specific disorder, or closely related set of disorders, for the purpose, in neonatal screening, of improving the outcome of the affected infant and, in antenatal screening, of providing parents of the affected fetus with the choice of terminating the pregnancy or preparing for the birth of a handicapped child.[2]

Screening in pregnancy is also conducted in order to provide treatment that will cure or ameliorate a condition in the mother or fetus or to prevent transmission of a condition from mother to fetus.

As best as we can determine, the routine use of prenatal screening for any condition was first initiated in 1916 at The Johns Hopkins Hospital, when J. Whitridge Williams directed that all pregnant women seen in the clinic be screened for syphilis.[3] It does not appear, however, that other obstetricians soon followed Williams's example. Prenatal screening for syphilis did not become widespread until it was legislatively mandated in the late 1930s to mid-1940s. Prenatal screening was initiated for Tay-Sachs disease and sickle cell disease in the 1970s and for neural tube defects in the 1980s.

Screening for phenylketonuria, initiated in the early 1960s, was the first widespread screening program to be conducted on newborns. Like prenatal screening for syphilis, PKU screening was legislatively mandated. In this case, however, the interval between the development of an effective test and legislation was much shorter. Within a few years of the introduction of a statewide voluntary screening program in Massachusetts, all states had either legislated or regulated PKU screening of all newborns.[4] Screening for other inborn errors of metabolism followed; tests for congenital hypothyroidism, galactosemia, homocystinuria, histidenemia, maple syrup urine disease, and tyrosinemia were introduced in the 1970s. Routine screening of newborns for sickle cell disease was also introduced in the 1970s and screening for hepatitis B virus in the 1980s. In 1988, Colorado became the first state to pass a law requiring every newborn to be screened for cystic fibrosis.[5]

Are there any lessons from these and other prenatal and newborn screening programs that can be applied to a study of HIV screening? Perhaps so. In this chapter we examine the experiences of six different screening programs—for syphilis, phenylketonuria, sickle cell disease, Tay-Sachs disease, neural tube defects, and hepatitis B virus—and note their similarities to and differences from screening for HIV. One characteristic of screening programs—whether or not the program has a disproportionate impact on minority groups—is of particular concern (see Chapters 2 and 14). Three of the six screening programs reviewed in this chapter—for Tay-Sachs disease, sickle cell disease, and hepatitis B virus— were selected because they have been carried out in minority populations with varying degrees of success.

Syphilis

Syphilis is a communicable disease caused by the spirochete *Treponema pallidum,* characterized by both active lesions and chronic deleterious effects including cardiovascular and central nervous system (CNS) symptoms. A pregnant woman with *T. pallidum* has a significant risk of transmitting syphilis to her fetus. Transmission to the fetus rarely occurs prior to the 12th week of pregnancy, and the rate of transmission varies with the time the woman was infected. Women infected shortly before or during pregnancy have the highest transmission rates. Without treatment, maternal infection increases the risk of stillbirth fourfold and the risk of infant death twofold. Surviving infants have a 20 percent incidence of infection.

Clinically, the symptoms of congenital syphilis vary, depending on whether they appear early (under 2 years of age) or late (over 2 years of age). Clinical manifestations of early congenital syphilis appear within the first 2 to 3 months of life, if at all, and include skin lesions, osteitis, periostitis, and lymphadenitis. Many infants show no clinical evidence of infection. If the infection is severe, however, there may be fever and neurologic symptoms. Late congenital syphilis can result in stigmata, such as a saddle nose, dish-shaped face, or corneal scars, and active lesions, including ocular lesions, CNS disease, nerve deafness, and skeletal lesions. The mortality rate in untreated children is up to 30 percent.

Prenatally, the demonstration of infection in the mother by a positive screening test supported by a confirmatory antibody test[6] causes the initiation of treatment. This treatment, generally involving the administration of penicillin,[7] cures the mother and either prevents transmission to or cures the fetus. Demonstration of the spirochete in the cord blood establishes a positive diagnosis in newborns, but failure to do so does not exclude infection.

Early in this century, the prevalence of syphilis and gonorrhea had reached such enormous proportions (far exceeding the current prevalence of HIV infection) that it was estimated that "morbidity of venereal disease exceed[ed] that of all other diseases combined."[8] Because of the stigma associated with these diseases, however, no accurate assessment of their prevalence was possible. As William Osler put it in 1917, "Syphilis . . . remains the despair of the statistician."[9] The best estimates of the extent of the problem, based on new cases of venereal disease in the army in 1909, neared 20 percent of the population.[10] In 1933, it was estimated that there were over 870,000 new cases a year in a U.S. population of 130 million.[11] Congenital syphilis was the leading cause of spontaneous abortions and stillbirth. In 1940, for example, it was estimated that women with syphilis transmitted the infection to at least 85,000 fetuses, resulting in 25,000 spontaneous abortions and stillbirths and 60,000 newborn cases each year.[12] Although testing to determine a pregnant woman's syphilis positivity was available as early as 1906–1907,[13] two major impediments stood in the way of an effective program to reduce the incidence of congenital syphilis—the onerous treatment options and the stigma of being shown to have the disease.

The first effective treatment for syphilis was developed by Paul Ehrlich in 1909, an accomplishment for which he won the Nobel Prize.[14] Salvarsan and, subsequently, neosalvarsan were arsenic compounds that, while effective against the spirochete, were very toxic (not infrequently resulting in death), difficult to administer (requiring intravenous injections),[15] painful, and expensive.[16] When these compounds were first introduced, there was wide disagreement among syphilologists on how to administer them properly. This disagreement culminated in a special meeting of the Health Section of the League of Nations in 1935 to study the problem. The Health Section recommended a 70-week schedule of arsenic and mercury compounds as standard treatment.[17] Not surprisingly, it has been estimated that less than one-quarter of patients were ever treated with the full 70-week course.[18]

There are no known reports in the medical literature on the use of arsenic compounds to prevent congenital syphilis until 1920. In May of that year, J. Whitridge Williams of The Johns Hopkins University Hospital (JHH) reported the results of clinical trials initiated in 1915 on the effects of salvarsan in pregnancy.[19] In this report, Williams argued that the only effective solution to congenital syphilis was to determine the Wasserman reaction in every pregnant woman who registered in the dispensary (of JHH) and to subject every positive patient to intensive antisyphilitic treatment. Williams argued further that the prenatal detection and treatment of syphilis could eliminate more prenatal and newborn deaths than any other obstetric intervention available.[20]

Despite Williams's successful experience and his strong claims with regard to the benefits of prenatal intervention, syphilis screening was not incorporated into routine obstetric practice for almost 20 years. A significant obstacle to such testing was the reluctance of private physicians to risk offending patients by suggesting a test for syphilis.[21] As a result, it took a legislative mandate to bring prenatal syphilis testing into routine obstetric practice.

Soon after his appointment in 1936 as U.S. Surgeon General, Thomas Parran launched a vigorous antisyphilis crusade, setting forth a five-point program for controlling syphilis, with special emphasis on controlling congenital syphilis. Parran's proposed program included mandatory blood tests before marriage and early in all pregnancies.[22] It was not until January 5, 1938, however, that the real impetus for syphilis screening legislation was generated. On that date, the *New York Post* published a front-page editorial entitled "13,000 Babies," strongly advocating mandatory prenatal screening for syphilis.[23] The figure of 13,000 referred to the estimated 4,000 infants born with, and 9,000 stillbirths caused by, syphilis in New York State annually. The editorial staff of the *Post* had discovered that although public prenatal clinics were requiring blood tests for syphilis, only half of New York City's practicing obstetricians were routinely testing their private patients.[24] As a result, "the very poorest women who were compelled to attend the clinics did not have as many syphilitic babies as the moderately well-to-do women who retained private physicians."[25] No doubt an additional obstacle to screening was that treatment protocols had not become less onerous than they were immediately following Ehrlich's introduction of salvarsan in 1909.

The editorial was followed by extensive lobbying on the part of organized medicine, welfare groups, and health organizations, spearheaded by Parran and the press.[26] Two months after the editorial was published, New York State's "Baby Health Bill" was signed and became the first U.S. law addressing the issue of congenital syphilis.[27] New York's law required physicians to test all pregnant women for syphilis and to record on the birth certificate that a test had been done or explain why it was not done. Women could refuse to take the test on conscientious, religious, or other grounds. Physicians, too, could refuse if they did not believe in blood tests or in the treatment of syphilis in pregnant women, in which case they would be targeted for extensive educational efforts.

Also in 1938, Congress passed the National Venereal Disease Control Act, which emphasized the national nature of the problem and provided for federal grants to state boards of health for the purpose of developing antivenereal measures.[28] These funds were instrumental in generating support for state syphilis programs.[29]

The scope of the congenital syphilis problem was large. In a 1940 publication of the U.S. Public Health Service (the *Report*), it was estimated that 1 million women of childbearing age in the United States had syphilis.[30] The *Report* noted that each year, women with syphilis transmitted it to at least 85,000 fetuses. Of these, 25,000 died before birth and 60,000 were born alive with syphilis.[31] Twenty years after Williams's initial suggestion, the *Report* recommended routine serologic tests for syphilis on all pregnant women.[32] The *Report* noted that "prenatal syphilis is a preventable disease; its prevention depends upon the routine, early and repeated use of the serologic test for syphilis and adequate, early, and continuous treatment of the mother up to the termination of the pregnancy."[33] Notwithstanding earlier recommendations for standard treatment for syphilis, at the time routine syphilis screening of pregnant women was legislated, no single treatment was used and the dosages and combinations of arsenicals and bismuth varied according to the predisposition of the physician and the stage of pregnancy. The *Report* stated, "[I]t is strongly recommended that the physician adopt and utilize the one [treatment] which to him seems the most convenient and desirable."[34]

The *Report*'s strongly worded recommendation for prenatal screening, coupled with Parran's forceful leadership and the commitment of federal funds, led many states to join the national campaign to eradicate congenital syphilis by law. By the end of 1945, 36 states had passed prenatal syphilis screening laws.[35] These laws immediately overcame the resistance of physicians to diagnosing syphilis in pregnant women and instituting treatment, resulting in a rapid decline of congenital transmission.[36]

At about the same time that states were passing mandatory syphilis screening legislation, a significant advance was made in the search for a better treatment. In 1943, Dr. John S. Mahoney of the U.S. Public Health Service found that penicillin was an effective treatment for syphilis. It was first made available to the Public Health Service for testing in 1944 but was practical only for inpatient care, since it required intramuscular injections at 2- to 3-hour intervals around the clock.[37] Not until the 1950s was it possible to treat syphilis effectively with a single injection of penicillin, and such treatment was recommended for congenital syphilis. With the introduction of antibiotic treatment for syphilis, congenital transmission fell even further. By the late 1950s, congenital syphilis had lost its central position as a major public health problem.

Although today congenital syphilis is not often seen in most areas of the country, in 1988 state health departments reported to the Centers for Disease Control (CDC) the highest number of cases in infants under 1 year of age since penicillin became widely used to treat syphilis in pregnant women. This increase was closely associated with the use of crack cocaine. As a result, the CDC now recommends screening all newborns in high-syphilis-prevalence areas for syphilis.[38] Because of a fivefold increase in congenital syphilis between 1986 and 1988, New York State now requires that all newborns or all new mothers (as well as all pregnant women) be screened.

Phenylketonuria

Phenylketonuria (PKU) is a hereditary metabolic disorder in which a deficiency of an intracellular enzyme results in the accumulation of the amino acid phenylalanine. PKU has an incidence in the United States of approximately 1 in 12,000 to 15,000 live births.[39] The primary characteristic of PKU is severe retardation; 95 percent of affected persons have IQs of less than 50. In addition, convulsions, hyperactivity, and eczema are common. Classically, PKU is not lethal. However, some data suggest that the life span is shortened, particularly in individuals affected with cofactor variants of PKU.

For the majority of infants diagnosed as having classical PKU today (approximately 95 percent), retardation can be prevented by the early restriction of dietary phenylalanine, optimally beginning before 4 weeks of age and continuing indefinitely, with regular monitoring of serum phenylalanine levels.[40] Later treatment will not reverse CNS damage but may improve some of the behavioral symptoms. For those few infants having a variant form of PKU in which a cofactor is deficient, other treatments can improve the outcome.[41]

The first newborn PKU screening programs in the United States began in the late 1950s in California and Cincinnati, Ohio.[42] It was not until 1961, however, when Dr. Robert Guthrie developed a simple bacteriologic assay test for PKU, that the impetus for mass screening programs occurred.[43] The Guthrie test allowed for detection of PKU in newborns by a simple and inexpensive heel prick before clinical symptoms of the disease became evident.

In July 1962, a large-scale pilot PKU screening program using an early version of the Guthrie test began in Massachusetts with the assistance of the Children's Bureau of the Department of Health, Education and Welfare. All the maternity hospitals in the state were invited on a voluntary basis to participate in the program. Educational programs for hospital staffs were instituted, in part, so that they would be prepared to explain the testing procedures to parents.[44] The screening program not only demonstrated the feasibility of mass screening but also had the ancillary effect of stimulating the voluntary adoption of PKU screening programs throughout Massachusetts. By the winter of 1962–1963, without a legislative mandate, all the state's maternity hospitals had voluntarily enrolled in the program and were soon screening all newborns for PKU.[45]

Notwithstanding the adoption of PKU screening as part of routine hospital practice in Massachusetts, Guthrie campaigned vigorously for mandatory screening legislation and enlisted the support of physicians; organizations representing retarded children, in particular the National Association for Retarded Children

(NARC);[46] and state health department officials. NARC in 1963 recommended "that State Associations emphasize the urgency of testing all newborns for metabolic disorders, including PKU," and in 1964 it strengthened its stand and went on record as recommending mandatory legislation for the screening of PKU.[47]

A critical view of the intense push to legislate PKU screening, rather than support its incorporation into routine medical practice, is that this push reflected the "professional evangelism" of a small but active group of physicians and medical researchers

> who had begun to build investigational interests and careers around the phenomena of the "inborn errors of metabolism." Some—not all—of the more actively disposed of these medical personalities involved themselves in the promotion of the PKU program. They became the advisors to legislators, government administrators, and voluntary organizations.[48]

In 1963, Massachusetts became the first state to enact a mandatory PKU screening law.[49] Following this success, and emphasizing the prevention of mental retardation rather than the genetic aspects of the screening, NARC organized an extensive lobbying effort to establish mandatory PKU screening legislation throughout the country.[50] The American Academy of Pediatrics (AAP), and organized medicine in general, strongly opposed a legislated approach.[51] AAP issued a commentary noting that there was "insufficient knowledge concerning either the correct and early diagnosis of inborn errors of metabolism, or their effective management, to warrant this kind of public health programming. The funds needed to support [PKU] legislation would be much better utilized to further research in the field."[52] Organized medicine lost this fight, however, and within the decade, 43 states enacted PKU-specific screening laws.[53] The remaining states set up active testing programs without statutory support.[54] In the overwhelming majority of these states PKU programs were mandatory, requiring physicians or other medical personnel to obtain blood samples from all newborns for testing (see Chapter 6). The statutes did not provide for the punishment of noncompliant parents.[55] In 1975, Maryland repealed its compulsory PKU screening law, replacing it with a statute and regulations requiring informed parental consent.[56]

In many respects, the Guthrie PKU test applied to populations embodies the central characteristics of the ideal screening program.[57] PKU has a known prevalence; the test is simple, safe and accurate; the cost of the test is low; and an effective treatment is available. As Levy notes, the "Guthrie test has served as a prototype for virtually all genetic screening—biochemical detection before the onset of clinical signs and thus early therapeutic intervention."[58]

Nevertheless, the rush to legislate PKU screening throughout the United States, despite opposition by the medical community and the apparent willingness of physicians (at least in Massachusetts) to incorporate the screening into routine medical practice, remains a largely unexplained phenomenon.[59] It is interesting to note that although successful PKU screening programs have been set up in at least 20 countries in addition to the United States, in most of these countries the programs are not legislated.[60]

Spurred on by the success of PKU screening and with the continued support of NARC, Guthrie subsequently developed and promoted other screening tests for inborn errors of metabolism, many of which became part of the statutory framework of the PKU legislation. For example, in 1974, New York State's PKU public health law was amended to include five more inherited metabolic disorders in its mandatory screening of newborns—maple syrup urine disease, homocystinuria, histidinemia, galactosemia, and adenosine deaminase deficiency.[61] At least 23 states have incorporated, by statute or regulation, at least one additional inborn error of metabolism into their mandatory prenatal screens (the most common of which is galactosemia).[62] Two more states encourage physicians to conduct voluntary newborn screening for several conditions without specific legislation, rules, or regulations.[63] One state supplements its mandatory PKU screening program with notice and information to physicians about other available tests.[64] Massachusetts, continuing its leadership role, has contracted with Connecticut, Maine, New Hampshire, Rhode Island, and Vermont to operate the Eastern Regional Newborn Screening Laboratory, which tests for galactose, leucine, methylalanine, thyroxine, and *Toxoplasma,* as well as for PKU.[65] These conditions are included in a routine Guthrie filter paper blood specimen test done on all newborns, without the consent of the parents, as part of a routine newborn screen.

Although the PKU program has screened millions of infants and has prevented retardation in several thousand,[66] it has been argued that PKU screening was introduced prematurely from a medical point of view and probably stymied further research.[67] Furthermore, mandatory PKU screening was enacted before the validity of the test had been demonstrated and prior to a clear understanding of the efficacy of dietary treatment.[68] Critics of legislated screening programs claim that at the time legislation was being enacted, the public and the legislatures were led to believe that a higher degree of certainty existed with respect to the medical understanding of PKU than was the case,[69] a claim that was affirmed by a National Academy of Sciences Committee for the Study of Inborn Errors of Metabolism.[70] As a result, some infants were incorrectly identified and treated as having PKU.[71] These criticisms had some merit but were (and are) probably applicable to only a small percentage of infants identified by the routine newborn test.[72]

Other shortcomings included the fact that few of the statutes provided either adequate quality assurance mechanisms or funding to care for infants identified as having PKU.[73] Finally, it was reported that even a decade after passage of the

PKU screening laws, almost one-half of a group of practicing pediatricians and family practitioners surveyed could not interpret an abnormal PKU test result correctly.[74]

Sickle Cell Disease

Sickle cell disease is an autosomal recessive hemolytic anemia occurring most frequently in blacks but also in persons of Mediterranean, Asian, Caribbean, Middle Eastern, and South and Central American origin. Sickle cell disease, the homozygous condition, is estimated to occur in as many as 1 in 400 African-American newborns.[75] Approximately 8 percent of American blacks are carriers of the sickle cell trait, the heterozygous condition.[76] Although most common in blacks, at least 10 percent of the cases occur in nonblacks.[77]

Sickle cell disease is characterized by sickle-shaped red blood cells that tend to clump and stick together in small blood vessels, leading to painful attacks known as "crises." Children with sickle cell disease have an increased susceptibility to severe bacterial infections, particularly those caused by *Streptococcus pneumoniae*.[78] The leading causes of death in infants and young children with sickle cell disease are overwhelming bacterial sepsis and disappearance of splenic function.

Screening for sickle cell hemoglobinopathies did not become an issue of public debate until the early 1970s, when an unusual series of events led to medical, public, and political awareness of the problem of sickle cell anemia.

In January 1970, Dr. Roland Scott wrote a letter to the editors of the *New England Journal of Medicine* in which he noted that little public health effort was being directed at the problem of sickle cell disease, even though it was more prevalent among blacks than more highly publicized disorders of children such as cystic fibrosis, childhood leukemia, and PKU.[79] According to Scott, the lack of consideration of sickle cell disease in research and health-care planning, the failure to recognize it as a community health problem, and the absence of volunteer efforts caused it to be the most neglected major health problem in the country. Implicit in Scott's argument was a suggestion of racial bias in the allocation of health resources. In his letter and in a subsequent Special Communication appearing in the *Journal of the American Medical Association,* Scott, emphasizing that the disease was incurable and without effective treatment, called for extensive education coupled with mass carrier screening programs of young blacks before marriageable age.[80] Furthermore, Scott noted that "it is not only because of its neglect that sickle cell anemia deserves higher priority. With the availability of a simple test for sickle trait carriers which makes screening possible, this may be the first hereditary illness which could be controlled by genetic counselling."[81]

Soon thereafter, Scott's appeal to the professional community was echoed in a public awareness campaign in the media. In November 1970, the first of a series of four prime-time television shows was aired in Hartford, Connecticut, on the subject of sickle cell disease.[82] Leonard D. Petricelli, president of a local television station, had learned about sickle cell anemia from his son, a deputy undersecretary of the U.S. Department of Health, Education and Welfare (HEW) (now the U.S. Department of Health and Human Services, DHHS), who was working on President Richard Nixon's annual health message. In anticipation of Nixon's speech and after having spoken to and gained the support of several black leaders in the community, Petricelli decided to produce the television shows.[83] The shows were well received in Hartford and stimulated a communitywide response to the problem of sickle cell disease.[84]

In February 1971, President Nixon singled out sickle cell disease for special attention in his health message and called for a vast increase in federal spending on sickle cell research, education, and screening programs.[85] Also in 1971, Connecticut passed the first sickle cell screening legislation in the country.[86] Other states quickly passed their own versions of this legislation.[87] These laws usually were introduced by black legislators and were passed by unanimous vote without debate. Even some local governments joined in. Seattle, for example, was

> swept along in this national tide of interest. Originally promoted by the Black Panther Party, mass sickle cell screening was begun by several health agencies both public and private. A barrage of publicity was unleashed in local newspapers, the "soul" radio station, and pamphlets, directing all black persons to be tested as a matter of urgency.[88]

By April 1973, 10 states had laws requiring mandatory screening for sickle cell disease,[89] notwithstanding the fact that no effective treatment was available.[90] The distribution of states with mandatory laws affected more than 40 percent of the total African-American population.[91] Four additional states passed voluntary sickle cell screening laws.[92]

The sickle cell screening statutes were not models of well-drafted legislation, and despite the initial enthusiasm, both the statutes and the screening programs quickly engendered much criticism.[93] Although the original proposal by Scott called for carrier screening of young adults, a hodgepodge of age groups was targeted in the legislation, including newborns, preschool children, marriage license applicants, and inmates of state institutions.[94] The statutes generally were a mishmash of confusion, some calling for carrier screening, some for disease screening, and some for both. For example, some states legislated the carrier screening of newborns, although the significance of carrier status is not relevant until persons are of reproductive age.

The original sickle cell laws also lacked provisions for ensuring confidentiality or providing funding for genetic counseling or educational programs.[95] The lack of confidentiality was not a trivial matter. Identification as having sickle cell trait or sickle cell disease resulted in documented cases of job discrimination, most notably in the military.[96] Other reported hazards of screening for sickle cell hemoglobinopathies included the inappropriate medication and treatment of persons whose symptoms were falsely attributed to sickle cell disease, delays in the adoption of children suspected of having the disease or trait, the exposure of nonpaternity, and insurance discrimination.[97] The lack of adequate education and counseling also had serious adverse consequences, largely in connection with the confusion between sickle cell trait or carrier status and sickle cell disease.

Initial supporters of sickle cell screening had been spurred on by the success of PKU screening, but "the immense difference between being able to control PKU and prevent retardation through diet and having only counseling on reproduction available for sickle-cell carriers was not fully appreciated until later."[98] This lack of an effective intervention fueled the growing criticism of the sickle cell statutes.

In addition to ambiguities concerning the rationale for screening, there were questions about who should and could be screening. A statute targeting African-Americans specifically, if challenged, would have had to demonstrate a compelling state interest in order to deal with the constitutional issue of suspect classification under equal protection (see Chapters 7 and 14). Some states went to great and awkward lengths to obviate this issue. For example, the New York statute mandating preschool testing required that urban schoolchildren submit evidence of a sickle cell test with their school medical records. The obligation for rural children, however, was optional at the discretion of the school physician, a policy that reflected the concentration of African-Americans in urban areas.[99] Finally, the fact that the majority of the statutes called for mandatory screening caused critics to raise questions about the purpose of the legislation. "The problem . . . is that no one is facing up to the eugenic implications of informing someone [that] he carries [the] sickle cell trait."[100] These considerations, coupled with the racial tension of the early 1970s, led to charges of racism and a growing opposition to the screening programs.

The combined failings of the sickle cell screening statutes would almost certainly have been deemed suspect and found unconstitutional had they been challenged in court. This challenge was not to come, however, for in 1972, passage of the National Sickle Cell Anemia Control Act[101] limited the use of federal funds to voluntary carrier screening programs and stopped the movement toward mandatory laws.[102] With the implicit promise of federal funding, many state legislatures amended their statutes to provide for voluntary testing; others opted for no state-sponsored testing at all, preferring private solutions to screening.[103]

Between 1978 and 1981, federal funding for voluntary genetic screening, including sickle cell hemoglobinopathies, increased significantly, enabling the expansion of existing programs and the establishment of others. By 1981, 42 statewide programs received federal funds.[104] Genetic screening was sharply curtailed, however, during the Reagan administration, with deep cuts to health programs and the "defunding" of a variety of categorical health programs including genetic and sickle cell screening. The Genetic Diseases Program was folded into the Maternal Child Health Services Block Grant. Federal funds were distributed to the states through the block grants, with significant curtailments on the use of funds imposed by DHHS.[105] As a result of this consolidation, as well as changes in the eligibility requirements for federal funding, 23 statewide genetics programs, including 17 sickle cell programs, became ineligible for federal funds.[106] By 1986, only eight statewide sickle cell screening programs were in operation.[107]

Today, support for mandatory, universal newborn screening for sickle cell disease is again growing. Recent clinical trials have demonstrated that a regimen of prophylactic penicillin in infants significantly reduces the mortality and morbidity of sickle cell disease. In 1988, a National Institutes of Health Consensus Conference (the Conference) found these findings so compelling that it recommended "the universal screening of all newborns for hemoglobinopathies," including sickle cell disease.[108] The decision to advocate a policy of universal rather than targeted screening was based in part on the experience of selective screening programs of high-risk infants such as the Georgia program. Georgia was criticized for failing to identify many affected infants.[109] Spokespersons for communities with large Hispanic populations testified about the practical difficulties of identifying all high-risk newborns. It was pointed out that even self-reporting of race or ethnicity is imperfect, since blacks from the Caribbean or Latin America often classify themselves as Hispanic. An additional consideration in the Conference's recommendation that screening be universal was, arguably, to avoid the racial fallout of the earlier experience with screening. Under the Conference's recommendations, states having only a small at-risk population would be given the limited option of implementing a targeted screening program if recommended by a state genetic planning committee or sickle cell advisory committee.[110]

As a result of the Conference's recommendations and increased federal funding (through the Genetic Services of the Health Services Resources Administration), 29 states and Puerto Rico have reinstituted programs or established pilot studies for sickle cell disease screening of newborns.[111]

Prenatal screening has been a less important aspect of the history of sickle cell screening than newborn screening. In the early 1970s, when carrier screening programs were being promoted, prenatal diagnosis of sickle cell disease was not available. A couple testing positive as carriers, therefore, had the limited choice of not having children or of running approximately a 25 percent risk of having a child with sickle cell disease. The advent of techniques that can diagnose sickle cell disease in the fetus has not, however, resulted in a groundswell of interest in prenatal testing or selective abortion of a fetus affected by sickle cell disease.[112]

Unlike Tay-Sachs disease, with its grimly predictable clinical course and ultimately fatal outcome, sickle cell disease has a quite variable course. Treatments are available, and are continually being developed to avoid or ameliorate symptoms of the disease and to extend the life span of affected individuals. It is difficult to estimate the extent to which either sickle cell carrier screening in pregnancy or prenatal diagnosis of sickle cell disease in fetuses is currently performed. No state programs mandate or offer prenatal sickle cell screening (see Chapter 6). Prenatal diagnosis, when it is performed, is generally conducted in the context of genetic counseling and proceeds only with informed consent.[113]

Tay-Sachs Disease

Tay-Sachs disease is a uniformly fatal, genetically transmitted, neurodegenerative disease associated with severe retardation and early blindness. It occurs predominantly in infants of Ashkenazi Jewish ancestry. The disease affects approximately 1 in 3,600 Jewish children compared with 1 in 360,000 non-Jewish children.[114] The carrier rate for Jewish individuals is estimated to be approximately 1 in 30 compared with 1 in 300 for non-Jews.[115]

In Tay-Sachs disease, the gene responsible for the production of the enzyme hexosaminidase A (Hex-A) is defective, leading to a failure to break down certain fatty substances in the brain. These substances accumulate and cause severe neurologic problems that become manifest at 4 to 6 months of age, when the child fails to reach normal milestones. This developmental lag is followed by deafness, blindness, convulsions, and generalized spasticity by 18 months, ending in death after 2 to 5 years.

Because there is no effective treatment or cure, the primary focus of screening programs is prevention of the birth of affected individuals, either by the identification of carriers prior to reproduction or, failing that, by the identification and termination of affected fetuses. After identification of an index couple by a simple and accurate Hex A assay of blood serum,[116] prenatal diagnosis for Tay-Sachs disease is generally done by assay of amniotic fluid for total Hex A and Hex A resistance to heat inactivation.[117] Today, earlier prenatal diagnosis using chorionic villus sampling is also available.

Tay-Sachs disease was the first condition for which large-scale carrier screening was conducted in the United States. In 1970, a community-based, voluntary, pilot screening program for carriers of Tay-Sachs disease among members of the Jewish community in the Baltimore–Washington area was instituted by Dr. Michael Kaback, then of The Johns Hopkins University. The medical, religious, and lay leaders of the community were involved in the planning and implementation of the screening program, which also enlisted the support of lay volunteers and local media in a massive educational effort.[118] More that 7,000 individuals volunteered for the carrier-detection blood test in the first 10 months.[119]

In 1974, Dr. Kaback initiated another Tay-Sachs prevention program in California, again involving extensive educational efforts. Carrier testing was offered in synagogues, schools, and community centers. In addition, education for physicians and the public, and counseling for affected couples, were made available.[120]

By the end of 1980, 73 cities and 13 countries had implemented community-based carrier-testing programs.[121] It is estimated that these screening efforts have contributed to a 60–85 percent decrease in the incidence of Tay-Sachs disease in Jewish infants in the United States.[122] The success of the focused education and screening in the Jewish community was dramatic, as evidenced by the fact that by 1984 more non-Jewish than Jewish Tay-Sachs babies were born.

Not everyone has deemed the U.S. Tay-Sachs program an unqualified success, however. At least one commentator has argued that a "public health" program that has the side effect of discouraging Jewish reproduction can hardly be considered benign by leaders of the Jewish community.[123] There is little evidence, however, that Tay-Sachs screening programs have had this effect. Notwithstanding the availability of sensitive tests, only a small percent of the adult North American Jews of reproductive age have volunteered to be screened.[124]

Currently, community-based Tay-Sachs screening has been largely replaced by testing of at-risk pregnant women, who are offered the test by their obstetricians. The husband is offered testing only if the wife is identified as a carrier. This shift in focus is not attributable to changes in obstetric technology, however. Prenatal diagnosis of Tay-Sachs disease was available from the beginning of interest in carrier screening. Thus couples identified as carriers always had the option of selective abortion.

Whether in pregnancy or at the community level, Tay-Sachs screening and testing have generally proceeded without state involvement or state funding. One notable exception is California, which has a state-sponsored Tay-Sachs program consisting largely of physician education, quality control of laboratories, and funds for testing of pregnant women (see Chapter 6).

Neural Tube Defects

Neural tube defects (NTDs) result from incomplete closure of an early fetal structure called the neural tube. NTDs constitute a spectrum of malformations ranging from uniformly fatal conditions to significantly or moderately disabling ones. The two major forms of NTD are anencephaly, the result of the incomplete neural tube closure in the developing head region, and spina bifida, the result of a lesion along the spinal cord.

Anencephaly is uniformly fatal and makes up 60 percent of all cases of NTD.[125] The natural history of spina bifida, however, is variable, depending on the location of the lesion and the degree of closure of the spinal column. Surviving infants experience disabilities ranging from weakness of the limbs to paralysis with incontinence and, occasionally, mental retardation. Repeated corrective surgery is not unusual. NTDs are significant because they are the most common group of birth defects in the United States, having an incidence of approximately 1 to 2 per 1,000 births.[126]

NTDs are believed to be caused by a combination of an inherited predisposition and environmental factors, with the defect manifesting at approximately 4 weeks gestational age. Unlike Tay-Sachs or sickle cell disease, there is no well-defined high-risk population for NTDs, a fact that precludes selective screening of pregnant women as an effective approach to identifying affected fetuses. Only 2 to 5 percent of affected children are born to parents with a family history of NTDs; the remaining 95 percent are born to couples not previously known to be at risk.[127]

In 1973, it was reported that maternal serum alpha-fetoprotein (MSAFP) levels are elevated in pregnancies where the fetus is affected with an open NTD. Alpha-fetoprotein (AFP) is a fetal serum protein normally secreted by the fetal kidneys and is usually present in the amniotic fluid and maternal serum in measurable amounts. In the case of an NTD, AFP enters the amniotic fluid and maternal serum at higher levels.

Because AFP is a normal fetal protein, testing for NTDs by measurement of MSAFP gives only an indication that the mother is at risk for having a fetus with an NTD. Only 1 of every 15 to 25 women with an initial elevated MSAFP level will have a fetus with an NTD.[128] As a result, it is necessary to follow up the initial MSAFP test with additional tests. Even in normal pregnancies, factors such as maternal age, gestational age at the time of the sampling, fetal sex and race, and multiple pregnancies influence MSAFP levels. A full AFP screening program includes a four-procedure testing protocol done in the second trimester, consisting of two blood tests for abnormal MSAFP levels, ultrasonography,[129] and amniocentesis for further measurement of AFP levels.[130] Even with this careful diagnostic chain of procedures, however, the fetus cannot be positively identified as having an NTD because other fetal abnormalities and complications are also associated with elevated MSAFP levels.[131] Although in a few instances interuterine treatment is possible, the alternatives when a defect is indicated are usually to allow the pregnancy to proceed, with preparation for the birth of an affected child, or to terminate the pregnancy.

By 1977, several companies had developed MSAFP test kits. Because of the inaccuracy of MSAFP tests alone in identifying affected fetuses, the unrestricted use of these test kits was met with widespread opposition. Groups opposed to the release of the AFP test kits by the Food and Drug Administration (FDA) included the American College of Obstetrics and Gynecology (ACOG), the American Academy of Pediatrics, the American Society of Human Genetics, the Spina Bifida Association of America, the Health Research Group, the Centers for

Disease Control, the Health Services Administration, the National Center for Health Care Technology, and antiabortion groups.[132]

Opposition came in part because of the fear that women would choose to terminate their pregnancies based solely on MSAFP testing without having the recommended confirmatory testing. An additional concern centered on the need to subject all pregnant women to screening, because there is no identifiable high-risk group for NTDs. Neither the medical community nor the laboratory facilities were prepared to deal with the volume of tests that would follow.[133] The ACOG position, as expressed in a 1982 Technical Bulletin, emphasized both concerns:

> Maternal serum [MS] AFP [alpha-fetoprotein] screening should be implemented *only* when it can be performed within a coordinated system of care that contains all the requisite resources and facilities to provide safeguards essential for ensuring prompt, accurate diagnosis and appropriate follow-through services. When such coordination and services are not possible, the risks and costs appear to outweigh the advantages and the program should not be implemented.[134] (emphasis added)

As a result of the controversy, the FDA failed to approve the MSAFP test kits as safe and effective for general use, and release of the kits was delayed for several years.[135] FDA approval for limited use of the kits came in 1983.[136]

In 1985, in spite of neither a significant improvement in the testing protocol nor an expansion of laboratory and genetic counseling resources, ACOG's Department of Legal Liability issued an unprecedented "Alert" to its members, substituting for its earlier medically driven position on screening for NTDs an apparently litigation-driven position. The Alert contained the following message:

> It is now imperative that you investigate the availability of these tests in your area and familiarize yourself with the procedure, location and mechanism of the follow-up tests to screen for neural tube defects. It is equally imperative that every prenatal patient be advised of the availability of this test and that your discussion about the test and the patient's decision with respect to the test be documented in the patient's chart.[137]

The resulting confusion as to which statement accurately reflected ACOG's position prompted a further elaboration in ACOG's September 1985 *Newsletter.* The *Newsletter*'s account attempted to soften the impact of the Alert without actually withdrawing it. According to the *Newsletter,* it was not in the purview of ACOG's legal department to set medical standards. The true ACOG position was that "the College has not, and does not recommend routine screening of maternal serum for AFP." The Alert was issued not to set medical standards but merely to present the facts. This backtracking, as has been pointed out, was undoubtedly advised so that the Alert could not be used in court as evidence of the standard of care.[138]

The latest installment in the evolving ACOG position was expressed in a 1987 editorial in *Obstetrics and Gynecology,* an ACOG publication. Citing greater understanding of MSAFP, improvement in ultrasonography and amniotic fluid analysis, the increase in the number of laboratories equipped to handle MSAFP screening, and the association of MSAFP levels with Down's syndrome,[139] the editorial endorsed routine MSAFP testing:

> We thus conclude that MSAFP screening for neural tube defects detection should now be undertaken in United States communities having expertise in ultrasound, genetic counseling, and amniocentesis. In communities in which these facilities are limited, it is still prudent to inform pregnant women of the availability of MSAFP screening. This obligation is probably most easily fulfilled by distributing patient information brochures. . . . Those communities not having appropriate facilities should attempt to develop a full scale MSAFP program, collaborating with an existing program, at a regional level.[140]

Because of the controversy associated with MSAFP screening, the interest in establishing state-sponsored screening programs has been limited. Since 1980, Vermont, without the benefit of prenatal screening legislation or regulations, had had an MSAFP screening program developed by the Vermont Department of Health Laboratory.[141] Mississippi, also without supporting legislation or regulations, has a limited MSAFP screening program that distributes information to physicians concerning the nature of NTDs and informed consent and counseling procedures. Mississippi advises that (the very low percentage of identifiable) high-risk women be tested.[142] In 1986, California legislatively established a prenatal AFP screening program.[143] Participation in the program by pregnant women is voluntary (see the Appendix to Chapter 6). Physicians are required to provide information about NTDs and the availability of the screening test, and to obtain either an informed consent or a signed refusal from their pregnant patients. In 1988, Hawaii's legislature enacted a prenatal screening statute that authorizes the state health department to ensure that prenatal screening services including those related to NTDs are made available to pregnant women. As of this writing, the program is not operational.[144]

Hepatitis B Virus

Hepatitis B virus (HBV) causes an infectious viral disease syndrome primarily affecting the liver. HBV can be manifested as chronic active hepatitis, cirrhosis, or hepatocellular carcinoma. Pregnant women infected with HBV may develop severe disease, jeopardizing the pregnancy itself, or become chronic carriers with few, if any, signs of infection. In the United States, there are over 200,000 new cases of HBV infection each year; 12,000 to 20,000 of those affected become chronic carriers.[145] The current estimate of the number of chronic carriers in the United States is 1 million.[146]

Vertical transmission of HBV represents one of the most efficient modes of HBV infection.[147] Most infants born to HBV-infected mothers become positive within the first 3 months of life, suggesting transmission at birth. Infants born to mothers positive for HBV surface antigen (HBsAg) and hepatitis B "e" antigen have a 70–90 percent chance of acquiring infection; 85–90 percent of infected infants become chronic HBV carriers. It has been estimated that 25 percent of children who become chronic carriers as a result of maternal transmission will die from hepatocellular carcinoma or cirrhosis of the liver.[148]

In 1983, it was established that the transmission of HBV from the HBsAg-positive mother to the newborn could be prevented by injecting the newborn with HBV immunoglobulin within 12 hours of birth, followed by injections of HBV vaccine during the immediate postpartum period and again at 1 and 6 months.[149]

Because substantial numbers of pregnant women infected with the virus are asymptomatic chronic carriers, identification of all infants in need of immunoglobulin and vaccine treatment is dependent upon the screening of pregnant women for evidence of HBV infection.

In 1984, the Immunization Practices Advisory Committee of the Public Health Service (ACIP) issued recommendations (the Recommendations) for prenatal HBsAg testing of certain pregnant women who were considered to be at substantially higher risk of HBV infection than the general population.[150] This high-risk group included women of Asian descent (who have the highest known carrier rate—approximately 8 percent), women born in Haiti or sub-Saharan Africa, and women with the following histories:

1. Work or treatment in a hemodialysis unit.
2. Work or residence in an institution for the mentally retarded.
3. Rejection as a blood donor.
4. Blood transfusion on repeated occasions.
5. Frequent occupational exposure to blood in medico-dental setting.
6. Household contact with an HBV carrier or hemodialysis patient.
7. Multiple households of venereal disease.
8. Percutaneous use of illicit drugs.[151]

Many physicians and hospitals implemented screening programs based on these Recommendations.

Follow-up studies on the effectiveness of screening based on the Recommendations, however, indicated that the ACIP criteria had a sensitivity of only 35–65 percent, meaning that many HBV-infected newborns were not being detected by selective screening programs.[152] For example, in a study of women attending a prenatal clinic in New Orleans, it was found that fully half of those found to be HBsAg-positive demonstrated none of the identifiable risk factors set forth in the Recommendations.[153] As a result of the low sensitivity of selective screening of only high-risk mothers, a 1988 editorial in the *Journal of the American Medical Association* recommended that the HBsAg test be added to the "prenatal panel" of routine laboratory tests for all pregnant women.[154] And in 1988, ACIP, citing major problems with its earlier Recommendations, reversed itself:

> It is now evident that routine screening of all pregnant women is the only strategy that will provide acceptable control of perinatal transmission of HBV infection in the United States. Screening the approximately 3.5 million pregnant women per year for HBsAg would identify 16,500 positive women and allow treatment that would prevent about 3,500 infants from becoming HBV carriers.[155]

ACIP further recommended that HBsAg testing be done early in pregnancy when other routine prenatal testing is done, for example, as part of "the routine prenatal 'panel.' "

It is not known to what degree these revised Recommendations have been adopted into medical practice. We are not aware of any legislative efforts to mandate HBV screening during pregnancy except for that of New York, which legislatively mandated the screening of all pregnant women, effective February 1990.[156] However, as noted in Chapter 6, both of the university hospitals with which the authors are affiliated have added HBV to their routine prenatal screening panels. We suspect that the practice of screening for HBV infection in pregnancy is now widespread and, as is the case at The Johns Hopkins University Hospital and Georgetown University Hospital, most pregnant women are unaware they are being tested.

Conclusion

We have reviewed the histories of six prenatal and newborn screening programs in order to try to determine what lessons are applicable to the proposed HIV screening of pregnant women and newborns. No single example emerges as the perfect prototype for HIV screening.

In many respects, *prenatal* screening for HIV resembles prenatal screening for NTDs or Tay-Sachs disease. No effective intervention to prevent the fetus from becoming affected or to treat the fetus in utero is (generally) available for any of these conditions, thus highlighting the alternative of termination of the pregnancy. A significant difference is that it is not yet possible to diagnose HIV prenatally, as it is with NTDs and Tay-Sachs disease. As a result, any decision to have an abortion made by an HIV-seropositive woman would have to be made on the basis of an approximately 30 percent probability of having an HIV-affected child (see Chapter 2). In this respect, prenatal screening for HIV is more akin to prenatal screening for sickle cell disease before the advent of recombinant DNA fetal diagnostic techniques.

HIV screening of *newborns* also evokes many features of sickle cell screening, although by contrast to sickle cell screening, the test for HIV infection in the newborn is less accurate and the treatment interventions are considerably less effective. One key problem with the early newborn sickle cell screening programs was that the ability to detect the disorder accurately was not coupled with the ability to treat the condition effectively. The recent experience with sickle cell screening, however, demonstrates that the "lack of treatment" objection to newborn screening is subject to change as effective treatments are developed.

The experience of screening programs such as sickle cell programs that target minority populations reveals several problems. If the disease is one for which no treatment exists, leaving abortion or mate selection as the key options, charges of eugenics and stigmatization result. Such programs can result not only in charges of eugenics but in actual racial discrimination, as was the case in the early sickle cell screening programs. Even today, when sickle cell screening of newborns has wide support because of the benefits of early medical intervention, the advocated policy calls for the testing of all infants rather than selective screening of African-American infants.

The rationale for universal newborn screening for sickle cell disease is based not only on the social and normative difficulties associated with selective screening, but also on public health objections. As illustrated in the case studies of both HBV screening and Tay-Sachs screening, selective screening is medically problematic. The experience with HBV showed that, even with a broad definition of the persons at risk, selective screening can fail to detect significant numbers of affected persons. As a result, it is currently recommended that all pregnant women be screened for HBV. The Tay-Sachs experience showcased another aspect of the problem. Over time, the at-risk population may shift, making the original criteria for selective screening less applicable. Screening of Jews for Tay-Sachs disease has been so successful that today the majority of infants born with the disease are not Jewish. Yet Tay-Sachs testing is so closely identified with the Jewish community that physicians generally fail to offer testing to their non-Jewish patients.

An important aspect of being identified as HIV seropositive is the stigmatization and adverse social and employment consequences that can follow (see Chapter 1). This stigmatization is not unlike that which affected identified syphilitics early in this century (and perhaps today as well) or those having sickle cell disease or trait during the 1970s. In contrast to the stigma associated with HIV, syphilis, and sickle cell disease or trait, the Tay-Sachs screening programs have not been associated with adverse social consequences. This is due, in part, to the efforts to educate the community and enlist widespread community support. Furthermore, unlike HIV or syphilis, the notion of "fault" has not been connected with having Tay-Sachs disease. Finally, the fact that HIV and sickle cell disease are strongly associated with racial minorities undoubtedly contributes to the stigmatization. As a result of these considerations, HIV screening programs would do well to anticipate and provide protection for the predictable results of positive HIV diagnoses, which include, but are not limited to, the areas of education, confidentiality, employment, housing, and insurance coverage (see Chapter 9).

Screening for the six diseases discussed in this chapter has been based sometimes on legislative or regulatory mandates and sometimes on incorporation into routine medical practice. For example, syphilis screening of pregnant women was legislated in almost every state in the country after a long and unsuccessful campaign to have screening incorporated into routine medical practice. The legislation was necessary to overcome reluctance on the part of physicians to offering the screening. Paradoxically, PKU screening of newborns was also mandated by state action, notwithstanding its apparently successful voluntary incorporation into routine medical practice in Massachusetts. In this case, the legislative route appears to have been sought as an insurance policy by the advocates of screening who could not predict whether all the states would follow Massachusetts' lead. There is little doubt that legislatively mandating syphilis and PKU screening resulted in a more rapid adoption of screening. In both cases, the ease of adoption of the legislative mandates reflected the availability of reasonably effective treatments and the fact that there was no selective screening of perceived "high-risk" groups.

From a governmental point of view, sickle cell screening has been more problematic, in part because of confusion about the risks of having the trait as opposed to the disease and, in part, because of the lack of an effective treatment. In the 1970s, mandatory screening—sometimes for the trait and sometimes for the disease—was tried briefly but was accompanied by such significant problems that very soon there was a rush to appeal or amend legislation to provide for voluntary screening. Significantly, now that an effective intervention is available, it is recommended that screening of all newborns for sickle cell disease be mandated by state law.

Screening for Tay-Sachs disease and NTDs has generally, but not always, been independent of government activity. California, where government involvement has been directed at ensuring that physicians offer the testing to all pregnant women, is one notable exception. The absence of widespread legislative mandates for Tay-Sachs disease reflects the success of private screening, although, as mentioned earlier, this success is increasingly limited to Jewish populations. The case for NTDs is somewhat more complex, but here, too, it is likely that many women are tested or offered testing by their physicians without a legislative directive, if only in reaction to the ACOG Liability Alert concerning NTDs. No doubt the fact that abortion is the only "treatment" option available in both cases is also a significant factor.

Except for New York's recent mandatory statute, prenatal screening for HBV has been a purely medical decision, notwithstanding the fact that the characteristics of prenatal screening for HBV are similar to those for syphilis. Presumably, the degree of physician compliance with professional recommendations to screen all pregnant women will determine whether HBV screening remains at the discretion of the physician or is incorporated into state screening policies.

Closely connected with the basis of authority to screen (medical or statutory) is the issue of consent. Prenatal testing for NTDs and Tay-Sachs disease has always been done on a voluntary basis. In both instances, the only prenatal "intervention" available is abortion. Less is known about how prenatal testing for sickle cell disease is currently conducted. Here again, the primary reason for prenatal testing is abortion. In many centers, prenatal testing follows conventional prenatal genetic testing procedures, which generally include the obligation to obtain informed consent. However, in other sites, sickle cell screening is done routinely. Confirmatory diagnostic techniques such as amniocentesis require informed consent.

Syphilis testing is the only prenatal screen that is legislatively mandated, reflecting the fact that testing permits both cure of the infection in the pregnant woman and prevention of the disease in the infant. However, as noted in Chapter 6, pregnant women are routinely screened for a number of conditions in addition to syphilis. Often this screening occurs without the active involvement or awareness of patients. These include conditions that are primarily of interest because of the risk they pose to the developing fetus, such as rubella and Rh factor, as well as diseases with medical implications for both mother and fetus, such as tuberculosis, gonorrhea, gestational diabetes, and herpes simplex. In each of these cases, effective interventions are available to prevent or markedly reduce associated harmful consequences.

For newborn screening, the prototype is PKU testing, which in most jurisdictions is performed on all infants without parental consent. However, unlike newborn HIV testing, there exists a highly effective intervention for babies identified through screening as having PKU. Additionally, the testing itself does not reveal medical information about the mother that is socially stigmatizing.

Increasingly, sickle cell disease is providing another model for newborn screening. In most jurisdictions where sickle cell testing has been adopted, it has also been instituted as a routine test not requiring parental consent. The benefits to infants identified through testing as having sickle cell disease, while significant, are arguably not as great as the benefits experienced by PKU infants. In addition, testing newborns does reveal medical information about the parents that is potentially socially significant—the presence of sickle cell trait. Testing can also lead to the identification of nonpaternity. For these and other reasons, some commentators have argued for prenatal consent requirements for newborn sickle cell testing programs, although the legislative trend is clearly running in the opposite direction.[157]

Notes

1. See, for example, Howard L. Minkoff "The Case for Routinely Offering Prenatal Testing for Human Immunodeficiency Virus," *American Journal of Obstetrics and Gynecology* 159 (4): 793–796, and Douglas Black, David Cox, Richard Doll et al., "HIV Testing on All Pregnant Women" (letter), *Lancet* (1987): 1277.
2. Neil A. Holtzman, Claire O. Leonard, and Mark R. Farfel, "Issues in Antenatal and Neonatal Screening and Surveillance for Hereditary and Congenital Disorders," *Annual Review of Public Health* 2 (1981): 219–251, at 219.
3. J. Whitridge Williams, "The Significance of Syphilis in Prenatal Care and in the Causation of Foetal Death," *Bulletin of The Johns Hopkins Hospital* 351 (1920): 141–145.
4. Lori Andrews, *State Laws and Regulations Governing Newborn Screening* (Chicago: American Bar Foundation, 1985).
5. *Hastings Center Report* 18 (1988): 48. Cystic fibrosis is the seventh condition in Colorado's newborn screening program.
6. P. J. L. Sequeira and J. O'H. Tobin, "Intrauterine Infections: Syphilis, Viral Diseases, Toxoplasmosis and Chlamydial Infections," in *Antenatal and Neonatal Screening*, ed. N. J. Wald (New York: Oxford University Press, 1984), 360–662.
7. Ibid., 362. Treatment of a pregnant woman who tests positive for syphilis depends on the status of the infection; that is, whether it is primary (less than 2 years old) or late benign or latent. It also depends on whether the patient can be trusted to return for a course of treatment or whether she should be treated with a single large injection. An additional factor is whether the woman is sensitive to penicillin; if she is, erythromycin is recommended.
8. Allan Brandt, *No Magic Bullet: A Social History of Venereal Disease in the United States Since 1880* (New York: Oxford University Press, 1985), 13.
9. Ibid.
10. Ibid.
11. William Allen Pusey, *The History and Epidemiology of Syphilis* (Baltimore: Thomas, 1933). The author based his estimates on a survey done by the Public Health Service in cooperation with the American Social Hygiene Association done the previous year. The author also makes the following estimate: "Among private patients of the average class . . . Johns Hopkins Hospital and the Mayo Clinic each find an incidence [of syphilis] of 5 percent. Taking many hospitals, the incidence of syphilis among admissions varies from 5 to 25 percent or more depending on the class of patients which these hospitals serve" (78).
12. U.S. Public Health Service (USPHS), *Syphilis in Mother and Child,* Supplement No. 7 to Venereal Disease Information (Washington, D.C.: Government Printing Office, 1940), 1.
13. Pusey, *History and Epidemiology of Syphilis,* 66. Development of the Wasserman test, the first practical test for syphilis, occurred in 1906–1907.
14. M. Marquardt, *Paul Ehrlich* (London: Heinemann, 1949).
15. In discussing the difficulty of administering salvarsan, one surgeon noted that "panic may seize even the fairly experienced if the goal [of finding the vein] is not reached on the first attempt; the tense attitude, the shrinking away, the sounds of remonstrance and disapproval from the patient are only too efficient in bringing

beads of sweat to the operator's forehead and in damaging the fine movements of the hands on which his success depends." And he noted further that "even the poor can scarcely be expected to submit with good grace to repeated barbarities in the name of good medicine" (John H. Stokes, "Certain Technical Refinements in Methods of Intravenous Injection," *Medical Record* 92 [1917]: 529–535).

16. The high cost of salvarsan can be explained by the fact that a German company held all rights to produce the drug. During World War I, by late 1915, when the Allies had blockaded Germany, so that supplies from the United States were cut off, the price of an ampule increased from $4 to $35. Later the Federal Trade Commission abrogated the German patent and licensed the production of salvarsan to three U.S. companies. Production in this country reduced the price to between $1.00 and $1.50 (Harry F. Dowling, "Comparisons and Contrasts bctwccn the Early Arsphenamine and Early Antibiotic Periods," *Bulletin of the History of Medicine* 47 [1973]: 247; see also Brandt, *No Magic Bullet,* 131). In the 1930s, the average cost of a course of treatment was between $305 and $380, but it could reach $1,000.

17. W. J. Brown, J. F. Donohue, N. Axnick et al., *Syphilis and Other Venereal Diseases* (Cambridge, Mass.: Harvard University Press, 1970), 15. See also H. Martenstein, "Inquiry in 5 Countries," *Quarterly Bulletin of Health Organizations* (League of Nations) 4 (1935): 129–246.

18. Brown et al., *Syphilis and Other Venereal Diseases.*

19. J. Whitridge Williams, "The Influence of the Treatment of Syphilitic Pregnant Women Upon the Incidence of Congenital Syphilis," *Bulletin of The Johns Hopkins Hospital* 33 (1922): 1–4.

20. Ibid., 13.

21. USPHS, *Syphilis in Mother and Child,* 7. A typical physician's comment was: "My patients do not have syphilis, and I will not insult any one of them by suggesting that she have a serologic test for syphilis performed." See also Williams, "Influence of the Treatment." Williams looked at the impact of many different levels of treatment of pregnant women on pregnancy outcome. The treatments ranged from "efficient" to "notoriously inefficient." Williams noted that "almost ideal results follow anything like efficient treatment of syphilitic women" and concluded that pregnant women were unusually amenable to antisyphilitic treatment." Women receiving "efficient" treatment had 10 of 11 live-born children born with negative Wasserman tests (one was lost to treatment).

22. Brandt, *No Magic Bullet,* 138.

23. *New York Post,* January 5, 1938, p. 1: "Here's our idea for the Legislature: The Post proposes that the state require by law that every doctor give every prospective mother a blood test as a mandatory part of routine prenatal care. . . . We think that New York should lead the nation in stamping out congenital syphilis and syphilitic stillbirth."

24. Edward C. Keinle, "Public Opinion and New York's 'Baby Health Bill.' " *Journal of Social Hygiene* 24 (1938): 487–492.

25. Ibid., 488.

26. See, for example, "Outlawing Syphilis" (editorial), *Journal of Social Hygiene* 24 (1938): 520–522. Syphilis is the only condition examined in this chapter that had organized medicine's support. Note also that passage of the "Baby Health Bill" was largely due to the almost unanimous support of women and women's groups, including the American Woman's Association, the Women's City Club of New York, and the State League of Women's Voters. Endorsement was also given by the

Children's Welfare Federation, comprising 50 New York hospitals and welfare organizations, the Maternity Center Association, state and city health departments, the State Medical Society, the New York Academy of Medicine, the State Charities Aid Association, the United Neighborhood Houses, and the Association for Improving the Condition of the Poor (Keinle, "Public Opinion," 488).

27. Walter Clark, "Administrative Aspects of the Prenatal and Premarital Examination Laws," *Journal of Social Hygiene* 24 (1938): 505. Rhode Island also passed a mandatory syphilis law for pregnant women in 1938.

28. Brandt, *No Magic Bullet,* 143–144.

29. Ibid. Prior to 1938, Congress had begun focusing attention on the seriousness of infectious diseases. The 1935 Social Security Act provided the Public Health Service with $8 million for state health programs, 10 percent of which was used for venereal diseases. According to Brandt, these funds represented the first federal money the state health departments had received since just after World War I.

30. USPHS, *Syphilis in Mother and Child.*

31. Ibid., 1. These 60,000 cases in infants represented approximately 10 percent of the new syphilis cases each year.

32. Ibid., 4. The "standard serological tests" recommended included all of the serologic tests for syphilis that were in common use in 1940 and that were shown to have acceptable specificity and sensitivity by the Committee on Evaluation of Serodiagnostic Tests for Syphilis.

33. Ibid., 11. Because transmission to the fetus was not believed to occur prior to the fifth month, early treatment was deemed essential. The earlier treatment was begun, the lower the incidence of congenital syphilis. Treatment of syphilis in pregnant women was to be directed entirely toward the fetus, "save for her ability to tolerate treatment," with proper care of the woman to await the delivery of a full-term, healthy infant (7).

34. Ibid., 9. It should be noted that unsuccessful treatment of the mother required treatment of the newborn. Such treatment was similar to that for pregnant women requiring weekly intravenous injections. The procedure was vividly described as one in which the infant was first to be laid on the table. If the infant "does not cry spontaneously during this maneuver it is desirable to make him do so; this brings out the jugular vein very prominently and makes intravenous treatment easier." The treatment recommended in this publication consisted of the administration of 34 doses of an arsenical and 43 doses of bismuth in a 72-week overlapping rotation (19).

35. A. Frank Brewer and Florence E. Olson, "Evaluation of California's Prenatal Law Requiring a Serologic Test for Syphilis," *American Journal of Syphilis, Gonorrhea and Veneral Disease* 31 (1947): 633–639, at 636. The current status of prenatal syphilis screening legislation is reviewed in Chapter 6.

36. Ibid. The infant mortality rate for syphilis dropped from 0.45/1,000 in 1939, the year California's prenatal screening bill was passed, to 0.15/1,000 in 1945. See also Brandt, *No Magic Bullet,* 150.

37. Brandt, *No Magic Bullet,* 12.

38. CDC, "Progress Toward Achieving the 1990 Objectives for the Nation for Sexually Transmitted Diseases," *Morbidity and Mortality Weekly Report* 39 (1989): 53–57.

39. The incidence of PKU was estimated to be only 1 in 20,000 when the PKU screening test was introduced. It should also be noted that the incidence varies markedly from country to country, from region to region within a country, and from one ethnic

group to another. For example, PKU is relatively common among Irish and Poles but is uncommon in U.S. blacks and Askenazi Jews (Harvey L. Levy and Marvin M. Mitchell, "The Current Status of Newborn Screening," *Hospital Practice* [1982]: 89–97).

40. See, for example, Holtzman et al., "Issues in Antenatal and Neonatal Screening," 220. See also American Academy of Pediatrics, Committee on Genetics, "Newborn Screening Fact Sheets," *Pediatrics* 83 (1989): 449–464. It should be noted that infants of untreated affected mothers may have microcephaly, retardation, and congenital heart disease even without having PKU. Studies to determine whether dietary treatment of the mother improves the outcome are under way.

41. American Academy of Pediatrics, "Newborn Screening Fact Sheets," 461–462.

42. Judith P. Swazey, "Phenylketonuria: A Case Study in Biomedical Legislation," *Journal of Urban Law* 48 (1971): 835–931, at 893.

43. Robert Guthrie, "Blood Screening for Phenylketonuria" (letter), *Journal of the American Medical Association* 178 (1961): 863; Robert Guthrie and Ada Susi, "A Simple Phenylalanine Method for Detecting Phenylketonuria in Large Populations of Newborn Infants," *Pediatrics* 32 (1963): 338. The screening test is based on a simple blood test. Shortly after birth, a drop of blood is absorbed on a piece of paper. Typically, the sample is mailed to a central laboratory for evaluation.

44. Robert A. MacCready and M. Grace Hussey, "Newborn Phenylketonuria Detection Program in Massachusetts," *American Journal of Public Health* 54 (1964): 2075–2081. This progress report of the Massachusetts PKU screening program does not mention whether a specific consent process was part of the program, but it did note that nurses were instructed on how to explain the test to parents and "in every instance physicians and parents cooperated."

45. Swazey, "Phenylketonuria," 894.

46. Committee for the Study of Inborn Errors of Metabolism, *Genetic Screening: Programs, Principles and Research* (Washington, D.C.: National Academy of Sciences, 1975), 44–87. It should be noted that NARC had supported Guthrie's research for the development of the PKU screening test (46).

47. National Association for Retarded Children, "Legislation for Mandatory Screening for Phenylketonuria (PKU) Recommended by NARC's Board of Directors," *Weekly Action Report*, no. 58 (January 4, 1964). NARC went even further and suggested a model law.

48. Swazey, "Phenylketonuria," 917, citing Joseph Cooper, *Creative Pluralism, Medical Research of the Committee on Government Operations* 90th Cong. (Washington, D.C.: Government Printing Office, 1967), 47–65. See also Peter Reilly, "State Supported Mass Genetic Screening Programs," in *Genetics and the Law*, ed. Aubrey Milunsky and George J. Annas (New York: Plenum, 1976), 1: 160. Reilly notes that "a few members of the medical research community became zealous advocates of screening."

49. Committee for the Study, *Genetic Screening*. The fact that Massachusetts was the first to enact a mandatory screen was not surprising, since the director of the State Health Department of Massachusetts was the chairman of NARC's Public Health Services Committee, of which Guthrie was also a member (46).

50. Ibid, 44–48. Actually, NARC initially rejected mandatory screening in favor of an approach characterized by health department recommendations. After encountering physician reluctance to adopt the recommendations voluntarily, however, NARC endorsed a mandatory approach.

51. Ibid.
52. "New Child Health Legislative Bills Proposed—Academy Subcommittee Issues Guidelines," *Bulletin of Pediatric Practice* (1967): 1–2.
53. Reilly, "State Supported Mass Genetic Screening Programs."
54. Ibid.
55. Ibid. Reilly also notes that no state statute required that affected children be placed on a low-phenylalanine diet.
56. Neil A. Holtzman, "Public Participation in Genetic Policymaking: The Maryland Commission on Hereditary Disorders," in *Genetics and the Law,* ed. Aubrey Milunsky and George J. Annas (New York: Plenum, 1984), 3: 247–255.
57. H. S. Cuckle and Nicholas J. Wald, "Principles of Screening," in *Antenatal and Neonatal Screening,* ed. Nicholas J. Wald (New York: Oxford University Press, 1984), 1–22.
58. Harvey L. Levy, "Problems in Genetic Screening which Confront the Law," in Milunsky and Annas, ed., *Genetics and the Law,* 1: 133.
59. Reilly, "State Supported Mass Genetic Screening Programs," 160. Of course, a possible explanation for the high rate of voluntary compliance of the Massachusetts physicians is that they believed it would obviate the "need" (and enthusiasm) for mandatory screening.
60. P. Reilly, "The Role of the Law," and M. O. Yeale, "Screening for Inborn Errors of Metabolism," both in *Neonatal Screening for Inborn Errors of Metabolism,* ed. H. Bickle, R. Guthrie, and G. Hammersen (New York: Springer-Verlag, 1980).
61. Ranject Grover, Doris Wethers, Syad Shahidi et al., "Evaluation of the Expanded Newborn Screening Program in New York City," *Pediatrics* 61 (1978): 740–749. The authors note that "the reasoning behind the selection of the particular conditions listed in the New York State law is not entirely clear but was apparently based partly on the ease with which certain other tests could be added [regardless of the need to be diagnosed at birth], and partly on political expediency. It was devised with consultation and expertise largely limited to the laboratory aspects of the program" (740). It should also be noted that sickle cell disease was included in New York's 1974 expanded mandatory newborn screening statute.
62. See Chapter 6 of this volume.
63. Vermont tests newborns for PKU, hypothyroidism, and galactosemia; Delaware tests, additionally, for homocystinuria and maple syrup urine disease.
64. New Hampshire statutorily requires only PKU testing, but it provides notice and information to physicians concerning other conditions for which testing is available. In addition, by virtue of its participation in the New England Regional Screening Program, newborns in New Hampshire are tested for galactosemia, hypothyroidism, MSUD, and homocystinuria (personal communication, Susan J. Moore, Newborn Screening Program Coordinator).
65. The Massachusetts newborn screening program is statutorily authorized under a provision aimed at combatting mental retardation.
66. Robert Guthrie, "Newborn Screening: Past, Present, Future," in *Genetic Disease: Screening and Management,* ed. Thomas P. Carter and Ann M. Willey (New York: Liss, 1986), 328. For example, New York's screening program screened 5.4 million newborns between 1965 and 1985, identifying 312 affected infants.
67. Swazey, "Phenylketonuria," 927.
68. Committee on Fetus and Newborn, "Screening of Newborn Infants for Metabolic Disease," *Pediatrics* 35 (1965): 499–503. "Another difficulty . . . [with PKU

screening] lies in the complete lack of uniformity of opinion as to what constitutes adequate control of dietary intake and what blood levels of phenylalanine should be maintained" (502). See also Holtzman et al., "Issues in Antenatal and Neonatal Screening," Even in the case of classical PKU, there is no consensus on the optimal duration of the restricted phenylalanine diet (222).

69. Samuel P. Bessman, "Legislation and Advances in Medical Knowledge—Acceleration or Inhibition?" *Journal of Pediatrics* 69 (1966): 334–338. See also Edwin W. Naylor, "Recent Developments in Neonatal Screening," *Seminars in Perinatology* 9 (1985): 232–249. Naylor notes that until the middle to late 1970s, the variant forms of PKU were not known; all that was known was that some cases of PKU were unresponsive to dietary therapy.

70. In *Genetic Screening,* the Committee for the Study of Inborn Errors of Metabolism concluded that "hindsight reveals that screening programs for [PKU] were instituted before the validity and effectiveness of all aspects of treatment, including appropriate dietary treatment, were thoroughly tested" (1–2).

71. Ara Tourian and James Sidbury, "Phenylketonuria and Hyperphenylalanemia," in *The Metabolic Basis of Inherited Disease,* ed. John B. Stanbury, James B. Wyngaarden, Donald S. Frederickson, et al. (New York: McGraw-Hill, 1983), 270–286. Hyperphenylalanemia has been associated with at least eight different causes, not all of which require dietary treatment. See also Bobbye M. Rouse, "Phenylalanine Deficiency Syndrome," *Journal of Pediatrics* 69 (1966): 246–249. The author reported that dietary treatment of "normal" infants falsely identified as having PKU resulted in generalized rash, poor development, and progressive weight loss and showed, generally, the signs of chronic malnourishment. The author speculated on whether such protein deficiency could lead to deficiencies in brain growth and subsequent learning ability (248). See also Edwin W. Naylor, "Screening for PKU Cofactor Variants," in Carter and Willey, eds., *Genetic Diseases,* 211–225. Naylor distinguishes classical PKU, for which dietary treatment is effective, from other forms of PKU and notes that their treatment management can be very different. He states that PKU must be viewed as a "heterogeneous collection of inborn errors. . . . It is no longer possible to routinely screen newborns for PKU, confirm the diagnosis, and initiate therapy, based solely on serum phenylalanine levels" (222).

72. Over 95 percent of infants who are identified as having PKU by the newborn screening test have classical PKU (Holtzman et al., "Issues in Antenatal and Neonatal Screening," 220).

73. Ibid., 248.

74. Neil A. Holtzman, "Rare Diseases, Common Problems: Recognition and Management," *Pediatrics* 62 (1978): 1056–1060.

75. American Academy of Pediatrics, "Newborn Screening Fact Sheets," 449–464. Sickle cell diseases, or sickle cell hemoglobinopathies, refer to a group of diseases characterized by genetic defects in the gene responsible for encoding hemoglobin. The most severe manifestations of the genetic defect is an anemia in persons who are homozygous for the defect. This homozygous condition is referred to in this chapter as sickle cell disease. Persons who are heterozygous—that is, having one normal and one affected gene—generally show few symptoms but are carriers for the trait. Should a person carrying the sickle cell trait marry another carrier (which, according to Rucknagel, occurs in one out of 150 marriages) the probability for each child of being heterozygous is 50 percent. (Donald L. Rucknagel, "The Genetics of Sickle

Cell Anemia and Related Syndromes," *Archives of Internal Medicine* 133 [1974]: 595–606).

The literature refers to both sickle cell disease and sickle cell anemia when discussing the homozygous condition and sickle cell trait or carrier status when discussing the heterozygous condition. A term encompassing both is sickle cell hemoglobinopathies.

76. Rucknagel, "Genetics of Sickle Cell Anemia and Related Syndrome."
77. Naylor, "Screening for PKU Cofactor Variants," 238; E. Naylor, "Recent Developments in Neonatal Screening," *Seminars in Perinatology* 9 (1985): 232–249.
78. Audrey K. Brown, Scott T. Miller, and Patricia Agatisa, "Care of Infants with Disease: The Ultimate Objective of Newborn Screening; Care of Infants with Sickle Cell Disease," *Pediatrics* (Suppl.), *Newborn Screening for Sickle Cell Disease and Other Hemoglobinopathies* 83 (1989): 897–900.
79. R. B. Scott, "Sickle Cell Anemia—High Prevalence and Low Priority," *New England Journal of Medicine* 282 (1970): 164–165. Not everyone shared Scott's view concerning the priority that sickle cell disease testing should receive. Dr. Lawrence E. Gary noted that maternal and infant mortality and hypertension all disproportionately affected blacks and were greater health risks than sickle cell disease. Hypertension, he noted, caused 13,500 deaths among blacks, while sickle cell disease caused only 340 ("The Sickle Cell Controversy," *Social Work* 19 [1974]: 263–272).
80. Scott, "Sickle Cell Anemia," 164. See also R. B. Scott, "Health Care Priority and Sickle Cell Anemia," *Journal of the American Medical Association* 214 (1970): 731–734.
81. Scott, "Health Care Priority," 734. Scott was optimistic about the use of genetic screens. He went on to say that "as suitable screening tests are developed for other conditions such as cystic fibrosis or muscular dystrophy, they too can be approached with similar preventive methods. Success in ameliorating one hereditary illness means that control of any hereditary illness will be limited only by the development of suitable tests for accurate mass screening of trait carriers" (734).
82. Barbara Culliton, "Sickle Cell Anemia: The Route from Obscurity to Prominence," *Science* 178 (1972): 138–142.
83. Ibid. In connection with the preparation of President Nixon's health message to Congress, the younger Petricelli had reviewed a statement on sickle cell anemia prepared by a summer intern in response to a letter from a woman whose son had the disease.
84. One of the shows contained an interview with Dr. Scott, who had been studying and treating sickle cell disease for 25 years at Howard University and who spoke of his dream of establishing a sickle cell center at Howard. As a result of the publicity, the citizens of Hartford spontaneously began to send in contributions to set up the Howard Center (Culliton, "Sickle Cell Anemia").
85. "National Health Strategy: The President's Message to the Congress Proposing a Comprehensive Health Policy for the Seventies," *Weekly Compilation of Presidential Documents* 7 (1972): 244–259.
86. Culliton, "Sickle Cell Anemia," 136, note 86. Connecticut's statute provided for voluntary screening.
87. See, for example, Reilly, "State Supported Mass Genetic Screening Programs," 173. Reilly notes that between 1970 and 1972, 12 states enacted sickle cell screening laws.

88. Mary L. Hampton, James Anderson, Blanche Lavizzo et al., "Sickle Cell 'Non-disease,' " *American Journal of Diseases of Children* 128 (1974): 158–161, at 158.

89. I. M Rutkow and J. M. Lipton, "Mandatory Screening for Sickle Cell Anemia" (letter), *New England Journal of Medicine* 289 (1973): 865–866, at 865. Included were the District of Columbia, California, Georgia, Illinois, Kentucky, Louisiana, Massachusetts, New York, and Virginia.

90. One author notes that "lay publicity and political support, plus the notion that since sickle cell anemia cannot be cured perhaps it should be 'treated' with genetic counseling, have created a great deal of pressure for educational programs, screening and genetic counseling efforts" (Rucknagel, "Genetics of Sickle Cell and Related Syndromes," 600).

91. Ira M. Rutkow and Jeffrey N. Lipton, "Some Negative Aspects of State Health Department Policies Related to Screening for Sickle Cell Anemia," *American Journal of Public Health* 64 (1974): 217–222, at 218.

92. Ibid. The four states were Arizona, Connecticut, Maryland, and Ohio.

93. President's Commission for the Study of Ethical Problems in Medicine and Biomedical and Behavioral Research, *Genetic Screening and Counseling: The Ethical, Social, and Legal Implications of Genetic Screening and Education Programs* (Washington, D.C.: Government Printing Office, 1983). "Early sickle-cell screening programs were ineffective and not readily accepted by the target population because they were often not community-based, did not build on education, were mandated in some states in a hasty manner, and seemed to be aimed at preventing the birth of minority children" (23).

94. Ibid.

95. Ibid. See also Loretta Kopelman, "Genetic Screening in Newborns: Voluntary or Compulsory?" *Perspectives in Biology and Medicine* 72 (1978): 83–89. The New York statute, for example, does not require the physician to inform parents that their child has either sickle cell trait or disease and does not provide funds for either counseling or follow-up.

96. Andrews, *State Laws and Regulations Governing Newborn Screening*, 149.

97. Ernest Beutler, Dane R. Boggs, Paul Heller et al., "Hazards of Indiscriminate Screening in Sickling" (correspondence), *New England Journal of Medicine* 285 (26): 1486–1487.

98. President's Commission, *Genetic Screening and Counseling*, 22.

99. Ibid., 427.

100. Barbara J. Culliton, "Sickle Cell Anemia: National Program Raises Problems as Well as Hopes," *Science* 178 (1972): 283–286, at 284 (citing an NIH official).

101. Public Law 92-294:86, Statute 136, sec. 1103: "The participation by any individual in any program or portion thereof under this title shall be wholly voluntary and shall not be a prerequisite to eligibility for receipt of any service or assistance from, or to participation in, any other program."

102. Reilly, "State Supported Mass Genetic Screening Programs," 21.

103. Ibid.

104. Jessica G. Davis, "Genetic Disease, Government, and Social Justice," in Milunsky and Annas, eds., *Genetics and the Law III*, 3: 385–393. The statewide programs took one of three forms: (1) state health department–sponsored programs; (2) university-based programs; and (3) regional programs in which the health departments of several states cooperated (386).

105. Ibid. DHHS specifically excluded genetic testing and counseling projects in cal-

culating the states' Maternal and Child Health [MCH] block grant allocation. Instead, funding earmarked for genetics testing was put into a special fund controlled by NIH that significantly restricted state eligibility requirements. None of the ineligible states used discretionary funds of the MCH grant to fund genetic services.

106. Ibid.

107. Personal communication, Dr. Marilyn H. Gaston, Deputy Chief of the Sickle Cell Disease Branch of the NIH National Heart, Lung, and Blood Institute.

108. Consensus Conference, "Newborn Screening for Sickle Cell Disease and other Hemoglobinopathies," *Journal of the American Medical Association* 258 (1989): 1205–1209. The National Heart, Lung, and Blood Institute, the Office of Child Health and Human Development, and the Genetic Disease Services Branch of the Health Resources and Services Branch of the Office of Medical Applications of Research sponsored an NIH Consensus Development Conference on Newborn Screening for Sickle Cell Disease and Other Hemoglobinopathies that brought together 400 biomedical investigators, clinicians, other health professionals, parents, and representatives of the public. The response to the Conference's recommendations has been mixed. The National Association of Sickle Cell Disease (NASCD), for example, has called for laws requiring state-supported screening of all at-risk newborns *without* informed consent. NASCD would leave the decision of who should be tested to the states but notes that in the vast majority of states, all newborns should be tested (J. Whitten, "Perspectives from the National Association for Sickle Cell Disease," *Pediatrics* 83 [Suppl.] [1989]: 906–907). In contrast, Holtzman, writing on behalf of the American Academy of Pediatrics (AAP), argues that because of the variability in the incidence of genetic disease by ethnic or racial group, the routine screening of all newborns for sickle cell disease would not be effective in predominantly white communities. Another factor reducing the effectiveness of a universal screening program is quality control of the screening process. Adding unnecessary screening would only exacerbate the existing problems of missed diagnoses. Because of these inefficiencies, coupled with limited state resources and differing community health needs, the AAP has reaffirmed its earlier position calling for the establishment of state advisory boards to review and approve new screening projects (Neil Holtzman. "Perspectives from the American Academy of Pediatrics," *Pediatrics* 83 [Suppl.] [1989]: 913–914).

109. Georgia, which began mandatory screening of African-American infants at 6 months of age in 1964, now has a policy of voluntary, targeted screening providing for the testing of "all newborns who are susceptible or are likely to have . . . sickle cell anemia or sickle cell trait." Screening is offered to newborns in 12 ethnic groups considered at risk. Newborns considered at risk are those "with either one or both parents of African, Arabian, Greek, Maltese, Portuguese, Puerto Rican, Sardinian, Sicilian, South and Central American, Southern Asian and Spanish origin," as well as infants where either one or both parents are of unknown heritage (Rules of the Department of Human Resources/Public Health of Georgia, Ch. 290-5-24.03 [c] [1983]). In spite of this targeted screening program, however, many affected infants are missed. Other criticisms of Georgia's selective screening program include noncompliance of hospitals (because targeted screening allows them to decide who is tested) and the potential stigmatization of newborns so identified (M. Harris and J. Eckman, "Approaches to Screening: Georgia's Experience with Newborn Screening: 1981–1985," *Pediatrics* 83 [Suppl.] [1989]: 858–860).

110. Gina Kolata, "Panel Urges Newborn Sickle Cell Screening," *Science* 236 (1987): 259–260.

111. Personal communication, Dr. Jane Lin-Fu, Chief, Genetic Disease Services Branch, Maternal and Child Health, NIH Heart, Blood and Lung Institute.

112. Although prenatal screening for sickle cell disease has been available for more than a decade, until recently it relied on the examination of fetal blood by fetoscopy, a procedure that was not widely available and that carried a 4 to 5 percent risk of fetal death. Recombinant DNA methodology, however, can now be used to analyze fetal DNA obtained by amniocentesis or chorionic villus sampling, procedures that are both widely available and less risky to the fetus (B. P. Alter, "Prenatal Diagnosis of Hemoglobinopathies: Worldwide Experience," in *Thalassemia: Recent Advances in Detection and Treatment,* ed. A. Cao, V. Carcassi, and P. T. Rowley [New York: Liss, 1982], 263–274).

113. Prenatal diagnosis also has been advocated as a method of minimizing infant morbidity and mortality by allowing time to educate the family and assisting the family in locating specialized medical facilities. The latter rationale, however, has been criticized as being less effective in identifying affected infants than universal screening of newborns (K. Anyane-Yeboa, "Hemoglobinopathy Screening During Early Pregnancy," *Pediatrics* [Suppl.] [1989]: 881–883). The Conference's recommendation, however, is that screening for hemoglobinopathies should include both prenatal maternal and neonatal screening as a continuum of health care (Consensus Conference, "Newborn Screening," 1207).

114. Michael M. Kaback, Ted J. Nathan, and Susan Greenwald, "Tay-Sachs Disease: Heterozygote Screening and Prenatal Diagnosis—U.S. Experience and World Perspective," in *Tay-Sachs Disease: Screening and Prevention,* ed. Michael M. Kaback (New York: Liss, 1977), 13–36.

115. Ibid.

116. Michael M. Kaback, Gloria Bailin, Phyllis Hirsch et al., "Automated Thermal Fractionation of Serum Hexosaminidase: Effects of Alteration in Reaction Variables and Implications for Tay-Sachs Disease Heterozygote Screening," in Kaback, ed., *Tay-Sachs Disease,* 197–212.

117. John S. O'Brien, Shintaro Okada, Dorothy L. Fillerup et al., "Tay-Sachs Disease: Prenatal Diagnosis," *Science* 172 (1971): 61; John S. O'Brien, "Pitfalls in the Prenatal Diagnosis of Tay-Sachs Disease," in Kaback, ed., *Tay-Sachs Disease,* 283–294. Noting a number of biological and methodological problems with the prenatal Hex A assay, O'Brien recommends that the amniotic fluid Hex A assays be followed by tissue culturing amniotic cells for 3 weeks and assaying Hex A levels and heat resistance in the resultant tissue culture fluid.

118. Kaback et al., "Tay-Sachs Disease," 27.

119. Ibid.

120. California considers its Tay-Sachs program the prototype for the development and delivery of similar genetic services to other defined populations in which specific genetic disorders occur, such as those afflicted by sickle cell disease, anemia, thalassemia, and cystic fibrosis.

121. Sherman Elias and George J. Annas, *Reproductive Genetics and the Law,* (Chicago: Year Book Medical Publishers, 1987), 67.

122. Michael Kaback. "Heterozygote Screening," in *Principles and Practice of Medical Genetics,* ed. Alan E. H. Emery and David L. Rimion (London: Churchill Livingstone, 1983), 1451–1457. See also Mark D. Ludman, Gregory A. Gra-

bowski, James D. Goldberg et al., "Heterozygote Detection and Prenatal Diagnosis for Tay-Sach and Type I Gaucher Diseases," in Carter and Willey, eds., *Genetic Disease*, 34 (citing a personal communication from M. Kaback).

123. Kaback, "Heterozygote Screening."

124. M. W. Steele. "Lessons from the American Tay-Sachs Programme" (letter), *Lancet* (1980): 914.

125. B. Gastel, J. Haddow, J. Fletcher et al., eds., *Maternal Serum Alpha Fetoprotein: Issues in the Prenatal Screening and Diagnosis of Neural Tube Defects* (Washington, D.C.: Government Printing Office, 1980), 1.

126. President's Commission, *Genetic Screening and Counseling*, 27.

127. Ibid.

128. D. J. H. Brock, A. E. Bolton, and J. M. Managhan, "Prenatal Diagnosis of Anencephaly Through Maternal Serum Alpha-Fetoprotein Measurement," *Lancet* 2 (1973): 923–926.

129. J. L. Simpson and H. L. Nadler, "Maternal Serum Alpha-Fetoprotein in 1987" (editorial), *Obstetrics and Gynecology* 69 (1987): 134–135.

130. E. O. Nightengale and S. B. Meister, eds., *Prenatal Screening, Policies, and Values: The Example of Neural Tube Defects* (Cambridge, Mass.: Harvard University Press, 1987), 11. See also George J. Annas, "Is a Genetic Screening Test Ready When the Lawyers Say It Is?" in *Judging Medicine,* ed. George J. Annas (Clifton, N.J.: Humana Press, 1988), 108–125. Approximately 5 percent of those screened show an elevated MSAFP level and are retested. If the MSAFP level is again elevated, ultrasonography is done to detect conditions other than NTDs and, in severe cases, to give further indications of NTDs. If no explanation for the elevated AFP level is found, amniocentesis is recommended. Approximately 5 to 10 percent of those undergoing amniocentesis show elevated AFP levels, and the majority are associated with NTDs. This procedure detects approximately 80–90 percent of anencephalies and 60–90 percent of all open spina bifidas (Annas, "Genetic Screening Test," 109).

131. Gerald J. Mizejewski and H. M. Risenberg, "Alpha-Fetoprotein: Use in Predicting Prenatal Distress," in *Alpha-Fetoprotein and Congenital Disorders,* ed. Gerald J. Mizejewski and Ian H. Porter (New York: Academic Press, 1985), 157–177. "It must be made clear that serum and amniotic fluid AFP determinations are not specific for a single birth defect, but rather for a wide range of fetal malformations" (157). These malformations include fetal distress (death), congenital nephrosis, Down's and Turner's syndromes, Fallot's teratology, and esophageal and intestinal atresias.

132. 45 Federal Register 74158 (November 7, 1980). See also President's Commission, *Genetic Screening and Counseling,* 29.

133. See Stephen J. Sepe, James S. Marks, Godfrey P. Oakley et al., "Genetic Services in the U.S. 1979–80," *Journal of the American Medical Association* 248 (1982): 1733.

134. American College of Obstetricians and Gynocologists, *Prenatal Detection of Neural Tube Defects,* ACOG Technical Bulletin, no. 99 (replaces no. 67, October 1982) (Washington, D.C., American College of Obstetricians and Gynecologists, 1986).

135. Annas, "Genetic Screening Test."

136. Simpson and Nadler, "Maternal Serum Alpha-Fetoprotein," 134. The limitations of the kits are marginal. After delaying approval of the kits, the FDA concluded that they should be released only to institutions that could ensure appropriate follow-up.

When the administration failed to sign off on the restrictions, however, the kits were released only with the requirement that the manufacturers must provide some educational support and monitor the outcomes.

137. Professional Liability Implications of AFP Tests: Special Notice to ACOG Fellows from the Law Department of ACOG, May 1985. This liability alert is the only one ever issued by ACOG.

138. Annas, "Genetic Screening Test," 112.

139. Irwin R. Merkatz, Harold M. Nitowsky, James N. Macri et al. "An Association Between Low Maternal Serum Alphafetoprotein and Fetal Chromosomal Abnormalities, *American Journal of Obstetrics and Gynecology* 148 (1984): 886–894.

140. Simpson and Nadler, "Maternal Serum Alpha-Fetoprotein," 135.

141. Vermont's Prenatal AFP Screening Program has developed the *AFP Screening Manual* for physicians and staffs, publishes the *AFP Newsletter,* and prints patient brochures. Additionally, it offers educational programs, counseling, and laboratory quality control. See the Appendix to Chapter 6 of this volume for further description. It recommends that all women be offered the test; approximately 40 to 50 percent of pregnant women are screened.

142. Information about Mississippi's AFP program is provided in Chapter 6 of this volume. The identifiable high-risk group is limited to couples with previously affected children or relatives and women with insulin-dependent diabetes mellitus.

143. California Health and Safety Code 289.7. See also Hawaii Revised Statutes, title 16–19, Ch. 281–344, Sec. 321–331 (1988 supplement).

144. Hawaii's recently passed statute gives the state health department the authority to "ensure that all pregnant women . . . are offered appropriate information, quality testing, diagnostic services, and follow-up services concerning neural tube defects and other disorders amenable to prenatal diagnosis." To date, no regulations have been promulgated.

145. See, for example, Jose A. Arevelo and Eugene A. Washington, "Cost-Effectiveness of Prenatal Screening and Immunization for Hepatitis B Virus," *Journal of the American Medical Association* 259 (1988): 365–368.

146. Paul R. Summers, Manoj K. Biswas, Joseph Pastorek et al., "The Pregnant Hepatitis B Carrier: Evidence Favoring Comprehensive Antepartum Screening," *Obstetrics and Gynecology* 69 (1987): 701–704.

147. ACOG and AAP, *Guidelines for Perinatal Care,* 2nd ed. (Washington, D.C.: ACOG and AAP, 1988) (the *Guidelines*), 138. Mothers with positive results on a test for HIV antibody or HBsAg are cautioned against nursing their infants until after the infants have received HBV immunoglobulin (200).

148. CDC, "Prevention of Perinatal Transmission of Hepatitis B Virus: Prenatal Screening of All Pregnant Women for Hepatitis B Surface Antigen," *Morbidity and Mortality Weekly Report* 37 (1988): 341–349. The antigens are inactive components of the hepatitis virus that can be detected with an antibody test.

149. R. Palmer Beasley, George Lee, and Cheng-Hsiung Roan, "Prevention of Perinatally Transmitted Hepatitis B Virus Infections with Hepatitis B Immunoglobulin and Hepatitis B Vaccine," *Lancet* 2 (1983): 1099–1104.

150. ACIP, "Recommendation on Postexposure Prophylaxis of Hepatitis B," *Morbidity and Mortality Weekly Report* 33 (1984): 285–290. A high maternal HBsAg level is a factor indicating an increased risk of transmitting the virus to the newborn. See also Mark A. Kane, Stephen C. Hadler, Harold S. Margolis et al., "Routine Prenatal Screening for Hepatitis B Surface Antigen" (editorial), *Journal of the American Medical Association* 259 (1988): 408–409.

151. ACIP, "Recommendation," 287. The "Recommendation" recognizes as risk factors for HBV infection many of the risk factors for HIV infection, including multiple episodes of STDs, IV drug use, rejection as a blood donor, repeated blood transfusions, prostitution, and sexual partners including men in the aforementioned groups (140).

152. Summers et al., "Pregnant Hepatitis B Carrier," 408.

153. Ibid.

154. "Routine Prenatal Screening for Hepatitis B Surface Antigen" (editorial), *Journal of the American Medical Association* 259 (1988): 408–409. See also the *Guidelines*, which notes that a "strong argument can be made . . . for the routine screening [of] all pregnant women for HBsAg rather than those considered at high risk," (139). The *Guidelines* urge hospitals and physicians to consider this approach.

155. CDC, "Prevention of Perinatal Transmission," 342. The problems with selective screening for HBV leading to the ACIP's recommendation that all newborns be screened were (1) concerns about the sensitivity, specificity, and practicality of the guidelines for selective screening; (2) lack of knowledge among prenatal health-care providers about the risks of perinatal transmission and about the selective screening procedures; (3) poor coordination of treatment and follow-up; (4) refusal of some public and private third-party payers to reimburse for HBV screening; and (5) impracticality of selective screening in some U.S. jurisdictions where HBV infection is highly endemic, such as parts of Alaska and certain Pacific islands.

156. Personal communication, Barbara Asheld, the Communicable Diseases Division, New York State Department of Health, New York State Public Health Law, sec. 2500(e). It is noted that as of 1988 (the time of the "Recommendation"), only one-third of U.S. hospitals performed the HBsAg test as an in-house procedure.

157. James E. Bowman, "Legal and Ethical Issues in Newborn Screening," *Pediatrics* 83 (1989): 894–896.

4

HIV Infection and Obstetric Care

JOHN T. REPKE AND TIMOTHY R. B. JOHNSON

As noted throughout this volume, the decision to screen for HIV in a pregnant population must take account of numerous social, legal, and ethical considerations, as well as more practical medical concerns. The purpose of this chapter is to explore those medical concerns that arise in obstetrics and prenatal care. Specifically, we examine five sets of issues: vertical transmission and obstetric management; the impact of HIV on pregnancy and the impact of pregnancy on HIV; counseling and education; risk of transmission of HIV to obstetric workers; and HIV screening in the obstetric context, including past and current screening policies of our prenatal clinical service.

Vertical Transmission and Obstetric Management

There is no question that HIV may infect the fetus. HIV has been found in cord blood as early as the 20th week of gestation.[1] A dysmorphic syndrome presumably related to very early fetal infection also has been described.[2] Unfortunately, as noted in Chapter 2, the rate of transmission from infected mother to fetus is not well established. True vertical infection has been estimated to occur in 30 to 65 percent of infants born to HIV-positive women.[3] In a European multicenter trial,[4] 75 percent of infants lost antibody to HIV by 1 year of age. Two of these children, however, had virus isolated from them confirming infection, suggesting that absence of maternal antibody does not necessarily ensure absence of infection. Recent experience suggests that in the United States, vertical infection occurs in about 30 percent of infants born to HIV-infected mothers (see Chapter 2).

Although transplacental viral transmission has been documented, many investigators feel that HIV infection often occurs at the time of delivery, similar to the major mode of transmission for hepatitis B. From an obstetric perspective, the central issue seems to be whether or not the route of delivery affects the rate of transmission. Recent data suggest that cesarean section may protect infants whose mothers have hepatitis B because of the total inoculum received at the time of vaginal delivery.[5] It is possible that the same mechanism may exist with HIV and that cesarean section in selected patients may be beneficial.[6] To date, however, there is insufficient evidence specific to HIV to suggest that cesarean delivery affords protection against transmission to the newborn. As a result, current obstetric thinking is that cesarean section does not benefit the fetus whose mother is HIV positive. It is unlikely that data on the protective potential of cesarean section will be forthcoming soon. Cross-sectional analysis might provide some insights, but variations in gestational age, stage of maternal disease at delivery, duration of labor, invasive procedures during labor, trauma to the fetus at the time of cesarean section, and even the amount of blood the fetus is exposed to at delivery would make interpretation of results difficult. Our speculation is that, barring some startling new insight into the mode of transmission of HIV, cesarean section is unlikely to provide protection against vertical transmission.

Along these same lines, it is possible that the amount of HIV that the fetus is exposed to at delivery in the birth canal is important and that efforts to prevent contamination of the fetus with maternal blood at the time of vaginal delivery or cesarean section might have a preventive effect. Unfortunately, this is not always possible and, perhaps more to the point, is frequently impossible. It is also possible that interventions such as the application of fetal scalp electrodes and fetal scalp blood sampling may increase the risk of transmission of HIV to the fetus. It is known that in women with active herpes, scalp electrode placement can lead to introduction of the herpes virus and disseminated neonatal herpes. In the absence of data to the contrary, it seems prudent to eschew such procedures except when absolutely necessary.

With one exception, the question of whether to avoid invasive procedures such as fetal scalp blood sampling has not been addressed satisfactorily in the obstetric literature. The one exception is invasive prenatal diagnostic procedures. It has been recommended in the obstetric literature that both amniocentesis and chorionic villus sampling not be carried out in women who are HIV-positive.[7] The concern with amniocentesis is that transabdominal puncture risks carrying maternal blood or tissue to the fetus through the amniotic sac, thereby increasing the risk of transmission of HIV. The reasoning with regard to chorionic villus sampling is similar, although in this procedure, puncture is transcervical rather than transabdominal. In both instances, the risks are theoretical; there are no data to support the current recommendation, nor is it likely that relevant data will be forthcoming soon. While in many cases forgoing prenatal diagnosis in the face of HIV seropositivity is likely to be an easy decision, for some women—for example, those at increased risk of carrying a fetus with Down's syndrome or sickle cell disease—the fact that the risk is primarily theoretical may make a complex decision more problematic.

Another technique potentially contraindicated in women infected with HIV is percutaneous umbilical blood sampling. In this technique, a needle is inserted through the maternal abdomen and into the umbilical cord of the fetus to take blood for serologic tests. At present, this technique is used for rapid diagnosis of certain conditions. In the future, it could be used to obtain fetal blood samples, which could then be tested for direct evidence of HIV infection in the fetus throughout gestation. However, there are some major drawbacks to using this technique as it is currently practiced. First, the technique carries a risk of fetal loss estimated to be in the range of 0.5 to 2 percent per procedure. Second, the risk of introducing HIV from the mother to a noninfected fetus at this time cannot be entirely eliminated. Perhaps in the future, through either pharmacotherapy or improved methods of sampling, this risk can be eliminated. However, currently, this is not the case.

Finally, there is potential for intervention with new or existing obstetric technologies as our knowledge of HIV continues to expand. There is, for example, the possibility of utilizing percutaneous umbilical access for direct administration of drugs that could potentially protect the noninfected fetus from infection. Maternal administration of pharmacologic agents that are capable of being passed transplacentally or of being injected directly into the umbilical vein may also prevent transmission of virus to the fetus. As noted in Chapter 2, in the near future it should be established whether identification of infected mothers will allow early neonatal intervention with pharmacotherapeutic agents that could minimize the risk of infection or delay the onset of clinically significant disease in infected newborns. Thus while our knowledge of HIV remains inadequate, it is expanding and may some day allow a better approach in obstetrics to the prevention of vertical transmission.

Impact of HIV on Pregnancy and Impact of Pregnancy on HIV

Pregnancy has long been known to alter cell-mediated immunity. The counseling of pregnant women should address not just the issue of vertical transmission, but also the impact of HIV on pregnancy and what effect pregnancy might have on the natural course of HIV infection. There are inadequate longitudinal data to answer these questions. Whether asymptomatic HIV carriers have healthier children than women with HIV-related illnesses or whether pregnancy accelerates the appearance of HIV-related illnesses in women is a question that remains unanswered.

Once again, longitudinal studies of pregnant women with HIV infection and pregnant women in various stages of illness in the HIV spectrum are necessary in order to answer these questions. One difficulty is that such research must be conducted in communities where HIV seroprevalence is relatively high; this constraint introduces various methodologic problems. As noted in Chapter 2, currently HIV infection occurs disproportionately among disadvantaged African-American and Hispanic women. This epidemiologic fact introduces into clinical investigations confounding variables such as education, socioeconomic status, and nutritional status, all of which have been demonstrated to have effects on the outcome of pregnancy. Additionally, such studies would include large numbers of patients with drug abuse problems. Drug abuse also has been associated with an adverse pregnancy outcome, as well as with many of the aforementioned risk factors. Based on our current knowledge of HIV infection, it is likely that the results of such studies will reveal that after controlling for other risk factors, the additional burden of HIV infection does not further affect the pregnancy outcome to a significant degree and only places the infant at risk for HIV infection via vertical transmission.

The other issue of whether or not HIV infection during pregnancy becomes a more aggressive disease, whose course is accelerated by the cell-mediated immunity alterations known to accompany pregnancy, is more complex.

Since so little is known about the impact of pregnancy on the course of HIV infection, a central question confronting obstetricians is whether and how to intervene. Currently, the primary intervention under consideration is maternal administration of zidovudine (AZT). It has been established that AZT delays the development of symptoms in asymptomatic, HIV-infected adults.[8] Delay of development or progression of HIV-related illnesses during pregnancy is of obvious benefit to the mother and, depending on the severity of the illness, may be of benefit to the fetus. Additionally, there is speculation that the use of AZT in pregnancy may reduce the risk of vertical transmission or at least lengthen the period from asymptomatic infection to HIV-related illness in the newborn.

Use of AZT in pregnancy is ethically problematic, however. Previous drug studies have demonstrated that the fetal period is one in which teratogenic, mutagenic, and carcinogenic effects of drugs can occur. At the same time, it is not possible to establish the efficacy of AZT in managing HIV infection in pregnancy and in preventing vertical transmission without exposing the fetus to unknown risks. Recently, a clinical trial of AZT in the third trimester of pregnancy was initiated and then (at least temporarily) discontinued because of reports that AZT may be carcinogenic.[9] Is it ethical to administer a potentially toxic substance to an HIV-positive, asymptomatic woman in her third trimester of pregnancy, knowing that adverse fetal effects may still occur, that the efficacy of drug treatment in this setting is unclear, and that there is about a 70 percent chance that the fetus is unaffected? Alternatively, is it ethical to deny HIV-positive, pregnant women efficacious medical intervention unless they terminate their pregnancies? It might be argued that the most appropriate course is to inform women of both the potential benefits and the unknown impact on the fetus of AZT and other HIV-related treatments, allowing women to make the final determination about treatment. But even here, a moral issue for obstetricians remains. How should obstetricians advise HIV-positive patients when their opinions are sought? Currently, the only clear indication for the use of AZT in pregnancy, outside a carefully monitored clinical trial, is the treatment of severe HIV-related illness. This use is akin to the administration of chemotherapy to a pregnant woman with cancer. It is appropriate and important that obstetricians explain the role of AZT and other medications in the management of HIV infection, as well as any reservations they may have concerning the use of these treatments during pregnancy, to their HIV-infected patients. If there are barriers to access, these too should be explained. Indeed, this information should be a routine component of HIV pre- and posttest counseling.

Counseling and Education

The education and counseling of patients on reducing the risks of heterosexual and vertical transmission of HIV remains a main goal of prenatal intervention. Prenatal care affords important opportunities to educate women about how they can protect themselves from contracting HIV, and about the relationship between HIV infection in women and HIV infection in infants. However, education and counseling require resources that are often in short supply in obstetric settings, particularly those that serve disadvantaged women. These resource constraints include inadequate access to experts and materials for training of staff, insufficient staff time and inadequate space for counseling, and the absence of financial reimbursement for counseling.

Patients and health care workers should be aware of data from hepatitis B transmission studies supporting the conclusion that individuals with multiple sexual partners tend to have sexual relations with other individuals who have had multiple sexual partners.[10] While having a large number of partners increases the risk of HIV infection, a reduced number of partners does not necessarily lessen the risk, depending on the population seroprevalence, sexual activity, and risk factors of the partner.[11] The use of condoms and spermicides, specifically nonoxynol-9, has been recommended as an effective means of preventing the spread of HIV. Undamaged latex condoms, when used in conjunction with nonoxynol-9, provide effective physical and chemical barriers to HIV. In vitro studies have demonstrated that intact latex condoms prevent the spread of HIV and that nonoxynol-9 concentrations in excess of 0.25 percent inactivate HIV.[12] It must be recognized, however, that these behaviors may be far less important than carefully choosing one's sexual partner.

The impact of providing pregnant women with information about these protective behaviors is unclear. The possibility of changing behavior during pregnancy has been explored in several studies, and there is a body of literature to suggest that pregnancy is a special time when women may be more willing to change their behavior (e.g., give up smoking). At the same time, it must be noted that this willingness to adopt healthier behaviors during pregnancy has been ascribed in the past to the protective impact of those behaviors on the fetus. The connection with fetal welfare is less direct in the case of HIV. Regardless of the impact on behavior change and the risk of transmission, from an ethical perspective, pretest and posttest counseling is a critical component of any HIV screening program and ought to be an integral element of screening in an obstetric setting (see Chapter 13). One recently published report suggests that an indigent inner-city population of pregnant women can be expected to elect HIV testing in high numbers when given the proper education and counseling.[13]

Risk to Obstetric Workers

With the exception of emergency rooms, no area of the hospital has greater potential for caring for patients whose medical background is unclear than labor and delivery units. Obstetricians, midwives, nurses, and their assistants often are exposed to blood products, amniotic fluid, and other products at the time of delivery and cesarean section. It is extremely difficult to protect health care workers completely. Data are becoming available on the risks of workers in different health care professions where exposure to body fluids is particularly likely to occur. A study at the Johns Hopkins Hospital suggests that transmission of HIV through a needle stick injury will occur in approximately 1 per 250 exposures. Based on a number of assumptions, it is estimated that, at an institution like the Johns Hopkins Hospital, 1 work-related seroconversion can be expected to occur every 6 years (Table 4.1)

Even this small potential for exposure has led to the establishment of patient care policies that protect hospital personnel from inadvertent HIV exposure. "Universal precautions," the name most often given to these rather extensive protective measures, has become the standard policy of many hospitals in the United States, including our own. The basis for these precautions is well found-ed. During the first 8 years of the HIV epidemic, there were 15 documented cases in the United States of health care workers infected by HIV as a direct result of their work.[14] At the same time, as suggested by the aforementioned Johns Hopkins projections, it can reasonably be assumed that transmission of

TABLE 4.1.   HIV Risk for Health Care Workers

Assumptions
  Transmission of HIV through needle stick injury = 1/250 exposure (0.4%)

U.S. Projections (1988)
  Total number who will acquire HIV in the work place = 20
  All 20 will acquire disease through blood exposure
  Preventable exposures = 40 percent of cases

Johns Hopkins Hospital
  Needle stick injuries with HIV-infected source = 38 cases
  Number of cases expected to convert = 1 every 6 years

HIV through needle stick injuries is a rare event. To put the problem of needle stick injuries in perspective, during the same 8-year period mentioned, 4,000 health care workers were hospitalized as a result of occupational hepatitis B exposure, resulting in 1,600 deaths.[15]

For surgeons, the risk of HIV infection in operating on an HIV-infected patient is estimated to be 1 in 4,500 to 1 in 130,000. In a low-risk patient of unknown HIV status, the risk is estimated to be 1 in 450,000 to 1 in 1.3 billion.[16] No comparable data are available yet on obstetric populations. However, in order to minimize the risk of HIV exposure among obstetric personnel, modifications in professional practice increasingly are being made. The changes implemented on our labor and delivery unit are illustrative. In addition to universal precautions, routine use of protective eye wear and waterproof gowns has begun. Also, newborn suctioning is no longer done by mouth but by devices that attach to wall suction. Other devices for this purpose are also available.[17] While disposable instruments may not be economically feasible, appropriate disinfection of instruments should further reduce the risk of HIV contamination.[18]

From a practical standpoint, these precautions have altered the obstetric environment. Throughout the 1970s, a move to a more natural approach to childbirth was made on most labor and delivery units. The requirements of universal precautions have reintroduced a more antiseptic atmosphere to the labor and delivery process. Also, there is concern that patients may be treated unequally. A patient who is presumed to be from a low-risk population for HIV seroprevalence may be managed somewhat differently from the patient who is thought to be from a high-seroprevalence population or who has been documented to be HIV-positive. Clearly, universal precautions must apply to all patients, but there is no question that differential treatment occurs. This raises significant ethical considerations, as well as significant medical concerns.

HIV Screening in the Obstetric Context

The concept of screening in an obstetric population is certainly not unprecedented. As noted in Chapter 8, it is current practice to test pregnant women for numerous illnesses based on population risk assessments. At our hospital, these screening tests include a hematocrit, hemoglobin, urine culture, a serologic test for syphilis, and hemoglobin electrophoresis. Generally, these tests are performed routinely; mothers are not informed that they are being done, and informed consent is not solicited. Theoretically, the right to refuse remains.

One notable exception is maternal serum alpha-fetoprotein (MSAFP) screening, a practice that obstetricians have adopted based on recommendations of the American College of Obstetricians and Gynecologists (see Chapter 3). Generally, this test is performed after informing women about its advantages and risks, and with their informed consent. MSAFP screening is used not only for the detection of neural tube defects. When correlated with maternal age, MSAFP test results provide additional information about the risk of chromosomal abnormalities. Positive MSAFP test results, suggestive either of neural tube defects or of chromosomal abnormalities, lead to further diagnostic testing (see Chapter 3). In many respects, MSAFP testing is similar to screening and counseling for genetic risk factors such as advanced maternal age, practices that are the standard of care in the United States. Procedures such as amniocentesis to investigate genetic risk factors are not routinely performed and require the informed consent of the mother.

Also recently introduced in our obstetric practice is routine screening during labor for substance and alcohol abuse. Patients are told that screening of the urine for substance abuse may improve pediatric newborn care, and that the test is performed on all patients during labor unless a patient specifically objects. Thus patients are given the right to refuse to have this test done if they so desire. The results of these tests have proved useful in initiating social work intervention to help prepare the mother and newborn for eventual discharge home. Prenatally, urine toxicology screens are performed on patients who acknowledge risk factors, or who are considered at increased risk for substance or alcohol abuse, at the discretion of physicians or nursing staff.

If HIV screening is to be made part of obstetric management, several key issues need to be addressed. These include whether to screen all or only some patients, the time for screening (at registration, at 28 weeks, during labor and delivery), the possibility of repeat screening, and when to screen nonparticipants in prenatal care who are probably at increased risk of HIV infection.

Until recently, the policy of our obstetric clinic, in conformity with the recommendations of both the Centers for Disease Control (CDC) and the U.S. Surgeon General, was to offer HIV testing to only high-risk women. A woman was defined as being at high risk if she answered yes to at least one question on a risk questionnaire administered at the time of registration. This instrument included questions about intravenous drug use, whether sex partners have used intravenous drugs or are bisexual, prostitution, and receipt of blood products.

Based on the results of a blind seroprevalence study of our patients, this policy was dropped in 1988. Pilot study data raised significant doubts about the efficacy of offering screening to only high-risk women. Of the 49 HIV-positive women identified, only 53 percent acknowledged risk factors for infection. Figure 4.1 presents the risk factors acknowledged by women found to be seropositive. The distribution of risk factors among all clinic patients who admitted being at risk is presented in Figure 4.2.

The extent to which the inefficiency we experienced during our period of targeted screening is the result of deliberate underreporting of risk behavior on the part of patients, as opposed to ignorance of patients about risk exposure, is unclear. Morrow-Tlucak and colleagues have shown that pregnant women who

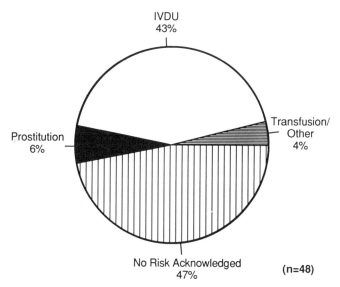

FIGURE 4.1   Hierarchical distribution of risk factors among HIV-seropositive women. (From M. Barbacci, G. A. Dallabetta, J. Repke et al. "HIV-screening in an inner-city prenatal population." Paper presented at the ICAAC Twenty-eighth Annual Meeting, Los Angeles, October 24, 1988)

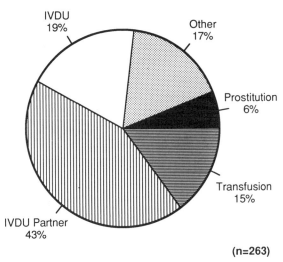

FIGURE 4.2   Hierarchical distribution of risk factors among clinic patients at risk for HIV infection. (From M. Barbacci et al. [1988])

abuse alcohol underreport their consumption habits, perhaps because of their knowledge of the effect of alcohol abuse on the fetus and their unwillingness to accept and admit their behavior.[19]

Our current policy is to offer testing to all obstetric patients. This decision was relatively easy to make, since the seroprevalence of HIV infection in our population of pregnant women approached 5 percent. The more difficult issue is whether our screening policy should be generalized to other settings and to groups of women with a much lower prevalence of HIV infection. For example, we do not routinely offer non-Jewish couples testing for Tay-Sachs disease. There is still a possibility that a non-Jewish couple could carry the gene for this disease. However, to screen all couples would be inordinately expensive, with a very low yield. The same argument might be made for HIV screening. At the same time, however, significant concerns have been raised regarding the possibility of discrimination and injustice if only high-risk populations are subjected to screening. These issues are dealt with elsewhere in this volume, especially in Chapters 6, 7, and 14.

The decision to require informed consent for testing, rather than to incorporate HIV testing in the panel of routine obstetric screens, reflects a larger hospital policy requiring consent for HIV testing by all patients. This policy was adopted primarily on ethical and legal grounds. The ethical and legal arguments for requiring informed consent for HIV testing are detailed in Chapters 7, 8, 12, and 14. Some states, ours included, have legislated informed consent requirements for HIV testing.

Testing is offered as close to the time of registration as possible. Currently, we do not offer a second screen late in pregnancy.

One new trend in obstetrics is to provide prepregnancy counseling as part of routine obstetric and gynecologic care. Prepregnancy programs are recommended to detect such problems as rubella nonsensitization in order to provide for rubella immunization. Incorporating HIV screening in the prepregnancy visit might be a good way of detecting women who are HIV-positive in advance of pregnancy and an ideal time to counsel HIV-infected women about the risks of vertical transmission and the potential risks of pregnancy. Such a screening policy recently has been suggested by a U.S. Public Health Service expert panel on prenatal care.[20]

Notes

1. E. Jovaisas, M. Koch, A. Schafer et al., "LAV/HTLV-III in a 20 Weeks Fetus," *Lancet* 2 (1985): 1129.
2. R. W. Marion, A. A. Wiznia, R. G. Hutcheon et al., "Human T-Cell Lymphotropic Virus Type III (HTLV-III) Embryopathy," *American Journal of Diseases of Children* 140 (1986): 638–640.

3. G. B. Scott, M. A. Fischl, N. K. Limas et al., "Mothers of Infants with the Acquired Immunodeficiency Syndrome: Evidence for Both Symptomatic and Asymptomatic Carriers," *Journal of the American Medical Association* 253 (1985): 363–366; Arye Rubenstein, "Pediatrics AIDS," *Current Problems in Pediatrics* 26 (1986): 362–409.

4. J. Q. Mok, C. Guaquinto, A. de Rossi et al., "Infants Born to Mothers Seropositive for Human Immunodeficiency Virus: Preliminary Findings from a Multicenter European Study," *Lancet* 1 (1987): 1164–1169.

5. F. Chiodo, E. Ricchi, P. Costigliola et al., "Vertical Transmission of HTLV-III" (letter), *Lancet* 1 (1986): 739.

6. Philip B. Mead, "Infection Control in the Era of AIDS," *Contemporary Obstetrics and Gynecology* 32 (1988): 116–122.

7. Howard Minkoff, "Care of Pregnant Women Infected with Human Immunodeficiency Virus," *Journal of the American Medical Association* 258 (1987): 2714–2717.

8. *Medical Letter* 28 (1986): 107; *Medical Letter* 29 (1987): 113.

9. John Modlin, personal communication, April 23, 1990.

10. B. B. Dan, "Sex and the Single Whirl: The Quantum Dynamics of Hepatitis B," *Journal of the American Medical Association* 256 (1986): 1344.

11. N. Hearst and S. B. Hulley, "Preventing the Heterosexual Spread of AIDS: Are We Giving Our Patients the Best Advice?" *Journal of the American Medical Association* 259 (1988): 2428–2432.

12. C. A. Rietmeijer, J. W. Krebs, P. M. Feorino et al., "Condoms as Physical and Chemical Barriers Against Human Immunodeficiency Virus," *Journal of the American Medical Association* 259 (1988): 1821–1823.

13. M. K. Lindsay, H. B. Peterson, T. I. Feng et al., "Routine Antepartum Human Immunodeficiency virus Infection Screening in an Inner-City Population," *Obstetrics and Gynecology* 74 (1989): 289–294.

14. Mead, "Infection Control."

15. Department of Labor and Department of Health and Human Services, "HBV/HIV Notice," *Federal Register* 52 (1987): 41818–41823.

16. M. D. Hagen, K. B. Meyer, and S. A. Pauker, "Routine Preoperative Screening for HIV," *Journal of the American Medical Association* 259 (1988): 1357.

17. R. A. Pretlow, "Hand Powered Apparatus for Aspiration of Meconium from the Airway," *Pediatrics* 79 (1987): 642.

18. L. S. Martin, J. S. McDougal, and S. C. Loskowski, "Disinfection and Inactivation of the HTLV III/LAV Virus," *Journal of Infectious Diseases* 152 (1985): 400.

19. C. B. Ernhart, M. Morrow-Tlucak, R. J. Sokol et al., "Underreporting of Alcohol Use in Pregnancy," *Alcoholism Clinical and Experimental* 12 (1988): 506–511.

20. Public Health Service, Expert Panel on the Content of Prenatal Care, "Caring for Our Future: The Content of Prenatal Care" (Public Health Service, Washington, D.C., 1989).

5

Maternal and Newborn HIV Screening: Implications for Children and Families

NANCY HUTTON AND LAWRENCE S. WISSOW

The overwhelming majority of AIDS cases among children are the result of mother–child transmission of HIV either during pregnancy or at the time of delivery. Thus two important reasons to consider HIV screening for women of childbearing age are the potential for slowing the advance of HIV infection from generation to generation and the early identification of infected infants who might benefit from medical intervention. The notion that these goals can be considered derives both from experience with other illnesses (Chapter 3) and from preliminary work in programs established to treat HIV-seropositive children. In this chapter, we argue that in the context of a system of ongoing, high-quality pediatric care, the benefits of HIV screening of pregnant women or newborns outweigh the risks. Technical and infectious disease–related issues are mentioned but are discussed more fully in Chapter 2. This chapter focuses on broader considerations for the child and his or her family.

Families Most Affected by Pediatric HIV Infection

Prior to the introduction of blood-product testing and treatment, the majority of pediatric HIV infections were attributable to transfusions. At the same time that blood products were becoming safer, however, HIV infection was spreading rapidly among intravenous drug users and their sexual contacts. As this newly exposed population began to have children, vertical transmission from mother to child became the predominant source of HIV infection among pre-teenage children (the risk factors among teenagers are similar to those among adults). As noted in Chapter 2, over half of all perinatal-associated AIDS cases develop in children born to mothers who have used intravenous drugs; in an additional one-fifth of cases, the child's mother, although not a drug user herself, is reported to have had a sexual partner who was a user now or at some time in the past.

In parallel with the problem of drug abuse, to which it is closely linked, perinatally acquired HIV infection has been most prevalent in poor, minority communities. Seventy-five percent of perinatally acquired AIDS cases involve African-American or Hispanic infants.[1] Anonymous seroprevalence surveys of childbearing women, using neonatal blood specimens, have found significant variation within states, with a higher prevalence in urban areas. In Massachusetts, the prevalence of HIV seropositivity was eight times greater among women delivering babies in inner-city hospitals than in suburban and rural hospitals.[2] A similar survey in New York found the highest concentration of HIV seropositivity in the poorest neighborhoods of New York City with the highest rates of intravenous drug use. In inner-city Baltimore, about 1 in 80 children are born to an HIV-infected mother.

Children born into families with substance abuse problems face a number of risks, even without considering HIV infection. There is a strong possibility that the family will not have a permanent home or a regular source of income. What housing is available may be substandard and possibly the site of drug-related activities or conflict. If a mother has used drugs or alcohol during pregnancy, her child may develop behavioral abnormalities that include irritability, difficulty in feeding, and extreme sensitivity to stimulation. Such infants can be extremely difficult to parent and may fail to develop the kinds of behaviors that normally elicit parental affection and nurturing. Drug-abusing parents have been noted to display parenting styles typical of adults who were themselves not nurtured as children. These styles are often based on the use of the infant as a means of support or gratification for the parent, and may include seductive touching, verbal abuse, and disruption of normal child exploratory activities.[3] Actively drug-abusing parents may also abandon their children, either for short periods or permanently.[4] Even if the mother herself is not a current user, the child may become a victim of physical conflict between the mother and a drug-abusing sexual partner.[5] Although a number of programs have been established to help such families by improving parenting skills and offering drug treatment, resources are relatively few compared with the level of need, and little is known about their efficacy.[6]

The level of social disruption discussed above is not universal among families with mother and child HIV infection. One of the tragedies of HIV infection derives from the extended asymptomatic period between contact with the virus and the manifestations of disease. In some cases, for example, a woman has been unknowingly infected with HIV during a sexual relationship with an intravenous drug-using man during an earlier, more tumultuous stage in her life. She succeeds, after a long struggle, in completing her education, finding a job, and locating decent housing. She establishes a more stable relationship. At a time when life seems relatively settled, she plans to and becomes pregnant, unaware that she risks infecting her mate and their newborn baby. The discovery of HIV infection at this point risks disrupting what may be a fragile step beyond a life of poverty and isolation.

It is important to emphasize that increasing numbers of women living in communities with a high prevalence of HIV infection are becoming infected through heterosexual contact. The proportion of pediatric AIDS patients whose mothers had sex partners with or at increased risk for AIDS rose from 11 percent of cases reported before 1985 to 21 percent of those reported in 1988.[7] For many of these women, their child's illness is the first indication of their own infection and health risk. Knowing that the number of reported AIDS cases always underestimates the number of people with HIV infection, we can presume that there are many women without known or acknowledged risk factors who are indeed infected and are bearing infected children. At the Johns Hopkins Hospital, about half of the pregnant women found to be seropositive after voluntary testing reported no risk factor for HIV infection.[8] These data are paralleled by the reporting of at least one pediatric AIDS case from nearly every state and the finding of seroprevalence rates of 1–2 per 1,000 among women of childbearing age even in states that have not been seen as foci of HIV infection.[9]

Clinical course of perinatal HIV infection

Infants who do acquire infection almost certainly develop HIV-related disease, but the age at which disease will develop, and how fulminant a course it will take, cannot be predicted during the newborn period. As with infection in older individuals, there appears to be a fairly broad spectrum of responses ranging from rapid, severe progression and death to extended periods with few or no symptoms. Case reports continue to document infection in children who are living to school age or beyond, some with little medical intervention.[10]

The Miami experience with 172 children diagnosed with vertically transmitted HIV infection was reported by Scott and colleagues in December 1989.[11] They found that 57 percent of these children had been diagnosed with clinical disease in the first year of life and 22 percent had been diagnosed in the second year. Diagnosis within the first year of life occurred much more frequently, however, among the subset of children followed prospectively from birth. Among these 26 children, 23 (88 percent) had evidence of clinical disease in the first year of life.

Historically, the earliest recognized and perhaps most immediately devastating pattern of illness resulting from perinatal HIV infection has been overwhelming pneumonia caused by *Pneumocystis carinii* (PCP). PCP often has a very sudden onset and a sharp downhill course leading to mechanical ventilation and a high mortality rate.[12] Most important, in groups of children identified as having HIV infection, PCP is the first sign of illness in about 8 to 9 percent.[13] In one cohort of seropositive children followed from birth to 18 months, PCP occurred in about 12 percent of those who proved to be infected.[14] When PCP is the first sign of infection, it occurs early in life; the mean age in one study was 5 months, with a range of 1 to 9 months.[15] Although data are not yet available for HIV-infected children, PCP prophylaxis does appear to be very effective both for children with cancer undergoing chemotherapy and for HIV-infected adults.

Although PCP is the most devastating early manifestation of perinatal HIV infection, most children develop subacute conditions, many of which may initially be attributed to other causes in the absence of knowledge of their seropositivity. These conditions include failure to thrive, generalized lymphadenopathy, liver and spleen enlargement, recurrent diarrhea, and lymphoid interstitial pneumonitis (LIP). In contrast to the course of PCP, among children in the Miami group LIP was diagnosed at a mean age of 13–14 months. The median survival for the 27 children in whom LIP was their presenting HIV disease was 72 months (6 years). Overall, half the population of perinatally infected children followed at the Miami center survived beyond the third year. This demonstrates that although some form of HIV disease will probably be diagnosed in the first 2 years of life in perinatally infected babies, often it may be relatively mild.

In 1989 Connor and colleagues[16] reported the status of 23 children with HIV infection that was not discovered until after the age of 4 years. Twenty-one were born to HIV-infected women. Four were transfused with HIV-infected blood during the newborn period (including 2 of 21 who also had maternal exposure). The ages at presentation ranged up to 10 years, and the oldest living child at the time of the report was 11 years. Five had died, four of whom had AIDS at the time of presentation. Four others with AIDS were still living up to 3 years later. Of particular note, six children had lymphadenopathy only, and nine were completely asymptomatic at the time their HIV infection was diagnosed. The mean age at diagnosis of this group was just over 6 years. This is in sharp contrast to reports early in the AIDS epidemic that all infants infected with HIV became seriously ill during infancy and died before the second year.

Although these findings paint a serious picture of the prognosis for children who are infected with HIV in the perinatal period, it is a picture that is becoming more consistent with that of other chronic illnesses with onset during infancy and early childhood. In other diseases, such as cystic fibrosis and sickle cell anemia, advances in early diagnosis, treatment of acute illnesses, and development of preventive strategies for specific disease-related symptoms have not only prolonged life but improved its quality. As the observations regarding the onset and course of HIV illness are extended to include the population of infants detected through screening rather than illness, we can expect to see a more optimistic assessment of the infected newborn's prognosis.

Potential Harms and Benefits of Knowing an Infant's HIV Status

Problems with diagnostic certainty

As discussed in Chapter 2, the current clinically available technology does not permit a firm serologic or laboratory diagnosis of HIV infection in children younger than 15 to 18 months old. Although most infants lose their passively acquired HIV antibody during the second 6 months of life,[17] some healthy children retain antibody for up to 18 months.[18] The most definitive laboratory procedure, HIV isolation from blood mononuclear cells, is not sensitive enough to detect all young infants with true HIV infection. In addition, it is a costly and complex process that requires weeks to complete and is not readily available to most pediatric health care providers. Detection of the HIV genome using the polymerase chain reaction (PCR) test holds great promise because it takes a relatively short time to perform and, theoretically, should be very sensitive yet specific. However, these characteristics of the test and its predictive value in populations of newborns at risk remain to be elucidated. In a recently published study, PCR was used to detect HIV infection in blood samples from 24 neonates ranging in age from birth to 16 days. Of the 12 infants who were later diagnosed with definite HIV infection, only 6 had positive PCR tests during this neonatal period.[19] At present, there is still no single test that reliably detects the presence of HIV infection during the newborn period. When the commonly available HIV antibody test is used as the newborn screen, approximately 70 percent of infants who test positive in the newborn period will later prove to be uninfected.[20]

On the other hand, while a healthy-appearing infant's status may not be known until the second year of life, the predictive value of a positive test is much greater among infants with symptoms suggestive of HIV infection. Although estimates vary, in one closely followed cohort,[21] over 75 percent of infants who were ultimately found to be infected had developed some symptoms by 6 months of age, and about 90 percent were symptomatic by 1 year. Thus if there is close medical follow-up of seropositive infants, the degree to which lack of specificity is a problem of screening depends on what interventions are planned for the infant during the period before symptoms occur. Until PCR or other specific tests for infant HIV infection are further examined and available for general use, serial clinical assessment, including a careful history and physical examination and selected laboratory tests, remain the most effective methods for detecting babies who may be developing symptomatic HIV disease.[22]

Interventions to improve quality of life and survival

Recurrent infections, pneumonia, failure to gain weight, episodes of diarrhea, or enlargement of lymph nodes may all signal the onset of HIV disease. Early detection of these conditions may increase longevity and improve the quality of life. For example, medications are available to treat specific infections other than the HIV itself, and extra nutritional support can partially overcome the effects of diarrhea and decreased intake. In some cases, the impact of nutritional intervention and treatment of secondary infections has been dramatic, with affected children able to return to normal levels of activity for months and, in some cases, years at a time. Zidovudine (AZT), the only generally available drug that appears to be effective in palliating AIDS, has been approved for use in children with known symptomatic disease, although questions regarding optimal dosage and the proper age or severity of illness for instituting therapy are still being addressed through clinical trials. The earlier a definitive diagnosis of HIV infection can be made, the earlier these interventions can be instituted. In adults, AZT has shown promise in delaying the manifestations of AIDS if given to infected but asymptomatic individuals. It is likely that this will prove to be the case among children as well, raising the issue of treatment early in childhood before an infant's true HIV status is known. The feasibility of such treatment ultimately will depend on the age at which initiation is considered necessary and the apparent toxicity of whatever minimal dose is determined to be effective. Other presymptomatic treatment, however, such as the use of trimethoprim-sulfamethoxasole (TMP-SMZ) for PCP prophylaxis, may be less problematic even in infants of ambiguous serostatus. TMP-SMZ has relatively little toxicity compared with AZT and may be able to prevent immediately devastating consequences until an age at which a definitive diagnosis can be made.

In the first 1 to 2 years of life, the requirements for close medical and psychosocial monitoring of children who may be infected with HIV overlap significantly with those for other children from similar social backgrounds. Current recommendations for health maintenance care include medical visits every 2 months during the first 6 months of life and every 3 months for the following year. Special problems or concerns can generate additional health care contacts above this basic level. This intensive approach is especially recommended for infants at high social risk because it affords opportunities to help parents learn about infant behaviors and understand infant needs.[23] Ideally, medical facility visits are combined with in-home parenting guidance or group parenting instruction and support.

Differences from routine health maintenance care include determination of immune status and modification of the childhood immunization schedule. In particular, inactivated polio vaccine is substituted for the oral live attenuated vaccine, based on the theoretical risk that an immunocompromised child (or adult caretaker with HIV infection) could develop paralytic polio from the oral vaccine. Additional immunizations not routinely given to all infants also are recommended, particularly those against pneumococcal disease and influenza,[24] as well as postexposure treatment for varicella.[25]

The Intensive Primary Care Program at the Johns Hopkins Children's Center is designed to offer comprehensive pediatric care to infants at risk for HIV infection using a team of health care providers that emphasizes outreach and addressing the needs of the family. Home visits are made in addition to clinic visits. Maintaining the health and optimal functioning of infants whose mothers are HIV seropositive requires a balance between concerns about HIV and the myriad other issues that need to be addressed in raising children. Emphasizing the infant's appropriate growth, development, behavior, and healthy appearance is necessary in order to remember that each newborn has greater than a two-thirds chance of having escaped infection.

The Hopkins program is representative of several such programs developed over the past few years to meet the needs of infants at risk of HIV infection. Eighty percent of the infants of HIV-infected women enrolled in the Hopkins program made more than the standard four pediatric visits during the first 6 months of life.[26] Individual visits usually involve at least two health-care professionals and last for at least an hour. Any complication, such as illness; homelessness; inability to access available social programs for food, housing, medical insurance, and subsistence income; or emotional turmoil due to the impact of the HIV diagnosis in the parent or child extends the time, effort, and complexity of these "well-child" visits. This intensive involvement with each family enables the primary health-care provider to make frequent assessments of the infant's HIV status, permitting definitive diagnosis as early as possible. It also offers intensive emotional support to families dealing with the overwhelming possibility that several family members may be affected by the same life-threatening disease.

For any child, a physician's approach to illness in the first months of life is very aggressive, gradually decreasing in intensity over the first few years. Almost any problem in a normal neonate will prompt a medical visit, and the threshold for diagnostic testing and presumptive treatment is very low. After the first few months of life, however, non-HIV-infected infants become less vulnerable to overwhelming infection and the threshold for treatment rises accordingly. In contrast, it is felt that children who may be infected with HIV continue to require close evaluation and aggressive treatment. Early, aggressive treatment of illnesses in children who truly are HIV-infected can prolong life and lessen morbidity. Hospital admission may be recommended for problems that would not require that level of care for non-HIV-infected children.

It should be stressed that given present diagnostic technologies, the only way to decide which infants should receive this special level of care is to include any child born to an HIV-seropositive mother (her serostatus may be determined by testing her or the infant). Screening programs probably require a combination of prenatal and neonatal testing, with the first attempting to get information that will be available at the time of birth, and the second examining infants whose mothers were not screened for any reason. This includes nearly all truly HIV-infected infants, but also two to three times that number of uninfected infants. Although the extra medical care these uninfected infants receive may be beneficial in some ways (especially if it is financed from special funds and allows them to receive care that their families otherwise could not afford), it also puts them at risk of suffering iatrogenic injury from aggressive care that they do not need. At the very least, they are likely to have additional blood tests to monitor their HIV antibody status in an attempt to determine as soon as possible if they are truly infected. Although the possibility exits that infants not infected with HIV experience more testing and hospitalization during their "indeterminate" phase than their low-risk peers, review of admission diagnoses in the Hopkins Intensive Primary Care cohort reveals that all hospitalizations would have occurred regardless of maternal HIV status.[27] In other words, the presenting problem was severe enough to warrant hospital admission. Within the same cohort, the infants who eventually were shown to have HIV infection accounted for the majority of the admissions. Several of these admissions occurred prior to confirmation of the HIV diagnosis.

Our experience and that of other clinicians caring for infants at risk of HIV emphasizes the need for accessible, approachable, and knowledgeable health care for all babies of HIV-infected women. For example, a 4-month-old infant followed in the Intensive Primary Care Program who had already been hospitalized twice for fever and significant irritability developed similar symptoms again. They were detected during a scheduled home visit by the team's visiting nurse practitioner, and the infant was referred to the clinic for evaluation. Her parents said they would otherwise have waited 2 more days for her scheduled appointment. She again underwent a battery of tests, including blood work, a spinal tap, and a chest x-ray. Potent parenteral antibiotic treatment was promptly initiated. The following day her blood culture was found to be positive for *Streotococcus pneumoniae*, indicating the presence of a life-threatening bacterial infection. Evaluation of her immune status confirmed that she had HIV infection. If she had remained untreated for a few more days, she could have developed meningitis or died from overwhelming sepsis. Instead, she is alive more than a year later, without recurrence of serious bacterial infection.

Opportunities to obtain experimental therapies

Identifying a child with HIV infection often makes that child eligible to participate in research protocols. This can be an advantage when the study offers access to otherwise unavailable treatment. Some research protocols offer no truly experimental treatments. Instead, they provide what otherwise would be an unavailable level of routine pediatric care in return for the opportunity to obtain data about the child's medical status on an ongoing basis. These data may be obtained through noninvasive (physical or developmental examinations) or invasive (blood-drawing) means. Other studies, however, involve potential risks, such as administration of AZT to determine its pharmacokinetics in infancy.

Any medical research in disadvantaged populations runs the risk that legitimate informed consent cannot be obtained, either because of communication barriers or because of the coercive effects of class and ethnic differences. These risks are exacerbated when the person from whom consent is sought is dependent on illegal drugs. Determinations of competence may be difficult to make in the case of parents who may or may not be under the influence of drugs at the time they have contact with the medical system (see Chapter 12). It may also be difficult for medical providers to accept the parents' formal status as proxy for the infant when parents have delegated the major responsibility for the child's care to another individual, often a grandparent but possibly a more distant relative. Children may also be placed under formal state supervision because they were either abandoned or abused. In these cases, the state may have limited authority to consent to medical care, but it is often uncertain whether that authority extends to consent for experimental treatment. Even if it does, medical personnel may be uncomfortable obtaining consent for potentially risky research from foster parents or social service workers who may have had only limited contact with the child.

HIV infection presents difficulties with obtaining valid parental consent beyond those generally associated with poverty and drug use (see also Chapter 12). It is not unusual to have multiple members of a family stricken with HIV-related illness; the most direct proxies for the child—the mother and father—may become seriously ill or demented or may die early in the child's life. There may be a need to formally designate alternative decision makers if the child is to receive experimental treatments.

Because it is so difficult to make a definitive diagnosis of HIV infection during the neonatal period, eligibility for research studies on perinatally acquired HIV infection has generally been based on the mother's HIV status rather than on the infant's infection status. This means that approximately two-thirds of the infants considered for participation in research protocols do not have HIV infection. The usual rationale for experimentation in general, and with children in particular, is that the benefits of participation, or the hope of benefits, outweigh the risks. These uninfected children may well benefit from research-based access to primary care, but they can gain no benefit from exposure to potentially toxic drugs. Knowing that a child was born to an HIV-positive mother places him or her at risk of being offered such opportunities that might seem reasonable to an altruistically minded adult but that would generally not be considered proper when consent can be given only by proxy.

Possibilities for increased social service intervention

The families affected by HIV infection have great social service needs, including the need for income supplementation, housing support, and child care. At best, the mother of a potentially infected child does not have a substance abuse problem of her own, her mate is a recovered addict, and they are not only supportive of each other but skilled in negotiating the steps required to secure health care, nutritional resources, subsistence income, and safe housing. However, even for those who can advocate for themselves, these resources are in short supply. Identification of an HIV risk or participation in special medical programs sometimes may help gain access to resources that would otherwise be unavailable.

Alternatively, identification of HIV status may increase the need for social services and simultaneously make those services more difficult to obtain. For example, placement issues often arise when mothers dependent on illegal drugs do not seem capable of caring for their newborn infants. Members of the extended family are often recruited to care for these children, but this arrangement may be jeopardized by the possibility that the child is infected with HIV. Health-care providers generally feel obligated to tell the substitute caretakers of the child's status (remembering that this is still a tentative diagnosis that has about a 70 percent chance of being wrong). This disclosure risks creating great tumult: it may be the first time the extended family knows of or must openly acknowledge the mother's drug use; it may cause the family to refuse to care for the child, either because of a perceived risk to themselves or because of the fear that they, in turn, will be socially stigmatized. The child may then be forced into the formal foster care system, which itself may have limited resources to care for sick children or those who are potentially infected. Indeed, one argument for maternal or infant HIV screening among high-risk populations is that the mother cannot care for her infant, necessitating foster care placement, knowledge that her HIV antibody test is negative may enable the placement to be made more easily.

AIDS has placed staggering burdens on the foster care and social service systems. New York officials estimate that by 1995 some 20,000 children in that city alone will have been orphaned because their parents have died of AIDS.[28] Boarder babies, newborns who have been abandoned or whose parents are too sick or disorganized to care for them, grow in numbers at many urban hospitals. Although only a minority, perhaps 1 in 10, are possibly infected with HIV, they are the most difficult to place in foster care.[29]

Infants potentially exposed to HIV compete for resources with the flood of infants born to mothers addicted to drugs. The impact of the increasing demand on social services agencies created by drug use during pregnancy is illustrated by data from Los Angeles County. In 1983, a handful of neonatal drug-exposure cases were reported to the county department of health services, constituting only a small fraction of all reports of child maltreatment. By 1987, the county had recorded over 1,300 reports of drug-exposed newborns; this total outnumbered reported cases of either physical abuse or child neglect for the same time period.[30]

The social effects of HIV labeling

Unfortunately, many case histories testify to the negative social impact on an infant identified as being HIV-seropositive. Even if the information is shared only with the parents, it can have a harmful effect. Parents who already have very low self-esteem may feel even more guilty and blameful if they know or believe that they have passed on a lethal disease to their newborn. If the information is divulged to others, both mother and child may be affected. Although there are no empirical studies on this point, anecdotal reports abound of mothers being expelled from their homes, beaten by their sexual partners, or having considered suicide when the fact that their infants are found to be HIV-seropositive is the first indication that they themselves are seropositive as well. In some cases, the belief that an infant is infected with HIV appears to increase the chance that the infant will be abandoned or rejected after birth. Such reactions are even more tragic given the inability to determine whether the infant is truly infected.

Confidentiality about an infant's HIV status is frequently difficult to maintain, even if the family is intact and the child will be cared for by his or her parents. Questions inevitably arise about the need to inform extended family members or others who may intermittently care for the infant, or an extended family member coming to a health-care visit may ask questions (such as why inactivated polio vaccine is being used) that would normally prompt a discussion of the risks of polio for HIV-infected patients.

Confidentiality is even harder to maintain if social service agencies become involved in a child's care. In response to worker and foster parent concerns, agencies are increasingly asking for disclosure of an infant's HIV status prior to placement. This information then becomes part of the child's social service record and may be discussed in hearings or conferences that are formally closed but that still may involve individuals who otherwise would not have had access to the test results. Social service records also may not include follow-up medical data, including later testing that either verifies or disproves the infant's presumptive diagnosis of HIV infection. Once the child is labeled as HIV-seropositive, it may be difficult to convince nonmedical personnel that he or she actually may be uninfected.

Disclosure issues are complicated by the ambiguity surrounding the risk to contacts of infected infants. Most evidence indicates that casual contact is not a means of transmission of HIV infection. In four published studies that examined groups of household contacts of patients with HIV seropositivity and/or AIDS or AIDS-related complex (ARC),[31] of 178 contacts who were not members of known risk groups or sexual partners of the index patient, none became HIV-seropositive or clinically ill. These contacts were estimated to have had household exposure to the index case ranging from a few months to over 3 years, although for most it was not possible to calculate the exact period of exposure. Four of the contacts studied were caretakers of infants who had apparently acquired HIV infection perinatally.[32]

In three other studies, however, 2 of 24 sexual partners[33] and 1 of 3 siblings of infant patients[34] were found to be seropositive. These three cases presumably represented sexual or perinatal transmission from the index patient. Additionally, a case has been reported in which a parent seroconverted while providing home care for a child with transfusion-acquired HIV infection.[35] The child's care included drawing blood from an indwelling catheter, changing ostomy bags, passing a nasogastric tube, and inserting a rectal tube. The parent did not recall having open lesions on her hands but did not always wear gloves or wash after caring for the child. From these initial series of observations, transmission of HIV in the home appears to parallel what has been observed in health care settings: the agent seems transmissible only by direct parenteral, mucous membrane, or open skin exposure.[36] The risk of exposure from urine, stool, tears, or saliva is felt to be very small. Still, current guidelines[37] suggest that HIV-seropositive children who lack control of bodily secretions, or who have behavioral problems such as biting, may be legitimately restricted in their placement with other children or in medical settings. In addition, many states have public health laws that prohibit children with contagious diseases from participating in normal day care settings. Thus although it would seem reasonable to consider not disclosing an infant's HIV status to substitute caretakers, there is considerable pressure to do so. Also, because a policy of general "universal precautions" is not appropriate to the home or day care setting, there is at least some doubt about the safety of persons who are unaware that they are caring for a child at risk for HIV and thus do not use proper precautions, such as gloving for diaper changes and methodical handwashing.

Summary: The Interests of Infants and Screening Policies

Early diagnosis of HIV infection permits more prompt and focused management of the immunodeficient child, including specific antiretroviral therapy, and thus holds the promise of both extending and improving the child's quality of life. HIV screening of pregnant women or newborns facilitates early diagnosis and early, aggressive intervention by identifying at-risk infants in need of careful monitoring. As a result, such screening clearly benefits the subset of newborns who have HIV infection, especially if it can prevent catastrophic illness from PCP in the first months of life. For these infants, the medical benefits of early diagnosis outweigh the social risks of being identified as HIV infected. One must weigh the benefit to this infected group against the possible harm to other newborns who would be singled out as at risk when in fact they are not infected with HIV. If the response to an at-risk newborn is to offer accessible, high-quality, comprehensive pediatric care during a particularly vulnerable stage of life, then one can argue that even these uninfected infants derive some benefit from being identified as special. Advances in test specificity, presymptomatic treatment, and social safeguards would further strengthen the case for prenatal and neonatal screening. Current limitations in these areas, however, suggest that for the foreseeable future, screening should be universally offered but remain voluntary, with the approach to the parent dictated by local seroprevalence and the existence of locally relevant, specific, individual risk factors.

Notes

1. Centers for Disease Control (CDC), "Update: Acquired Immunodeficiency Syndrome—United States, 1981–1988," *Morbidity and Mortality Weekly Report* 38 (1989): 229–236.

2. R. Hoff, V. Berardi, B. Weiblen et al., "Seroprevalence of Human Immunodeficiency Virus Among Childbearing Women: Estimation by Testing Samples of Blood from Newborns," *New England Journal of Medicine* 318 (1988): 525–530.

3. Ira Chasnoff, W. J. Burns, S. H. Schnoll et al., "Maternal–Neonatal Incest," *American Journal of Orthopsychiatry* 56 (1986): 557–580.

4. Jane Gross, "Grandmothers Bear a Burden Sired by Drugs," *New York Times,* April 9, 1989, p. A1.

5. P. Kerr, "Addiction's Hidden Toll: Poor Families in Turmoil," *New York Times,* June 23, 1988, p. A1.

6. N. R. Lief, "The Drug User as a Parent," *International Journal of Addictions* 20 (1985): 63–97; J. S. Musick, V. Bernstein, C. Percansky et al., "A Chain of Enablement: Using Community-Based Programs to Strengthen Relationships Between Teen Parents and Their Infants," *Zero-to-Three* 8 (1987): 1–6.

7. CDC, "Update: Acquired Immunodeficiency Syndrome—United States."

8. Marguerite Barbacci, Thomas Quinn, Richard Kline et al., "Failure of Targeted Screening to Identify HIV+ Pregnant Women" (Abstract M.B.P. 5), *Proceedings of the 5th International AIDS Conference* (1989): 222.

9. Hoff et al., "Seroprevalence of Human Immunodeficiency Virus."

10. E. M. Connor, M. Wright, M. Boland et al., "Prolonged Incubation Period in Children with Human Immunodeficiency Virus infection" (HIV) (Abstract 1040), *Pediatric Research* 25 (1989): 176A.

11. Gwendolyn Scott, Cecelia Hutto, R. Makuch et al., "Survival in Children with Perinatally Acquired Human Immunodeficiency Virus Type 1 Infection," *New England Journal of Medicine* 321 (1989): 1791–1796.

12. M. L. Bagarazzi, Edward M. Connor, G. D. McSherry et al., "*Pneumocystis Carinii* Pneumonia (PCP) Among Human Immunodeficiency Virus (HIV) Infected Children: Ten Years Experience" (Abstract 980), *Pediatric Research* 27 (1990): 166A.

13. Ibid.; Scott et al., "Survival in Children."

14. S. Blanche, C. Rouzioux, M. Moscato et al., "A Prospective Study of Infants Born to Women Seropositive for Human Immunodeficiency Virus Type 1," *New England Journal of Medicine* 320 (1989): 1643–1648.

15. Bagarazzi et al., "*Pneumocystis carinii* Pneumonia (PCP)."

16. Connor et al., "Prolonged Incubation Period."

17. European Collaborative Study, "Mother-to-Child Transmission of HIV Infection," *Lancet* 2 (1988): 1039–1042; Nancy Hutton, unpublished data.

18. Ibid.

19. Martha Rogers, C.-Y. Ou, M. Rayfield et al., "Use of Polymerase Chain Reaction for Early Detection of the Proviral Sequences of Human Immunodeficiency Virus in Infants Born to Seropositive Mothers," *New England Journal of Medicine* 320 (1989): 1649–1654.

20. Blanche et al., "Prospective Study"; European Collaborative Study, "Mother-to-Child Transmission"; Hutton, unpublished data; R. Ryder, W. Nsa, S. Hassig et al., "Perinatal Transmission of the Human Immunodeficiency Virus Type 1 to Infants of Seropositive Women in Zaire," *New England Journal of Medicine* 320 (1989): 1637–1642.

21. Blanche et al., "Prospective study."

22. Scott et al., "Survival in Children."

23. D. L. Olds, C. R. Henderson, R. Chamberlin et al., "Preventing Child Abuse and Neglect: A Randomized Trial of Nurse Home Visitation," *Pediatrics* 78 (1986): 65–78.

24. CDC, "General Recommendations on Immunization," *Morbidity and Mortality Weekly Report* 38 (1989): 205–227.
25. American Academy of Pediatrics, "Varicella-Zoster Infections," *Report of the Committee on Infectious Diseases, 21st Edition* (1988): 456–462.
26. Nancy Hutton, Arlene Butz, Mary Joyner et al., "Health Care Utilization by HIV At Risk Infants" (Abstract S.D. 793). *Proceedings of the 6th International Aids Conference* 3 (1990): 288.
27. Arlene Butz, Nancy Hutton, Mary Joyner et al., "HIV Risk Infants: Hospitalization Patterns" (presented at the Hopkins AIDS Conference, Baltimore, April 1990).
28. B. Lambert, "AIDS Legacy: A Growing Generation of Orphans," *New York Times,* July 17, 1989, p. A1.
29. S. Daley, "Foster Care and AIDS: Joy and Pain," *New York Times,* May 7, 1988, p. 29; C. L. Hays, "Hospitalization of Sick Infants Faulted in Suit," *New York Times,* July 14, 1989, p. B1.
30. Personal communication, M. Durfee, Medical coordinator, Child Abuse Prevention Program, Los Angeles County.
31. G. Friedland, B. Saltzman, M. Rogers et al., "Lack of Transmission of HTLV-III/LAV Infection to Household Contacts of Patients with AIDS or AIDS-Related Complex with Oral Candidiasis," *New England Journal of Medicine* 314 (1986): 344–349; J. Jason, S. McDougal, G. Dixon et al., "HTLV-III/LAV Antibody and Immune Status of Household Contacts and Sexual Partners of Persons with Hemophilia," *Journal of the American Medical Association* 255 (1986): 212–215; J. Kaplan, J. Oleske, J. Getchell et al., "Evidence Against Transmission of Human T-Lymphotropic Virus Type III/Lymphadenopathy-Associated Virus (HTLV-III/LAV) in Families of Children with Acquired Immunodeficiency syndrome," *Pediatric Infectious Disease Journal* 4 (1985): 468–71; D. Lawrence, J. Jason, J. Bouhasin et al., "HTLV-III/LAV Antibody Status of Spouses and Household Contacts Assisting in Home Infusion of Hemophilia Patients," *Blood* 66 (1985): 703–705.
32. Kaplan et al., "Evidence Against Transmission"
33. Jason et al., "HTLV-III/LAV Antibody and immune status"; Lawrence et al., "HTLV-III/LAV Antibody Status."
34. Kaplan et al., "Evidence Against Transmission."
35. CDC, "Apparent Transmission of Human T-Lymphotropic Virus Type III/Lymphadenopathy-Associated Virus from a Child to a Mother Providing Health Care," *Morbidity and Mortality Weekly Report* 35 (1986): 76–79.
36. S. Weiss, W. Saxinger, D. Rechtman et al., "HTLV-III Infection Among Health Care Workers: Association with Needle-Stick Injuries," *Journal of the American Medical Association* 254 (1985): 2089–2093.
37. American Academy of Pediatrics, "Health Guidelines for the Attendance in Day-Care and Foster Care Settings of Children Infected with Human Immunodeficiency Virus," *Pediatrics* 79 (1987): 466–471.

III

LEGAL ISSUES

6

Prenatal and Newborn Screening: State Legislative Approaches and Current Practice Standards

KATHERINE L. ACUFF

Any efforts to screen pregnant women and newborns for HIV do not occur in a vacuum but in the context of current screening practices. This chapter focuses on two ways that large-scale screening efforts can be and have been established. First, it examines legislatively established screening programs to determine whether HIV screening can be accommodated under existing authority. Because screening is a state issue, there is a great degree of variability in the answer to this question. No recommendation are made on advisability of a legislative approach to HIV screening, however, beyond an insistence that any screening program for HIV be wholly voluntary. Second, because only a limited number of conditions are screened for by force of legislative authority, professional practice guidelines and medical practices at two university hospitals are examined to get a rough idea of the scope and procedures by which pregnant women and newborns are currently screened.

This review, coupled with an examination of the case histories of six screening efforts in Chapter 3, shows that there is no single right way to approach screening. There are successes—and failures—in both legislated and medically driven screening efforts. The goal of this chapter is to elucidate some of the characteristics of successful screening programs that transcend the manner in which they have been established.

Current Legislative Status of Screening Programs

All 50 states and the District of Columbia have established by statute, regulation, or informal policy screening programs that cover prenatal or newborn screening or both.[1] State screening programs vary greatly in the elaborateness of the authorizing legislation, as well as with regard to such issues as whether screening must be voluntary or mandatory and whether specific provisions for informed consent are made.

In order to determine if prenatal and newborn HIV screening could be implemented within the authority granted to the state health departments under current legislation or regulations, the legal apparatus governing screening was reviewed. (All jurisdictions will be referred to hereafter as "states.")[2]

Table 6.1 is a summary of the prenatal and newborn conditions for which the states screen. A more detailed review of the legislative materials is presented in the Appendix to this chapter. In addition to identifying the types of conditions for which screening programs exist, this section discusses some of the features of the legislative authority for screening.

Prenatal screening

The most widespread condition subject to state-mandated prenatal screening is syphilis. In 45 states, a prenatal syphilis test is required by state law, with some states providing that a woman may refuse on the basis of religious objections or on other grounds. Ohio also mandates screening for gonorrhea, and South Carolina requires screening for rubella titer, Rh factor, and a hemoglobin determination that detects sickle cell disease as well as other hemoglobinopathies. Five states have no prenatal screening legislation and rely on good medical practice to include screening of pregnant women for syphilis.

In all states with syphilis legislation, the responsibility for syphilis screening is given to individual physicians (or other medical care providers) and is generally mandated to occur at the time of the first prenatal visit or shortly thereafter. Some states require a subsequent test during pregnancy. Typically, the statutes set forth no penalties for failure to comply with the requirement. Occasionally, however, a statute includes enforcement language. California, for example, makes the failure to obtain a blood sample for syphilis testing a misdemeanor, although it provides no punishment for noncompliance. Texas makes the failure to take a blood sample for a syphilis test a misdemeanor punishable by a fine of $200 to $500.

Two states—California and Hawaii—have comprehensive legislation aimed at prenatal testing by amniocentesis for genetic disorders.[3] Interestingly, neither state includes syphilis in its umbrella prenatal legislation, which probably reflects the very different origins of the two programs. Legislation for syphilis testing, enacted some 40 to 50 years ago, targets a treatable infection and is generally found tucked away among the statutory provisions dealing with venereal or communicable disease control. California's and Hawaii's prenatal screening programs (enacted in 1978 and 1988, respectively), on the other hand, deal primarily with untreatable genetic conditions.

California's prenatal diagnosis legislation states that "the participation by an individual in this program shall be wholly voluntary and shall not be a prerequisite to eligibility for, or receipt of, any other service or assistance from, or to participation in any other program." The statute's scope is quite broad, with the population covered including, but not limited to, the following:

1. Women 35 years of age or older.
2. Women having had a previous Down Syndrome child or a child with any other genetic disorder.
3. Pregnancies where one parent is a translocation carrier.
4. Women who are carriers of an X-linked disease.
5. Pregnancies where both parents are carriers of an autosomal trait (for a disease or defect).
6. Pregnancies where the parents have a previous child who has a neural tube defect.

During the 10-year period from July 1, 1976, to June 30, 1986, over 79,000 women received prenatal diagnosis services in the 20 prenatal diagnosis service centers licensed by the state.[4] As a result of its prenatal program, 30 to 40 percent of all the prenatal testing done in the United States is performed in California.[5]

Within its comprehensive prenatal screening program, California operates a separate Alpha-Fetoprotein (AFP) Screening Program in which all physicians are required by statute to offer every pregnant woman information about prenatal screening for neural tube defects (NTDs). The regulations require that all clinicians give a detailed patient brochure to every pregnant woman at the first prenatal visit (if this is at or before 20 weeks of gestation). This brochure is distributed by the state and is currently available in English, Spanish, and Asian languages. After reviewing the brochure, the pregnant woman is asked to sign an informed consent or a refusal document. At the eight state-designated AFP Prenatal Diagnosis Centers, evaluation of the test results, genetic counseling, and confirmatory tests are provided.[6] The California AFP Screening Program began in April 1986, and within the first 6 months, approximately half of those eligible to participate—some 37,000 women—elected to be screened.[7]

Newborn screening

The most extensive statutory screening efforts have been made in conjunction with screening of newborns for inborn errors of metabolism, genetic diseases, or heritable diseases, the prototype being screening for phenylketonuria (PKU). Currently, all 50 states and the District of Columbia provide by statute, regulation, or otherwise for PKU screening of newborns.[8]

Although the statutory and regulatory form of newborn screening statutes varies to some degree in the United States, typically the authorizing legislation mandates screening for PKU, or for PKU with a few additional conditions specified, and in most instances includes a catchall clause allowing the testing for additional disorders upon the recommendation of the department of health or a specially appointed commission or advisory board.

The degree of specificity in the statutes varies substantially. For example, Alabama's statute provides simply that all newborns be tested for hypothyroid-

TABLE 6.1. Screening Programs in the 50 States and the District of Columbia

State	Prenatal	Newborn
Alabama	SYP[a]	PKU, HT, SC
Alaska	SYP	PKU, GAL, CAH, BIO
Arizona	SYP	PKU, GAL, HT, MSUD, BIO, CF, HC, SC[b]
Arkansas	SYP	PKU, HT, SC
California	SYP; MSAFP offered	PKU, HT, SC, BIO
Colorado	SYP	PKU, HT, GAL, HC, MSUD, SC, CF[c]
Connecticut	SYP	PKU, HT, GAL
Delaware	SYP	PKU, HT, GAL, HC, MSUD, SC, BIO (pilot)
District of Columbia	—	PKU, GAL, HT, HC, MSUD, SC
Florida	SYP	PKU, HT, GAL, MSUD, SC
Georgia	SYP	PKU, GAL, TYR, SC (targeted)
Hawaii	SYP[d]	PKU, HT
Idaho	SYP	PKU, GAL, HT, MSUD, HC, TYR, BIO
Illinois	SYP	PKU, HT, GAL, SC
Indiana	SYP	PKU, HT, GAL, HC, MSUD, SC
Iowa	SYP	PKU, HT, GAL, MSUD, HC
Kansas	SYP	PKU, HT, GAL, SC
Kentucky	SYP	PKU, HT, GAL, SC (pilot)
Louisiana	SYP	PKU, HT, GAL, SC
Maine	SYP, Rh	PKU, HT, GAL, MSUD, HC
Maryland	SYP	PKU, HT, GAL, MSUD, HC, BIO, TYR, SC PKU, HT, GAL, MSUD, HC, TP, SC, CAH
Michigan	SYP	PKU, HT, GAL, MSUD, BD, SC
Minnesota	—	PKU, HT, GAL, SC
Mississippi	MSAFP offered to high-risk groups only	PKU, HT, SC
Missouri	SYP	PKU, HT, GAL, SC
Montana	SYP	PKU, HT, other amino acidopathies
Nebraska	SYP	PKU, HT, BIO
Nevada	SYP	PKU, HT, GAL, MSUD, BIO, TYR, HC, SC
New Hampshire	—	PKU, HT, GAL, HC, MSUD
New Jersey	SYP	PKU, HT, GAL, SC
New Mexico	SYP	PKU, HT, GAL
New York	SYP, HEP B	PKU, HT, GAL, HC, MSUD, SC, SYP
North Carolina	SYP	PKU, HT, GAL, CAH, SC (nonwhites)
North Dakota	SYP	PKU, HT
Ohio	SYP, GON	PKU, HT, GAL, HC
Oklahoma	SYP	PKU, HT (SC and GAL pilots in 1990)
Oregon	SYP	PKU, HT, GAL, MSUD, HC, TYR, BIO
Pennsylvania	SYP	PKU, HT, SC (pilot)
Rhode Island	SYP	PKU, HT, GAL, MSUD, HC, SC
South Carolina	SYP, RUB, Rh	PKU, HT, SC
South Dakota	SYP	PKU, HT, SC
Tennessee	SYP	PKU, HT, SC
Texas	SYP	PKU, HT, GAL, SC, TP, CHL
Utah	SYP	PKU, HT, GAL
Vermont	SYP, MSAFP offered	PKU, HT, GAL, HC, MSUD

TABLE 6.1.   (*Continued*)

State	Prenatal	Newborn
Virginia	SYP	PKU, HT, GAL, HC, MSUD, SC
Washington	SYP	PKU, HT
West Virginia	SYP	PKU, HT, GAL
Wisconsin	—	PKU, HT, GAL, MSUD
Wyoming	SYP	PKU, HT, GAL, HC, MSUD, SC, CF, BIO

[a]SYP = syphilis; PKU = phenylketonuria; HT = congenital hypothyroidism; SC = sickle cell and other hemoglobinopathies; HC = homocystinuria; GAL = galactosemia; MSUD = maple syrup urine disease; BD = biotinidase deficiency; TYR = tyrosinemia; TP = toxoplasmosis; CHL = chlamydia; CAH = congenital adrenal hyperplasia; HEP B = hepatitis B.

[b]Only PKU, GAL, and CH are authorized by Arizona's regulations. The other four conditions screened—MSUD, HC, SC, CF, and BIO—are screened by virtue of the fact that Arizona is a participant in a regional screening pact whereby all newborn screening is evaluated by a central laboratory in Denver, Colorado. If Denver chose to stop screening for MSUD, for example, so would Arizona.

[c]In 1988, Colorado became the first state to add cystic fibrosis to its newborn screening program. New Mexico and Arizona also screen for cystic fibrosis because it sends its newborn samples to Colorado for testing.

[d]Hawaii passed legislation in 1988 establishing a prenatal screening program; as of September 1989 no regulations had been promulgated.

ism, PKU, and sickle cell trait and/or hemoglobinopathies. It also includes a provision allowing for parental waiver of the test on religious grounds. It contains no catchall language allowing for expansion to cover screening for other conditions such as HIV. Six states have similar disease-specific language.[9]

Maryland's statute was drafted in an apparent effort not only to set forth specific guidelines for screening but also to retain a great deal of flexibility. The statute established the Hereditary and Congenital Disorders Program to be monitored by the State Commission on Hereditary and Congenital Disorders, with the authority to give advice on the need for rules, regulations, and standards for the detection and management of hereditary and congenital disorders. Maryland's statute, however, leaves little room for interpretation as to the types of disorders the statute is intended to include. It defines a "hereditary" disorder as "any disorder that: (1) Is transmitted through the genetic material deoxyribonucleic acid (DNA); or (2) Arises through the improper processing of the information in the genetic material."

The Maryland statute defines a "congenital" disorder as a significant structural or functional abnormality of the body that is present at birth. It specifically carves out from the definition of congenital disorder conditions that result from "(i) an intrauterine infection; or (ii) a birth injury."

The establishment of screening programs for hemoglobinopathies, including sickle cell disease, is provided by statute (or regulations) by 30 states and Puerto Rico.[10] This number is up sharply since the 1988 National Institutes of Health (NIH) Consensus Conference on Newborn Screening for Sickle Cell Disease and Other Hemoglobinopathies, which recommended the screening of all newborns.[11] In 26 of the states, the District of Columbia, and Puerto Rico, all newborns are screened.[12] In Massachusetts and New Jersey, pilot screening programs were expanded to statewide screening of all newborns in 1990. In four states, pilot screening programs of all newborns in high-prevalence areas have been established, with expansion to statewide screening anticipated by the end of 1991.[13] In North Carolina and Georgia, selective screening of the nonwhite population is done. Although the authority for sickle cell screening is sometimes contained in the general newborn screening statutes, it is often provided in separate sickle cell–specific legislation. In most jurisdictions, statutory language provides for mandatory screening of newborns, generally allowing a parent to object only upon religious grounds. Maryland's statute is unique in requiring parental consent to newborn screening.

Discussion of legislative authority

Could the existing legislation or regulations related to prenatal and newborn screening be interpreted to encompass HIV screening? For most states the answer is, probably not. However, the likelihood varies with the statutory language.

As discussed above, prenatal screening legislation is largely restricted to screening for syphilis. In 44 states, the syphilis legislation is disease specific (although other conditions may be named) and does not include provisions for expansion to include other diseases such as HIV. As a result, the authority for prenatal HIV screening would not be likely to come from these statutes.

An exception to the usual narrowly drafted prenatal screening legislation is that of Oregon, which provides that physicians shall obtain blood samples from pregnant women at the time of the first prenatal visit "for such tests related to *any infectious condition* which may affect a pregnant woman or fetus, as the division shall by rule require" (emphasis added). This provision appears broad enough to include prenatal HIV screening. Oregon's statute provides that any such screening must be made with the consent of the woman and that "no sample shall be taken without such consent." Any HIV screening that could be authorized under Oregon's statute would have to be voluntary.

As discussed above, two states—California and Hawaii—are currently offering screening to pregnant women under the authority of comprehensive prenatal screening programs. For both of these programs, the conditions targeted are hereditary or developmental disorders rather than infectious diseases. As a result, because HIV is an infectious disease, it would not be easily accommodated within the scope of the legislation. If such a legislative stretch were attempted, HIV testing would have to be voluntary, in keeping with the other prenatal screening programs covered under these laws.

Two states—Vermont and Mississippi—are unusual in having prenatal maternal serum alpha-fetoprotein (MSAFP) screening programs without the benefit of specific authorizing legislation, rules, or regulations. These "programs" generally consist of providing informational materials for physician and patient education, as well as setting standards for MSAFP testing procedures. All testing is voluntary and is conducted with the informed consent of the patient.

The authority for creating Vermont's and Mississippi's MSAFP programs is evidently grounded in the broad statements of purpose for the state health departments contained in the legislation creating the departments.[14] Should Vermont and Mississippi attempt to informally establish similar HIV testing programs without the benefit of legislation or rulemaking, however, it is uncertain whether the programs could withstand legal challenge. At issue is whether the formal rulemaking procedures required by each state's administrative procedure act[15] would be triggered (and, perhaps, should have been triggered in the case of the MSAFP screening program as well).[16] Such formal rulemaking requirements would not necessarily preclude HIV screening, but it would require public notice and comment on the proposed rules and could be a significant barrier to an HIV screening program.

With respect to the screening of newborns, the statutory language in some of the screening legislation may be, in some cases, sufficiently broad to encompass newborn HIV screening. The pivotal factor is the language of the catchall clauses, which varies substantially. Several states limit the conditions that can be added to only other inborn errors of metabolism,[17] to congenital or metabolic disorders generally,[18] or to those conditions resulting in mental retardation; in any of these cases, screening for HIV is precluded.[19] Florida, in addition to limiting its catchall clause to disorders resulting in mental retardation, provides that the screening test be accepted by current medical practice.

The Maryland statute includes "congenital disorders" in the scope of its newborn screening statute, but it defines "congenital" so as to specifically exclude conditions that result from intrauterine infections.[20] If literally interpreted, this express exclusion of "intrauterine infection" from the Maryland definition of "congenital" would appear to preclude the implementation of a state-supported HIV screening program under the statute.[21]

A few states have language that could be read to allow incorporation of HIV screening in newborns, at least if certain conditions are met. The broadest statutes are those of Hawaii and New York, which provide that newborn screening may be undertaken for "any other disease that may be specified by the department of health." A literal reading of this would permit HIV screening. Kansas allows newborn testing for "other diseases as may be appropriately detected with the same procedures for which laboratory services are required." Because it is possible to test for HIV antibodies in dried blood on filter papers—the method used for inborn errors of metabolism such as PKU—HIV could fall within the scope of this statute as well.[22] Massachusetts's catchall language provides that newborns can also be tested for "such other specifically treatable genetic or biochemical disorders or *treatable infectious diseases* which may be determined by testing," as specified by the department of health (emphasis added). This is the only statute that provides expressly for expansion to cover infectious diseases. Whether HIV screening could be covered would seem to depend on the development of accurate diagnostic tests for newborns, as well as on improvement of HIV treatments for newborns. Several other states allow expansion to other "preventable diseases."[23] If it becomes possible to prevent transmission of intrapartum HIV infection of the newborn, HIV screening could be accomplished under these statutes.

Current Medical Practice with Respect to Prenatal and Newborn Screening

Screening programs authorized by the government by no means exhaust the number or kinds of screening tests currently performed on pregnant women and newborns. Many screening tests are performed routinely by obstetricians and pediatricians without benefit of legislation or public health regulation. Unfortunately, there have been no empirical studies documenting medical practice with regard to screening tests in pregnancy or among newborns. In an attempt to capture some sense of the range of screening tests currently being used with which HIV testing can be compared, I looked at two sources—pronouncements on screening by the American Academy of Pediatrics (AAP) and the American College of Obstetricians and Gynecologists (ACOG) and the practices of the obstetric and newborn services of Johns Hopkins and Georgetown University hospitals.

Pronouncements of professional organizations

AAP and ACOG, supported by the March of Dimes, have set forth in *Guidelines for Perinatal Care,* 2nd ed., 1988 (the *Guidelines*), certain recommendations for prenatal and newborn screening.[24] As the editors note, the *Guidelines* are not intended to set practice standards, at least in the legal sense:

> The Guidelines should not be viewed as a body of rigid rules. They are general and intended to be adapted to many different situations, taking into account the needs and resources particular to the locality, the institution, or type of practice. . . . The purpose of these guidelines will be well served if they provide a firm basis on which local norms may be built.[25]

At the same time, however, the recommendations in the *Guidelines* do provide insight into professional standards and the state of the field of screening.

Prenatal screening recommendations

According to the *Guidelines,* candidates for prenatal genetic screening include certain couples at increased risk for producing genetically abnormal offspring because of advanced parental age, the presence of a birth defect in the parents, previous offspring or near relatives, or a history of abortions or stillbirths. In addition, a family history of Huntington's disease or hemophilia is an indication for screening. Finally, in a single-sentence example of "autosomal recessive diseases sufficiently common enough to warrant screening," the *Guidelines* recommend the screening of Jews to identify carriers of Tay-Sachs, blacks to identify carriers of sickle cell disease, and individuals of Italian, Greek, or Oriental descent to identify carriers of thalassemia.[26] The *Guidelines* summarize the indications for screening for congenital defects:

1. *Cytogenetic indications*
   a. Advanced maternal age (35 years or older at the expected time of delivery);
   b. Previous offspring with a chromosomal aberration, particularly autosomal trisomy;
   c. Chromosomal abnormality in either parent, particularly a translocation; and
   d. Need to determine fetal sex when there is a family history of a serious X-linked condition for which specific intrauterine diagnosis is not available.

2. *Single gene disorders* (i.e., conditions such as inborn errors of metabolism, hemoglobinopathies, cystic fibrosis, and Duchenne muscular dystrophy that are detectable in chorionic villi, amniotic fluid, or amniotic fluid cells) in a sibling or risk of such disorders because of parents' carrier status.

3. *Multifactorial disorders in a first-degree relative.*
   a. Neural tube defects
   b. Insulin-dependent maternal diabetes.[27]

In addition, the *Guidelines* discuss at some length the benefits and limitations of MSAFP screening, noting that a comprehensive screening program can identify both NTDs and chromosomal disorders such as trisomy 21. A successful MSAFP screening program "should include the provision of information to the patient,[28] accurate and prompt laboratory testing, access to consultants for sonography and for complex prenatal diagnosis, support services, and competent counseling on the available options, including pregnancy termination."[29] It is also noted that because the success of a screening program is dependent on these several factors, efficient coordination is necessary to ensure that the time span from screening to decision is relatively short.

Prenatal screening for certain infectious diseases is also addressed. The *Guidelines* recommend that all pregnant women be screened for syphilis, tuberculosis, and rubella. Furthermore, it is recommended that high-risk women be tested routinely for gonorrhea, chlamydia, and herpes simplex virus. Although the *Guidelines* note the ineffectiveness of screening only high-risk women for hepatitis B virus (HBV), they stop short of recommending the screening of all pregnant women as part of routine medical practice and defer this decision to individual physicians and hospitals.

With respect to HIV screening, the *Guidelines* advise that pregnant women believed to be at increased risk of HIV infection be routinely counseled and strongly urged to undergo testing for HIV antibody. Women at high risk are described in the *Guidelines* as current or former intravenous drug users; sexual partners of persons with clinical or serologic evidence of HIV infection; persons living in high-risk areas of the United States or from countries where there is a known or suspected high prevalence of HIV infection among women; those who have been engaged in prostitution, have had multiple sexual partners, or are being treated for sexually transmitted diseases; and those who received transfusions between 1978 and 1985. The *Guidelines* emphasize that

> the identification of HIV-infected pregnant women as early in pregnancy as possible is important to ensure appropriate medical care for them; to plan medical care for their infants, and to provide counseling about family planning, future pregnancies, and the risk of sexual transmission of HIV to others.[30]

The *Guidelines* further note that there are a plethora of social and ethical concerns connected with AIDS and HIV infection and state that

> because of their extreme significance to the patient and her family, it is important to ensure that the patient understands the potential implications of HIV antibody testing before she undergoes the test and that she agrees to be tested and to receive the counseling necessary after the test results are available.[31]

The discussion of HIV testing in the *Guidelines* differs from the discussion of screening for other conditions in several noteworthy respects. For example, the *Guidelines* recommend that physicians "urge" prenatal testing when a woman is suspected to be at high risk for HIV infection, but the document is not similarly explicit about professional duties to advocate testing for other conditions. At the same time, however, patient consent is recognized as an important component of HIV testing, although there is no specific discussion of consent issues in the testing of pregnant women for other diseases or conditions, such as Tay-Sachs disease or sickle cell disease. Additionally, suspected HIV infection is the only situation in which counseling is specifically encouraged, although the *Guidelines* do set forth the criteria for adequate genetic counseling in general, and state that "counseling is obligatory before antenatal diagnostic studies are performed."[32]

In obstetrics, the *Guidelines* are supplemented by several ACOG technical bulletins that address issues related to prenatal screening, some of which expand on the recommendations included in the *Guidelines*.[33] For example, one technical bulletin specific to testing for HIV discusses at some length the purpose and importance of counseling:

> Testing for HIV antibody is an important addition to counseling in certain circumstances. Testing without counseling (aside from anonymous serosurveys and screening of blood products) serves no individual or public health goals and should be discouraged. When combined with counseling, however, testing can perform many functions. In particular, it enables women to make informed decisions about their reproductive health and behavior. . . . Testing should be offered to women in risk groups who are either pregnant or contemplating pregnancy.[34]

ACOG's view of which women are at risk for HIV mirrors that described in the *Guidelines* but, additionally, states that women with uncertain drug or sexual histories should be offered testing.

If a pregnant woman tests HIV antibody-positive, ACOG advises that "reproductive options, including induced abortion as a valid choice for HIV-infected women, should be discussed."[35] ACOG also recommends that pregnant women who are HIV-positive be screened for other similarly transmitted organisms, such as chlamydia and HBV, as well as other conditions such as tuberculosis, cytomegalovirus, and toxoplasmosis.

Newborn screening recommendations

With respect to newborn screening, the *Guidelines* recommend that all newborns be screened, at a minimum, for the persistent hyperphenylalanemias, including PKU, and for congenital hypothyroidism. For a number of other inborn errors of metabolism, the *Guidelines* acknowledge the availability of screening tests but note that because the laboratory results are unlikely to be available prior to the manifestation of symptoms, other diagnostic means should be utilized. Included in this category are several conditions such as maple syrup urine disease (MSUD), galactosemia, and congenital lactic acidosis for which some states routinely test newborns.

Current screening practice at Johns Hopkins and Georgetown University hospitals

The screening practices at Johns Hopkins and Georgetown University hospitals were reviewed not because they are believed to be representative of screening practices generally or because their patient population is deemed typical, but simply because the authors of this book have associations with these universities. Nevertheless, it is believed that reviewing their screening practices gives some insight into routine obstetric and pediatric practice. Table 6.2 shows the conditions for which screening is performed at Johns Hopkins and Georgetown and the categories of patients tested.

It is notable that the screening practices of the two institutions are very similar, conform closely to the screening recommendations of the *Guidelines,* and follow the general directives of the *Guidelines* concerning testing newborns for inborn errors of metabolism. One clear difference is the inclusion of a toxicology screen for substance abuse of all pregnant women at Johns Hopkins, a test not addressed in the *Guidelines* and that may reflect a difference in the patient populations of the two institutions.

As discussed in the previous section, the *Guidelines* recommend offering HIV screening to all high-risk patients. Georgetown appears to follow this recommendation providing for HIV screening at a physician's discretion. Johns Hopkins takes a different approach, shifting the burden of determining the risk to the

TABLE 6.2. Prenatal and Newborn Screening Practices at Johns Hopkins Hospital in Baltimore and Georgetown University Hospital in Washington, D.C.[a]

Screening	Groups Screened
Johns Hopkins Hospital	
Prenatal	
Syphilis (at first and third trimesters)	All
Gonorrhea (at first and third trimesters)	All
Atypical blood group antibodies	All
Hemoglobin electrophoresis[b]	Persons at risk (usually blacks)
Antibodies for rubella	All
Tuberculosis	All
Hepatitis B	All
Tay-Sachs disease	Carrier status testing in Jewish parents
Ultrasound (16th week)	All clinic patients; as indicated with other patients
MSAFP (16th week)	Offered to all; informed consent required
Gestational diabetes (28th week)	All
Substance abuse	All; informed refusal[c]
HIV antibody test	Offered to all; informed consent required[d]
Newborn	
PKU	All
Congenital hypothyroidism (CH)	All
Galactosemia	All
Homocystinuria	All
MSUD	All
Sickle cell hemoglobinopathies	All
Biotinidase	All
Rh factor	If mother is RH[-]
Syphilis	All
Georgetown University Hospital	
Prenatal	
First visit	
Hematocrit/hemoglobin	All
Blood type	All
Atypical blood group antibodies	All
Syphilis	All
Rubella	All
Sickle cell preparation	If black
Hemoglobin electrophoresis	If sickle cell preparation is positive or if there is increased risk of a hemoglobinopathy
Hepatitis B	All
Tay-Sachs disease	Carrier status testing in Jewish parents
Chlamydia	Depending on risk
Gonorrhea	Depending on risk
Group B streptococcus	All
MSAFP (16 weeks)	All offered
Genetic amniocentesis (16 weeks)	Recommended for high-risk groups
Ultrasound (18–20 weeks)	All offered
Diabetic screening	Recommended to all, depending on the risk;[e] informed consent required

132

TABLE 6.2.   (*Continued*)

Screening	Groups Screened
Newborn[f]	
PKU	All
CH	All
Sickle cell hemoglobinopathies	All
Rh factor	If mother is RH $^-$

[a]I would like to thank Dr. John Repke at Johns Hopkins Hospital and Dr. Jon Katz, Dr. Bashari Freij, and Dr. John Queenen at Georgetown University Hospital for their help in generating the information for this table.

[b]This identifies sickle cell disease and trait, as well as hemoglobin C trait and thalassemia.

[c]Patients are told that they will be screened for substance abuse and that all patients are routinely so screened, but they have the right to refuse.

[d]The informed consent form is a part of the HIV laboratory test requisition form.

[e]The offering of HIV antibody testing is strongly practitioner dependent.

[f]There is no written policy concerning newborn screening at Georgetown. Newborns are screened for hepatitis and/or syphilis without informed consent at the clinician's discretion. If the physician believes the newborn is at risk for HIV, the mother is asked to give informed consent for testing. If testing is refused, the mother is approached again, counseled, and again asked to consent to the testing of the newborn. Upon a second refusal, the medical team assumes that the newborn is positive in terms of its medical care.

pregnant woman. All Johns Hopkins obstetric patients are offered HIV testing. Both institutions require informed consent prior to any HIV testing. And at both Johns Hopkins and Georgetown, newborns may be tested for HIV only upon the informed consent of the mother.

Conclusion

This chapter has focused on the statutory and medical practice context for screening pregnant women and newborns for HIV. It does not provide any clear answers to the questions concerning HIV screening, but it does offer some information worthy of consideration.

First, with regard to the role of the state in authorizing testing, it appears that for most jurisdictions, existing prenatal screening legislation is too narrowly drawn to accommodate HIV screening. Most states would likely have to pass new legislation.

Second, legislation is by no means the only, or even the predominant, route to ensuring adoption of policies regarding prenatal or newborn screening. Although professional screening recommendations usually parallel legislatively mandated screening, many other testing procedures have been incorporated into routine medical practice based upon the pronouncements of professional organizations, without the spur of legislative mandate. Notable here is the case of HBV screening of newborns for which the Immunization Practices Advisory Committee of the Public Health Service (ACIP), with the support of ACOG and AAP, has issued universal screening recommendations. Indeed, with respect to HIV, professional organizations, such as ACOG, and official health agencies, such as the Centers for Disease Control (CDC), have already taken positions concerning HIV testing of pregnant women and newborns. Although no empirical data are available, it is likely that HIV testing of pregnant women and newborns is currently being done in many centers.

A third mechanism for accomplishing routine screening is the combination of the first two. Notwithstanding the fact that PKU legislation was passed in more than 40 states over the strong objection of AAP, it is also the case that professional organizations can (and have) urge(d) passage of legislation to ensure that testing be done. The prime example here is prenatal screening for syphilis, in which a variety of professional organizations, spearheaded by the U.S. Surgeon General, led a crusade for the passage of mandatory syphilis testing of pregnant women (see Chapter 3). Additionally, a 1987 NIH Consensus Conference of professionals that recommended the screening of all newborns for sickle cell disease led to responses to re-fund dormant state sickle cell programs, to pass new legislation, or to establish pilot screening programs.[36]

The recommendations made in this volume for HIV testing of pregnant women and newborns are based on the current scientific and medical knowledge concerning the disease. Because changes in methods of identifying HIV seropositivity in the fetus and in the newborn, and improvements in the availability of treatment interventions, will undoubtedly occur, modifications are built into the recommendations based on a variety of anticipated scenarios. It is hoped that the screening recommendations will be endorsed by professional organizations and incorporated into good medical practice as soon as possible. As a result of the flexible nature of the recommendations, it is essential that the vehicle by which the recommendations are put into effect is capable of responding quickly to changed circumstances. For this reason, a legislated approach may lack the flexibility needed unless it is drafted broadly and the testing is tied to the advice of an advisory board in contact with professional organizations.

APPENDIX **REVIEW OF SCREENING STATUTES**

Alabama

Prenatal

Code of Alabama § 22-11A-16 (Michie Supp. 1987) provides that physicians shall obtain blood samples from every pregnant woman at the time of the first prenatal visit for a standard serologic test for syphilis.

Newborn

Code of Alabama § 22-20-3 (Michie Supp. 1987) provides that all newborns be tested for hypothyroidism, PKU and sickle cell anemia, sickle cell trait, and/or abnormal hemoglobin.

Parents may object on religious grounds.

Alaska

Prenatal

Alaska Statutes § 18.15.150 (West 1986) provides that physicians shall obtain blood samples from all pregnant women at the time of their first professional visit or within 10 days after the visit for a standard serologic test for syphilis.

The woman may object on religious grounds.

Newborn

Alaska Statutes § 18.5.200 (West 1986) provides for the screening of all new-borns for PKU. It also provides that the health department "administer and provide services for the testing for other heritable diseases that lead to mental retardation and physical handicaps as screening programs accepted by current medical practice and as developed."

7 Alaska Administrative Code 27.510 (1984) provides additionally for the testing of all newborns for biotinidase, galactosemia, and congenital adrenal hyper-plasia.

Arizona

Prenatal

Arizona Revised Statutes Annotated § 36-693 (1988) provides that physicians shall obtain from all pregnant women a blood sample at the first prenatal visit for a standard serologic test for syphilis.

Newborn

Arizona Revised Statutes Annotated § 36-694 (West 1989 Replacement) provides that all newborns shall be tested for "metabolic disorders" as specified by the rules and regulations of the department of health services.

Arizona Revised Statutes Annotated § 36-797.41 (West 1989 Replacement) provides that the state will make every effort to detect, as early as possible, sickle cell anemia according to regulations set forth by the department. It does not specify the testing of newborns.

Arizona Official Compilation, Administrative Rules and Regulations 9-14-511 et seq. (1982). R9-14-513 provides specifically for the testing of all newborns for PKU, galactosemia, and hypothyroidism.*

R9-14-511 states as its purpose "to cause every newborn, with the consent of his parent or legal guardian, to be tested for metabolic disorders for which early and appropriate treatment can provide prevention or substantial amelioration of mental retardation."

Arkansas

Prenatal

Arkansas Code of 1987 Annotated § 20-16-507 (Michie) provides that physicians shall obtain blood samples from every pregnant woman during gestation or at delivery for a standard serologic test for syphilis.

Newborn

Arkansas Code of 1987 Annotated § 20-15-301 et seq. (Michie) provides for the testing of all newborns for PKU and hypothyroidism and, in addition, for the testing of "all non-Caucasian newborn infants" for sickle cell anemia.

Parents may object to such tests on religious grounds.

Arkansas "Rules and Regulations Pertaining to the Testing of Newborn Infants for Phenylketonuria, Congenital Hypothyroidism, and Sickle Cell Anemia" provides for the testing of all newborns for PKU, congenital hypothyroidism, and sickle cell disease.

California

Prenatal

California Health and Safety Code § 3220 et seq. (West 1987) requires physicians to obtain a blood sample for a syphilis test from each pregnant woman at the time of the first prenatal visit. The regulations are set forth in *17 California Administration Code 1125 et seq.*

California Health and Safety Code § 304 et seq. (West 1987) provides that physicians shall obtain a blood sample from pregnant women at the time of their first prenatal visit or upon delivery to determine their Rh status unless the woman objects to the test on religious grounds.

---

*By statute and regulation, Arizona's health department is authorized to screen for three conditions (PKU, galactosemia, and hypothyroidism). Because it is part of a regional testing agreement with Colorado, its newborns are also automatically tested for maple syrup urine disease, homocystinuria, biotinidase deficiency, and sickle cell disease.

California Health and Safety Code §§ 290 et seq. (West 1987). In 1978, California passed legislation creating a wholly voluntary prenatal diagnosis program. Under this legislation, criteria for eligibility are established that include, but are not limited to, the following:

1. Women 35 years of age or older.
2. Women having had a previous Down Syndrome child or a child with any other genetic disorder.
3. Pregnancies where one parent is a translocation carrier.
4. Women who are carriers of an X-linked disease.
5. Pregnancies where both parents are carriers of an autosomal trait (for a disease or defect).
6. Pregnancies where the parents have a previous child who has a neural tube defect.

Prenatal Maternal Serum Alpha-Fetoprotein Screening

The California AFP Screening Program began in 1986. By regulation, physicians must give brochures to pregnant women at the time of the first visit, and the patient is asked to sign an informed consent/refusal document.

Newborn

California Health and Safety Code § 309 (West 1897) provides that a genetic disease unit shall evaluate and prepare recommendations on the implementation of tests for the detection of hereditary and congenital diseases, biotinidase deficiency, and hereditary hemoglobinopathies. The State Department of Health Services shall implement a program for the detection of PKU, galactosemia, hypothyroidism, and sickle cell anemia.

Sickle Cell Disease

California's State Sickle Cell Program began in 1972. This program today, in addition to providing counseling and education, makes available to all at-risk couples a prenatal test for sickle cell disease. At-risk couples are defined as those in which both partners are carriers of the S gene.

Tay-Sachs Disease

This program involves mass blood testing projects performed in the community and provided on a voluntary basis. According to the descriptive materials provided by the Newborn Screening Section, this "program serves as a prototype for the development and delivery of similar genetic services to other defined populations where specific genetic disorders occur (i.e., sickle cell anemia, thalassemia, and cystic fibrosis)."

Colorado

Prenatal

Colorado Revised Statutes § 25-4-201 (Bradford 1987 Replacement) provides that physicians shall obtain a blood sample from every pregnant woman at the first prenatal visit for a standard serologic test for syphilis.

Newborn

Colorado Revised Statutes § 25-4-1004 (Bradford 1987 Replacement) provides that all newborns shall be tested for PKU, hypothyroidism, abnormal hemoglobins, galactosemia, homocystinuria, maple urine disease, cystic fibrosis, biotinidase deficiency, and "such other conditions as the board of health may determine meet the criteria set forth in paragraph (c)." Paragraph (c) sets forth the following criteria:

   (I)   The condition for which the test is designed presents a significant danger to the health of the infant or his family and is amenable to treatment;
   (II) The incidence of the condition is sufficiently high to warrant screening;
   (III) The test meets commonly accepted clinical standards of reliability, as demonstrated through research or use in another state or jurisdiction; and
   (IV) The cost–benefit consequences of screening are acceptable within the context of the total newborn screening program.

5 Code of Colorado Regulations (1977). The existing regulations predate the legislation and provide for only PKU testing of newborns.

Connecticut

Prenatal

Connecticut General Statutes Annotated § 19a-90 (West 1989) provides that physicians shall obtain blood samples for all pregnant women within 30 days of the first prenatal examination and during the final trimester for a standard serologic test for syphilis.

Newborn

Connecticut General Statutes Annotated § 19a-55 (West 1989) provides that all newborns shall be tested for PKU, hypothyroidism, galactosemia, and "such other tests for inborn errors of metabolism as shall be prescribed by the department of health services."*

Parents may object to the test on religious grounds.

*Although Connecticut does not screen newborns for sickle cell disease, under the authority of a statute or regulations, the Maternal and Child Health Division of the Connecticut Department of Health has a grant that covers the screening of most high-risk newborns in four separate programs (personal communication, Dr. V. Bapat).

Delaware

Prenatal

Delaware Code Revised Annotated § 707 (Michie 1983 Replacement) provides that every physician shall obtain a blood sample from every pregnant woman at the time of the first prenatal examination for a standard serologic test for syphilis.

Failure to obtain such a sample is punishable by a fine of up to $1,000 or imprisonment of not more than 1 year, or both.

Newborn

Delaware has no laws or regulations pertaining to newborn screening. Its program is purely voluntary, with the state health department having the Newborn Screening Coordinator to function as a resource person and monitor of screening generally. Currently, a health department brochure describes and recommends testing all newborns for the following conditions: PKU, maple syrup urine disease, homocystinuria, hypothyroidism, galactosemia, and hemoglobinopathies. Additionally, there is currently a pilot screening program for biotinidase deficiency. All samples are sent to Maryland to be tested (personal communication, Betsy Voss, Newborn Screening Coordinator, November 14, 1989).

District of Columbia

Prenatal

There is no statute on testing for syphilis.

Newborn

District of Columbia Code Annotated § 6-311 et seq. (Michie 1988) provides "for the early identification of certain metabolic disorders in newborns."

§ 6-312(1) states that "the term 'metabolic disorder' means a disorder which results in a defect in the function of a specific enzyme or protein." *§ 6-313* provides for the testing of every newborn for galactosemia, homocystinuria, hypothyroidism, maple syrup urine disease, PKU, and sickle cell hemoglobinopathy.

Florida

Prenatal

Florida Statutes Annotated § 383.08 (West 1989) provides for a serologic test for syphilis at the time of the first professional visit.

Newborn

Florida Statutes Annotated § 383.14 (West 1989) provides for the screening of all infants "for phenylketonuria and other metabolic, hereditary, and congenital disorders known to result in significant impairment of health or intellect, as screening programs accepted by current medical practice become available and practical in the judgment of the [D]epartment [of Health and Rehabilitative Services]."

The statute also establishes the Infant Screening Advisory Council, whose purpose is to advise the department about conditions for which testing should be included under the screening program.

Florida Administration Code § 10D-76.01 et seq. (1986) provides that all infants shall be screened for PKU, hypothyroidism, galactosemia, and "designated disorders" unless parents object. Parents may refuse testing (no reasons given) in writing.

Georgia

Prenatal

Code of Georgia Annotated, ch. 17 § 31-17-4 (Michie 1989) provides that physicians shall obtain a blood specimen for a syphilis test from every pregnant woman. The statute does not state when the sample should be taken, nor does it provide for refusal or punishment for physician noncompliance.

Newborn

Code of Georgia Annotated, ch. 12 § 31-1-6 (Michie 1989) provides that the Georgia Department of Human Resources shall promulgate rules and regulations concerning the testing of newborns for disorders caused by PKU, galactosemia, tyrosinemia, homocystinuria, maple syrup urine disease, hypothyroidism, "and such other inherited metabolic disorders as may be determined in the future to cause mental retardation if undiagnosed and untreated."

Code of Georgia Annotated, ch. 12 § 31-12-7 (Michie 1989) provides for testing for PKU, sickle cell anemia, and sickle trait. An opinion of the attorney general of Georgia provides that "if clearly defined and articulable guidelines are provided, the department may restrict such testing under this statute to 'susceptible' persons" (Opin. Att. Gen. No. 81-10).

Official Compilation Rules and Regulations of the State of Georgia, Rules of Department of Human Resources, Public Health, ch. 290-5-24-0 (1988) provides for the testing of all newborns for PKU, galactosemia, hypothyroidism, homocystinuria, maple syrup urine disease, tyrosinemia, and sickle cell disease.

Parents may object to such tests on religious grounds.

Hawaii

Prenatal

Hawaii Revised Statutes § 325-51 (1988) provides that physicians shall obtain blood specimens from all pregnant women during gestation or delivery for a standard serologic test for syphilis. It also provides that "every pregnant woman shall permit the sample of the woman's blood to be taken."

Violation of this statute is punishable by an administrative fine not to exceed $1,000.

Hawaii Revised Statutes § 321-331 (1988) provides authority for the department of health to establish a prenatal screening program "to ensure that all pregnant women . . . are offered appropriate information, quality testing, diagnostic services, and follow-up services concerning neural tube defects and other disorders amenable to prenatal diagnosis." It further states that the purpose of prenatal screening "is to obtain vital information for the pregnant woman and her family as well as for the providers of her health care." The program is voluntary.

Newborn

Hawaii Revised Statutes § 321 (1988) provides that all newborns shall be tested for PKU, hypothyroidism, "and any other disease that may be specified by the department of health."

A parent or guardian may object on religious grounds. The written objection is to be make a part of the newborn's medical record.

Hawaii Administrative Rules, ch. 11-143 (December 18, 1986) provides that all newborns shall be tested for PKU and congenital hypothyroidism.

A parent or guardian may refuse the test on religious grounds. The refusal must be indicated on a special refusal form that includes the medical implications of the refusal. One copy is to be included in the newborn's medical record and another copy sent to the department of health.

Idaho

Prenatal

General Laws of Idaho Annotated § 39-1001 (Michie 1989) provides that physicians shall obtain a blood specimen from every pregnant woman within 15 days of her first prenatal examination for a standard serologic test for syphilis.

Violation of this section shall be a misdemeanor unless the physician requests such a sample and is refused. No reasons for a legitimate refusal are given in the statute.

Newborn

General Laws of Idaho Annotated § 39-909 (Michie 1989) provides for the testing of all newborns for PKU and "such other tests for preventable diseases as prescribed by the state board of health and welfare."*

Idaho Regulations, title 2, ch. 12, "Rules Governing Procedures and Testing to Be Performed on Newborn Infants" (1980) do not indicate the conditions to be tested, specifying only "the tests and/or procedures that must be performed on newborn infants for early detection of mental retardation, developmental disabilities, blood amino acid levels, and prevention of infant blindness."

§§ 02.12100–12.12499 pertain to the requirements concerning testing newborns for PKU and "other preventable diseases."

Parents may object on religious grounds.

Illinois

Prenatal

Illinois Statutes Annotated, ch. 111 ½ § 4801 (Smith-Hurd 1989) requires physicians to test every pregnant woman for syphilis at the time of the first examination and in the third trimester. This provision shall not apply to any woman who objects on religious grounds.

Newborn

Illinois Statutes Annotated, ch. 111 ½ §§ .4903 et seq. (Smith-Hurd 1989) provides that the "Illinois Department of Public Health shall promulgate and enforce rules and regulations requiring that every newborn be subjected to tests for phenylketonuria, hypothyroidism, galactosemia and such other metabolic diseases as the Department may deem necessary from time to time."

77 Illinois Administrative Code 661 (1987) "Newborn Metabolic Screening and Treatment Code" provides that all newborns be tested for PKU, hypothyroidism, galactosemia, congenital adrenal hypoplasia, and biotinidase deficiency.†

Indiana

Prenatal

Indiana Statutes Annotated § 16-1-11-12 (Michie 1986) provides that physicians

---

*Under a regional agreement with Oregon, Idaho tests for PKU, hypothyroidism, galactosemia, maple syrup urine disease, homocystinuria, tyrosinemina and biotinidase (personal communication, Mary Jane Webb, Genetic Services Program Manager, Idaho Department of Health and Welfare).

†Illinois began routine screening of all newborns for sickle cell disease in 1988 (personal communication, Sydney Kling, Administrator, Genetic Diseases Program, Division of Family Health, State Department of Public Health).

who diagnose the pregnancy of a woman shall obtain a blood sample for a standard serologic test for syphilis.

Newborn

Indiana Statutes Annotated § 12-8-6-1 (Michie 1986) provides that all newborns shall be tested for PKU, hypothyroidism, hemoglobinopathies, including sickle cell anemia, galactosemia, maple syrup urine disease, homocystinuria, and "inborn errors of metabolism that result in mental retardation and are designated by the board." (The "board" refers the state board of health.)

Parents may object in writing on religious grounds.

Indiana Administrative Code § 410, 3-3-3 (1988) provides for testing for PKU, hypothyroidism, galactosemia, maple syrup urine disease, homocystinuria, and hemoglobinopathies.

Iowa

Prenatal

Iowa Code Annotated § 140.11 (West 1989) provides that physicians shall obtain a blood sample from all pregnant women within 14 days of the first prenatal visit for a standard serologic test for syphilis.

Iowa Code Annotated § 136.1 et seq. (West 1989) establishes a birth defects institute to "initiate and conduct investigations of the causes, mortality, methods of treatment, prevention and cure of birth defects and related diseases and to develop and administer genetic and metabolic screening programs and other related activities where the programs will aid in the prevention or treatment of a particular genetic or metabolic defect or disease." Additionally, the birth defects institute is given responsibility for "developing screening and educational programs for sickle cell anemia and other genetic blood disorders."

§ 136A.4 defines genetic and metabolic screening as "the search through testing for persons with genetic and metabolic diseases so that early treatment or counseling can lead to the amelioration or avoidance of the adverse consequences of the diseases."

Newborn

Iowa Administrative Code § 641-4.1 et seq. (1988) provides for the testing of all newborns for hypothyroidism, PKU, galactosemia, maple syrup urine disease, and hemoglobinopathies.

The physician is given the duty of informing the parents of the type of specimen, how it is obtained, the nature of the disease being screened, and the consequences of treatment and nontreatment.

Parents may refuse (no grounds given), and such refusal shall be documented and become part of the medical record.

§ 641-4.6 establishes a voluntary maternal serum AFP screening program. Under this program, patients desiring this screening test will have the specimens tested in a central laboratory with test kits approved by the birth defects institute. A sliding fee scale is available for patients with incomes below 150 percent of the federal poverty level.

Kansas

Prenatal

Kansas Statutes Annotated § 65-153f (Michie 1988 Supp.) provides that physicians shall obtain a blood sample from all pregnant women within 14 days after diagnosis of the pregnancy for a standard serologic test for syphilis.

Violation of this provision is a misdemeanor punishable by a fine of $10 to $100.

Newborn

Kansas Statutes Annotated § 65-180 (1988 Supp.) provides for the testing of newborns for PKU, hypothyroidism, and "such other diseases as may be appropriately detected with the same procedures for which laboratory services are required."

Kansas Statutes Annotated (1987) § 65-1, 10 (1988 Supp.) provides that the secretary of health and environment is authorized to establish a statewide program of blood tests for sickle cell trait and sickle cell anemia. It does not specify that all newborns are to be tested. (Kansas began testing all newborns for sickle cell disease in 1990. Personal communication, Kay Domingo, Special Health Services, Kansas Department of Health and Environment.)

Kansas Administrative Regulations, ch. 28-4-501 et seq. (1987) provides for the testing of all newborns for PKU, congenital hypothyroidism, and galactosemia.

Parental refusal to take part in the testing procedure shall be documented in the child's record at the institution or the physician's office or both. The regulations do not specify the grounds for refusal.

Kentucky

Prenatal

Kentucky Revised Statutes Annotated § 214.160 (Michie 1988) provides that physicians shall obtain a blood sample from every pregnant woman at the time of the first prenatal visit for a serologic test for syphilis.

Newborn

Kentucky Revised Statutes Annotated § 214.155 (Michie 1988) provides for the testing of all newborns for "inborn errors of metabolism, including but not limited to [PKU]."

Parents may refuse such tests in writing on religious grounds.

902 Kentucky Administrative Regulations § 4:030 (1987) provides for the testing of all newborns for PKU, galactosemia, and hypothyroidism.*

Louisiana

Prenatal

Louisiana Revised Statutes § 40:1091 (West 1987 Supp.) provides that physicians shall obtain blood samples from every pregnant woman at the time of the first prenatal examination or as soon as possible thereafter for a standard test for syphilis.

Newborn

Louisiana Revised Statutes § 40:1299 (West 1987 Supp.) provides for the establishment of programs to "combat the effects of sickle cell anemia and to combat mental retardation in children suffering from a genetic defect which causes phenylketonuria, congenital hypothyroidism, and galactosemia."†

Maine

Prenatal

Main Revised Statutes Annotated § 1231 (West 1988 Supp.) provides that physicians shall obtain a blood sample from every pregnant woman at the time of the first prenatal visit for a standard serologic test for syphilis and Rh factors.

The woman must consent to the test.

Newborn

Main Revised Statutes Annotated, title 22 § 1532 (West 1988 Supp.) provides for the testing of newborns for "the presence of metabolic abnormalities which may be expected to result in subsequent mental deficiencies."

---

*In 1989, Kentucky received federal funds to establish a targeted newborn sickle cell screening program. All newborns born at ten hospitals with the highest nonwhite patient populations are routinely screened for hemoglobinopathies. In addition, the state has developed a program wherein newborns considered to be at-risk who were not screened at birth are screened at the first well-baby visit at approximately 2 weeks (personal communication, Darlene Goodrich, Sickle Cell Program, Kentucky Department of Health Services).

†Screening for galactosemia was discontinued after 1990 (personal communication, Charles Meyers, Genetic Diseases Branch, Department of Health and Human Resources).

Ch. 283, "Rules and Regulations Relating to Testing Newborn Infants for the Detection of Causes of Mental Retardation" requires that all newborn specimens be tested for PKU, homocystinuria, maple syrup urine disease, galactosemia, and hypothyroidism. The regulations also provide that "other disorders may be added to this list as cost effective screening procedures become available." Samples are sent to the Regional Screening Laboratory in Massachusetts for testing.

Parents who refuse testing on religious grounds must do so in writing, which shall be made a part of the infant's medical record.

Maryland

Prenatal

Maryland Public Helath Code Annotated § 18–307 M(Michie 1987 Replacement) provides that a blood sample shall be taken from every pregnant woman at the time of her first prenatal examination for a standard serologic syphilis test.

The woman may refuse the test on religious grounds.

Newborn

Maryland Public Health Code Annotated § 13-101 to 13-111 (Michie 1987 Replacement). In 1973, Maryland created the State Commission on Hereditary and Congenital Disorders, with the responsibility to oversee all state efforts to detect and manage hereditary disorders.*

§ *13-101(c)* Congenital Disorder.—(1) "Congenital disorder" means a significant structural or functional abnormality of the body that is present at birth. (2) "Congenital disorder" does not include a condition that results from: (i) An intrauterine infection; or (ii) A birth injury.

§ *13-101(d)* Hereditary Disorder.— "Hereditary disorder" means any disorder that: (1) Is transmitted through the genetic material deoxyribonucleic acid (DNA); or (2) Arises through the improper processing of the information in the genetic material.

Massachusetts

Prenatal

Massachusetts General Laws Annotated, ch. 111 § 121A (Michie 1989 Supp.) requires physicians to obtain from all pregnant women at the time of the first examination blood specimens for a syphilis test.

---

*The Newborn Screening Laboratory has the following screening protocol: at birth, all newborns are screened for biotinidase, galactosemia, and hemoglobinopathies (including both disease and trait); at either birth or 1 to 4 weeks there is screening for homocytonuria, hypothyroidemia, maple syrup urine disease, and PKU; and between 1 and 4 weeks, infants are screened for tyrosinemia (personal communication, Sue Kruchko, Birth Defects Registry Coordinator, Hereditary Disorders Division, Maryland Department of Health and Mental Hygiene).

Newborn

Massachusetts General Laws Annotated, ch. 111 § 110A (Michie 1989 Supp.) provides for the testing of newborns for PKU, cretinism, and such other specifically treatable genetic or biochemical disorders or treatable infectious diseases that may be determined by testing, as specified by the commissioner of the Department of Public Health.

Parents may object to such tests on religious grounds.

The Massachusetts Department of Health has a Newborn Screening Program-Protocol that provides for the screening of all newborns via blood filter papers for PKU, galactosemia, maple syrup urine disease, homocystinuria, hypothyroidism, and toxoplasmosis.*

Michigan

Prenatal

Michigan Compiled Laws Annotated 333.5251 (West 1989) provides that physicians shall obtain a blood sample from every pregnant woman at the time of the first prenatal visit for a standard venereal disease test approved by the department.

Newborn

Michigan Compiled Laws Annotated 333.5431 (West 1989) provides that all newborns be tested for PKU, galactosemia, hypothyroidism, maple syrup urine disease, biotinidase deficiency, sickle cell anemia, "and other treatable but otherwise handicapping conditions as designated by the department."

Michigan Administrative Code R 325.1471 et seq. (1979) provides for the laboratory standards for such tests.

Minnesota

Prenatal

Minnesota does not have a statute for screening pregnant women for syphilis.

Newborn

Minnesota Statutes § 144.125 (1988) provides that all newborns be tested for hemoglobinopathy, PKU, "and other inborn errors of metabolism in accordance with rules prescribed by the state commissioner of health."

---

*Massachusetts, by contracts with Connecticut, Maine, New Hampshire, Rhode Island, and Vermont, operates a regional screening laboratory that screens for all the above-listed conditions. Massachusetts established a statewide program to screen all newborns for sickle cell disease beginning in April 1990 (personal communication, Dr. Rodney Hoff, Director of Newborn Screening, Massachusetts Department of Public Health).

Minnesota Rules §§ 4615.0300 et seq. (1987) provides for the testing of new-borns for the "metabolic diseases" PKU, galactosemia, and hypothyroidism.

§ 4615.0500 provides that parents shall be informed that their newborn(s) will be screened, the reasons for such screening, and their right to refuse this screen-ing on religious grounds.

Mississippi

Prenatal

Mississippi does not have a statute for screening pregnant women for syphilis.

The state distributes information (included in Appendix C to "Rules and Regulations Governing Newborn Screening") to physicians concerning MSAFP screening for NTDs in which it states the criteria for high risk to be "couples who have a neural tube defect themselves, or couples who have parents, siblings, or other children with a neural tube defect and women with diabetes mellitus." It also provides that informed consent for the MSAFP test shall be obtained at the time of the screen, as well as extensive counseling guidelines including informa-tion that the test is voluntary, that positive results may lead to other tests and difficult decisions, and that no treatment in utero is possible.

Newborn

Mississippi Code of 1972 Annotated §§ 41-21-201 et seq. (Harrison 1988 Supp.) provides for a newborn screening program designed to detect hypothyroidism, PKU, hemoglobinopathy, and galactosemia "which may result in mental retarda-tion or medical complications in children."

Parents may refuse such tests on religious grounds.

"Rules and Regulations Governing Newborn Screening: Phenylketonuria, Hypo-thyroidism, and Hemoglobinopathies" (June 8, 1987) provides that all newborns shall be tested for PKU, hypothyroidism, and hemoglobinopathies.

Parents may object on religious grounds.

Missouri

Prenatal

Revised Statutes of Missouri, title 12 § 210.030 (1988) provides that physicians shall obtain a blood sample from every pregnant woman at the time of the first prenatal visit for a standard serologic blood test.

Newborn

Missouri Revised Statutes, title 12 §§ 191.300 et seq. (1988) provides for the establishment of a genetic advisory committee to advise the health department in

all genetic programs, including metabolic disease screening programs, hemophilia, sickle cell disease, and cystic fibrosis programs.*

Missouri Revised Statutes, title 19, ch. 33 §§ 191.331 et seq. (1988) provides
that all newborns shall be tested for PKU "and such other metabolic diseases as
are prescribed by the division."

Missouri Code of State Regulations 13-50-143.010 (1976) states that the "metabolic diseases" covered are PKU, primary hypothyroidism, and galactosemia.

Parents may object on religious grounds. The objection shall be in writing and
filed in the office of the attending physician or other health professional, hospital, or public health facility, with a copy sent to the department of health.

Montana

Prenatal

Montana Code Annotated § 50-19-101 et seq. (1987) provides that "every
female" seeking prenatal care is required to submit a blood specimen for a
standard serologic test for syphilis. The woman may refuse such a test only upon
judicial satisfaction (by affidavit or other proof) that the test is contrary to the
tenets or practices of her religion and that the public health or welfare will not be
injured.

Newborn

Montana Code Annotated §§ 50-19-201 et seq. (1987) provides that all newborns
shall be tested for such inborn metabolic errors as the department of health shall
require. There is no provision for parental objection.

Administrative Rules of Montana (3/31/88) provides that "'tests for inborn
errors of metabolism' include laboratory tests for phenylketonuria, detection of
other aminoacidopathies, and thyroxine level for hypothyroidism." There is no
provision for parental objection.

Nebraska

Prenatal

Revised Statutes of Nebraska § 71-1116 (1986 Reissue) provides for the mandatory testing of all pregnant women for syphilis. It requires every physician (or
other person authorized to practice obstetrics) to obtain a blood sample at the

---

*Missouri added sickle cell screening of all newborns to its routine screening panel in 1989
(personal communication, Nancy Althouse, Special Needs Bureau, Bureau of Family Health, Missouri Division of Health).

time of the first visit to be tested for syphilis. There is no provision for refusal to submit to the test. No penalty is stated for a physician's failure to comply.

Newborn

Revised Statutes of Nebraska §§ 71-519 to 71-524 (1986 Reissue) provides that "all infants shall be screened for phenylketonuria, primary hypothyroidism, biotinidase deficiency, and such other metabolic diseases as the Department of Health may from time to time specify."

There is no provision for parental refusal. With respect to enforcement, the statute provides the following:

> In addition to any other remedies which may be available by law, a civil proceeding to enforce section 1 of this act (providing for the testing) may be brought in the district court of the county where the infant is domiciled or found. The attending physician, the hospital, the Attorney General, or the county attorney of the county where the infant is domiciled or found may institute such proceedings as are necessary to enforce such section.

The Nebraska Department of Health's *"Rules and Regulations Relating to the Screening for Newborn Metabolic Diseases," title 181, ch. 2 (1989)* supplement the statute. No other diseases are specified within the regulations.

Nevada

Prenatal

Nevada Revised Statutes Annotated § 442.010 (Michie 1986) provides that physicians shall obtain blood samples from every pregnant woman during the third trimester for a standard serologic test for syphilis.

The statute also provides that if such a test shows that the pregnant woman is infected with syphilis, she shall immediately commence treatment for syphilis and shall continue treatment until discharged by a licensed physician.

Violations of the statutes are considered misdemeanors.

Newborn

Nevada Revised Statutes Annotated § 442.115 (Michie 1986) provides for the testing of newborns for "preventable inheritable disorders leading to mental retardation."*

Parents may object if either one files a written objection with the person or institution responsible for making the examination or tests.

---

*There are no state regulations. Nevada currently screens for seven conditions: PKU, maple syrup urine disease, tyrosinemia, galactosemia, hypothyroidism, biotinidase, and homocystinuria. As of October 1, 1990, all newborns are being screened for hemoglobinopathies (personal communication, Janet Knozen, Management Assistant, Maternal and Child Health, Nevada State Health Division).

New Hampshire

Prenatal

New Hampshire Revised Statutes Annotated § 132:18 (1987 Supp.). The prenatal test for syphilis was repealed in 1986.

Newborn

New Hampshire Revised Statutes Annotated §§ 132:10-a et seq. (1987 Supp.) provides that all newborns shall be tested for PKU.*

New Jersey

Prenatal

New Jersey Statutes Annotated § 26:4-49.1 (West 1987) requires the physician to take a blood sample at the time of a woman's first prenatal visit. There is no provision for the woman's refusal or for a penalty for physician noncompliance.

Newborn

New Jersey Statutes Annotated § 26:2-110 et seq. (West 1987) provides for the testing of all newborns for PKU, congenital hypothyroidism, and galactosemia.

New Jersey Administrative Code, title 8, ch. 28 (1985) establishes a birth defects registry. It does not specify the diseases to be tested.

New Mexico

Prenatal

New Mexico Statutes Annotated § 24-1-10 (Michie 1987) provides that every physician shall obtain a blood sample from every pregnant woman at the time of first examination.

Newborn

New Mexico Statutes Annotated § 24-1.6 (Michie 1987) provides that the department of health shall adopt tests for the detection of PKU and "other congenital diseases" to be given to all newborns. The department shall consider the recommendations of the New Mexico Pediatrics Society of the American Academy of Pediatrics in determining the conditions to be screened.

Parents, after having been informed of the reasons for the tests, may waive the requirements for the tests in writing.

---

*New Hampshire participates in the New England Regional Screening Program and screens all newborns for PKU, galactosemia, hypothyroidism, maple syrup urine disease, and homocystinuria (personal communication, Susan J. Moore, Program Coordinator).

79-Health and Environment Department (HED)-1 et seq. (1979): "Newborn Screening Program Regulations" provides for screening for PKU, galactosemia, hypothyroidism, homocystinuria, maple syrup urine disease, sickle cell anemia, and "any other congenital disease or condition for which testing may hereafter be required, on the basis of a formal recommendation made to the Department by the New Mexico Pediatrics Society and adopted by the Department"*

New York

Prenatal

New York Public Health Law § 2308 (McKinney 1988) requires physicians to test every pregnant women for syphilis at the time of the first examination.† There is no punishment for failure to do so.

Newborn

New York Public Health Law §§ 2500 et seq. (McKinney 1988). § 2500(a) provides for the testing of newborns for "phenylketonuria, homozygous sickle cell disease, hypothyroidism, branched-chain ketonuria, galactosemia, homocystinuria and such other diseases and conditions as may from time to time be designated by the commissioner in accordance with rules or regulations prescribed by the commissioner."‡

There is no provision for parental refusal or for a penalty for physician non-compliance.

Official Compilation of Codes, Rules, and Regulations of the State of New York, title 10, §§ 69.1 et seq. (1987) provides for the "testing for phenylketonuria and other diseases and conditions," without expanding on the conditions set forth in the statute.

The regulations provide for parental refusal on the grounds of religious beliefs but do not require physicians to notify parents of the testing requirement or the right of refusal.

---

*The regulations are not up to date. New Mexico currently screens for hypothyroidism, galactosemia, and PKU. The state no longer screens for maple syrup urine disease, homocystinuria, or sickle cell hemoglobinopathies (personal communication, Hope Young, Lab Scientist, New Mexico Health and Environment Department).

†After a fivefold increase in the incidence of congenital syphilis between 1986 and 1988 related to the use of crack cocaine, New York has recently begun testing all newborns for syphilis (CDC, "Congenital Syphilis—New York City 1986–1988," *Morbidity and Mortality Weekly Report* 38 [1989]: 825–829). Notwithstanding the prenatal syphilis screening statute on the books, because of the significant number of pregnant women who do not receive prenatal care, New York adopted new legislation providing for mandatory screening of either women at the time of delivery or their newborns or both (see *Official Compilation of Codes, Rules, and Regulations of the State of New York, title 10, §§ 69.2*).

‡As of February 1990, new legislation in New York authorized the mandatory screening of all pregnant women for HBV (see *New York Public Health Law § 2500 [e]*). Regulations had not been promulgated.

North Carolina

Prenatal

General Statutes of North Carolina § 130A-165 (Michie 1988) provides that every pregnant woman shall have a blood sample taken during pregnancy for a serologic test for syphilis.

Newborn

North Carolina has no statute or regulations for screening newborns.

General Statutes of North Carolina § 130A-129 (Michie 1988) provides that the health department shall establish and administer a sickle cell program that includes provisions for voluntary testing.

North Dakota

Prenatal

North Dakota Century Code Annotated § 23-07-07.1 (Michie 1989) provides that physicians shall, "with the consent of the patient," obtain a blood sample at the time of the first professional visit or within 10 days thereafter for a syphilis test.

Newborn

North Dakota Century Code Annotated §§ 25-17-01 et seq. (Michie 1989) provides that the state department of health shall carry out a program of education and testing for PKU and other metabolic diseases causing mental retardation for which appropriate methods of detection, prevention, or treatment are available.
    Parents may object on religious grounds.

North Dakota "Newborn Metabolic Screening: Guidelines for Hospitals and Clinics" states that all newborns are to be tested for PKU and congenital hypothyroidism.

Ohio

Prenatal

Ohio Revised Code Annotated § 3701.50 (Anderson 1989) provides that physicians shall obtain specimens from a pregnant woman within 10 days of the first examination for tests for syphilis and gonorrhea.
    The woman may waive the test if she submits an affidavit stating that her objection is on religious grounds and if the public health department is satisfied that the public health and welfare will not be injuriously affected by the waiver.

Newborn

Ohio Revised Code Annotated § 3701.501 (Anderson 1989) provides for the testing of all newborns for PKU, homocystinuria, galactosemia, and hypothyroidism. "Tests for other genetic, endocrine, or metabolic disorders may be required if the following conditions are met:

1) A determination is made under rules adopted by the public health council that the disorders cause disability if undiagnosed and untreated and are treatable;

2) No additional blood samples or specimens are required to conduct the test."

Parents may object to the tests on religious grounds.

Ohio Administrative Code, ch. 3701-45-01 (1988) provides that the public health laboratories shall provide screening and testing of newborns for PKU, homocystinuria, galactosemia, hypothyroidism, or other genetic, endocrine, or metabolic disorders.

Oklahoma

Prenatal

Oklahoma Revised Statutes, title 63 § 1-515 et seq. (West 1989 Supp.) provides that physicians shall obtain blood samples from every pregnant woman at the time of the first prenatal visit for a standard serologic test for syphilis.

Newborn

Oklahoma Revised Statutes, title 63 § 1-533 (West 1989 Supp.) provides for the establishment of an educational program concerning PKU and related inborn metabolic disorders.

Oklahoma Revised Statutes, title 63 § 1-534 (West 1989 Supp.) provides that the state board of health shall establish rules and regulations "pertaining to such tests as accepted medical practice shall indicate, and is authorized to make such testing mandatory if sufficient evidence exists that the public has been negligent in accepting such practice."

Oklahoma Procedures for Newborn Metabolic Disorder Screening (July 9, 1987), Rules and Regulations provides that all newborns shall be tested for PKU and hypothyroidism.*

A parent may object to such test on religious grounds. The written objection shall be included in the newborn's medical record, with a copy sent to the Newborn Screening Program.

---

*Oklahoma conducted a pilot screening program in April 1990 for sickle cell disease and galactosemia. A statewide program for the testing of all newborns began in April 1991 (personal communication, Mary Ann Kaufman, Director of Genetics, Maternal and Child Health, Oklahoma State Department of Health).

Oregon

Prenatal

Oregon Revised Statutes § 433.017 (Butterworth 1987) provides that physicians shall obtain a blood sample from all pregnant women at the time of the first prenatal visit "for such tests related to any infectious condition which may affect a pregnant woman or fetus, as the division shall by rule require."

It also provides that physicians shall request the consent of the woman and that "no sample shall be taken without such consent." There is no provision for punishment for physician noncompliance.

Newborn

Oregon Revised Statutes § 433.285 (Butterworth 1987) sets forth Oregon's policy to control metabolic diseases. It provides that "in the interest of public health and the prevention of mental retardation, every infant, shall be given tests approved by the Health Division for the detection of the disease of phenylketonuria and other metabolic diseases."

Parents may object on religious grounds.

Oregon Administrative rules, ch. 333, div. 24.-210 (1986) provides that every infant shall be tested for PKU, maple syrup urine disease, hypermethioninemia, tyrosinemia, galactosemia, and hypothyroidism.*

Pennsylvania

Prenatal

Pennsylvania Statutes Annotated, title 35. § 521.13 (Purdon 1989) requires physicians to test for syphilis at the time of the first prenatal examination.

The statute provides that should the woman dissent from having the blood test done, the physician shall be obligated to "explain to the woman the desirability of the test." Additionally, the physician is obligated to note on the birth certificate whether or not the test was performed and, if not, whether it was not done because, "in the opinion of the physician, the test was not advisable or because the woman dissented."

Newborn

Pennsylvania Statutes Annotated, title 35-621 et seq. (Purdon 1989) provides for the testing of every infant for PKU and for "such other metabolic diseases of the newborn which may lead to mental retardation or physical defects" and which

---

*Oregon also screens for homocystinuria and biotinidase (personal communication, Dr. P. Miyahira, Newborn Screening, Oregon State Health Department).

may be approved by the Advisory Health Board of the State Department of Health.

28 Pennsylvania Code § 29.11 et seq. (Rules and Regulations) provides for the testing of all newborns for PKU and hypothyroidism.*

Parents may object on religious grounds. The objection shall be made in writing and entered in the child's medical record.

Rhode Island

Prenatal

General Laws of Rhode Island, ch. 23-11-8 (Michie 1986) provides that physicians have a duty to obtain blood specimens from all pregnant women within 30 days of the first professional visit for the purpose of a syphilis test.

Violation of this law constitutes a misdemeanor. Physicians in violation shall be fined up to $100 for each offense. A breach of confidentiality is punishable by imprisonment not to exceed 6 months or a fine of not more than $250.

Newborn

General Laws of Rhode Island, ch. 23-13-14 (Michie 1986) (Newborn Metabolic Testing Program) provides that newborns shall be tested for metabolic diseases as the department of health shall provide. The department of health is to make such rules and regulations as accepted medical practice shall indicate.

General Laws of Rhode Island, ch. 23-13-15 (Michie 1986) (Newborn Sickle Cell Disease Testing Program) provides for the testing of all newborns.

Parents may object on religious grounds.

Rhode Island's *"Rules and Regulations Pertaining to the Fee Structure for the Metabolic Disease Testing Program" (February 1988)* are expressed in general language and do not specify the conditions to be tested except for sickle cell disease. The rules define "metabolic disease" as "inborn errors of metabolism which have their origin in mutational events that alter the genetic constitution of an individual and/or disrupts normal functions through some other disease mechanism and such other conditions including sickle cell disease."†

*Pennsylvania began a pilot newborn sickle cell screening program in April 1990 in Philadelphia County. The pilot program ended in December 1990 but as of May 1991 sickle cell screening continues to be limited to Philadelphia because of insufficient funds to expand the program statewide (personal communication, Alice Gray, Follow-up Coordinator, Neonatal Metabolic Screening Program, State Department of Health).

†In practice, Rhode Island screens for PKU, hypothyroidism, galactosemia, maple syrup urine disease, homocystinuria, and sickle cell disease (personal communication, Amy Zimmerman, Chief of Newborn Screening, Rhode Island Department of Health).

South Carolina

Prenatal

Code of Laws of South Carolina of 1976 § 44-29-120 (Revised 1985) provides that physicians shall obtain blood samples from pregnant women within 3 days of the first prenatal visit for a standard serologic test for syphilis, rubella, Rh factor, and a hemoglobin determination.

Violation of this section is a misdemeanor punishable by a fine of not more than $100 or imprisonment for not more than 30 days.

Newborn

Code of Laws of South Carolina of 1976 § 44-37-30 (Revised 1985) provides that all newborns shall be tested for inborn metabolic errors and hemoglobinopathies.*

Parents may object to such tests in writing on religious grounds.

South Dakota

Prenatal

South Dakota Codified Laws §§ 34-23-9 et seq. (Michie 1989) provides that physicians shall obtain blood samples from pregnant women at the first prenatal examination for a standard serologic test for syphilis.

Newborn

South Dakota Codified Laws § 34-24-18 (Michie 1989) provides that testing of newborns shall include, but not be limited to, PKU and hypothyroidism.

§ 34-24-17 provides that parents may object to such tests on religious grounds.

Administrative Rules of South Dakota, title 44:19 (1988) provides laboratory standards for testing for PKU and hypothyroidism.

Tennessee

Prenatal

Tennessee Code Annotated §§ 68-5-601 et seq. (Michie 1988) provides that physicians shall obtain blood samples from every pregnant woman within 10 days of the first prenatal visit for standard serologic tests for syphilis and rubella.

A woman may refuse such tests in writing, stating her religious tenets and practices affirmed under the penalty of perjury.

---

*South Carolina currently screens all newborns for PKU, hypothyroidism, and hemoglobinopathies (personal communication, Rose Alferd, Genetic Screening, South Carolina Department of Health).

Tennessee has a comprehensive genetic and metabolic screening statute that is potentially applicable to both prenatal and newborn screening.

Tennessee Code Annotated §§ 68-5-501 et seq. (Michie 1988) provides for the establishment of a genetics program to ensure the availability of genetic services to citizens of the state, as well as for genetic and metabolic screening. Birth defects are defined as "those abnormalities of body structure or function present at birth which adversely affect the intellectual capacity, health, or abilities of affected individuals." According the statute, "genetic disorders are those conditions caused by an alteration or abnormality in the genetic material which may adversely affect the health and functional abilities of affected individuals."

§ 68-5-504 states that the genetic testing services

> shall be provided only to: born children; unborn children whose testing would result in treatment; men; nonpregnant women; and those pregnant women whose testing would result in treatment for themselves or their unborn children. Induced abortions shall not be regarded as treatment. Therefore, procedures or services designed to search out disorders in unborn children which are not treatable shall not be provided for . . . it being the finding of the general assembly that the use of this program to abort unborn children is against the public policy of the state of Tennessee.

Rules of the Tennessee Department of Public Health (1974), ch. 1200-15-1 et seq. provides for the testing of newborns for PKU.*

Texas

Prenatal

Texas Revised Civil Statutes Annotated, art. 4445a (Vernon 1985) requires the physician or other person attending a pregnant woman to test for syphilis at the time of the first examination.† It does not include a provision to test for other venereal diseases.

Newborn

Texas Revised Civil Statutes Annotated, art. 4447e (Vernon 1985) aims to "combat mental retardation in children suffering from phenylketonuria and other heritable diseases."

Texas Revised Statutes Annotated, art. 4447e-1 (Vernon 1985) mandates a program to detect hypothyroidism in newborn infants.

Texas Administrative Code Annotated, title 25 §§ 37.51 et seq. (1985) provides

---

*Tennessee has screened all newborns for hemoglobinopathies since March 1989 (personal communication, Susan Ericson, Tennessee Department of Health).

†Prenatally, Texas tests for syphilis, gonorrhea, chlamydia, and rubella titers (personal communication, Louise Brown, Texas Department of Health).

that all newborns shall be tested for PKU, galactosemia, sickling hemo-globinopathies, and congenital hypothyroidism.

The regulations provide for two exceptions: if the parent objects on the basis of religious conflict or if certain medical considerations indicate the need to delay testing.

Utah

Prenatal

Utah Code Annotated § 26-6-20 (Michie 1987) provides that physicians shall obtain a blood specimen from every pregnant woman at the time of the first prenatal examination or within 10 days thereafter for a syphilis test.

The statute shall not apply to any woman who objects on the grounds that she is a "bona fide member of a specified, well recognized religious organization whose teachings are contrary to such tests."

There is no provision for punishment for physician noncompliance.

Newborn

Utah Code Annotated § 26-10-6 (Michie 1987) provides that each newborn shall be tested for PKU and "other metabolic diseases which may result in mental retardation or brain damage and for which a preventive measure or treatment is available and for which a laboratory diagnostic test method has been found reliable."

Parents may object to such tests on religious grounds.

Administrative Rules of the State of Utah R 440-5 (1987–1988), "Rules Pertaining to the Testing of Newborn Infants for Phenylketonuria and Other Metabolic Diseases Which May Result in Mental Retardation or Brain Damage," provides that all newborns shall be tested for PKU.*

Vermont

Prenatal

Vermont Statutes Annotated, title 18 § 1102 (1988 Supp.) provides that the practitioner shall obtain a blood sample from every pregnant woman prior to the third month of gestation for a standard serologic test for syphilis.†

---

*Utah screens for PKU, hypothyroidism, and galactosemia. Utah began developing a pilot screening program for hemoglobinopathies in 1990 (personal communication, Gloria Schow, Genetic Nurse Consultant, Program Director, Metabolic Screening Program, Utah Department of Health).

†Without the benefit of a prenatal screening statute or regulations, Vermont has an AFP screening program described in the *AFP Screening Manual* developed by the Vermont Department of Health Laboratory. This program was begun in 1980. AFP screening is offered to all pregnant women, and 40 to 50 percent agree to be tested (personal communication, Dr. Carol P. Walters, Program Coordinator, Vermont Newborn Screening Program).

Newborn

Vermont has neither a newborn screening statute nor regulations. It does screen, however, relying on a manual called *Newborn Screening: For Your Baby's Health,* which describes the Vermont Newborn Screening Program as developed by the Vermont Department of Health Laboratory. Beginning in 1965, when PKU testing was initiated, the program was administered by the Medical Center Hospital of Vermont. In 1989, this responsibility was transferred to the Vermont Regional Genetics Center, which is under contract by the Department of Health.

Virginia

Prenatal

Code of Virginia Annotated § 32.1-57 (Michie 1988 Supp.) provides that physicians attending every pregnant woman shall obtain a blood specimen within 15 days of the first prenatal examination for a standard serologic test for such venereal diseases as the public health board shall designate.

Newborn

Code of Virginia Annotated § 32.1-65 (Michie 1988 Supp.) provides that all newborns shall be tested for biotinidase deficiency, PKU, hypothyroidism, homocystinuria, galactosemia, and maple syrup urine disease, "and each infant determined at risk shall be subject to a screening test for sickle cell diseases."

Parents may object to such tests on religious grounds.

Virginia currently has a draft of "Regulations Governing the Newborn Screening and Treatment Program," which is all that is in place now. The regulations do not specify what conditions are to be screened, other than referring to such newborn screening test "as specified by the Code of Virginia in § 32.1-65."

Parents may object to such tests in writing on religious grounds. The written objection shall be incorporated in the medical record.

Washington

Prenatal

Revised Code of Washington Annotated § 70.24.090 (1988) provides that physicians shall obtain a blood sample from every pregnant woman at the time of the first examination for a test for syphilis. In addition, in the event that the pregnant woman's initial visit to the physician occurs after the fifth month of gestation, the physician is required to advise and urge the patient to "secure a medical examination and blood test before the fifth month of any subsequent pregnancies." There is no provision for refusal or punishment for physician noncompliance.

Newborn

Revised Code of Washington § 70.83.010 (1988) declares that it is the policy of the state to detect PKU and "other preventable heritable disorders leading to developmental disabilities or physical defects."

Washington Administrative Code, ch. 248-102 (1977) provides for the testing of all newborns for PKU and hypothyroidism.

The rules also provide for an informed refusal. That is, "the parent, parents, or guardian shall be informed that a blood specimen is to be taken from the infant in compliance with State law prior to obtaining the specimen," and that "in the event that a parent, parents or guardian refuse to allow such testing because of religious tenets or practices, a signed refusal shall be sent to Health Services Division in lieu of the specimen for the newborn."

West Virginia

Prenatal

West Virginia Code § 16-4A-1 et seq. (Michie 1985 Replacement) provides that the physician shall obtain from every pregnant woman at the earliest opportunity a blood sample to be tested for syphilis. There is no provision for refusal or for punishment for physician noncompliance.

Newborn

West Virginia Code § 16-22-1 et seq. (Michie 1985 Replacement) provides that all newborns shall be tested for PKU, galactosemia, and hypothyroidism. No provision is made for parental refusal. The statute also provides that any person in violation of the provisions of the statute "shall be guilty of a misdemeanor, and, upon conviction thereof, shall be fined not less than twenty-five and not more than fifty dollars."

There are no regulations concerning newborn screening.

Wisconsin

Prenatal

Wisconsin has no statute that provides for the screening of pregnant women for syphilis.

Newborn

Wisconsin Statutes Annotated §§ 146.01 et seq. (West 1989) provides for the testing of all newborns for PKU, galactosemia, maple syrup urine disease, congenital hypothyroidism, sickle cell anemia, "or other causes of congenital disorders."

Parents may object on religious grounds. The statutes provide that the parents or the legal guardian must be fully informed of the purposes of the testing and be given a reasonable opportunity to object.

There are no regulations concerning newborn screening.

Wyoming

Prenatal

Wyoming Statutes Annotated § 35-4-501-503 (Michie 1988 Replacement) provides that physicians shall obtain blood specimens from all pregnant women at the time of their first prenatal visit to be tested for syphilis. There is no provision for refusal or for punishment for physician noncompliance.

Newborn

Wyoming Statutes Annotated §§ 35-4-801 et seq. (Michie 1988 Replacement) provides for the metabolic screening of newborns. It states that every newborn "shall be given medical examinations for the detection of remedial inborn errors of metabolism." The specific tests to be done are to be determined by a committee.

The statute also provides that "informed consent of the parents shall be obtained and if any parent or guardian of a child objects to the mandatory examination the child is exempt."

Wyoming Department of Health and Social Services Regulations, ch. 36, "Mandatory Screening of Newborn Infants for Inborn Errors of Metabolism," provides for the screening of all newborns for PKU, hypothyroidism, galactosemia, homocystinuria, maple syrup urine disease, sickle cell anemia, and "any other disease caused by an inborn error of metabolism for which testing may hereinafter be required on the basis of action by the designated committee."*

The regulations also provide that no "mandatory testing" shall be done without the consent of a parent or guardian. Objections may be made on any grounds but must be in writing.

Notes

1. Except for a prenatal syphilis statute, Vermont has no statute or regulations concerning prenatal or newborn screening. The state does, however, have a voluntary AFP screening program for all pregnant women (with a 40–50 percent testing rate) and a voluntary newborn screening program. The Vermont Department of Health Laborato-

---

*The state currently screens for the same eight conditions as Colorado by virtue of using the same laboratory facilities. These conditions are PKU, homocystinuria, biotinidase, galactosemia, maple syrup urine disease, hypothyroidism, hemoglobinopathies, and cystic fibrosis (personal communication, Lawrence Goodmay, Genetic Program Manager, State Department of Health).

ry has published a manual that recommends screening for PKU, congenital hypothyroidism, galactosemia, homocystinuria, and maple syrup urine disease.

2. The citations to the legislative authority for each state are omitted from this discussion. Full citations and brief descriptions are contained in the Appendix to this
chapter.

3. Although California and Hawaii are the only states to have legislated prenatal screening programs, Vermont has had an AFP screening program since 1980 (see note 1).
Vermont's program includes three counties in northern New York as well (personal
communication, Dr. Carol Walters, Director of AFP and Newborn Screening, Vermont Department of Health). Mississippi, also without statutory or regulatory authorization, does limited AFP screening for women considered to be at high risk—that
is, if there has previously been a birth of an affected infant to the pregnant woman or
close family members or if the woman is diabetic (personal communication, Dr.
Daniel R. Bender, Director, Genetics Project, Mississippi Department of Health).

4. Much of the information about California's screening programs is contained in a
document printed by the Family Health Division of the California Department of
Health Services called *Genetic Disease Branch: Review of Current Programs* (January 1, 1987).

5. In order to cover the costs of the relatively expensive prenatal diagnosis program,
California assists women in filing for third-party payments and provides subsidies to
women who are unable to afford the services.

6. Medi-Cal picks up the $40 fee for those women unable to pay for the service.

7. George C. Cunningham, "Review of Current Programs," State of California, Department of Health Services, January 1, 1987.

8. Forty-eight states and the District of Columbia have statutorily established their own
PKU screening programs. In North Carolina, screening is based on public health
regulations; in Vermont, it is based on a departmental protocol only.

9. In addition to Alabama, six states have statutes with disease-specific newborn screening language, with no catchall provision. These states are Arkansas, Iowa, Louisiana,
New Hampshire, New Jersey, and Texas. Notwithstanding the PKU-specific language
of New Hampshire's statute, by virtue of the state's participation in the New England
Regional Newborn Screening Program, all New Hampshire newborns are automatically screened for galactosemia, hypothyroidism, maple syrup urine disease, and
homocystinuria.

10. In some of these states, screening began in 1990, (personal communication, Dr. Jane
Lin-Fu, Genetic Services, Maternal and Child Health, NIH). Kentucky, Oklahoma,
Utah, and Pennsylvania established pilot newborn screening programs in 1990. In
Pennsylvania, there are no statutes or regulations concerning sickle cell screening.
Pilot screening is being done by the health department pursuant to a federal grant.

11. Prior to the conference and legislation authorizing federal funding of statewide
screening for sickle cell disease (in fiscal year 1986 and reauthorized for fiscal years
1988, 1989, and 1990), only eight states were attempting statewide screening (personal communication, Dr. Marilyn H. Gaston, M.D., former Deputy Chief of the
Sickle Cell Disease Branch of the National Heart, Lung, and Blood Institute of NIH).

12. These states are Alabama, Arizona, Arkansas, California, Colorado, Delaware, Dis-
trict of Columbia, Florida, Illinois, Indiana, Iowa, Kansas, Louisiana, Maryland,
Michigan, Minnesota, Mississippi, Missouri, Nevada, New Jersey, New York,
Rhode Island, South Dakota, Tennessee, Texas, Virginia, and Wisconsin.

13. The states are Kentucky, Oklahoma, Pennsylvania, and Utah.

14. Courts tend to give broad deference to governmental action aimed at the public's health and welfare.

15. Mississippi Code of 1972 Annotated §§ 25-43-1 et seq. (Harrison 1988 Supp); Vermont Statutes Annotated, title 3 § 801 et seq. (1988).

16. This, in turn, depends on whether a voluntary, primarily educational screening program would properly fall into the statutory definition of the "rule" contained in the respective administrative procedure acts. Vermont defines "rule" as "each agency statement of general applicability which implements, interprets, or prescribes law or policy." Similarly, Mississippi's statute defines "rule" as "each agency statement of general applicability that implements, interprets or prescribes law or policy or describes the organization, procedure or practice requirements of any agency."

17. These states are Connecticut, Illinois, Kentucky, Maine, Missouri, Montana, Nebraska, Ohio, Oklahoma, Oregon, and Rhode Island.

18. These states are Maryland, New Mexico, Texas, and Wisconsin.

19. These states are Florida, Georgia, Indiana, Mississippi, Nevada, North Dakota, Pennsylvania, and Utah.

20. Actually, the situation is even more complicated. As noted in Chapter 2 of this volume, it is currently estimated that the majority of maternal–fetal transmission occurs as a result of intrapartum as opposed to intrauterine infection. Strictly speaking, then, only a minority of infants contracting HIV infection in utero would be covered by the exception.

21. A narrower reading of this language would limit screening to conditions similar in kind to those specifically mentioned—that is, hereditary conditions.

22. H. Farzadegan, Thomas Quinn, and Frank Polk, "Detecting Antibodies to Human Immunodeficiency Virus in Dried Blood on Filter Papers" (correspondence), *Journal of Infectious Diseases* 155 (1987): 1073–1074.

23. These states are Idaho, Iowa, Michigan, Nevada, and Wyoming.

24. According to the editors, the first edition of the *Guidelines* set a precedent by exemplifying the cooperative efforts of two disciplines—obstetrics and pediatrics— dedicated to the improvement of pregnancy outcomes. The second edition has several new sections, including sections on the impact of AIDS on prenatal and newborn treatment. It should be noted that in addition to the recommendations included in the *Guidelines,* ACOG has issued a series of technical bulletins dealing with prenatal screening issues, as discussed later in this chapter. The *Guidelines'* editors note that "the segments related to obstetric practice do not replace the ACOG Standards for Obstetric-Gynecologic Services, but rather expand on the principles suggested therein." According to a spokesperson at AAP, the *Guidelines* accurately reflect the AAP's recommendations with respect to newborn screening. AAP has, however, recently published fact sheets on newborn screening in which it fails to make any specific recommendations about what tests should be done. Rather, it notes that because the knowledge concerning newborn screening is changing rapidly, it has attempted to present only consensus viewpoints. It recommends that "pediatricians who desire additional information should contact the specialists in their region or those involved at the national level" (American Academy of Pediatrics, Committee on Genetics, "Newborn Screening Fact Sheets," *Pediatrics* 83 [1989]: 449–464).

25. *Guidelines,* ii.

26. Ibid., 234–243.

27. Ibid., 242.

28. The *Guidelines* do not elaborate on what information is to be provided.

29. *Guidelines,* 240–241.
30. Ibid.
31. Ibid., 157.
32. Ibid., 236.
33. See, for example, American College of Obstetricians and Gynecologists, *Gonorrhea and Chlamydial Infections,* ACOG Technical Bulletin, no. 89 (Washington, D.C.: American College of Obstetricians and Gynecologists, November 1985); ACOG Committee Statement, "State-of-the-Art Opinion in Obstetrics and Gynecology," September 1986; *Prenatal Detection of Neural Tube Defects,* ACOG Technical Bulletin, no. 99 (Washington, D.C.: American College of Obstetricians and Gynecologists, December 1986); *Genital Human Papillomavirus Infection,* ACOG Technical Bulletin, no. 105 (Washington, D.C.: American College of Obstetricians and Gynecologists, June 1987); *Antenatal Diagnosis of Genetic Disorders,* ACOG Technical Bulletin, no. 108 (Washington, D.C.: American College of Obstetricians and Gynecologists, September 1987); *Human Immune Deficiency Virus Infections,* ACOG Technical Bulletin, no. 123 (Washington, D.C.: American college of Obstetricians and Gynecologists, December 1988); and *Perinatal Herpes Simplex Virus Infections,* ACOG Technical Bulletin, no. 122 (Washington, D.C.: American College of Obstetricians and Gynecologists, November 1988).
34. ACOG, *Human Immune Deficiency Virus.*
35. Ibid.
36. Personal communication, Dr. Jane Lin-Fu, Chief of Genetic Services Branch, Bureau of Maternal and Child Health, NIH.

7

Legal Issues in Nonvoluntary Prenatal HIV Screening

ANITA L. ALLEN

Early reports of AIDS, ARC, and HIV infection in pregnant women and infants quickly spawned proposals for prenatal testing.[1] The Centers for Disease Control recommended that AIDS testing of pregnant women be undertaken only with consent and always in conjunction with counseling and confidentiality.[2] Nevertheless, the expectation that vigorous voluntary measures would not attract universal participation,[3] even by high-risk and symptomatic women,[4] prompted calls that officials or health-care providers require every pregnant woman to undergo testing.[5] This chapter identifies legal issues raised by nonvoluntary testing or screening of pregnant women for evidence of AIDS, ARC, or HIV. Nonvoluntary AIDS testing options range from very coercive (e.g., governmentally mandated testing of all pregnant women and testing mandated as a condition for receiving prenatal care) to mildly coercive (e.g., routine AIDS testing of blood obtained for other pregnancy-related purposes without advance patient notification or informed consent). Regardless of the extent of coercion contemplated, calls for nonvoluntary testing raise important legal questions. This chapter focuses broadly on two such questions. First, may public authorities lawfully require pregnant women to submit to HIV antibody or other AIDS testing against their will? Second, do public and private health-care providers who implement nonvoluntary prenatal AIDS testing not mandated by law thereby expose themselves to civil liability of aggrieved patients? After highlighting federal constitutional concerns raised by governmentally sponsored, nonvoluntary prenatal AIDS testing, the chapter identifies state law concerns raised by both governmental and privately sponsored testing.[6]

The unsettled character of pertinent state and federal strictures bars definitive answers to legal questions posed by prenatal testing. However, as concluded below, nonvoluntary prenatal AIDS-related testing raises more legal concerns than public health concerns it can presently abate. Nonvoluntary testing is and will remain a legally problematic interference with autonomy and privacy as long as AIDS has no fully effective treatment or cure and as long as less intrusive, less discriminatory measures can educate pregnant women and protect their sex partners and health-care providers from infection.

It will take court battles to decide whether and to what extent state and federal laws permit the interference with autonomy and privacy that nonvoluntary prenatal AIDS testing entails. Because Congress has not prohibited or clearly preempted state regulation of prenatal AIDS testing,[7] states are free to enact testing programs. But the courts will measure the validity of state and local testing initiatives against the U.S. Constitution, state constitutions,[8] state statutes, and the principles of common law tort[9] and contract[10] liability. Recently enacted statutes in a few states specifically prohibit most nonvoluntary AIDS testing.[11] But a number of states have enacted or considered mandatory AIDS-testing legislation that requires mandatory HIV antibody testing when donating blood or sperm, when being tested for syphilis, when imprisoned, when obtaining a marriage license, or when undergoing surgery.[12] States may soon require that public and private health-care providers routinely offer AIDS testing to all pregnant patients. Significantly, private providers are already routinely testing pregnant patients for the HIV antibody, arguably without informed consent.[13]

The outcome of any future legal battles over prenatal AIDS-related testing is difficult to predict on the basis of the scattered cases brought thus far by victims of unwanted AIDS testing in other contexts. However, it should be noted that plaintiffs have typically lost suits claiming that nonconsensual testing violated their rights under state or federal law. For example, citing the exigencies of military and prison life, federal courts have upheld the constitutionality of government action subjecting military personnel, civilian employees of the military, and federal prisoners to nonconsensual testing aimed at identifying AIDS carriers. Federal district courts and courts of appeal have approved nonvoluntary AIDS testing in these contexts[14] and in the context of public hospital employment,[15] leaving open questions about the legality of nonvoluntary AIDS testing away from military, penal, and public employment settings.

Observers detect a trend in the federal courts toward tolerating nonvoluntary testing, whether to detect substance abuse or AIDS.[16] Accordingly, out of deference to legislative policymakers and practices designed to protect and educate the public, the U.S. Supreme Court could someday hold that the Constitution permits nonvoluntary AIDS testing during pregnancy. This holding would force opponents of testing to seek legal relief in state and federal legislation. However, at least one federal appeals court has refused constitutional approval of AIDS testing measures not rationally tailored to meet the present health emergency.[17] It is plausible to suppose that the Supreme Court would likewise condemn as unconstitutional nonvoluntary prenatal AIDS testing that imposed weighty burdens on pregnant women while furthering no equivalent public interests.

Constitutional Constraints on Screening

The power to protect

In the United States, personal liberty is accorded a substantial measure of constitutional protection from governmental interference. In addition, the Constitution recognizes substantive rights that government cannot abridge without a compelling justification. However, in American jurisprudence, individual liberty is not accorded absolute protection. Local, state, and federal authorities may interfere with individual liberty to promote the public welfare. The federal and state governments have regulatory and police powers under the Constitution strong enough to permit intervention in the form of coercive laws that are necessary to protect public health.

The Supreme Court confirmed the legitimacy of the power to protect public health early in the present century. In *Jacobson* v. *Massachusetts,* the Court upheld mandatory smallpox vaccination laws promulgated by state authorities.[18] Arguing that the liberty of the individual must at times be subject to restraint "under the pressure of great dangers," the Court asserted that "a community has the right to protect itself against an epidemic of disease which threatens the safety of its members."[19]

The power of government to protect public health through coercion is limited, but American courts have historically shown great deference to a state's power to control the spread of infectious disease. For example, courts have upheld statutes requiring suspected prostitutes to undergo tests for sexually transmitted diseases.[20] During widespread outbreaks of venereal disease, bubonic plague, cholera, leprosy, smallpox, scarlet fever, and tuberculosis,[21] public disease control has been accomplished through mandatory vaccination,[22] reporting,[23] quarantine,[24] detention, examination,[25] and sterilization.[26] Reacting to the AIDS crisis, policymakers have discussed not only mandatory testing, but also reporting requirements, surveillance, contact tracing, quarantine, and the regulation of bathhouses, erotic book stores, and sex shows.[27]

In other areas of health law unconnected to the control of infectious disease, similar deference is shown to the government's interest in protecting public health through coercion. In recent cases concerning the right of individuals to be free of court-ordered medical treatment and forced feeding, courts have subscribed to the view that states have a legitimate interest in protecting life, protecting third parties, preventing suicide, and maintaining the integrity of the medical profession.[28] With a frequency and in situations that inspire fears about patriarchal and totalitarian abuses of power, recent courts have ordered policy detention of pregnant women—and even surgery—ostensibly to protect the well-being of the unborn.[29]

Limitations on public power

Individual liberty is not absolute in the face of a public health emergency, but neither is the power of government to act for the public good. Limitations on state and federal governments are established by the Constitution, statutes, and judicial decisions. The Supreme Court has found in the equal protection and due process clauses of the Fourteenth Amendment the requirement that measures adopted to protect public health or safety have at least a minimally rational relationship to legitimate state interests.[30] Accordingly, in determining the constitutional validity of state action to protect the public health, the Court has traditionally applied a "minimum rationality" standard. Under this standard, state action is presumed constitutional if it has a reasonable relationship to a legitimate state interest and, in the language of the law, is not arbitrary, capricious, or otherwise unreasonably oppressive.

In practice, the minimum rationality standard offers more protection to individuals when it comes to public health and safety than its name suggests.[31] Moreover, an expressly higher standard may apply in some instances. In the wake of the Supreme Court's explicit recognition of a fundamental right to privacy, many courts have suggested that health measures infringing privacy-related liberties and bodily integrity must be given strict judicial scrutiny.[32] The application of the courts' "strict scrutiny" standard asks authorities to demonstrate both a compelling governmental interest overriding fundamental rights and reliance on the least restrictive means of furthering that interest.

State interests

Government has a legitimate and, indeed, a compelling interest in halting the spread of the deadly AIDS virus. The difficult question is whether the government lawfully may further its compelling interest through nonvoluntary testing. The usual public health arguments for mandatory and routine testing of pregnant women refer to the need of hospitals and other medical facilities to protect efficiently against the spread of infection to health-care workers, and the need of public health officials and researchers to monitor the dimensions of the present crisis.[33] The policy is also defended by appeal to paternalistic and beneficent goals related to the care of the affected populations of pregnant women, fetuses, newborns, spouses, and sex partners.[34] Perhaps the strongest argument for prenatal AIDS testing is that it can provide pregnant women with information they may deem pertinent to decision making.[35] Knowledge of seropositivity obtained as a consequence of nonvoluntary testing may affect the choices some pregnant women make regarding abortion, amniocentesis (or other procedures capable of increasing the risk of maternal–fetal HIV transmission), child care, safe sex, and future pregnancies.[36] It is uncertain whether a governmentally mandated AIDS testing program aimed at pregnant women based on these objectives would survive constitutional challenges.[37]

Protecting the unborn and fetal rights

Public health and moral arguments for mandatory AIDS testing in pregnancy often lay particular emphasis on the health needs of the unborn. Some contend that protecting the well-being of the unborn is sufficient justification for non-voluntary prenatal AIDS testing. From a legal perspective, whether it is or is not depends on any fetal rights and legitimate governmental interests in fetal protection that courts recognize. The legal community is presently at odds over how best to characterize the legal status of the fetus. The unborn clearly matter in American law, but there is wide disagreement concerning the weight to give to claims based on their health in the face of competing claims about the rights of pregnant women. On the one hand, the Anglo-American legal tradition has never accorded full legal personhood status to the unborn. The Supreme Court has never held that they are citizens of the United States, equal to fully born persons for all legal purposes. On the other hand, the unborn are taken into account in the allocation of property rights and the attribution of criminal and civil responsibility. The unborn can be bequeathed property. It is a crime in many states to kill a fetus *en ventre sa mère,* and states may prohibit the abortion of a viable fetus. Negligently killing a fetus can give rise to civil liability for wrongful death. Wrongful birth actions in the law of torts are premised on injurious acts or omissions regarding the unborn, including failure to abort. In July 1989, a Florida woman was convicted of child abuse for using cocaine while pregnant. She joined a host of other women who have faced prosecution and loss of parental rights for substance abuse, use of alcohol, or failure to heed medical advice.[38]

Many of these long-standing features of the law and recent developments are controversial. Some lawyers would doubtless agree with legal philosopher Ronald Dworkin that under the best interpretation of constitutional law the fetus is not a constitutional person. If a human being at all, the fetus "is in a unique situation politically as well as biologically . . . sufficient to deny it constitutional status."[39] Other lawyers are less confident about categorically denying constitutional personhood to the unborn but reject intervention in pregnancy on practical grounds. Martha Field is persuaded that while the state has a strong and legitimate interest in newborns, "coercive governmental regulation has little to offer in the field of pregnancy."[40]

If incremental advances in AIDS research eventually offer correspondingly incremental advances in the ability of health-care providers to reduce the threat of HIV infection by testing or treating pregnant women or fetuses, prenatal AIDS testing policy will become yet another battleground for the fetal personhood debate. In the meantime, it is doubtful that nonvoluntary testing programs are even minimally justified from the perspective of the public interest in halting the contagion. Arguing the potentially greater efficacy of voluntary, educative measures,[41] opponents of mandatory and routine AIDS testing assert that coercive prenatal HIV antibody testing lacks sufficient utility to serve as the basis for a policy rationally tailored to meet present dangers. Sympathetic courts may agree and may be persuaded that the Constitution precludes mandatory AIDS testing in pregnancy at this time.

Equal protection

AIDS-related equal protection challenges have already been brought to federal courts in suits by or on behalf of military personnel or employees, prison inmates, and schoolchildren diagnosed as having AIDS. AIDS testing programs aimed at pregnant women can be expected to face constitutional equal protection challenges as well.[42]

The equal protection clause of the Fourteenth Amendment provides that "no State shall make or enforce any law which shall . . . deny to any person within its jurisdiction the equal protection of the laws."[43] The due process clause of the Fifth Amendment imposes comparable equal protection obligations on the federal government.[44] The equal protection of laws requires that state and federal initiatives treat similarly situated classes of persons similarly in the allocation of socioeconomic or political benefits and burdens. For government—or for private interests with governmental functions or sufficiently close ties to government to render their acts the legal equivalent of state action—to single out pregnant women from the population at large for mandatory or routine AIDS testing would seem to raise a question of discriminatory, unequal treatment.

Yet it is extremely doubtful that pregnant women opposed to nonvoluntary testing would prevail in equal protection challenges. In general, courts strongly presume the constitutionality of state rules and programs.[45] They subject most constitutional equal protection challenges to a minimum level of scrutiny, upholding legislation whose discriminatory classifications are reasonable in view of legitimate public purposes. Legislation is struck down only if it is deemed clearly erroneous or arbitrary. In particular, courts invalidate legislation deemed to impose burdens that are arbitrarily less inclusive or more inclusive than logically required to achieve government objectives.

Prison inmates segregated because of AIDS have complained, virtually without success in the courts, of stigmatization, invasion of privacy, and loss of liberty.[46] They have been isolated as required by correctional facility policies aimed at protecting non-AIDS-infected inmates and prison staff from AIDS infection, and at protecting AIDS victims from abuse by non-AIDS-infected inmates and exposure to other diseases. Courts have typically concluded that "because AIDS positive inmates are not similarly situated to the general prison population, the equal protection clause does not apply."[47] Moreover, they have denied that AIDS victims as such are a "suspect class" subject to invidious discrimination and have refused to subject their claims to heightened scrutiny. According to one court, "so long as there are legitimate governmental ends, and the means are rationally related to the ends, the equal protection clause is not violated."[48] Military personnel and employees have been similarly unsuccessful, either because discriminatory treatment is held to have a rational basis or because military and governmental immunities bar their suits against branches of the armed forces, military officers, and government bureaucrats.[49] But schoolchildren with AIDS have succeeded in court when they have protested segregation or exclusion from public schools or training facilities on equal protection grounds.[50]

Arguably, since AIDS currently rages in populations other than pregnant women, it would be arbitrary for officials to attempt to fight the epidemic by singling out pregnant women. The classification "pregnant women" could be described as arbitrarily underinclusive, because it fails to bring other groups of AIDS victims and carriers within the ambit of testing programs.[51] Yet maternal–fetal HIV transmission is costly as well as potentially deadly. According to the Supreme Court, the Constitution permits piecemeal solutions to acute phases of a problem.[52] While the equal protection clause does not require that government address every aspect of a problem or fail to address public problems at all,[53] individual rights require a logical nexus between legitimate state ends and discriminatory burdens.

Viewed in another light, the classification of pregnant women inherent in a coercive prenatal AIDS testing program could be aptly described as unconstitutionally overinclusive rather than underinclusive.[54] For the most part, pregnant women are not HIV infected, do not have AIDS or ARC, and do not fit into any high-risk category. To impose testing nonetheless on all pregnant women would appear to be irrational in economic cost–benefit terms and would "burden some who are not similarly situated with regard to the purposes" of HIV testing.[55] The governmentally imposed burden of these women would involve more than a needle puncture. It would include lost autonomy, false positives, false negatives and consequent stigma, personal turmoil, or unnecessary abortion.

In equal protection cases, courts strictly scrutinize state legislation creating classifications that impair fundamental rights. Under the strict scrutiny analysis, the challenged classification "must serve important governmental objectives and must be substantially related to achievement of those objectives."[56] Coercive prenatal AIDS testing legislation would appear to penalize women exercising fundamental rights of procreative privacy and access to medical care. In the absence of a compelling state interest, a court would be expected to invalidate legislation impairing fundamental rights. For example, in *Skinner* v. *Oklahoma,* the fundamental right of procreation led the Court to sustain an equal protection challenge of a mandatory sterilization law.[57] And in *Memorial Hospital* v. *Mar-*

icopa County, the impairment of the fundamental right to access to essential health care was grounds for invalidating legislation under the equal protection clause.[58]

Courts also give strict scrutiny in the equal protection context to state legislation imposing benefits and burdens on certain suspect classes. In keeping with the historic purpose of the Fourteenth Amendment to address invidious racial discrimination, state action premised on racial classification[59] or national origin is presumptively invalid and has been frequently invalidated under the courts' strict scrutiny standard. *Korematsu* v. *United States,* the notorious Supreme Court decision upholding the exclusion of Americans of Japanese ancestry from certain public areas during the Second World War, is cited as a dramatic exception to the rule that explicit racial classifications do not survive the Supreme Court's application of strict scrutiny.[60] In *Korematsu,* compelling national interests connected with the exigencies of war supposedly justified explicit race-based distinctions among similarly situated citizens.

Nonvoluntary prenatal AIDS testing would have a de facto disproportionate impact on racial minorities, despite the absence of any explicitly racial classification. The greatest reported incidence by far of AIDS in women is among women of color. Studies indicate that the AIDS epidemic has struck black (51 percent) and Hispanic (21 percent) women hardest.[61] Because more than 70 percent of the women who would test positive for the AIDS virus in a mandatory prenatal testing program would be black or Hispanic, the bulk of those who suffered hardship as a consequence of testing, data collection, and disclosures would be black or Hispanic.

Courts should be reluctant to stigmatize groups already stigmatized through racial discrimination.[62] A definite stigma attaches to having AIDS, worsened by the association of the disease with homosexuality,[63] drug use,[64] and prostitution. Depending on the design of the program, mandatory and routine testing could mean that information about a person's HIV antibody status is obtained and reported to public authorities. Publication of a person's HIV status can result in subsequent discrimination in the areas of employment, insurance, housing, education, and the community.[65] Mandatory and routine testing can lead to feelings of extreme isolation and guilt and to the psychological effects of being faced with an incurable disease.[66] Even though confidentiality of records and test results is strictly protected in many states,[67] this does not address the adverse psychological and emotional effects on the individual or the damage that would occur if the results were disclosed willfully, negligently, or in the sincere belief that disclosure is in the public's best interest.[68] Because of the burdensome effects of a mandatory or routine testing scheme, it is likely that the atmosphere of cooperation and trust between physician and patient would be seriously eroded, creating further hurdles for women seeking medical care.[69]

Whether universal or limited to high-risk individuals or communities, coercive prenatal AIDS testing legislation would have a disparate impact on traditionally disadvantaged racial minorities. Unfortunately, the Supreme Court has held that facially race-neutral government action must have a *discriminatory purpose* as well as a *disparate impact* if it is to be invalidated under the equal protection clause. Under the leading case of *Washington* v. *Davis,* courts must validate rationally defensible government action with a disparate negative impact on racial minorities in the absence of evidence of a discriminatory intent.[70] The Court reserves its strict scrutiny in racial classification cases for invalidating discriminatory state action provably prompted by racial animosity. Given the prevalence of racial prejudice in the United States, where it is known that the substantially certain consequence of a policy initiative is a disparate negative impact on racial minorities, critics of the Court have urged that it is foolish to demand special proof of discriminatory intent.

Minority women are members of disfavored racial groups and the disfavored gender. The Supreme Court has never unequivocally declared that gender is a suspect classification entitled to strict scrutiny. However, gender classifications have often been subjected to a medium rather than a minimum level of scrutiny.[71] Recognizing the pernicious effects of gender bias, courts have required that states justify discriminatory classifications by reference to fair and substantial state interests instead of merely rational ones.[72] This would seem to be of great significance to the constitutionality of mandatory and routine AIDS testing of pregnant women, since in the world as we know it, all pregnant persons are women. On its face, "discrimination based on a woman's pregnancy is . . . discrimination because of her sex."[73] This philosophically appealing line of analysis is not, however, the law. The Supreme Court has yet to overrule its holding that under the equal protection clause, discrimination on the basis of pregnancy does not equal discrimination on the basis of gender.[74]

Courts would have ample policy grounds for electing medium scrutiny for their reviews of mandatory and routine prenatal AIDS testing programs. The arbitrariness of singling out pregnant women for AIDS testing suggests that the rights of these citizens are being compromised thoughtlessly, perhaps because they are devalued as mere women or "vessels" for the unborn.[75] Regrettably, the adverse implications of prenatal testing policies may seem less important to policymakers when those who are most likely to suffer are poor, female members of racial minority groups. Minority women are still stereotyped as less capable than white men and women and as most in need of paternalism. Black and Hispanic women are also stereotyped as licentious and irresponsible, fitting objects of vigorous social control. Unless mandatory testing is performed across a broader base of individuals, such as all persons receiving hospital services, the decision to impose a prenatal testing regime is a distinct threat to egalitarian principles.

Constitutional privacy

Women's constitutional privacy rights would pose the greatest legal roadblock to a governmentally mandated prenatal testing program. The Supreme Court has distinguished three facets of privacy, each of which is potentially diminished by mandatory and routine prenatal testing: physical privacy, decisional privacy, and informational privacy. Briefly, physical privacy, protected under the Fourth Amendment, is freedom from unreasonable governmental search and seizure. Decisional privacy is freedom to make appropriately private choices without governmental interference. And, finally, informational privacy is freedom to limit access to information about oneself through confidentiality and record secrecy.

The Fourth Amendment

Governmentally mandated AIDS testing of pregnant women may run afoul of the Fourth Amendment. While the U.S. Constitution does not expressly provide for a right to privacy, the Fourth Amendment is an important source of privacy protection in the Bill of Rights. The Fourth Amendment provides for the "right of the people to be secure in their persons . . . against unreasonable searches and seizures."[76] The Supreme Court has repeatedly interpreted these words to mean that an individual's reasonable expectations of privacy may not be subject to arbitrary interference by agents or instrumentalities of local, state, and federal governments.[77] To measure the reasonableness of a privacy intrusion, the courts have balanced "the nature and quality of the intrusion on the individual's fourth amendment interest . . . against the importance of the governmental interest alleged to justify the intrusion."[78]

For more than two decades, it has been recognized that "mandatory blood testing is a search and seizure that must comply with the standard of reasonableness imposed by the fourth amendment."[79] Nonetheless, mandatory blood tests have been upheld as reasonable interferences with Fourth Amendment privacy. In *Schmerber* v. *California,* the Supreme Court considered the constitutionality of a blood test ordered by police over the protests of a suspected drunk driver.[80] Employing a "balancing test," the Court weighed the individual's privacy interest in not undergoing the test against society's interest in conducting the nonconsensual procedure to enforce its accident laws. Although it recognized that "the integrity of an individual's person is a cherished value in our society," the Court upheld the involuntary procedure as minimally intrusive.[81] Courts have also upheld mandatory premarital blood tests designed to detect sexually transmitted diseases. By contrast, the Supreme Court has invalidated police-ordered stomach pumping and surgery as unconstitutional intrusions that shock the conscience.[82]

Premarital and drunk driver blood testing is widely accepted. Recent courts have validated blood tests to detect drug and alcohol use.[83] A federal district court in Louisiana held in 1989 that Fourth Amendment privacy does not place a public hospital nurse—with needle-handling responsibilities and admittedly in a high-risk group for AIDS—beyond the reach of a mandatory AIDS testing requirement.[84] Critics believe that government AIDS testing policies can be deeply intrusive, implicating weighty constitutional values of personal security and privacy if they mandate testing of low-risk individuals or individuals with a low probability of transmitting disease to others.

Future courts may agree. A mandatory blood testing program for the AIDS virus was recently struck down by the U.S. Court of Appeals as an unconstitutional interference with personal security. In *Glover* v. *Eastern Nebraska Community Office of Retardation,* the Eighth Circuit Court affirmed a lower court decision in a class action brought by the employees of a public agency providing services for the mentally retarded.[85] Class members sought to invalidate an agency testing policy on Fourth Amendment grounds.

The controverted agency policy required employees whose work brought them into close contact with mentally retarded clients to submit to blood testing for HIV antibodies and hepatitis B virus. The targeted employees were also required to notify a personnel officer if they knew or suspected that they had either disease and to disclose medical records detailing any treatments. The stated purpose of the challenged policy was to create a safe environment for working, training, and living. The agency feared the risk of disease transmission from workers to clients. Retarded clients occasionally bit and scratched, and workers sometimes assisted clients with personal hygiene.

The Eighth Circuit Court nevertheless found no error in the district court's conclusion that the risk of disease transmission in the agency was "minuscule, trivial, extremely low, extraordinarily low, theoretical, approaching zero."[86] Balancing the employees' interests in not being tested against the employer's interest in testing to avert unlikely injury, the court concluded that the agency's testing policy was unconstitutional. Attorneys for the agency were unsuccessful in arguing that employees of a highly regulated state agency have a lowered expectation of privacy, that the state has not just an interest but a strong and compelling interest in protecting its "particularly susceptible population" of retarded clients, that employee blood tests constitute administrative searches, and that the reliability of the tests makes them reasonable. The case represents a significant departure from the analyses that have led other circuits to uphold breathalyzer and urine testing to detect drug or alcohol consumption. The *Glover* case illustrates that courts are capable of deciding that the governmental interest in safety fails to justify a mandatory testing policy. Plainly, it is not enough that a population targeted for testing poses a theoretical risk to others. The government is required by the Constitution to show that its testing policy makes more than a minimal contribution to the reduction of the hazard.

While employee transmission of AIDS is unlikely in most settings, maternal–fetal transmission occurs in approximately one-third of all cases. At first glance, it might appear that the case for mandatory prenatal testing is therefore stronger than was the case for mandatory employee testing in the human services sector considered in *Glover*. But the case for mandatory testing of pregnant women is actually weaker. To guard against the extremely low risk of worker-to-client transmission in the human services sector, an employee who tested positive for the AIDS virus could have been transferred to a new job. Mandatory testing in the context of *Glover* had potential lifesaving consequences. Unlike an AIDS virus–infected agency employee, however, an AIDS virus–infected pregnant woman cannot be transferred to a new job to eliminate the risk she poses to her child. In key respects, her job as gestator is sole. AIDS testing in pregnancy cannot yet save the lives of the unborn, though it can terminate and prevent potential lives. Where it leads HIV-positive women to choose abortion over the risk of giving birth to a fatally sick child, AIDS testing in pregnancy is a factor in terminating pregnancies. AIDS testing also may be a factor in preventing women from considering new pregnancies.

Policymakers must begin to look to the future, when medical developments make it possible to offer meaningful protection to the unborn. When that day arrives, the question of whether women have a constitutionally reasonable expectation of privacy in their own bodies, barring governmentally mandated AIDS testing and treatment, will be sharply raised. Some will argue that the health benefit to be gained for the unborn from testing, combined with the health and economic benefits to be gained for society, far outweigh the burden to pregnant women of a needle prick. However, the burden pregnant women would face is more onerous than a needle prick. The full burden is interference with autonomy and the consequential burdens of stigma, privacy invasion, and discrimination. The ultimate issue will thus be the extent to which it is constitutionally reasonable that the lives of women can be controlled to protect the fetus and promote legislated ends. The full constitutional determination of the issue extends beyond the parameters of the Fourth Amendment.

Decisional privacy

In addition to the specific privacy protections of the Fourth Amendment, the Supreme Court in *Griswold* v. *Connecticut* recognized a general, fundamental constitutional right of privacy. The precise boundaries of the right have not been drawn. However, the Court has already declared that many important choices relating to birth control,[87] sterility,[88] abortion,[89] marriage,[90] and childrearing[91] are appropriately private choices. In *Griswold,* the Court held that a right of privacy broad enough to protect the decision to use contraception subsists in the "penumbra" of the Bill of Rights and the Fourteenth Amendment.[92] According to the *Griswold* decision, a sphere of private conduct free from coercive governmental interference is implied by the First Amendment guarantee of free association, the Third Amendment prohibition against military appropriation of private homes, the Fourth Amendment limitation on search and seizure, and the Fifth Amendment constraint on compulsory self-incrimination. Moreover, both the Ninth Amendment's reservation of unenumerated rights against the federal government and the Fourteenth Amendment's guarantee of liberty accord with the traditional expectation of a private realm of autonomous choice and bodily integrity.

After *Griswold,* the right to privacy was relied on in *Roe* v. *Wade* and *Doe* v. *Bolton* to establish that blanket state prohibition of abortion is unconstitutional.[93] Subsequent abortion cases, through *Thornburgh* v. *American College of Obstetricians and Gynecologists* in 1986, emphasized that constitutional privacy includes "freedom to care for one's health and person" and that the right to privacy is a fundamental aspect of Fourteenth Amendment liberty.[94]

Because the right is fundamental, governmental interference with constitutional privacy is given strict judicial scrutiny. As previously noted, under the Supreme Court's strict scrutiny analysis, interference with private choices is deemed warranted only if it is the least restrictive means of promoting a compelling state interest. Thus, for example, in *Roe* v. *Wade* the Court found that states could have no compelling interests in restricting access to medically safe abortion in the first trimester; but it suggested that they might have compelling interests in public, fetal, and maternal health sufficient to justify regulation of second trimester abortion and prohibition of third trimester abortion.[95] In 1989, the decision in *Webster* v. *Reproductive Health Services* signaled the demise of *Roe*'s trimester analysis limiting intervention on behalf of the fetus to the period after viability. Flatly contradicting *Roe,* in the *Webster* case U.S. Supreme Court Chief Justice William Rehnquist opined in dicta that "the State's interest in potential life is compelling before viability."[96] It seems likely that the Rehnquist Court will rethink the constitutional right of privacy. In the meantime, the *Griswold* and *Roe* decisions and the doctrine of a fundamental right to privacy stand.

The right to privacy is closely associated with the concept of bodily integrity. It is also associated with the highest regard for human dignity, individual choice, and self-determination. Many courts have maintained that the constitutional right to privacy guarantees or is premised on bodily integrity. A California court recently announced that "the constitutional right of privacy guarantees to the individual the freedom to choose to reject, or refuse to consent to, intrusion of his bodily integrity."[97] In like fashion, a Massachusetts state court recently asserted that "the law implicitly recognizes that a person has a strong interest in being free from nonconsensual invasion of his bodily integrity."[98]

Nonconsensual prenatal AIDS testing compromises bodily integrity and self-determination. Until and unless the Supreme Court addresses it squarely, the question of whether constitutional privacy rights would invalidate a local, state, or federal government requirement that unconsenting pregnant women be tested for AIDS has no definitive legal answer. At first glance, mandatory and routine prenatal screening for signs of the AIDS virus would appear to be inconsistent with the decisional privacy "right of an individual to be free in action, thought, experience, and belief from government compulsion."[99] Many legal commentators continue to believe, after reflection, that women's interests in privacy and autonomy override the governmental interest in mandatory prenatal testing.

However, past courts have authorized nonvoluntary medical procedures on pregnant women considerably more intrusive than blood tests. Prior to *Roe* v. *Wade,* a New Jersey court appointed a guardian for a fetus and ordered the guardian to consent to blood transfusions over the mother's objections as necessary to save the lives of the mother and the fetus.[100] *Roe* v. *Wade* points toward the argument that prenatal intervention on behalf of the fetus in the first and possibly the second trimester of pregnancy would be unwarranted and unconstitutional. Under *Roe,* the state has no compelling interest in the life of the fetus prior to the third trimester. However, some commentators defend the notion that even if a woman has a constitutional right to abortion under *Roe* v. *Wade,* once she chooses not to abort, she becomes a proper object of intervention designed to protect the health and well-being of her future child.

Several lower courts have embraced the argument that states may assert a constitutionally compelling interest in the life of the fetus after viability or as soon as any abortion rights have been waived, whichever happens first. In highly publicized cases since *Roe* v. *Wade,* courts have sought to protect the welfare of fetuses by overriding pregnant women's medical decisions. When a Georgia woman refused a cesarean delivery and a blood transfusion on religious grounds, a state court ordered her to submit to surgery if her physician found that cesarean delivery would be less risky than natural childbirth for her 39-week-old fetus. A New York State court held in 1985 that a pregnant woman's interest in the exercise of her religious beliefs was not sufficient to override the state's significant interest in protecting the life of an 18-week-old fetus and stated that the fetus could be regarded as a human being to whom the court stood in a *parens patriae* relationship.[101] The court noted that "the state has a significant interest in protecting the potential of human life represented by an unborn fetus which increases throughout the course of pregnancy, becoming compelling when the fetus reaches viability."[102]

National attention was drawn to the question of coercive pregnancy interventions in a 1987 case, *In re A.C.* A federal district court in the District of Columbia granted a hospital a declaratory order to perform a cesarean delivery over the objections of a terminally ill woman who was 26 weeks pregnant. The court held that the mother's fundamental penumbral privacy right against bodily intrusion was properly subordinated to the interests of the unborn child and the state. Distinguishing the case from abortion, the court cited the compelling state interest language of *Roe* v. *Wade* and reasoned that "as a matter of law, the right of a woman to an abortion is different and distinct from her obligations to the [viable] fetus once she has decided not to timely terminate her pregnancy."[103] In a footnote, the court stated that "this case does not present facts indicating that A. C.'s good health was being sacrificed to save her child's life, although her condition was clearly affected."[104] It appeared to be of little consequence to the court that the woman's autonomy was being sacrificed even if her health was not. Tragically, the mother and child died shortly after the operation.

Pregnancy intervention has been authorized where it has been perceived necessary to save the life of the unborn (or to prevent fetal abuse), never simply to convey information to the pregnant woman or third parties. Only in the rarest instances would the information so obtained save or improve the quality of a life. For this reason, the constitutionality of governmentally mandated testing is doubtful in the light of women's rights of privacy. Because of the privacy concerns, it would appear that the goals of mandatory and routine testing are best pursued through noncoercive educational measures.[105] Evidence is already at hand that mandatory and routine testing would be less efficacious for reducing maternal–fetal and sexual transmission of disease than intensive education efforts and social services realistically targeted at high-risk populations. To protect the safety of health-care personnel, health-care providers can introduce policies aimed at the patient population generally, rather than at pregnant women.

It should be noted that as long as there is no cure for AIDS, both pro-life and pro-choice proponents have something to fear in mandatory and routine AIDS testing in pregnancy. Several studies recommend giving seropositive pregnant women the option of abortion.[106] Reproductive free choice would arguably be threatened in a context in which officials tested pregnant women without their consent for a maternal–fetal transmittable, fatal disease and offered information about abortion. Yet not providing such information could expose new mothers and their health-care providers to civil liability for wrongful birth and life.[107] In any case, policymakers who urge prenatal AIDS testing in the hope that it will lead to abortion may be disappointed. The cultural and religious importance of giving birth outweighs problems of illness and disability, including AIDS, in the minds of some women of color.[108] Some blacks view both the AIDS epidemic and abortion as threatening genocide, abortion more palpably.[109] Moreover, it is not clear who would pay for poor women's abortions. In many communities, public abortion funding is not available to those otherwise eligible for publicly supported gynecologic and obstetric are. In 1977 in *Maher* v. *Roe,* the Supreme Court upheld the constitutionality of state legislation banning public subsidy of abortions.[110] Four years later, in *Harris* v. *McRae,* the Court upheld the constitutionality of federal legislation prohibiting Medicaid funding for elective abortion.[111] In 1989, in *Webster* v. *Reproductive Health Services,* the Court revisited the question of state abortion funding and upheld the constitutionality of state legislation categorically prohibiting the use of public funds, employees, or facilities for abortion.[112]

Notwithstanding the cultural and economic forces against abortion, abortion opponents may base strong opposition to testing pregnant women for AIDS on the fear that positive and false-positive results will lead women to elect abortion. Since not all infants born of infected mothers are infected,[113] and since some infants live a number of years though infected, the possibility that even a few women may be pressed to choose abortion on account of maternal seropositivity is troubling.

Informational privacy

A final aspect of constitutional privacy remains to be considered. Critics of mandatory and routine AIDS testing have often premised their objections on the importance of informational privacy.[114] It has been argued that mandatory and routine screening inevitably lead to data collection, the use of personal data for public purposes, and unwarranted disclosure of private medical facts. These consequences, it is argued, amount to the invasion of constitutional privacy rights. An extreme libertarian version of the argument maintains that information collection by the government is an inherent invasion of privacy rights. More typically, it is argued that government data collection makes it likely that private or confidential medical information will be publicly disclosed. Whether intentional or inadvertent, the results of unwanted disclosure of a positive AIDS status can have disastrous consequences for individuals and their families. The Supreme Court has fallen short of recognizing a separate and distinct constitutional right to informational privacy. The interest in informational privacy is sometimes protected under the rubric of decisional privacy. In its abortion cases, the Court has stressed that mandatory nonanonymous and onerous state reporting and record-keeping practices can abridge women's fundamental right to decisional privacy.[115]

The Court has come closest to recognizing an independent right of information privacy in *Whalen* v. *Roe,* a case upholding the constitutionality of a New York statute requiring that information precisely identifying the recipients of certain prescription drugs be filed and maintained for 5 years by the State Health Department.[116] Although the statute was enacted to curb the illegal sale or distribution of prescription drugs, the plaintiffs alleged that physician and pharmacist compliance with the statute could lead to the publicization of private medical information and to the perception that individuals with legitimate needs for medication were drug addicts. A unanimous Court held that where a state implements procedures, as New York had, that "evidence a proper concern with, and protection of, the individual's interest in privacy," a concern for prospective unwarranted disclosures is no basis for declaring its laws unconstitutional. Following *Whalen,* it would appear that a coercive governmental testing policy that included meaningful informational privacy safeguards could be constitutionally valid despite the chance of burdensome information leaks.

Writing for the *Whalen* Court, Justice John Paul Stevens observed that the statutory or regulatory duties to avoid unwarranted disclosure of data collected for public purposes "arguably [have] roots in the Constitution." Many lower courts have construed *Whalen* as positing that a constitutional right of privacy "exists in certain types of personal information."[117] Indeed, most courts have "concluded that a constitutional right of confidentiality is implicated by disclosure of a broad range of information."[118] While lower courts have recognized a constitutional right of informational privacy, they have made it clear that the right is not an absolute one. Defining the scope of legitimate state interference with the informational privacy right has been left to "a case by case method, balancing the individual's rights to confidentiality against the government's interest in limited disclosure."[119]

Recognizing a constitutional right to informational privacy, a Wisconsin district court denied the state's summary judgment motion in a case brought by the inmate of a correctional facility alleging that Health Service Unit medical personnel discussed his positive AIDS test results with nonmedical staff.[120] Despite the trend in the lower courts to assert a constitutional privacy right to personal information, informational privacy arguments against mandatory testing of pregnant women rest on ambiguous precedence. In *Plowman v. U.S. Dept. of the Army,* a case involving nonconsensual AIDS testing and information disclosure, a Virginia district court refused to rely on *Whalen* as the basis of an informational privacy right.[121] The right was claimed by a civilian employee of the Department of the Army in Korea who alleged that army personnel tested him for the AIDS virus without his consent and then disclosed the positive test result. Because he brought his claim against the army and an army officer in his official capacity, both traditionally protected by governmental immunity, the court was unwilling to recognize a constitutional right in the absence of "controlling authority [confirming] the extension of the constitutional [privacy] right . . . to medical information."[122]

State Law Constraints

Courts regard the U.S. Constitution as a potential constraint on nonvoluntary prenatal AIDS testing initiatives sponsored by government—Congress, state legislatures, agencies, and government-affiliated health-care providers. It does not follow that private health-care providers are at liberty to impose nonvoluntary prenatal testing requirements that public providers could not. On the contrary, many state constitutions have provisions closely modeled after the Fourteenth Amendment but applicable to private and public entities alike. Furthermore, nonvoluntary prenatal AIDS testing procedures may violate privacy rights set forth in state constitutions or created by state statutes expressly prohibiting nonconsensual AIDS-related testing and breach of confidentiality. State tort and contract laws are additional legal strictures for prudent health-care providers.[123]

The range of potential common law tort and contract liabilities for private health-care providers is suggested by the handful of early cases like *Plowman* and *Aviles* (see note 9) brought against public entities, blood banks, and individuals as a result of nonvoluntary HIV antibody testing.[124] Future victims and would-be victims of nonvoluntary prenatal AIDS testing might choose to pursue contract claims. For example, plaintiffs might pursue claims of wrongful interference with a contract in cases where prenatal testing is thought to have proximately caused a loss of employment. They might also bring charges of breach of contract or warranty, where it is alleged that a nonvoluntary AIDS tester failed to carry out the express and implied duties of the patient–provider relationship.

A more promising direction for nonvoluntary testing plaintiffs is suggested by early state-law claims brought against private and public sector HIV testers alleging (1) battery and negligence, (2) invasion of privacy, breach of confidence, and defamation, and (3) infliction of emotional distress.[125] If faced with HIV testing requirements, pregnant women alleging injuries in these familiar tort categories could elect to fight back aggressively with class actions for money damages against individual physicians, institutional providers, or administrative agencies. They could even seek equitable relief in the form of injunctions against nonconsensual testing on the grounds that it presents the likelihood of irreparable harm. The success of individual or class plaintiffs seeking legal or equitable remedies would depend on the plausibility of particular claims and the predilections of particular courts.

Battery, negligence, and informed consent

Generally speaking, a medical examination, treatment, or operation performed without informed consent is unlawful battery or medical malpractice.[126] Civil liability for battery—defined as nonconsensual, intentional, harmful, or offensive physical contact—arose out of the law's recognition that individuals have an interest in personal autonomy and bodily integrity. Civil liability for negligence, the basis for most medical malpractice claims, has similar origins. In the absence of informed consent, even beneficial, well-intended medical care is tortious. Failure to secure informed consent for the provision of health care is also tortious where harm or offense results from failure to explain fully the purposes and effects of a prescribed course of treatment.[127] Procedures that exceed the scope of informed consent are civil wrongs as well. As one court colorfully summarized the rule of informed consent, "every competent person is the final arbiter of whether or not he gets cut, by whom he gets cut, and where he gets cut."[128]

Voluntary HIV testing in pregnancy preceded by education and counseling would normally raise no legal problem of informed consent.[129] However, nonvoluntary testing, such as mandatory testing, testing required as a condition of care, and routine testing without meaningful opportunities to withhold consent, is legally problematic. Although mandatory testing raises ethical and policy questions, courts are not likely to find health-care providers liable for mandatory testing implemented in accordance with local, state, or federal requirements. Liability could conceivably result from private providers' conditionally mandatory HIV testing requirements that elevate AIDS-related testing to a "take it or leave it" precondition of receiving prenatal care. Most pregnant women do not view prenatal care as an option and may not have realistic alternatives for care. Conditionally mandatory testing is legally problematic because courts could be persuaded that such testing imposed on women with few prenatal care options is effectively nonconsensual, in violation of the rule of informed consent.

If not mandated by law, routine prenatal AIDS testing *without advance notification* poses a problem under the law's informed consent requirement. The *Plowman* court implied that HIV blood tests "extracted for the purposes of other, arguably consensual diagnostic tests" are not serious privacy invasions.[130] Even if this is correct, surely informed consent is absent where patients have provided blood samples for undisclosed or partially disclosed purposes, only later to discover that the HIV antibody test was performed. An undisclosed hospital policy of performing patient-identified (i.e., nonanonymous) AIDS-related tests on blood samples taken from pregnant women for other diagnostic purposes should raise concern about whether the rule of informed consent has been deceitfully sidestepped. Given the foreseeable adverse implications of testing positive for HIV, patients are plausibly ascribed a right to know in advance that they will be tested, even if no additional amount of blood or needle punctures are medically necessary. Thus if a blood sample is routinely obtained from a pregnant woman and is utilized for the unauthorized purpose of HIV antibody testing, the possibility of liability for injuries linked to lack of informed consent cannot be foreclosed. The situation is closely analogous to cases in which physicians are found liable after obtaining consent to perform one type of surgery (e.g., a hysterectomy) and concurrently performed another for which consent was not obtained (e.g., an appendectomy).[131]

Routine prenatal HIV testing, if not mandated by law, also raises legal and ethical concerns. Routine AIDS-related testing *with advance notification* and an opportunity to refuse takes patients' informed consent into account, but in a way that may not be meaningful. If health-care providers do not call attention to the AIDS test, the special burdens of AIDS testing, and the right to refuse testing, patients may fail, to their detriment, to appreciate material facts bearing on their treatment.[132] To make a right of refusal meaningful to the poor, poorly educated black and Hispanic women who are most likely to test positive for HIV, an actual, culturally responsive discussion of testing and its consequences could be required. Otherwise, routine AIDS testing risks becoming the practical and therefore the legal equivalent of compulsion.

Routine testing procedures can be conducted anonymously or nonanonymously. The results of nonanonymous testing can be either communicated to the patient or withheld. Providers may elect to withhold test results where the purpose of testing is research. (It has been argued that providers are obligated by an ethical or a legal "duty to warn" to disclose positive results to test takers or third parties. There is only limited legal authority for a duty to warn strangers of peril.)[133] As a practical matter, anonymous routine testing for research purposes of samples taken from women who have not consented to testing and are not notified would rarely result in personal legal injury or liability. It is worth considering whether a class of women tested anonymously could cry foul and successfully claim injury if statistical data obtained through secret, anonymous testing were put to uses that harmed their collective legal interests. The case of legal injury would seem strongest where deceit was involved: where patients were told, untruthfully, that AIDS testing would not be performed without their consent, after which the blood of those who refused testing was tested anyway on an anonymous or undisclosed basis.

Privacy, defamation, and confidentiality

Mandatory and routine AIDS testing compromises rights of privacy and related rights recognized under state law. The common law precedent or statutes of many states recognize four distinct invasion of privacy torts, in addition to breach of confidence and defamation. Successfully alleging any one the four privacy torts—intrusion, unreasonable publicity given to private life, false-light publication, and commercial appropriation—plaintiffs may recover in privacy suits against public or private actors.[134] Scholarly critics of the privacy tort complain that its elements are vague and that plaintiffs are seldom victorious. However, plaintiffs are sometimes successful, even with novel privacy claims.[135] The basic legal requirement for a favorable judgment is to show injuries to sensibilities or reputation resulting from conduct that reasonable persons of ordinary prudence view as highly offensive.[136] Of special concern in the AIDS-related testing context are highly offensive bodily intrusion and embarrassing publications.

The intrusion tort is premised on the idea that persons are entitled to limit access to their bodies, homes, and aspects of their personal lives otherwise shielded in seclusion. Nonvoluntary prenatal AIDS testing involves both a bodily intrusion and an informational one. The bodily intrusion is a needle puncture and extraction of blood. In cases involving unprivileged bodily searches, past courts have been willing to find that even short-lived physical contacts that occur in public places can be intrusions on a woman's reasonable expectation of seclusion.[137] Moreover, prying for private information, whether or not any information is actually obtained, can amount to an intrusion in the eyes of the law.[138] Unauthorized viewing or disclosure of patient information revealing the results of AIDS testing is also conceivably a tortious intrusion on seclusion.[139]

The dissemination of patient information and records could potentially lead to lawsuits alleging liability for unreasonable publication of private facts. The right to privacy encompasses the right to control information about oneself, subject to legal privileges, including the privilege of the media to publish newsworthy stories. Although several states have enacted legislation to provide for privacy in AIDS testing procedures,[140] the possibility exists that those with access to samples, diagnostic reports, or medical records would deliberately pass information on patient seropositivity (whether accurate or not) along to unauthorized third parties. The consequences could prove disastrous to the affected individual in areas of employment, social ties, housing, education, and insurance.[141] Where private information is disseminated, victims may have an action for publication of embarrassing private facts. Where misinformation is disseminated, whether orally or in print, an action for false-light publication may also be appropriate.[142] Liability for defamation—libel or slander—to redress reputational injury is also possible where AIDS-related falsehoods are disseminated. This could become relevant if a false-positive enzyme-linked immunosorbent assay (ELISA) test result were misrepresented as definitive or if a person with a positive ELISA test were described as "dying of AIDS." Traditional common law creates a strong presumption that slander relating to venereal or communicable diseases is injurious.[143]

Breach of confidence is increasingly recognized as a separate tort, distinct from privacy invasion.[144] In fact, where the defendant has a confidential relationship to the plaintiff, such as the physician–patient relationship, some courts have held that breach of confidence rather than invasion of privacy is the more appropriate rubric.[145] Absent legal requirements to disclose disease status, physicians and other health-care personnel[146] may be held liable for improper disclosures.[147] Some states require confidentiality in the physician–patient relationship by statute. Moreover, while most states have not enacted legislation protecting the confidentiality of persons undergoing voluntary, routine, or mandatory AIDS testing, a few have.[148] Confidentiality is also protected to a degree by rules of evidence and procedure that limit the use of information obtained in confidence. Problems of confidentiality with respect to positive AIDS test results are well known.[149] Acts of violence and discrimination against AIDS victims and their families have been widely publicized in the media. Thus some women may wish to decline voluntary testing, even where anonymity or confidentiality is promised, to avoid the consequences of identification and disclosure. If limited access to information cannot be ensured, the invasion of privacy and breach of confidence torts will serve as practical barriers to mandatory testing. Physicians, hospitals, and other health-care providers may be unable to tolerate exposure to the legal risks of mandatory testing of pregnant women.

The commercial appropriation tort has little obvious application to AIDS-related testing. However, this privacy tort was relied on, without ultimate success, in *Anderson v. Strong Memorial Hospital* by a New Yorker photographed and later recognized when the photograph was published in a local newspaper reporting or advertising the defendant hospital's services for AIDS victims.[150] In New York, a privacy statute is the basis of rights against commercial appropriation of a person's name, likeness, or identity. In construing the statute, one preliminary issue for the New York court was whether the plaintiff, who had consented in advance to a silhouette of his face appearing in print, was sufficiently recognizable in the photograph. But beyond the likeness issue, the court had to decide whether, if the photograph was a likeness, publishing the photograph was a commercial appropriation. The plaintiff alleged that his photograph had been put to a commercial purpose—advertising a health-care facility. Finally, the court considered whether the newspaper was privileged in publishing the plaintiff's photograph as news. Although the plaintiff did not prevail, the court did not hold that the media may publish the photographs of AIDS patients or individuals seeking HIV antibody screening without consent on the grounds that the AIDS epidemic is newsworthy.

Infliction of emotional distress

In a number of reported cases, AIDS victims have included infliction of emotion distress among the allegations made against health-care providers responsible for nonconsensual testing or breach of confidence. Infliction of emotional distress has also been alleged against employers or institutional authorities responsible for deprivation of benefits, liberty, and privacy.[151] In most states, outrageous conduct, whether intentional or negligent, is actionable if it is the provable cause of emotional distress. In the *Plowman* case, a former government employee charged intentional infliction of emotional distress against a military officer who allegedly "ratified unwarranted, nonconsensual AIDS tests."[152] The court dismissed Plowman's claims because of the absolute immunity of the military officer discharging discretionary duties in a foreign country. Nonetheless, the court pointed toward a potentially powerful theory of liability for private persons against private sector testers when it hinted that nonconsensual AIDS testing of civilians was not necessarily wise or appropriate.

Conclusion

AIDS is a potentially fatal disease. The best known treatment for AIDS, the retroviral drug azidothymidine (AZT), has been licensed for ameliorating the symptoms of adult and childhood AIDS. But no treatment is known specifically to alleviate AIDS, ARC, or HIV infection in pregnant women or the unborn.[153] Against this background, members of the health-care, public health, and pol-icymaking communities have nonetheless contemplated coercive mandatory and routine prenatal AIDS testing measures.

As long as the social benefits to be gained from coercive prenatal testing are limited in relation to its foreseeable costs to autonomy and privacy, courts in-terpreting state constitutions, statutes, and the common law could be fairly expected to side with injured plaintiffs seeking compensation for loss of privacy, breach of confidentiality, emotional distress, or injury to reputation. In addition, the doubtful purpose of mandatory testing today has negative implications for its constitutionality under federal law. It remains to be seen whether governmentally sponsored mandatory prenatal testing would survive constitutional challenges premised on violation of the Fourth or Fourteenth amendments.

The day may come when prenatal testing or treatment can significantly reduce the incidence and severity of pediatric AIDS. Should that day arrive—and we must hope it will—the woman who eshewed appropriate, affordable prenatal care would be the exception rather than the rule. At the same time, the courts would be unlikely to declare mandatory AIDS testing and treatment requirements illegal. Indeed, in cases where pregnant women openly refused voluntary AIDS care for themselves or their fetuses, the courts could be expected to order testing and treatment not specifically mandated by statute, much as they now order controversial surgery, blood transfusions, and incarceration for the protection of the unborn.[154]

Notes

1. See Padraig O'Malley, ed., "Special Issue on AIDS," *New England Journal of Public Policy* 4 (Winter–Spring 1988): 9, 43–44.

2. Centers for Disease Control (CDC), "Recommendations for Assisting in the Preven-tion of Perinatal Transmission of Human T-Lymphotrophic Virus Type III/ Lymphadenopathy Associated Virus and Acquired Immunodeficiency Syndrome," *Mortality and Morbidity Weekly Report* 34 (1985): 721, 725.

3. See Bernard Lo, Robert Steinbrook, Molly Cooke et al., "Voluntary Screening for Human Immunodeficiency Virus (HIV) Infection: Weighing the Benefits and Harms," *Annals of Internal Medicine* 110 (1989): 727.

4. According to the CDC, the high-risk groups include (1) nonmedical intravenous drug users, (2) prostitutes, and (3) sex partners of intravenous drug users, bisexual men, men with hemophilia, or men who have other evidence of HIV infection ("Recommendations," 723).
   Women who are HIV positive may be more likely to become symptomatic during or after pregnancy (Department of Health and Human Services [DHHS], *Report of the Surgeon General's Workshop on Children with HIV Infection and Their Families,* DHHS Publication HRS-D-MC 87-1 [Rockville, Md.: DHHS/PHS, 1987], 18). Obstetric complications in AIDS and deaths have been reported (Lisa M. Koonin,

"Pregnancy-Associated Deaths Due to AIDS in the United States," *Journal of the American Medical Association* 261 [1989]: 1306).

5. See Kathleen Nolan, "Ethical Issues in Caring for Pregnant Women and Newborns at Risk for Human Immunodeficiency Virus Infection," *Seminars in Perinatology* 13 (1989): 55, rejecting compulsory interventions but citing nonvoluntary testing proposals, including K. Krasinski, W. Borkowsky, D. Bebenroth et al., "Failure of Voluntary Testing for HIV to Identify Infected Parturient Women in a High Risk Population," *New England Journal of Medicine* 318 (1988): 185, and D. Ghitelman, "What to Tell a Patient Who Tests HIV Positive," *Medical Economics* 64 (1987): 79–93. See also "M.D.s Urge More Testing for AIDS. Suggest Screening Pregnant Women," *Miami Herald,* February 27, 1988, p. 1A. See Mary E. Guinan and Ann Hardy, "Epidemiology of AIDS in Women in the United States: 1981 Through 1986," *Journal of the American Medical Association* 257 (1987): 2039–2042 (screening recommended because women might not be aware of the risks).

But see Richard F. Duncan, "Public Policy and the AIDS Epidemic," *Journal of Contemporary Health, Law and Policy* 2 (1986): 169. See Kenneth R. Howe, "Why Mandatory Screening for AIDS Is a Very Bad Idea," in *AIDS, Ethics, and Public Policy,* ed. Christine Pierce and Donald Van De Veer (Belmont, Calif.: Wadsworth, 1988), 140–150. In general, mandatory testing is expensive and has numerous other practical drawbacks (Paul D. Cleary, Michael J. Barry, Kenneth H. Mayer et al., "Compulsory Premarital Screening for the Human Immunodeficiency Virus," *Journal of the American Medical Association* 258 [1987]: 1757–1761; CDC, "Recommendations," 724). Identification of AIDS carriers through mandatory prenatal testing will arrest the spread of disease only if infected pregnant women are willing and able to identify their partners, change their own sexual behavior, and undergo abortion. Mandatory testing appears to have ethical drawbacks as well (Ronald Bayer, Carol Levine, and Susan M. Wolf, "HIV Antibody Screening: An Ethical Framework for Evaluating Proposed Programs," *Journal of the American Medical Association* 256 [1986]: 1770).

6. The constitutionality of AIDS testing and related practices has been considered by numerous legal commentators. See, for example, Susan Levy, "The Constitutional Implications of Mandatory Testing for Acquired Immunodeficiency Syndrome—AIDS," *Emory Law Journal* 37 (1988): 217, 232–245; Patricia S. Atkins, "The Constitutional Implications of Mandatory AIDS Testing in the Health Care Industry," *Southwestern University Law Review* 17 (1988): 787–822; David J. Schmitt, "The Constitutional Ramifications of a Universal, Mandatory Program for the Acquired Immunodeficiency Syndrome," *Creighton Law Review* 9 (1988): 859–981; Michael Closen, Susan Marie Connor, Howard Kaufman et al., "AIDS: Testing Democracy—Irrational Response to the Public Health Crisis and the Need for Privacy in Serologic Testing," *John Marshall Law Review* 19 (1986): 835–840; Note, "The constitutional Rights of AIDS Carriers," *Harvard Law Review* 99 (1986): 1274; and Alexander G. Gray, Jr., "The Parameters of Mandatory Public Health Measures and the AIDS Epidemic," *Suffolk University Law Review* 20 (1986): 505, 516. See Peter J. Nanula, "Protecting Confidentiality in the Effort to Control AIDS," *Harvard Journal on Legislation* 24 (1986): 316, 330–333; Gretta J. Heaney, "The Constitutional Right of Informational Privacy: Does It Protect Children Suffering from AIDS?" *Fordham Urban Law Journal* 14 (1986): 927; and Deborah Jones Merritt, "The Constitutional Balance Between Health and Liberty,"

Hastings Center Report 16 (1986): 2–10. See Jennifer Terry, "The Body Invaded: Medical Surveillance of Women as Reproducers, *Socialist Review* 19 (1989): 13. Legal commentators have not limited their attention to constitutional law. See Michael Closen, Donald H. J. Hermann, Patricia J. Horne et al., *AIDS: Cases and Materials* (Houston: John Marshall, 1989), and Harlon Dalton and Scott Burris, eds., *AIDS and the Law: A Guide for the Public* (New Haven, Conn.: Yale University Press, 1987). See also "Mandatory AIDS Testing: Public Health and Private Rights" (symposium), *West's Federal Rules Decisions* 124 (1989): 288–312; Harold L. Hirsh, "AIDS and the Law," *Journal of Legal Medicine* 10 (1989): 169–210; "Current Legal Issues in AIDS" (symposium), *Ohio State Law Journal* 49 (1989); Paul Reidinger, "Testing, Testing: Drug, AIDS Testing Upheld," *American Bar Association Journal* 75 (1989): 96; Martha S. Swartz, "AIDS Testing and Informed Consent," *Journal of Health Politics, Policy and Law* 13 (1988): 607–621; Andrew Ayers Martin, "Title VII Discrimination in Biochemical Testing for AIDS and Marijuana," *Duke Law Journal* 1988 (1988): 129–153; John Howard, "HIV Screening: Scientific, Ethical, and Legal Issues," *Journal of Legal Medicine* 9 (1988): 601–610; Theodore Falk, "AIDS Public Health Law," *Journal of Legal Medicine* 9 (1988): 529; Karen A. Clifford and Russell P. Iuculano, "AIDS and Insurance: The Rationale for AIDS-Related Testing," *Harvard Law Review* 100 (1987): 1805–1825; Deborah Jones Merritt, "Communicable Diseases and Constitutional Law: Controlling AIDS," *New York University Law Review* 61 (1986): 739; Bernard M. Dickens, "Legal Rights and Duties in the AIDS Epidemic," *Science* 239 (1988): 580–586; William J. Curran, Mary E. Clark, and Larry Gostin, "AIDS: Legal and Policy Implications of the Application of Traditional Disease Control Measures," *Law, Medicine and Health Care* 15 (1987): 27–35; Larry Gostin and William J. Curran, "AIDS Screening, Confidentiality, and the Duty to Warn," *American Journal of Public Health* 77 (1987): 361; Larry Gostin and Andrew Zeigler, "A Review of AIDS-Related Legislative and Regulatory Policy in the United States," *Law, Medicine and Health Care* 15 (1987): 14; Michael Mills, Constance B. Wofsy, and John Mills, "The Acquired Immunodeficiency Syndrome: Infection Control and Public Health Law," *New England Journal of Medicine* 314 (1986): 931–936; and Joni N. Gray and Gary Melton, "The Law and Ethics of Psychological Research on AIDS," *Nebraska Law Review* 64 (1985): 637.

7. "Congress may preempt state regulation expressly, or by enacting a regulation with which it in fact conflicts, or by enacting a system of regulations so comprehensive as to displace all state regulations even if they do not conflict with any specific federal one" (Geoffrey R. Stone, Louis M. Seidman, Cass R. Sunstein et al., *Constitutional Law* [Boston: Little, Brown, 1986], 318, citing *Pacific Gas and Electric* v. *State Energy Resources Conservation Commission,* 461 U.S. 190 [1983]).

8. The constitutions of several states guarantee rights of privacy. See, for example, California Constitution, art. I, sec. 1 ("All people are by nature free and independent and have inalienable rights. Among these are enjoying and defending life and liberty, acquiring, possessing, and protecting property, and pursuing and obtaining safety, happiness and privacy"); Florida Constitution, art. I, sec. 23 (1980) ("every natural person has the right to be let alone and free from governmental intrusion into his private life"); and Montana Constitution, art. II, sec. 10 ("The right of individual privacy is essential to the well-being of a free society and shall not be infringed without a compelling state interest"). State supreme courts could conceivably interpret state constitutions as barring intrusive, nonconsensual blood testing, information disclosure, and reputational injury.

9. Intentional infliction of emotional distress was alleged in *Plowman* v. *U.S. Dept. of the Army*, 698 F. Supp. 627 (E.D. Va. 1988) (nonconsensual HIV antibody testing of a civilian employee of the military). Claims of intentional infliction of emotional distress, negligence, tortious invasion of privacy, and injury to reputation were brought in *Aviles* v. *United States*, 696 F. Supp. 217 (E.D. La. 1988) (HIV antibody test conducted on a U.S. Coast Guard member during a mandatory physical examination) but dismissed for lack of federal subject matter jurisdiction.

10. Cases charging breach of confidence have sometimes alleged that the action was also a breach of contract. See, for example, *Horne* v. *Patton*, 287 So. 2d 824 (Ala. 1973) (a physician who disclosed personal information to the plaintiff's employer invaded the plaintiff's privacy and breached an implied contract of confidentiality embodied in the physician–patient relationship), citing state and federal cases. See also *Anderson* v. *Strong Memorial Hospital*, 531 N.Y.S.2d 735, 740 (Sup. 1988), recognizing an implied covenant of confidentiality and trust in the physician–patient relationship, whose breach is actionable at law. See *Plowman* v. *U.S. Dept. of the Army*, 698 F. Supp. 627 (E.D. Va. 1988), dismissing breach of employment contract claims against the military and a military officer in a suit by a civilian employee alleging nonvoluntary HIV testing and information disclosure.

11. Several states, including California, Wisconsin, New York, Massachusetts, and Illinois, have enacted legislation banning certain nonvoluntary AIDS, ARC, and HIV antibody testing and information abuses. California law prohibits HIV testing without written informed consent (California Health and Safety Code, sec. 199.35 [Deering 1985]). Wisconsin also makes informed consent a prerequisite of HIV testing 1985 (Laws of Wisconsin 672, sec. 103.15). New York State courts have held that state and local statutes categorically ban nonconsensual AIDS testing. See, for example, *Doe* v. *Roe*, 526 N.Y.S.2d 718 (Sup. 1988); but see *People* v. *Toure*, 523 N.Y.S.2d 746 (Sup. 1988) (an incarcerated rape defendant may not block disclosure to the victim of the results of testing for sexually transmitted diseases). Illinois limits nonvoluntary testing at blood banks and alternative test sites but does not require informed consent in common treatment and therapeutic contexts (Donald H. J. Hermann and George F. De Wolfe, "HIV Antibody Testing Without Patient's Informed Consent: Illinois Abandons Patient's Rights," *Journal of Health and Hospital Law* 21 [1988]: 263–267; Madeleine M. Weldon-Linne, C. Michael Weldon-Linne, and Julie Murphy, "Aids-Virus Antibody Testing: Issues of Informed Consent and Patient Confidentiality," *Illinois Bar Journal* 75 [1986]: 206, 208).
See also Gilbert Gaynor, "Executive Action Against AIDS: A Proposal for Federal Regulation Under Existing Law," *Ohio State Law Journal* 49 (1989): 999; Thea Foglietta Silverman, "AIDS Update 1989," *Whittier Law Review* 10 (1988): 441–458; and Hilary E. Lewis, "Acquired Immunodeficiency Syndrome: State Legislative Activity," *Journal of the American Medical Association* 258 (1987): 2410–2414.

12. See Gostin and Ziegler, "Review of AIDS-Related Legislative and Regulatory Policy in the United States," 5, and Closen et al., "AIDS: Testing Democracy," 922–927. Mandatory HIV testing programs are currently in place in many areas. Blood centers test all blood, blood products, and live organ donations for the antibodies to the HIV virus. On October 24, 1985, the military began testing all active-duty personnel, in addition to recruits for the National Guard, the reserves, ROTC programs, and military academies (Dalton and Burris, *AIDS and the Law*, 226). Federal prisoners are screened for HIV, as are state prisoners in more than a dozen states (ibid., 239; T. Hammett, *1988 Update: AIDS in Correctional Facilities*

[Washington, D.C.: National Institute of Justice, U.S. Department of Justice, 1988], 3).

13. See Howard L. Minkoff and Sheldon H. Landesman, "The Case for Routinely Offering Prenatal Testing for Human Immunodeficiency Virus," *American Journal of Obstetrics and Gynecology* 159 (1988): 793–794, and Sheldon Landesman, Howard Minkoff, Susan Holman et al., "Serosurvey of Human Immunodeficiency Virus Infection in Parturients," *Journal of the American Medical Association* 258 (1987): 2701, 2703. These studies recommend that HIV testing, accompanied by counseling, consent, and privacy, be routinely offered to all pregnant women where there is both seroprevalence and poor identification of people at risk.

A California bill would require blood specimens already taken for syphilis screening to be tested for HIV except where the woman being tested refuses in writing. Georgia would require that every pregnant woman or any high-risk group of pregnant women, as designated by the Department of Health and Human Services, be tested for a sexually transmitted disease. Illinois would require the initial examination of pregnant women to include a blood test for exposure to AIDS. Washington would require all women seeking prenatal care to be tested for AIDS, pre-AIDS, or the AIDS antibody, and would make it the duty of the attending physician to ensure that the examination occurs and that a report is filed by the local health officer. Rhode Island would require that all persons having a blood test or being treated by a physician, hospital, or clinic be tested for the AIDS antibody, including those being tested (1) prior to application for a marriage license, (2) for pregnancy, (3) for any sexually transmitted diseases, (4) in conjunction with an abortion clinic, and (5) as part of a drug dependency program, including all persons admitted to a hospital as an in-patient. Positive tests should be reported to the department of health.

14. *Plowman* v. *U.S. Dept. of the Army,* 698 F. Supp. 627 (E.D. Va. 1988) (nonconsensual HIV antibody testing of a civilian employee of the military); *Aviles* v. *United States,* 696 F. Supp. 217 (E.D. La. 1988) (HIV antibody test conducted on a U.S. Coast Guard member during a mandatory physical examination).

15. *Leckelt* v. *Board of Commissioners of Hospital District No. 1,* 714 F. Supp. 1377 (E.D. La. 1989).

16. Leonard Glantz, "A Nation of Suspects: Drug Testing and the Fourth Amendment," *American Journal of Public Health* 79 (1988): 1427–1431.

17. *Glover* v. *Eastern Nebraska Community Office of Retardation,* 867 F.2d 461 (8th Cir. 1989).

18. *Jacobson* v. *Massachusetts,* 197 U.S. 11 (1905). See also *Hanzel* v. *Arter,* 625 F. Supp. 1259 (S.D. Ohio 1985).

19. *Jacobson* v. *Massachusetts,* 197 U.S. at 28.

20. *Ex parte Clemente,* 61 Cal. App. 666, 215 P. 698 (Cal. Dis. Ct. App. 1923).

21. See Larry Gostin and William J. Curran, "Legal Control Measures for AIDS: Reporting Requirements, Surveillance, Quarantine, and Regulation of Public Meeting Places," *American Journal of Public Health* 77 (1987): 214, citing *State ex rel. Kennedy* v. *Head,* 185 S.W.2d 530 (Tenn. 1945) and *Ex parte Caselli,* 204 P. 364 (Mont. 1922) (venereal disease); *Greene* v. *Edwards,* 265 S.E.2d (W. Va. 1980) (tuberculosis); *Crayton* v. *Larrabee,* 220 N.Y. 493 (N.Y. 1917), *aff'd* 1147 N.Y.S. 1105 (smallpox); *People* v. *Tait,* 103 N.E. 750, 752 (1913) (scarlet fever); *Kirk* v. *Wyman,* 83 S.C. 372, 65 S.E. 387 (1909) (leprosy); and *Hurst* v. *Warner,* 102 Mich. 238 (Mich. 1894) (cholera). See also *Jew Ho* v. *Williamson,* 103 F. 10 (N.D. Cal. 1900) (bubonic plague).

22. *Jacobson* v. *Massachusetts* 197 U.S. 11 (1905).
23. See, for example, California Health and Safety Code, sec. 3123; Florida Statutes Annotated, sec. 381.231; New Jersey Revised Statutes, sec. 26:4–15; New York Public Health Law, sec. 2101(1).
24. *Jew Ho* v. *Williamson,* 103 F. 10 (N.D. Cal. 1900).
25. *Reynolds* v. *McNichols,* 488 F.2d 1378 (10th Cir. 1973) (the court upheld a city "hold and treat" ordinance challenged by a prostitute. The ordinance authorized limited detention in jail without bond for the purpose of examination and treatment of one reasonably suspected of having a venereal disease when the prostitute was arrested and charged with solicitation).
26. *Buck* v. *Bell,* 274 U.S. 200 (1927) (the Court upheld a law authorizing the compulsory sterilization of a mentally impaired woman to prevent another generation of "imbeciles"). But see *Wentzel* v. *Montgomery General Hospital, Inc.,* 293 Md. 685, 447 A.2d 1244 (1982), *cert. denied,* 459 U.S. 1147 (1983) (right to privacy and bodily integrity to be free of sterilization).
27. For a thorough discussion, see Gostin and Curran, "Legal Control Measures for AIDS," 214–218. Also see *Broadway Books* v. *Gene Roberts,* 642 F. Supp. 486 (E.D. Tenn. 1986) (upholding an AIDS ordinance regulating the time, place, and manner of business for sex shops over equal protection challenge). See Catherine Damme, "Controlling Genetic Diseases Through Law," *University of California Davis Law Review* 15 (1982): 805 n. 10., citing *City of New Orleans* v. *Dukes,* 427 U.S. 297, 303 (1976); and *Massachusetts Board of Retirement* v. *Murgia,* 427 U.S. 307, 314–16 (1976).
28. *In re Colyer,* 660 P.2d 738 (Wash. 1983).
29. Janet Gallagher, "Prenatal Invasions and Interventions: What's Wrong with Fetal Rights," *Harvard Women's Law Journal* 10 (1987): 9.
30. See Laurence H. Tribe, *American Constitutional Law* (Mineola, N.Y.: Foundation Press, 1988), 1439–1450.
31. "Although . . . compelled blood tests . . . have sometimes been upheld on a showing of clear necessity, procedural regularity, and minimal pain, in each case the matter has been taken with enough seriousness to warrant a conclusion that an aspect of personhood was at stake, and that the government's burden was to provide more than minimal justification for its action" (ibid., 1331–1332).
32. *Satz* v. *Perlmutter,* 362 So. 2d 160 (1978), citing *Union Pacific Railway* v. *Botsford,* 141 U.S. 250 (1891) (privacy premised on bodily integrity); *Superintendent of Belchertown* v. *Saikewicz,* 373 Mass. 728, 370 N.E.2d 417 (1979): *Wentzel* v. *Montgomery General Hospital,* 293 Md. 685, 447 A.2d 1244 (1982) (sterilization and bodily integrity); *Bartling* v. *Superior Court of Los Angeles,* 163 Cal. App. 3d 186, 209 Cal. Rptr. 220 (1984) ("The constitutional right of privacy guarantees to the individual the freedom to reject, or refuse to consent to intrusions of his bodily integrity"); *Foody* v. *Manchester Memorial,* 482 A.2d 713 (1984) (privacy encompasses bodily integrity); *Riese* v. *St. Mary's Hospital,* 196 Cal. App. 3d 1388, 243 Cal. Rptr. 241 (1987) (life-sustaining treatment); *Severns* v. *Wilmington Medical Center,* 421 A.2d 1334; *In re A.C.,* 533 A.2d 611, 539 A.2d 203 (1988).
33. Lo et al., "Voluntary Screening for Human Immunodeficiency Virus (HIV) Infection," 727.
34. Ibid. See also Frank S. Rhame and Dennis G. Maki, "The Case for Wider Use of Testing for HIV Infection," *New England Journal of Medicine* 320 (1989): 1248. For arguments against routine AIDS counseling and HIV testing of women not in

designated high-risk groups, see CDC, "Recommendations," 721, 724. The argument that women's sex partners can be protected through mandatory testing is weakened by data indicating that female-to-male transmission occurs, but much less commonly than male-to-female transmission (Guinan and Hardy, "Epidemiology of AIDS in Women," 2039).

35. P. A. Clay Stephens, "U.S. Women and HIV Infection," *New England Journal of Public Policy* 4 (1988): 381, 389.

36. Knowledge of seropositivity does not always lead pregnant women to elect abortion and decide against repeat pregnancies. In one study of seropositive women, the rate of elective abortion and the rate of repeat pregnancies were nearly identical (Peter Selwyn, E. Schoenbaum, K. Davenny et al., "Prospective Study of HIV Infection and Pregnancy Outcomes in IV Drug Users," *Journal of the American Medical Association* 261 [1989]: 1289; see also Howard Minkoff, Deepak Nanoa, Rachel Menez, et al., "Pregnancies Resulting in Infants with AIDS or ARC: Follow-up of Mothers, Children, and Subsequently Born Siblings," *Obstetrics and Gynecology* 69 [1987]: 288, and Ann Sunderland, G. Moroso, and M. Berthaud, "Influence of HIV Infection on Pregnancy Decisions" (Abstract 6607), in *Programs and Abstracts of the 4th International AIDS Conference, Stockholm, June 1988.*

37. See generally Levy, "Constitutional Implications," 217.

38. *New York Times,* September 10, 1989, p. 5. Similar cases have been brought in Massachusetts, Florida, South Carolina, Virginia, and Illinois (*Chicago Tribune,* May 14, 1989, zone c, p. 2, zone d, p. 1; *Newsday,* July 1, 1989, p. 6). For a discussion of wrongful birth actions, see Chapter 8 of this volume.

39. Ronald Dworkin, "The Great Abortion Case," *New York Review of Books,* June 29, 1989, pp. 49–53.

40. Martha A. Field, "Controlling the Woman to Protect the Fetus," *Law, Medicine and Health Care* 17 (1989): 114–129.

41. Institute of Medicine, National Academy of Sciences, *Confronting AIDS: Update 1988* (Washington, D.C.: National Academy Press, 1988), 110. The National Academy of Sciences stated that the most compelling way of significantly reducing the spread of the AIDS antibody is through education.

42. See Charles Spiegel, "Privacy, Sodomy, AIDS and the Schools: Case Studies in Equal Protection," in *1986 Annual Survey of American Law* (New York: New York University School of Law, 1987), 221–253.

43. U.S. Constitution, amend. XIV, sec. 1.

44. *Bolling* v. *Sharpe,* 347 U.S. 497 (1954).

45. Tribe, *American Constitutional Law,* 1436–1443.

46. *Powell* v. *Department of Corrections,* 647 F. Supp. 968 (N.D. Okla. 1986) (a homosexual with AIDS treated differently from homosexuals without AIDS was not denied equal protection); *Doe* v. *Coughlin,* 71 N.Y.2d 48, 518 N.E.2d 536, 523 N.Y.S.2d 782 (1987) (conjugal visitation rights denied an AIDS victim); *Baez* v. *Rapping,* 680 F. Supp. 112 (S.D. N.Y. 1988) (prison use of a "precaution sheet" identifying an AIDS victim and segregation upheld); *Lewis* v. *Prison Health Services, Inc.,* Civil Action No. 88-1247 (E.D. Pa. November 22, 1988); *Muhammed* v. *Carlson,* 845 F.2d 175 (8th Cir. 1988), *cert. denied,* 109 S. Ct. 1346 (1989).

47. *Lewis* v. *Prison Health Services, Inc.,* Civil Action No. 88-1247 (E.D. Pa. November 22, 1988).

48. Ibid. See also *Massachusetts Board of Retirement* v. *Murgia,* 427 U.S. 307, 312 (1976).

49. *Aviles* v. *United States,* 696 F. Supp. 217 (E.D. La. 1988).
50. A mentally retarded girl was successful in *Martinez* v. *School Board of Hillsborough County, Florida,* 861 F.2d 1502, 692 F. Supp. 1293 (1988). In addition to the equal protection clause, the court relied heavily on the federal Education of the Handicapped Act and the Rehabilitation Act of 1972, 87 Stat. 394 (1973) (codified 29 U.S.C., sec. 794 (1982). See *Ray* v. *School District of DeSota County,* 666 F. Supp. 1524 (1987).
51. But see *Williamson* v. *Lee Optical,* 348 U.S. 483, 488–90 (1955).
52. Ibid.
53. *Dandridge* v. *Williams,* 397 U.S. 471, 486 (1970).
54. *New York Transit Authority* v. *Beazer,* 440 U.S. 568 (1979).
55. Tribe, *American Constitutional Law,* 1450.
56. *Craig* v. *Boren,* 429 U.S. 190, 197 (1976).
57. *Skinner* v. *Oklahoma* 316 U.S. (1942).
58. *Memorial Hospital* v. *Maricopa County,* 415 U.S. 250 (1974).
59. *Washington* v. *Davis,* 426 U.S. 229 (1974).
60. *Korematsu* v. *United States,* 323 U.S. 414 (1944). See also *In re Griffiths,* 413 U.S. 717 (1973).
61. See CDC, "Acquired Immunodeficiency Syndrome (AIDS) Among Blacks and Hispanics—United States," *Morbidity and Mortality Weekly Report* 35 (1985): 655. See also "Women with HIV," in *Report of the President's Commission on the Human Immunodeficiency Virus Epidemic* (Washington, D.C.: President's Commission, 1988), 13, and Venetia Porter, "Minorities and HIV Infection," *New England Journal of Public Policy* 4 (1988): 371. See Dalton and Burris, *AIDS and the Law,* 281–283 (impact of AIDS on minorities).
    For a broad discussion of minority women's reproductive health problems and practices, including their less frequent use of prenatal screening, see Laurie Nsiah-Jefferson, "Reproductive Laws, Women of Color, and Low Income Women," in *Reproductive Laws for the 1990's,* ed. Sherrill Cohen and Nadine Taub (Clifton, N.J.: Humana Press, 1989), 23, 32–34, and Mary Sue Henifin, Ruth Hubbard, and Judy Norsigian, "Prenatal Screening," in *Reproductive Laws for the 1990's,* 155–183.
62. See Gostin and Ziegler, "Review of AIDS-Related Policy," 10.
63. Lawrence K. Altman, "Who's Stricken and How: AIDS Pattern Is Shifting," *New York Times,* February 5, 1989, p. 1.
64. Over half the CDC-reported cases of women with adult AIDS involved women who have been intravenous drug users (CDC, "HIV/AIDS Surveillance Report," September 26, 1988). In specific studies, the percentage has been as high as 77 percent (Arye Rubinstein and Larry Bernstein, "The Epidemiology of Pediatric Acquired Immunodeficiency Syndrome," *Clinical Immunology and Immunopathology* 40 [1986]: 118; see also Guinan and Hardy, "Epidemiology of AIDS in Women," 2039–2042, and DHHS, *Report of the Surgeon General's Workshop on Children with HIV Infection and Their Families,* 34). European studies also link intravenous drug use to infant AIDS (J. Q. Mok, C. Giaquinto, A. DeRossi et al., "Infants Born to Mothers Seropositive for HIV," *Lancet* [1987]: 1164, 1167).
    See generally Ellie E. Schoenbaum, D. Hartel, P. Selwyn et al., "Risk Factors for HIV Infection in IV Drug Users," *New England Journal of Medicine* 321 (1989): 874, 875 (associating the higher prevalence of HIV infection among black and Hispanic intravenous drug users to needle sharing with strangers).

65. Ronald Bayer, *Private Acts, Social Consequences: AIDS and the Politics of Public Health* (New York: Free Press, 1989), 72–100, 137–168. See Institute of Medicine, *Confronting Aids*, 6 ("fear of discrimination is a major constraint to widespread acceptance of many potentially effective public health measures").

66. Many AIDS patients suffer severe psychological disorders, including paranoia, suicidal tendencies, depression, and heightened fears of rejection and abandonment by family and friends (Dalton and Burris, *AIDS and the Law*, 283–284).

67. See New York Health Law, sec. 206; Colorado rules and Regulations for Communicable Disease Control, rule 2.8; Texas. Revised Civil Statutes, art. 4419b-I, sec. 3.06 (communicable disease confidentiality statute).

68. Even the release of a negative test result could be damaging because of the assumption that the person undergoing the testing is in a high-risk group.

69. Discouraging high-risk individuals from seeking testing, counseling, and treatment would contravene present public policy (Gostin and Ziegler, "Review of AIDS-Related Policy," 10).

70. *Washington* v. *Davis*, 426 U.S. 229, 240 (1976).

71. *Frontiero* v. *Richardson*, 411 U.S. 677 (1973).

72. *Reed* v. *Reed*, 404 U.S. 71 (1971).

73. *Nashville Gas Co.* v. *Satty*, 434 U.S. 136 (1977).

74. *General Electric Co.* v. *Gilbert*, 429 U.S. 125 (1976); *Gedulgig* v. *Aiello*, 417 U.S. 484 (1974). But see *Newport News Shipbuilding and Dry Dock Co.* v. *Equal Employment Opportunity Commission*, 462 U.S. 669, 684 (1983).

75. Gallagher, "Prenatal Invasions and Interventions," 9.

76. U.S. Constitution, amend. IV.

77. *Katz* v. *United States*, 389 U.S. 347 (1967).

78. *O'Connor* v. *Ortega*, 480 U.S. 709, 719 (1966). See also *Winston* v. *Lee*, 470 U.S. 753 (1985) (balancing test applied to determine whether invasion of the body cavity or of bodily fluids was unreasonable under the Fourth Amendment). In *Plowman* v. *U.S. Dept. of the Army*, the court speculated that the government's nonconsensual testing and information disclosures were not offensive to the Fourth Amendment, since "the blood sample necessary for plaintiff's HIV test had already been extracted for the purpose of other, arguably consensual diagnostic tests" and because "the Army surgical personnel had a medical need to know a patient's HIV status in the event that surgical procedures became necessary" (698 F. Supp. 627, 636 [E.D. Va. 1988]). The court relied on *United States* v. *City and County of San Francisco*, No. 84-7089 (N.D. Cal. August 28, 1987) (unpublished opinion) and *Local 1812, American Federation of Government Employees* v. *United States Dept. of State*, 662 F. Supp. 50 (D.D.C. 1987).

79. *Glover* v. *Eastern Nebraska Community Office of Retardation*, 867 F.2d 461 (8th Cir. 1989), citing *Schmerber* v. *California*, 384 U.S. 757, 767–768 (1966).

80. *Schmerber* v. *California*, 384 U.S. 757, 767–768 (1966).

81. Ibid.

82. In *Rochin* v. *California*, 342 U.S. 165 (1952), the policy ordered that the stomach of a suspected narcotics dealer be pumped to retrieve two capsules of morphine. The Supreme Court found that the police had violated the defendant's due process rights because such action "shocks the conscience" and "is bound to offend even hardened sensibilities." In another case, *Winston* v. *Lee*, 470 U.S. 753 (1985), the Court held that surgery to remove a bullet needed for evidence in a criminal case would violate the defendant's constitutional rights. The Court refused to distinguish be-

tween minor and major surgery, saying that less drastic intrusions would have to be decided on a case-by-case basis.

83. See, for example, *Shoemaker v. Handel*, 795 F.2d 1136 (3rd Cir. 1986) (administrative search exception applies to validate warrantless breath and urine testing of employees in the heavily regulated horse-racing industry), and *Division 241 Amalgamated Transit Union (AFL-CIO) v. Suscy*, 538 F.2d 1264 (7th Cir. 1976) (no reasonable expectation of privacy exists with regard to submitting to blood and urine tests following a bus driver's involvement in a serious accident or when suspected of being intoxicated or under the influence of narcotics).

84. *Leckelt v. Board of Commissioners of Hospital District No. 1*, 714 F. Supp. 1377 (E.D. La. 1989).

85. *Glover v. Eastern Nebraska Community Office of Retardation*, 867 F.2d 461 (8th Cir. 1989).

86. Ibid., 465.

87. *Griswold v. Connecticut*, 381 U.S. 479 (1965).

88. *Buck v. Bell*, 274 U.S. 200 (1927).

89. *Roe v. Wade*, 410 U.S. 113 (1973).

90. *Zablocki v. Redhail*, 434 U.S. 374 (1978).

91. *Pierce v. Society of Sisters*, 268 U.S. 510 (1925).

92. *Griswold v. Connecticut*, 381 U.S. 479 (1965). The court wrote that "specific guarantees in the Bill of Rights have penumbras, formed by emanations from those guarantees" that protect a persons's right to engage in private activity free from governmental interference (ibid., 484).

93. *Roe v. Wade*, 410 U.S. 113 (1973); *Doe v. Bolton*, 410 U.S. 179 (1973).

94. *Thornburgh v. American College of Obstetricians and Gynecologists*, 476 U.S. 747 (1986). Under the express language of the Fourteenth Amendment, no state may "deprive any person of life, liberty, or property, without due process of law."

95. *Roe v. Wade*, 410 U.S. at 163.

96. *Webster v. Reproductive Health Services*, 109 S. Ct. 3040 (1989), reversing 851 F.2d 1071 (8th Cir. 1988).

97. *Bartling v. Superior Court of Los Angeles*, 163 Cal. App. 3d 186, 209 Cal. Rptr. 220 (1984) ("The constitutional right of privacy guarantees to the individual the freedom to reject, or refuse to consent to intrusions of his bodily integrity").

98. *Superintendent of Belchertown v. Saikewicz*, 373 Mass. 728, 370 N.E.2d 417, 424 (1979).

99. *Schmerber v. California*, 384 U.S. 757 (1966).

100. *Raleigh Fitkin-Paul Morgan Memorial Hospital v. Anderson*, 201 A.2d 537 (N.J. 1964).

101. *In the Matter of Jamaica Hospital*, 128 Misc. 2d 1006, 491 N.Y.S.2d 898, 899–900 (1985).

102. Ibid.

103. *In re A.C.*, 533 A.2d 611, 614–615 (App. D.C. 1987).

104. Ibid., 615, n. 4. In a subsequent review of *In re A.C.*, the District of Columbia Court of Appeals decided that a pregnant woman has a right to bodily integrity that almost always outweighs the rights of the fetus (—— F.2d —— [D.C. Cir. April 26, 1990] [en banc]).

105. Institute of Medicine, *Confronting AIDS*, 110.

106. See, for example, Benjamin P. Sachs, Ruth Tuomala, and Fredaric Frigoletto, "Acquired Immunodeficiency Syndrome: Suggested Protocol for counseling and

Screening in Pregnancy," *Obstetrics and Gynecology* 70 (1987): 408, 410; B. J.
Thomson and A. G. Dalgleish, "Human Retroviruses and Paediatric Disease,"
Archives of Disease in Childhood 62 (1987): 634; and Anthony J. Pinching and
Donald J. Jeffries, "AIDS and HTLV-III/LAV Infection: Consequences for Obstetrics and Perinatal Medicine," *British Journal of Obstetrics and Gynecology* 92
(1985): 1216. Some studies do not specifically recommend offering patients the
option of abortion (see, for example, Howard Minkoff, "Care of Pregnant Women
Infected with Human Immunodeficiency Virus," *Journal of the American Medical
Association* 258 [1987]: 258). One study accuses health-care practitioners of over-
emphasizing the abortion option, even to the point of offering third-trimester abortions (Stephens, "U.S. Women and HIV Infection," 390).

107. See *Harbeson* v. *Parke-Davis, Inc.*, 98 Wash. 2d 460, 656 P.2d 483 (1983) (detailing the parameters of action for wrongful birth and wrongful life.)

108. See Constance B. Wofsy, "Human Immunodeficiency Virus Infection in Women,"
Journal of the American Medical Association 257 (1987): 2074, 2075.

109. See Harlon L. Dalton, "Aids in Blackface," *Daedalus* 118 (1989): 205, 220.

110. *Maher* v. *Roe*, 476 U.S. 747 (1986).

111. *Harris* v. *McRae*, 448 U.S. 297 (1980).

112. *Webster* v. *Reproductive Health Services*, 109 S. Ct. 3040 (1989), reversing 851
F.2d 1071 (8th Cir. 1988).

113. See Schoenbaum et al., "Risk Factors," 874, 875.

114. Nanula, "Protecting Confidentiality," 316; Heaney, "Constitutional Right of Informational Privacy," 14. See also Chapter 9 of this volume.

115. *Thornburgh* v. *American College of Obstetrics and Gynecology*, 476 U.S. 747
(1986).

116. *Whalen* v. *Roe*, 429 U.S. 589 (1977).

117. See *Plowman* v. *U.S. Dept. of the Army*, 698 F. Supp. 627 (E.D. Va. 1988), citing
cases.

118. See *Woods* v. *White et al.*, 689 F. Supp. 874 (W.D. Wis. 1988), citing *Kimbelin* v.
United States Dept. of Justice, 788 F.2d 434, 438 (7th Cir. 1986), *Fadjou* v. *Coon*,
633 F.2d 1172, 1176 (5th Cir. 1981), *United States* v. *Westinghouse Electric Corp.*,
638 F.2d 570, 577 (1980), and *Borucki* v. *Ryan*, 658 F. Supp. 325, 330 (D. Mass.
1986).

119. *Borucki* v. *Ryan*, 827 F.2d 836, 846 (1st Cir. 1987).

120. *Woods* v. *White et al.*, 689 F. Supp. 874 (W.D. Wis. 1988).

121. *Plowman* v. *U.S. Dept. of the Army*, 698 F. Supp. 627 (E.D. Va. 1988).

122. Ibid., 663.

123. See note 8 (state constitutions), note 9 (tort law), note 10 (contract and breach of
confidence law), and notes 11–13 (state statutes and proposed legislation).

124. See note 9.

125. See notes 9 and 10.

126. See *Gray* v. *Grunnazle*, 423 Pa. 144, 223 A.2d 663 (1966) (failure to warn a patient
of the risk of paralysis in a spinal operation constituted battery).

127. See, for example, *Belair* v. *Carter*, 13 Ohio App. 2d 113, 234 N.E.2d 311 (1960)
(failure to warn a patient of the risk of radiation burns held to be a battery).

128. See *Jones* v. *Irvin*, 602 F. Supp. 399 (S.D. Ill. 1985) (a physician could be liable for
failure to advise a patient of the proper dosage of medicine, which caused her to
suffer a serious adverse reaction).

129. "In the context of ordinary medical therapy, the doctrine of informed consent is

usually defined as a duty to warn a patient of: 1. material risks; 2. possible complications expected; 3. unexpected risks of the proposed treatment; 4. reasonable alternatives to the treatment; 5. risks and comparative benefits of the alternatives; and 6. in most cases, the effects of nontreatment" (Weldon-Linne et al., "AIDS-Virus Antibody Testing," 208).

130. *Plowman v. U.S. Dept. of the Army*, 698 F. Supp. 627, 636 (E.D. Va. 1988).

131. See *Pratt v. Davis*, 118 Ill. App. 161 (1905) (a physician removed a patient's ovaries and uterus without her consent).

132. See chapter 12 of this volume for a discussion of ethical issues in obtaining meaningful informed consent. See Chapter 8 of this volume for a discussion of the relation between informed consent and the standard of medical care in the context of medical malpractice.

133. But see *Tarasoff v. Regents of the University of California*, 551 P.2d 334 (Cal. 1976).

134. *Restatement (2d) of Torts*, sec. 652 A–I.

135. See, for example, *Phillips v. Smalley Maintenance Services*, 435 So. 2d 705 (Ala. 1983).

136. *Restatement (2d) of Torts*, sec. 652B, comment b.

137. See, for example, *Bennett v. Norban*, 151 A.2d 476, 477 (Pa. 1959).

138. *Phillips v. Smalley Maintenance Services*, 435 So. 2d 705 (Ala. 1983).

139. Nanula, "Protecting Confidentiality," 323.

140. California (1985 California Legislative Services, ch. 1519, sec. 199.35–38), Wisconsin (1985 Laws of Wisconsin 73, sec. 103.15, sec. 146.025), Florida (1985 Laws of Florida, ch. 85-52, sec. 381.606).

141. Closen et al., "AIDS: Testing Democracy," 903–916; Mills et al., "Acquired Immunodeficiency Syndrome," 932.

142. AIDS patients may have "a civil claim for damages against the person making the wrongful disclosure" (Mills et al., "Acquired Immunodeficiency Syndrome," 932).

143. *Restatement (2d) of Torts*, sec. 572 (liability without proof of special damages for imputation of loathsome diseases).

144. *Hammonds v. Aetna Casualty & Surety Co.*, 243 F. Supp. 793, 801 (N.D. Ohio 1965) ("The unauthorized revelation of medical secrets, or any confidential communication given in the course of treatment, is tortious conduct which may be the basis for an action in damages"). See also *Tower v. Hirschhorn*, 397 Mass. 581, 588 (1986) (a physician divulged confidential medical information about a patient without her consent).

145. *Tuscon Medical Center, Inc. v. Rowles*, 520 P.2d 518 (Ariz. 1974) (medical information qualifying for the physician–patient privilege did not lose its privileged status by being incorporated into hospital medical records).

146. See generally Natula, "Protecting Confidentiality," 315.

147. *Humphers v. Interstate*, 696 P.2d 527 (Or. 1985) (physician's disclosure of a birth mother's identity to an adult daughter adopted as an infant constituted breach of confidence rather than invasion of privacy).

148. See, for example, California Health and Safety Code, sec. 199.20–23 (West 1985); Wisconsin Statutes Annotated, sec. 146.025 (West 1986).

149. See *South Florida Blood Service v. Rasmussen*, 500 So. 2d 533 (Fla. 1987).

150. *Anderson v. Strong Memorial Hospital*, 531 N.Y.S.2d 735 (Sup. 1988).

151. 150. *Plowman v. U.S. Dept. of the Army*, 698 F. Supp. 627, 637 (E.D. Va. 1988).

152. Ibid., 637.

153. There is currently no cure or highly effective treatment for either adult or pediatric AIDS (Mills et al., "Acquired Immunodeficiency Syndrome," 934). AZT, licensed for use in the treatment of children in 1989, appears to ameliorate the symptoms of mental deterioration without, however, altering the fatal course of AIDS. In the meantime, AIDS victims have had to fight for access to new drug treatments. See, for example, *Weaver* v. *Reagen,* 701 F. Supp. 717 (W.D. Mo. 1988) (class action to obtain Medicaid coverage for Retrovir).

154. Opponents of pregnancy interventions in the first two trimesters argue that they are inconsistent with *Roe* v. *Wade,* 410 U.S. 113 (1973), which held that the state may not assert a compelling interest in fetal life until viability—roughly, the third trimester. Were the view expressed by Chief Justice Rehnquist in *Webster* v. *Reproductive Health Services* that the state has a compelling interest in the fetus at every stage of pregnancy to prevail, the Supreme Court could easily find that legislated prenatal testing requirements are valid notwithstanding women's claims to privacy, autonomy, and bodily integrity.

8

Legal Issues in Voluntary Screening for HIV Infection in Pregnant Women

PATRICIA A. KING

Those who provide medical care for women of reproductive age[1] are understandably concerned about the nature and extent of their legal obligations to screen for HIV infection, particularly if their patients are pregnant.[2] Information provided by screening tests may be relevant to the pregnant woman's health care, including management of her pregnancy; may be pertinent to the pregnant woman's and, in some circumstances, the biological father's assessment of reproductive risks; and has implications for the health status of the fetus.

In general, the physician's legal obligation is grounded in the physician's fiduciary obligation to the patient and the patient's right to self-determination.[3] Specifically, the legal standard of care for physicians, including the obligation owed to pregnant women, is that a physician "must have and use the knowledge, skill and care ordinarily possessed by the members of the profession in good standing."[4] Applying this legal standard in the context of HIV infection and pregnancy is complicated. First, legal precedents governing the physician's obligations about disclosure and counseling are of relatively recent origin.[5] The requirements that exist are broadly stated, constrained by the exigencies of litigation and focused on physical risks of harm. They therefore offer physicians limited guidance for a range of therapeutic dilemmas. Moreover, although this chapter focuses only on the obligations of physicians, a variety of people may be involved in the patient's care. This fact raises the question of who, in addition to the patient's personal physician, has fiduciary obligations. Courts have not resolved this question, but they have been willing to expand the circumstances in which the physician–patient relationship exists.[6]

Second, HIV infection has social, psychological, and ethical dimensions that extend far beyond those found elsewhere in medicine, with the possible exception of medical genetics. As a result, the legal precedents are of especially limited value in the HIV context. For example, the prevalence of HIV infection varies dramatically from one part of the country to another, thus putting at issue the question of whether the legal standard will be applied in a manner that takes account of the national prevalence of HIV infection or some prevalence of infection based on smaller geographical units.

Third, whether a woman is at risk of HIV infection has implications for the pregnant woman's reproductive decisions. In other contexts, the general legal standard has been interpreted to include making available in a timely fashion appropriate diagnostic procedures and information concerning reproductive risks to pregnant women. Finally, the legal obligation of the physician may extend beyond the boundaries of the traditional physician–patient relationship. Information about the pregnant woman offers a basis for predicting the risk of HIV infection in her fetus. Several questions are raised. For example, what responsibilities, if any, does a physician have to the unborn child? Does the physician have an obligation to disclose the unborn child's risk of harm to the genetic father?

This chapter analyzes and evaluates the legal standard of care in connection with voluntary screening for HIV infection in pregnant women. It suggests that physicians may be potentially liable for (1) failure to diagnose, (2) failure to inform adequately, and (3) failure to provide appropriate counseling in screening for HIV infection.[7] From the perspective of avoiding possible legal liability, the chapter concludes that health-care professionals should routinely offer HIV testing to all pregnant women in circumstances that permit them to decide whether to consent to or refuse the test.

Requisite Knowledge, Skill, and Care

In general, physicians have an obligation to possess and use expert knowledge, skill, and care in the interest of their patient's well-being. This obligation is judged in accordance with customary professional standards.[8] One commentator summarizes the standard of conduct applicable to a physician's conduct as follows: "(1) a reasonable or ordinary degree of skill and learning; (2) commonly possessed and exercised by members of the profession; (3) who are of the same school or system as the defendant; (4) and who practice in the same or similar localities; (5) and exercise of the defendant's good judgment."[9] Historically, the professional standard took account of where the physician practiced. Courts reasoned that physicians who practiced in small or rural communities did not have the same resources or opportunities to stay abreast of changes in medical practice as did physicians in less isolated environments. In some states, dissatisfaction with local standards that were thought to be too narrow, and thus too lax, led to the adoption of similar locality rules. As a result, a physician could also be held to the standard of reasonable practitioners in localities that were essentially like his or her own. Modern communication and educational techniques and technologies, however, have lessened the differences in resources and opportunities among physicians. As a result, more and more courts, particularly in cases involving specialists, have abandoned geographical boundaries altogether and have applied national standards. Since many of the health professionals involved in the private care of pregnant women are likely to be specialists, their conduct will typically be governed by national standards.

If we assume that physicians will be judged in accordance with national standards, vexing questions remain about what the national standard requires in the context of HIV infection. The prevalent modes of transmission of HIV are through sexual intercourse and intravenous drug use. As a consequence, it is possible for anyone engaging in such behaviors to be exposed to the virus. As a practical matter, however, the virus is concentrated in specific urban areas with similar demographic patterns. As a result, persons engaging in these behaviors are at especially high risk in communities that already have a high prevalence of HIV infection. Physicians in high-prevalence areas may have adopted practices that would rarely be found in low-prevalence areas. Assume, for example, that in high-prevalence areas, physicians offer HIV screening to all pregnant women. Assume, further, that physicians in low-prevalence areas offer screening for HIV infection to only pregnant women whose medical or social history indicates a higher than average risk for HIV infection. It is possible, however, that a pregnant woman in a low-prevalence area with no known risk factors is in fact infected with HIV. In any subsequent lawsuit for negligent failure to diagnose the infection, an important issue will be whether the physician should have acted on the basis of prevalence data for his or her locality or national prevalence data in deciding whether to offer the screening test. The defending physician will argue that any governing standard should take account of the community's characteristics, particularly prevalence data, and the behavior of reasonable physicians practicing with awareness of those data. The defending physician will also argue that the costs associated with screening exceed the potential benefit of the identification of HIV infection in a very small number of persons. Alternatively, the plaintiff might counter the defendant's arguments by asserting that national HIV incidence data, in light of the costs of administering the test, are high enough to warrant universal voluntary screening for all despite the low prevalence of the virus in a particular community.[10] The plaintiff's argument might be strengthened if she could further demonstrate that it was routine to screen universally on a voluntary basis for other conditions with similar frequencies of occurrence.[11]

Knowledge to be possessed

Every American household should have received from the federal government a mailing on the subject of HIV infection.[12] Minimally, it would seem that physicians should have knowledge equivalent to the knowledge possessed by the educated public. Moreover, physicians should have knowledge of data issued by the Centers for Disease Control and of guidelines issued by relevant professional bodies. Professionally generated information and guidelines for practice may be reliable authorities in civil lawsuits.[13] Finally, those physicians possessing superior knowledge will be judged by what they actually know even if others in the profession would not generally be aware of such information.

Exercising reasonable care: utilization of skills and knowledge

In addition to possessing the requisite knowledge, the individual practitioner must use this special knowledge and skill appropriately. There are two related, yet distinct, issues that face physicians with respect to screening pregnant women for the presence of HIV. First, physicians want to identify with the greatest possible accuracy those women who should be tested for HIV infection—a diagnostic function. Second, physicians want to know what questions should be asked of pregnant women and what information should be disclosed to them in order to meet counseling obligations.

Who should be tested?

Whether physicians have exercised reasonable care with respect to a diagnostic function is judged by professional standards. In determining which patients should be tested, physicians have basically two options. They can treat everyone alike and offer HIV testing to all patients. Alternatively, they can attempt to identify some appropriate subset of patients who should be offered HIV testing. In the context of HIV infection and pregnancy, that patient subset might consist of high-risk as distinct from low-risk women. A woman might be high risk in terms of her behavioral patterns and/or because she lives in a high-prevalence area. On balance, for reasons developed below, from a legal liability perspective, I believe that physicians would be prudent to discuss and offer HIV screening to all patients.

The identification of patients as high or low risk is a more complicated matter than is usually encountered with respect to the utilization of screening and diagnostic tests. The risk–benefit assessment is harder to make about the possibility of HIV infection, especially with asymptomatic patients. Ordinarily, the decision to offer particular patients screening tests involves balancing the benefits of screening against the physical risks of intervention to the patient and the costs to society. For many medical problems, physicians have access to easily obtainable information that provides some guidance for making the assessment. For example, amniocentesis for the purpose of determining whether a fetus has Down's syndrome is recommended in the absence of other risk factors for pregnant women who have reached age 35. The patient's age is not hard to obtain, and typically patients are willing to disclose it. With other genetic conditions, the birth of a child suffering from Down's syndrome signals a need to screen for the disability and to counsel the woman in future pregnancies.

Balancing the benefits against the risks of HIV testing is often uncomplicated as well. For example, it may be known that the pregnant woman is an intravenous drug user. In the vast majority of cases, however, determining who should be tested for HIV infection is difficult. The woman may not have symptoms that might alert a physician to the possibility of HIV infection. A woman may not know or have reason to know that she is at risk of being infected. She may not believe that she has had sexual intercourse with a person who was infected. In addition, although it is possible to identify pregnant women who are at high risk of being infected with HIV by taking an adequate medical and/or social history, in many instances a woman will be reluctant to disclose the information that is predictive of risk. The data are very personal and private. A woman may not want, for example, to discuss her sexual habits, or whether she uses or has used drugs. She may also worry that if she has been exposed to the virus, the information will be disseminated to others in a way that will be harmful to her interests. For all these reasons, an adequate medical or social history might be difficult to obtain.

In view of the difficulty of obtaining pertinent information from patients, a physician practicing in what is perceived to be a low-prevalence area might conclude that attempting to identify high-risk women by their social history is not fruitful and might offer HIV testing to only those patients with obvious or easily discernible risk factors. In addition to the liability risks discussed above, there are factors that suggest that a physician should be cautious in adopting this course of action. Clearly, some pregnant women in low-prevalence areas with no discernible risk factors will be infected. Moreover, physicians will have enormous difficulty in determining whether they practice in high- or low-prevalence areas, especially without the assistance of public health officials. Finally, in a nation with a population as mobile as our own, there is no reason to assume that HIV infection will be confined to those groups or geographical areas already identified as high risk.

Some might argue that offering screening tests to all pregnant patients in low-risk areas is practicing defensive medicine—a practice that should not be encouraged.[14] In the context of HIV infection and pregnancy, however, this argument is not compelling. First, we need to bear in mind that HIV infection is not entirely a biomedical problem. The only foreseeable means of reducing HIV transmission in the near future is by promoting behavioral changes. For a large number of women, their only point of contact with the health-care community is during pregnancy. Thus screening is important for the educational opportunities that it presents.[15] Women can learn about HIV infection; the means of reducing the risk of exposure; and, if seropositive, how to reduce the risk to third parties, including potential offspring. To the extent that HIV infection in women is closely associated with racial, ethnic, class, and behavioral factors, offering testing to all pregnant women not only reduces the likelihood of discrimination and divisiveness in our society concerning HIV infection, but makes it all the more important that educational opportunities are taken advantage of.

Second, and perhaps more important, offering HIV screening to all women affirms their autonomy in making decisions about their bodies and their reproductive options. As Lo et al. point out, "Respecting patient preferences is particularly appropriate when the decisions involve personal issues, such as childbearing, and when medical knowledge is uncertain."[16]

Counseling and disclosure

LEGAL REQUIREMENTS IN GENERAL. The law imposes on physicians two general duties: to disclose information about therapeutic procedures sufficient to allow the patient to make an informed decision, and to obtain consent prior to the initiation of the procedure. There is disagreement concerning the standard by which to judge these duties. Whether physicians have provided legally adequate information (as well as adequate diagnosis) is judged by professional standards in the majority of American jurisdictions. Specifically, a physician's disclosure is judged with reference to what a reasonably prudent physician would have disclosed in the same or similar circumstances. In a significant minority of jurisdictions, however, the determination of whether adequate information has been provided is judged by what a reasonably prudent patient would have considered material under the circumstances. This standard has been referred to as a "lay" or "patient-oriented standard."[17] Under this standard, juries rather than medical experts formulate the standard of disclosure. As Alexander Morgan Capron has pointed out concerning the related area of genetic counseling,

> The lay standard is particularly appropriate . . . because the conduct in question—the comprehensible conveying of information from one person to another—is a matter jurors are capable of determining without medical expertise. Furthermore the adequacy of the informing process turns on value preferences more properly derived from the individual counselee or from community standards of reasonableness than from professional norms of a clinical subspecialty.[18]

For reasons developed below, the lay standard seems particularly appropriate for HIV counseling as well.

Jurisdictions vary in what they require to be disclosed. In general, they require some disclosure about the hazards or risks of the procedure, the nature of the procedure, the anticipated benefits, and the alternatives.[19] There is also a simple requirement that consent be obtained, and, for the most part, the consent need not be in writing. There is no requirement that the patient comprehend what has been disclosed.

Law has shaped the discussion of the ethical requirements of informed consent. The litigation process, in turn, has helped to mold the nature and character of the legal requirements. The President's Commission for the study of Ethical Problems in Medicine and Biomedical and Behavioral Research summarized this impact:

The litigation process has shaped the legal doctrine of informed consent. The nature of the cases coming before the courts led to a particular perspective on the character, failings, and potential of relationships between patients and health care providers. The existence of an injury led courts to concentrate on whether there had been disclosure of the particular risks of the medical procedure rather than to an evaluation of the process of the patient–professional communication as a whole. The need to avoid giving undue weight to a patient's after-the-fact, speculative, and potentially self-serving testimony regarding materiality and causation led to an objective standard that can contradict individual patients' particular values or desires. And the need to identify legal responsibility and potential financial liability led to a particular view of the appropriate roles of members of the health care team. Taken together, these have brought the current law to an uneasy compromise among ethical aspirations, the realities of medical practice, and the exigencies of the litigation process.[20]

LEGAL REQUIREMENTS IN THE HIV CONTEXT. Legal precedents are not easily applied in the context of HIV infection. This is so because, arguably, HIV infection is also not like other medical areas. Lori Andrews points out that "the social, psychological, and ethical impact of medical genetics extends far beyond that of other areas of medicine." Thus legal precedents may not be able to handle all the legal issues raised by genetics.[21] In this regard, HIV infection resembles medical genetics more closely than other infectious diseases with respect to identifying persons as having the disease. As with genetics, the revelation of HIV status can stigmatize and lead to discrimination against the affected person. The stigma potential is enhanced because of the close association of HIV infection with groups—gay persons, African-Americans, Hispanics, and the poor—who are already oppressed and discriminated against in this society. In a real sense, HIV infection, like a genetic disease, is immutable. There is no way to eliminate the condition. At some stage, HIV infection is asymptomatic. In this regard, it resembles genetic predispositions or late-onset disorders. The question of how individuals respond when told of having a fatal or serious illness while apparently healthy is not well understood. At least for HIV-infected women, there is also the inextricable link between having the disease and making the reproductive decisions typically required with a genetic disease or trait.

In reality, the interaction between physician and patient is complex and difficult to analyze in a simplistic way. Physicians must solicit as well as disclose information. Indeed, effective solicitation of information is critical if physicians are to discharge their disclosure functions adequately. The information sought and disclosed may relate to separate events in the treatment process. For example, information may be related to the decision of whether to undergo a screening test (identification of patients to be screened). In addition, disclosure may be required after test results are known, and the content might vary, depending on whether the results were positive or negative. Disclosure may vary according to the interest of the pregnant woman being addressed. For example, disclosure may be related to the pregnant woman's personal interests in health and privacy, or they may be related to her reproductive risks.

Moreover, disclosure of information may range from minimal to disclosure that will result in fully informed consent by the patient. For example, the physician could merely tell the patient that testing is routinely performed unless an objection is made. Alternatively, the physician might provide more complete disclosure by engaging in intense face-to-face discussion with the patient. In this discussion, the physician could inform the patient of the risks and benefits of the procedure, as well as those associated with information obtained from the procedure, including the possibility that the results, if positive, might be disseminated to others. Finally, physicians might aim for a level of disclosure somewhere between the two extreme positions just described. For example, a physician might hand out a printed brochure containing comprehensive information that invites the patient to take the initiative to discuss the matter further with the physician.[22]

Most informed consent cases do not take account of the complexities described above. For example, the cases have traditionally concerned the failure to give sufficient information about the physical risks of a procedure or process that has resulted in harm to the patient. In contrast, the administration of an HIV test presents minimal risks of physical harm. The risks in HIV screening are those associated with information obtained from the test. The significant risks are that the information will be revealed to third parties who may take adverse action against the patient or that the patient will suffer psychological harm. Indeed, an enormous worry is that the patient who should be tested will decline to do so out of fear of the social and psychological consequences.

This latter point raises the question of whether physicians have special obligations to patients whom they believe are at very high risk of having the infection—an issue that is not well developed in the case law. In at least one jurisdiction, the court concluded that if a person refuses a recommended procedure, the physician has a legal obligation to call to her attention the risks of not having the procedure.[23] Physicians, however, should be cautious in warning about the risks of refusing the screening tests. Patients do have the right to refuse treatment.[24] From the patient's perspective, the information produced by the test may not be particularly desirable. HIV infection in pregnant women is found disproportionally among African-American and Hispanic women.[25] These women are disproportionally from lower socioeconomic groups with myriad problems—such as poor nutrition and unhealthy living conditions—that may be as worrisome as the possibility of HIV infection. These women often have inadequate access to health and social services, and where such resources exist, they often do not meet the cultural needs of users, thus spawning mistrust. For example, they may not be covered by private health insurance. State Medicaid plans may not cover the drugs or other services these patients will need if they test positive.

Finally, if the women who test positive are also intravenous drug users, there may not be an adequate number of treatment slots to meet their needs.[26] Since these women are often vulnerable, physicians should be especially sensitive to avoid coercing them by making access to necessities or medical treatment conditional on participation in HIV screening programs.[27]

The informed consent cases furnish inadequate guidance in that they require patients to be informed of alternative procedures. Yet the only alternative to screening for HIV infection is to wait and see if the patient is in fact infected. A meaningful alternative from the patient's perspective is not related to the test but is an attempt to determine whether the test can be administered in a manner likely to reduce the risk of disclosure of positive results. Patients might like to know about alternative anonymous screening sites. Existing precedents do not address the question of whether a physician should be required to provide such information.[28] Finally, and of some significance in HIV screening, the legal cases have generally not involved posttest counseling obligations.[29]

THE SPECIAL DILEMMA OF POSTTEST COUNSELING. If a pregnant woman decides to be screened for HIV infection, the physician's obligation undoubtedly includes posttest counseling irrespective of the test results. For persons who test negatively, it is important for them to understand, especially if they engage in high-risk behavior, that they can be infected but may not have converted. Moreover, there is always the possibility of a false-negative result. Finally, patients, especially those engaged in high-risk behavior, should be told that they can still become infected unless they institute significant behavior changes. The nature and extent of the counseling connected with a negative result will clearly be structured by the characteristics of the individual woman.

For women who test positive, the obvious initial step is to conduct confirmatory tests.[30] If such tests are also positive, then the physician minimally needs to advise the woman concerning her own health prospects,[31] the likelihood that her fetus is also affected,[32] and her reproductive options. As Osterholm and MacDonald point out, counseling about abortion is a controversial issue. Such counseling should be especially culturally sensitive and specific. Moreover, counseling about future pregnancy also has cultural implications that must be taken into account.[33]

SPECIAL LEGISLATION. Some states have promulgated legislation specifically directed at the issue of disclosure and counseling in HIV testing. While a few of these states require informed consent without further specification,[34] most give explicit requirements. For example, Florida requires informed consent that must be "preceded by an explanation of the test, including its purpose, potential uses, and limitations and the meaning of its results." Maine goes further. It requires informed consent prior to the administration of the test. Informed consent is defined as voluntary consent with an actual understanding of the nature of the test, the purposes for which the results may be used, to whom the results may be disclosed, and the reasonably foreseeable risks and benefits resulting from the test.[35] In addition, Maine requires that those tested be offered pretest and posttest counseling. The pretest counseling must include the nature, purpose, and reliability of the test; to whom the results may be disclosed; and the reasonably foreseeable risks and benefits of the test. Minimum posttest counseling requirements include the discussion of the test results, their significance, and their reliability. The subject must also be made aware of the social and emotional consequences of the result, supplied with information about medical care and support services, and given information on preventive practices and risk reduction plans. Washington has a requirement directed at health-care practitioners attending a pregnant woman to see that she receives AIDS counseling. AIDS counseling is defined as "counseling directed toward increasing the individual's understanding of acquired immunodeficiency syndrome and changing the individual's behavior."[36]

Despite the presence of special legislation, it is evident that it is exceedingly difficult, if not impossible, to integrate legal informed consent requirements into medical practice. Brody suggests that this is especially true of primary care settings.[37] To say that legal informed consent requirements give inadequate guidance is not to say that informed consent should not be an ingredient of good medical practice. It does suggest that greater emphasis is needed on understanding the requirements of medical care and how issues of autonomy and disclosure might be successfully integrated into it. How to accomplish that task is clearly beyond the province of this chapter. It is evident, however, that using a lay standard more clearly approximates the ideal than the professional standard. Brody notes:

> The reasonable patient standard docs a much better job of indicating the centrality of respect for patient autonomy and the desired outcome of the informed consent process, which is revealing the information that a reasonable person would need to make an informed and rational decision. This standard is particularly valuable when modified to include the specific informational and decisional needs of a particular patient.[38]

The difficulty of extrapolating from existing legal precedents and the characteristics of HIV infection suggest, therefore, that physicians should offer HIV screening to pregnant women in a manner that maximizes their participation in the decision-making process. The prospect of expanded liability in the area of reproductive risks provides an additional reason for adopting patient-oriented procedures.

Counseling About Reproductive Risks

In the vast majority of American jurisdictions that have considered the matter, a physician is obligated to provide legally adequate information to parents about their reproductive risks.[39] Failure to provide such information may result in liability to the parents if a disabled child is born. These suits are called "wrongful birth suits." Among jurisdictions that recognize such suits, there is a lack of uniformity about the proper measure of damages. Some courts permit recovery for the extraordinary expenses resulting from a child's impairment but not for the costs that would ordinarily be incurred in raising a child. Other courts allow recovery for only parental pain and suffering resulting from the birth of a disabled child. At least one court permits recovery for all the costs of raising the child.[40]

In most wrongful birth suits, both parents have been the plaintiffs. One interesting unanswered question is the extent to which the legal obligation of physicians to provide information about reproductive choices extends to prospective fathers as well as prospective mothers. Since reproductive information is of concern to the prospective father, the obligation to provide such information may also extend to the father individually, despite the fact that subsequent physical interventions will involve only the pregnant woman. In *DiNatale* v. *Lieberman*,[41] the court expressed its reasons for permitting the father to sue:

> Even though a father has no legally enforceable right to either compel or prevent an abortion, he has a right to participate in the decision. He shares the mother's right to seek damages for the negligent wrongful birth because he shares the legal obligation to provide for the child's care and support. The father's right is not dependent upon the mother's cause of action but is his individually. (Citations omitted)[42]

Interestingly, the court cited a Florida statute giving the father the right to be notified in the event of his wife's abortion. Thus the justification for disclosing reproductive risks to fathers is perhaps strongest where the father has a right to notification about abortion. In states with such a notification requirement, disclosure might include providing the reasons for abortion. Even in states without a notification requirement, a physician might urge a pregnant woman to notify the father because she will need comfort and support in carrying out her decision to terminate the pregnancy.

Where the woman does not want to terminate her pregnancy, the biological father would seem to have a strong interest in learning about his reproductive risks. The father should have the opportunity to prepare for the birth of a disabled child for whom he will have to provide. In other situations, the interest of the father in participating in decision making for the fetus has been recognized. For example, the National Commission for the Protection of Human Subjects of Biomedical and Behavioral Research's *Report and Recommendations: Research on the Fetus* specified that, in some circumstances, research on the fetus requires the informed consent of the mother and no objection by the father.[43]

In the context of HIV infection of pregnant women, understanding the nature of this potential obligation to the genetic father, as well as fulfilling the obligation, is vastly more complicated. Available information about risk factors and the characteristics of infected women suggest that many pregnant women will not be married, or may not even know who the biological father is or the whereabouts of the biological father if his identity is known. Consequently, the physician will have the difficult task of identifying and perhaps contacting the biological father.

Moreover, in the HIV context, disclosing reproductive risks to the genetic father of necessity reveals the pregnant woman's health status and the prospect of infection for the father. For a variety of reasons, a pregnant woman may not want the genetic father to know that she is infected or that he is at risk. As a result, the physician will have to decide whether to respect the patient's confidentiality or fulfill an obligation to the genetic father.

While existing law may not require physicians to undertake maximum efforts to locate and disclose to genetic fathers their reproductive risks, where possible, physicians should consider doing so. Minimally, the issue should be raised with pregnant women, and they should be encouraged to involve the father, if he is available, in the decision.

A child may also have a cause of action against a physician for failure to properly inform the child's parents of their reproductive risks. This action is called a "wrongful life action," since the child is arguing that he or she should not have been born. A significantly smaller number of jurisdictions, however, allow the child to recover.[44]

A very small number of jurisdictions by statute,[45] or by judicial opinion,[46] deny recovery to both parents and children. The statutes, in particular, seem to be the result of the connection between these lawsuits and the abortion controversy. The connection goes back to *Gleitman* v. *Cosgrove*.[47]

In *Gleitman,* the New Jersey Supreme Court denied recovery to both the parents and the child for birth defects that resulted from the mother's exposure to rubella during pregnancy. The plaintiffs asserted that the mother would have had an abortion but for the fact that the defendant physician had negligently reassured her that the disease would not affect the fetus. In denying recovery, the New Jersey Supreme Court was clearly troubled by the prospect of allowing causes of action predicated on the assertion that the pregnant woman was denied the opportunity to obtain an abortion. The Supreme Court's legalization of abortion in *Roe* v. *Wade*[48] has had an impact on some courts, including those in New Jersey,[49] and gradually a few have permitted at least parents to bring a cause of action. Despite the decision in *Roe* v. *Wade,* the controversial link with abortion remains.

The problem is that there is no recovery in negligence for failure to adequately inform patients of risks if the failure to inform does not result in physical injury. The claim in wrongful birth and wrongful life cases is that the injury is the birth of a disabled child and that the injury could have been prevented if the parents had been given the opportunity to abort. Thus a claim for recovery must be based on the lack of opportunity to abort in order to claim injury, at least as long as fetuses cannot be treated in utero.[50] Parents who were not given information about fetal impairments but who would have used the time to prepare for the birth of a disabled child would have no basis for recovery in negligence.

It is likely that the debate about the appropriateness of wrongful birth suits in particular will continue. Moreover, counseling of pregnant women who may have been infected with HIV might help fuel the debate. HIV infection is life-threatening, and many woman, because of their own infection, will not be able to care for their infected children. Moreover, it is not yet possible to screen fetuses directly for the presence of the virus. Thus a pregnant woman who is told that she is positive may choose to abort what could be a normal, healthy fetus. Despite the fact that approximately 70 percent of the offspring of infected mothers will not be infected, the incentives for abortion will be high. For those who question the value of screening pregnant women, prenatal diagnosis of genetic disease, and counseling where no therapy can be offered to the fetus or child, the appropriate care of pregnant women at risk of HIV infection provides an opportunity to advocate against screening. Yet in screening for HIV infection, unlike genetic screening, the pregnant woman's own health-care needs may require that she be advised about the availability of HIV testing. In the event that she wants to be tested for her own health needs, she will also have available to her information about her reproductive risks. She may be disadvantaged, however, in those jurisdictions that do not permit tort recovery for failure to advise about reproductive risks if she needs a physician's help in evaluating her reproductive risks.

Conclusion

In sum, a physician may have difficulty balancing the benefits and risks in trying to decide whether a particular woman should be tested for the presence of HIV infection. Yet a physician may be legally liable for failure to advise a pregnant woman (and possibly the prospective father and the child after birth) about her reproductive and personal health risks. A possible approach, and one consistent with ethical norms, might be to make all pregnant women aware of the opportunity to be screened for HIV infection during pregnancy. This view is affirmed by Capron, who suggests that "adherence to proper procedures of disclosure and consent will not merely reduce or eliminate the risk of liability but also greatly diminish the probability that the injured party will initiate suit."[51]

Finally, the characteristics of HIV infection itself urge that physicians adopt a patient-oriented approach to the issue of making the screening test available to all pregnant women. There is a strong argument that HIV infection is not like other diseases. Kenneth Keniston writes:

AIDS is sui generis: in its initial invisibility to its victims, in its prolonged latency, in its protean symptomatology, in its apparent invariant virulence, in the cruelty of the processes by which it destroys. . . . And even if we agree to call AIDS a disease of a new and different kind, this definition must not monopolize its meaning. AIDS has

214

behavioral and social roots as well as biomedical causes. . . . Only a definition of this condition as also a behavioral problem can legitimize policies that might be effective in the coming years.[52]

Notes

1. As of November 7, 1986, the vast majority of women with AIDS were of reproductive age (Mary Guinan and Ann Hardy, "Epidemiology of AIDS in Women in the United States: 1981 Through 1986," *Journal of the American Medical Association* 257 (1987): 2039–2042. As of that date, there were 27,140 reported cases of full-blown AIDS in adults. Of that number, 1,819 (6.7 percent) were women. The primary transmission category for these women was intravenous drug use. The second largest category was heterosexual contact with a person at high risk of being infected with HIV. Over 70 percent of the women with AIDS were of black or Hispanic origin (ibid).

2. This chapter focuses on voluntary screening for HIV infection in pregnant women. Voluntary screening makes available information concerning a woman's health status. It also provides information pertinent to decisions about marriage, sexual relationships, and present and future childbearing. It should be noted, however, that decisions about pregnancy and childbearing may be affected by factors other than the perceived risk to pregnant women and fetuses of HIV infection. For example, childbearing may be related to self-esteem or rehabilitation (Peter Selwyn, Rosalind Carter, Ellie Schoenbaum et al., "Knowledge of HIV Antibody Status and Decisions to Continue or Terminate Pregnancy Among Intravenous Drug Users," *Journal of the American Medical Association* 261 [1989]: 3567–3571). Moreover, there are data that suggest that, at least among intravenous drug users, many pregnancies are unplanned and regular contraceptive usage is rare (ibid., 3571).

Screening newborns for HIV infection can also provide information about maternal status. When such screening is done anonymously, information about the prevalence of the virus in the general population of childbearing women can be obtained. In one study, researchers concluded that 1 of every 476 women giving birth in Massachusetts was infected with the HIV virus. The prevalence of HIV infection varied according to the type and location of maternity hospitals; rates were highest in inner-city hospitals, lower in mixed urban and suburban hospitals, and lowest in suburban and rural hospitals (Rodney Hoff, Victor P. Berardi, Barbara Weiblen et al., "Seroprevalence of Human Immunodeficiency Virus Among Childbearing Women," *New England Journal of Medicine* 318 [1988]: 525–530).

3. Lori B. Andrews, *Medical Genetics: A Legal Frontier* (Chicago: American Bar Foundation, 1987), 1.

4. W. Keeton, D. Dobbs, R. Keeton et al., eds., *Prosser and Keeton on the Law of Torts,* 5th ed. (St. Paul: West, 1984), sec. 32, 187.

5. The term "informed consent" was first used in 1975 in *Salgo* v. *Leland Stanford Jr. University Board of Trustees,* 154 Cal. App. 2d 560, 317 P.2d 170 (1957).

6. Andrews, *Medical Genetics,* 106. See *Coffe* v. *McDonnell Douglas Corp.,* 8 Cal. App. 3d 551, 105 Cal. Rptr. 358, 503 P.2d 1366 (1972) (the company was liable for its failure to establish a mechanism to review the results of tests ordered in the preemployment physical examination by the company physician), and *Wilmington General Hospital* v. *Manlove,* 54 Del. 15, 174 A.2d 135 (1961) (the hospital was

liable for aggravated injuries produced by a delay in getting medical attention after a child was turned away by the hospital's emergency room).

7. For an article agreeing with this conclusion, see Donald H. J. Hermann, "Liability Related to Diagnosis and Transmission of AIDS," *Law, Medicine and Health Care* 15 (1987): 36–45. Although it is important that health-care professionals understand the potential legal liability, such considerations should not dictate their practices and professional judgments (see George J. Annas, "Is a Genetic Screening Test Ready When the Lawyers Say It Is?" *Hastings Center Report* 15 [1985]: 16–18).

8. In at least one well-known case, a court did not follow customary professional standards. In *Helling* v. *Carey,* 83 Wash. 2d 514, 519 P.2d 981 (1974), the court ruled that the defendant practitioners should have administered a glaucoma test despite the fact that it was not the professional custom of that specialty to administer this test to individuals under age 40. The court considered significant the facts that the test was efficacious and inexpensive, that no judgment factor was involved, and that the test was harmless if the physical condition of the eye permitted it to be given.

9. Allan H. McCoid, "The Care Requirement of Medical Practitioners," *Vanderbilt Law Review* 12 (1959): 549, 559.

10. For an article suggesting this result, see Howard L. Minkoff and Sheldon H. Landesman, "The Case for Routinely Offering Prenatal Testing for Human Immunodeficiency Virus," *American Journal of Obstetrics and Gynecology* 159 (1988): 793–796.

11. Ibid., 794. Geographic variation is generally a problem for medicine. Research has shown the wide variation in utilization of particular procedures along geographic lines. Why such geographic variation occurs is not well understood, although it has clear implications for the quality of medical care (see Mark R. Chassin, Jacqueline Kosecoff, R. E. Park et al., "Does Inappropriate Use Explain Geographic Variations in the Use of Health Care Services?" *Journal of the American Medical Association* 258 (1987): 2533, and John Wennberg, "Dealing with Medical Practice Variations: A Proposal for Action," *Health Affairs* 3 [1984]: 1).

12. Department of Health and Human Services, *AIDS Knowledge and Attitudes: August 1988, Provisional Data from the National Health Interview Survey,* DHHS Publication (PHS) 89-1250 (Washington, D.C.: Government Printing Office, 1988).

13. For example, Exception 18 of Rule 803 of the Federal Rules of Evidence states:

> To the extent called to the attention of an expert witness upon cross-examination or relied upon by the expert witness in direct examination, statements contained in published treatises, periodicals, or pamphlets on a subject of history, medicine, or other science or art, established as a reliable authority by the testimony or admission of the witness or by other expert testimony or by judicial notice. If admitted, the statements may be read into evidence but may not be received as exhibits.

14. Some, however, urge wider HIV testing. For example, Frank S. Rhame and Dennis G. Maki argue that wider testing is justified because many Americans are not aware of their status and our goal should be to inform all who are infected of this fact. Thus they recommend HIV testing for all adult Americans under age 60 ("The Case for Wider Use of Testing for HIV Infection," *New England Journal of Medicine* 320 [1989]: 1248–1254).

15. I am not arguing that the best way to educate Americans about HIV and the importance of certain precautions connected with sexual encounters and drug use is to do so only in connection with mass screening. I am urging that there is a role for face-to-face discussion as well as mass education efforts. For pregnant women in particular,

health care is already being provided for the pregnancy. Educational about HIV infection should be a significant part of the promotion of better health and life-style for the pregnant woman and the fetus.

16. Bernard Lo, Robert Steinbrock, Molly Cooke et al. "Voluntary Screening for Human Immunodeficiency Virus (HIV) Infection: Weighing the Benefits and Harms," *Annals of Internal Medicine* 110 (1989): 727–733. Physicians should also bear in mind that in some instances the professional standard is considered as evidence of what ought to be done, and what ought to be done is ultimately a question of reasonableness. See *Helling* v. *Carey,* 83 Wash. 2d 514, 519 P.2d 981 (1974), and the discussion of the lay standard in the text on pp. 206–207. See generally G. Annas, S. Law, R. Rosenblatt, et al., *American Health Law* (Boston: Little, Brown, 1990), 403–404.

17. President's Commission for the Study of Ethical Problems in Medicine and Biomedical and Behavioral Research, *Making Health Care Decisions: The Ethical and Legal Implications of Informed Consent in the Patient–Practitioner Relationship* (Washington, D.C.: Government Printing Office, 1982), 3: Appendix L, 195–196.

18. Alexander Morgan Capron, "Tort Liability in Genetic Counseling," *Columbia Law Review* 79 (1979): 618, 629. A variation of the lay standard would be formulated with reference to what a particular patient would want to know. Although an approach that focuses on individual preferences would seem the best way to affirm individual self-determination, courts have been extremely reluctant to use this approach. To date, only two courts have adopted it (*Scott* v. *Bradford,* 606 P.2d 554 [Okla. 1979], and *McPherson* v. *Ellis,* 305 N.C. 255, 287 S.E.2d 892 [1982]). See generally Ruth R. Faden and Tom L. Beauchamp, *A History and Theory of Informed Consent* (New York: Oxford University Press, 1986).

19. President's Commission, *Making Health Care Decisions.* See also Chapter 13 of this volume.

20. President's Commission for the Study of Ethical Problems in Medicine and Biomedical and Behavioral Research, *Making Health Care Decisions: The Ethical and Legal Implications of Informed Consent in the Patient–Practitioner Relationship* (Washington, D.C.: Government Printing Office, 1982), 1: 29. The report notes that lawsuits require the naming of defendants that have some prospect of being able to pay damages. Thus the cases have typically involved physicians and institutions. As a result, other health-care professionals who may be involved in disclosing information to patients and obtaining informed consent have rarely been the subject of lawsuits. As a consequence, the legal obligations of other health-care professionals have not been well articulated. This may change to the extent that these other health professionals obtain or are covered by liability insurance.

21. Andrews, *Medical Genetics,* 1.

22. For one person's account of the administration of a questionnaire concerning risk factors for HIV infection that proved extremely troubling see McIlvane, "In Doctor's Office, On Trial for AIDS," *New York Times,* September 27, 1987, p. 28.

23. In *Truman* v. *Thomas,* 27 Cal. 3d 285, 165 Cal. Rptr. 308, 611 P.2d 902 (1980), the California Supreme Court affirmed a jury verdict and held that a physician breached his obligation to provide due care by failing to inform a patient of the material risks of not consenting to a recommended procedure. One commentator urges that physicians be very aggressive concerning HIV screening: "We believe it is no longer tenable to do less than strongly recommend an HIV test to all patients who acknowledge any sexual contact with homosexual men, any needle sharing, or multiple unsafe hetero-

sexual contacts. Physicians should vigorously elicit such histories" (Rhame and Maki, "The Case for Wider Use of Testing," 1253).

24. A few legal commentators have already suggested that the right of pregnant women to refuse genetic diagnostic tests should be limited. They raise the possibility that pregnant women who are at risk of delivering a disabled child and refuse a genetic screening test should be liable for prenatal abuse. See, for example, John Robertson, "Procreative Liberty and the Control of Conception, Pregnancy and Childbirth," *Virginia Law Review* 69 (1983): 405, and Margery Shaw, "Conditional Prospective Rights of the Fetus," *Journal of Legal Medicine* 5 (1984): 63.

25. Social settings of drug use and different practices related to injection may help explain the higher prevalence of HIV infection among African-Americans and Hispanics. A recent study examined the relation of intravenous-drug-use practices, heterosexual behavior, and race or ethnic background to HIV infection. In this study, injecting drugs in shooting galleries and sharing needles with strangers—behaviors associated with an increased risk of HIV infection—were more frequent among African-Americans and Hispanics. The study concluded that "strategies to prevent AIDS should be culturally sensitive and should target specific social settings in which drugs are used, specific injection behaviors, cocaine use, and certain sexual behavior in order to be most effective" (Ellie Schoenbaum, D. Hartel, P. Selwyn et al., "Risk Factors for Human Immunodeficiency Virus Infection in Intravenous Drug Users," *New England Journal of Medicine* 321 (1989): 878).

26. A recent survey of drug-treatment providers in New York City revealed that "54% categorically exclude pregnant women, 67% refuse to treat pregnant Medicaid patients, and 87% will not treat pregnant women on Medicaid who are addicted to crack cocaine" (Wendy Chavkin and Nicholas Freudenberg, Letter, *New England Journal of Medicine* 321 [1989]: 1266). For all women, there are three basic obstacles to receiving prenatal care: lack of resources to pay for the care, lack of access to transportation, and lack of knowledge of or ambivalence about pregnancy (Annas et al., *American Health Law*, 927–929 n. 14).

27. For an excellent article cautioning against this and other practices that might coerce a pregnant woman, see Mary Sue Henifin, Ruth Hubbard, and Judy Norsigian, "Prenatal Screening," in *Reproductive Laws for the 1990's,* ed. Sherrill Cohen and Nadine Taub (Clifton, N.J.: Humana Press, 1989), 155–184.

28. What a physician might disclose to a patient if the physician wished to adopt a patient-oriented approach is a difficult issue and beyond the scope of this chapter. Several commentators, however, have made recommendations in this regard. The following typifies the suggestions that have been made, although the reader is cautioned that the information is dated and the suggestion has deficiencies.

> The information the counselors are instructed to provide is as follows. If the patient is human immunodeficiency virus antibody-positive, the exact risk of an infant's developing AIDS-related illness is unknown, but may be as high as 65%. The patient is offered the option to terminate the pregnancy; if this is unacceptable, pediatric follow-up with a specialist is arranged. The patient is strongly advised not to breast-feed, because transmission of the virus through breast milk is possible. If the woman is human immunodeficiency virus antibody-positive but has no covert illness, she should enter the health-care system with the understanding that they will be able to take rapid advantage of advances in care as soon as they are made available. Knowledge about the length of time a woman is antibody-positive may

also affect her prognosis. Affected women are advised to have their other children evaluated and followed. Counseling services are made available to discuss the issues of future childbearing. Changes in the patient's lifestyle will be emphasized, with a discussion of safe sex practices to prevent spread to sexual partners and other intimate contacts.

The patient is informed that the disadvantages of being tested include mental anguish, particularly while awaiting the results and if the test is positive but the patient asymptomatic. It is explained that her quality of life may be altered appreciably, with potential adverse effect on her insurability and/or her infant's insurability. Even though medical records are confidential, we cannot guarantee that insurance companies will not gain access to test results and use this knowledge. Her employability may be affected. Last, but by no means least, her interpersonal relationships with her health-care providers, family, and friends may all change as a result of being human immunodeficiency virus-positive.

Benjamin Sachs, Ruth Tuomala, and Frederic Frigoletto, "Acquired Immunodeficiency Syndrome: Suggested Protocol for Counseling and Screening in Pregnancy," *Obstetrics and Gynecology* 70 (1987): 410. Also see Lo et al., "Voluntary Screening," 731.

29. For a discussion of posttest counseling, see Chapter 13 of this volume.
30. For a description of follow-up care, see Sachs et al., "Acquired Immunodeficiency Syndrome," 732.
31. Preliminary data indicate that pregnancy itself does not adversely affect the health of an HIV-infected woman (Lisa M. Koonin, Tedd V. Ellerbrock, Hani K. Atrash et al., "Pregnancy-Associated Deaths Due to AIDS in the United States," *Journal of the American Medical Association* 261 [1989]: 1306–1309; Sheldon H. Landesman, Howard Minkoff, and Anne Willoughby, "HIV Disease in Reproductive Age Women: A Problem of the Present," *Journal of the American Medical Association* 261 [1989]: 1326–1327; Peter Selwyn, E. Schoenbaum, K. Davenny et al., "Prospective Study of Human Immunodeficiency Virus Infection and Pregnancy Outcomes in Intravenous Drug Users," *Journal of the American Medical Association* 261 [1989]: 1289–1294).
32. The rate of perinatal transmission ranges from 22 to 39 percent in the medical literature (Gwendolyn Scott, Cecilia Hutto, Robert W. Makuch et al., "Survival in Children with Perinatally Acquired Human Immunodeficiency Virus Type I Infection," *New England Journal of Medicine* 321 [1989]: 1791–1796). In this study, the survival rate of infected children was a median of 38 months from the time of diagnosis.
33. Michael Osterholm and Kristine MacDonald, "Facing the Complex Issues of Pediatric AIDS: A Public Health Perspective," *Journal of the American Medical Association* 258 (1987): 2736–2737. Selwyn et al. also note that counseling of HIV-infected pregnant women must address not only perinatal transmission, but also the sociocultural and behavioral contexts in which reproductive decision making takes place. They also note that some pregnant women who are HIV infected do not have Medicaid coverage for abortion. They confirm that reproductive counseling in the HIV context is a personnel-intensive process that is costly, and they advocate additional research to appreciate fully the relationship between HIV infection and reproductive behavior ("Knowledge of HIV Antibody Status"). For a detailed discussion of the elements of counseling, see Chapter 13 of this volume.
34. California Health and Safety Code, 199.22(A) (1989).

35. Maine Revised Statutes Annotated, title 5, sec. 19201 5-A (1989).
36. Revised Code of Washington Annotated, sec. 70.24.320 (3) (1975 & Supp. 1988). Other states with consent statutes covering HIV testing include Delaware (Delaware Code Annotated, title 16, sec. 1202 [1983 & Supp. 1988]), Georgia (Code of Georgia Annotated, sec. 31-17A [1985 & Supp. 1988]), Illinois (Illinois Annotated Statutes, ch. 111, sec. 7304, 7305, 7309 [Smith-Hurd 1988]), Massachusetts (Massachusetts General Laws Annotated, ch. 111, sec. 70F [West 1983 & Supp. 1989]), Missouri (Annotated Missouri Statutes, sec. 191.674 [Vernon 1983 & Supp. 1988]), Oregon (Oregon Revised Statutes, sec. 433.045 [1989]), and Wisconsin (Wisconsin Statutes Annotated, sec. 146.025 [West 1989]). The Illinois statute is especially interesting and illustrates the ambivalence that some legislatures have about allowing the patient to make an informed decision. This statute, originally passed in 1987, stated that HIV testing could not be performed without the written consent of the subject. In 1988, however, in a surprise move, the Illinois legislature passed an amendment to the original statute stating that written informed consent, information, and counseling are not required for performance of an HIV test "when in the judgement of the physician, such testing is medically indicated to provide appropriate diagnoses and treatment to the subject of the test, provided that the subject of the test has otherwise provided his or her consent to such physician for medical treatment" (Donald H. J. Hermann and George F. De Wolfe, "HIV Antibody Testing Without Patient's Informed Consent: Illinois Abandons Patient's Rights," *Journal of Health and Hospital Law* 21 [1988]: 263–267).
37. Howard Brody, "Transparency: Informed Consent in Primary Care," *Hastings Center Report* 9 (1989): 5–9.
38. Ibid., 6.
39. For a listing of states giving parents this cause of action, see Note, "Wrongful Birth Actions: The Case Against Legislative Curtailment," *Harvard Law Review* 100 (1987): 2017, 2018 n. 5.
40. *Azzolino* v. *Dingfelder*, 315 N.C. 103, 112 S.E.2d 528 (1985), *cert denied*, 479 U.S. 835 (1986).
41. See *Di Natale* v. *Lieberman*, 409 So. 2d 512 (Fla. Dist. Ct. App. 1982) (where because of the extraordinary expenses required for the care of a disabled child resulting from prenatal negligence, the father could maintain a cause of action for negligent wrongful birth). Capron makes a similar point: "When the subject matter of the counseling is the reproductive decision to be made by a couple, the man has as much of an interest in being adequately informed as the woman does, even if any subsequent physical invasion involves solely her person" ("Tort Liability in Genetic Counseling," 629, n. 36).
42. *Di Natale* v. *Lieberman*, 409 So. 2d at 513.
43. National Commission for the Protection of Human Subjects of Biomedical and Behavioral Research, *Research on the Fetus: Report and Recommendations* (Washington, D.C.: Department of Health, Education and Welfare, 1975), 73–76.
44. See, for example, *Pitre* v. *Opelousas General Hospital*, 530 So. 2d 1151 (La. 1988); *Continental Casualty Co.* v. *Empire Casualty Co.*, 713 P.2d 384 (Colo. Ct. App. 1986); *Procanik* v. *Cillo*, 97 N.J. 339, 478 A.2d 755 (1984); *Harbeson* v. *Parke Davis, Inc.*, 98 Wash. 2d 460, 656 P.2d 483 (1983); and *Turpin* v. *Sortini*, 31 Cal. 3d 220, 643 P.2d 954, 182 Cal. Rptr. 337 (1982). Most courts refuse to award general damages for a child's claim. They have allowed special damages for the extra expenses associated with the child's disabilities.
45. See, for example, Idaho Code, sec. 5-334 (Supp. 1986), Minnesota Statutes, sec.

145.424 (Supp. 1987), Annotated Missouri Statutes, sec. 188.130 (Vernon Supp. 1987), South Dakota Codified Laws Annotated, sec. 21-55-2 (Supp. 1986), and Utah Code Annotated, sec. 78-11-24 (Supp. 1986). See also Note, "Wrongful Birth Actions," 2019 n. 8.

46. See *Hickman v. Group Health Plan, Inc.,* 396 N.W.2d 10 (Minn. 1986); *Azzolino v. Dingfelder,* 315 N.C. 103, 337 S.E.2d 528 (1985), *cert denied,* 479 U.S. 835 (1986).

47. *Gleitman v. Cosgrove,* 49 N.J. 22, 227 A.2d 689 (1967).

48. *Roe v. Wade,* 410 U.S. 113 (1973).

49. *Berman v. Allan,* 80 N.J. 421, 404 A.2d 8 (1979) (overruling *Gleitman* in part).

50. Adrienne Asch makes a very powerful point about recognition of wrongful birth and wrongful life claims:

> Commitment to access and choice for women commits us to support those women who believe that they were denied testing or adequate counseling and, thus, bore a child with a disability whom they would have aborted had they known. We can support such suits only because they may be one of the few ways to compel the medical profession to inform and care for women responsibly during pregnancy. For this reason alone, feminists as well as advocates of disability rights can accept such actions.

"Reproductive Technology and Disability," in Cohen and Taub, ed., *Reproductive Laws for the 1990's,* 93.

51. Capron, "Tort Liability in Genetic Counseling," 672.

52. Kenneth Keniston, "Introduction to the Issue, Living with AIDS: Part II," *Daedalus* 118 (1989): ix–xxxii.

9

Legal Protections of Confidential Medical Information and the Need for Antidiscrimination Laws

MADISON POWERS

HIV antibody screening programs have the potential to produce large quantities of highly sensitive, personal medical information that, if revealed to third parties, may result in injury to the personal, social, and economic interests of those screened. The collection, storage, and use of such information by health-care providers, public health officials, and researchers increase the likelihood of such information being improperly disclosed and harmful to a variety of individual interests.

Reasons frequently cited for the expansion of programs for collection of HIV information are providing individuals with information necessary for making important medical and personal decisions, providing physicians with information necessary to evaluate and implement timely treatment plans, protecting others from harm, providing information useful for changing high-risk behaviors, determining the prevalence of the disease and assessing further service and research needs, and directing research aimed at finding a cure or vaccine.

Balancing confidentiality interests against other social and individual concerns is uniquely problematic in the case of HIV screening for pregnant women and newborns. First, in any screening program designed to gather information relevant to the newborn's potential HIV status, the information generated also reveals personal information about the health status of the mother. Second, since newborn screening detects the presence of only maternal antibodies, the potential for harm from disclosure of test information exists for the majority of newborns who will not develop HIV infection. Third, because a newborn begins his or her illness while in a state of total dependence on others for care, and often requires a broad range of medical and social services, there may be many persons with a legitimate need to know the specific details of confidential medical information.[1]

This chapter examines some of the confidentiality interests of persons screened for evidence of HIV infection, the limits of existing legal approaches to their protection, and current proposals for the development of a comprehensive confidentiality and antidiscrimination policy. Although many of the concerns discussed are relevant to all persons screened for HIV infection, the chapter attempts to show how those concerns may be different, or in some instances less widely appreciated, in cases involving pregnant women and newborns.

The first section discusses the special character of the interests at stake in the context of HIV screening and argues for the need to move beyond the traditionally accepted rationale for legal protection of confidential medical information. The second section discusses recent constitutional decisions that define the minimum requirements a governmentally sanctioned screening program must incorporate for protection of confidential medical information. It is argued that such protections are unlikely to be responsive to the principal concerns raised by most HIV screening programs. The third section describes statutory and common law duties of confidentiality generally. It is argued that the limited range of persons under the duty of confidentiality and the obstacles to the enforcement of this legal duty are serious impediments to the protection of confidential medical information. The fourth section examines the major exceptions to the duty of confidentiality and outlines proposals for addressing the problems associated with those exceptions. The fifth section argues that the limited application of the duty of confidentiality, the vast number of exceptions, and the difficulties of enforcement mean that many important interests are not adequately protected by confidentiality policies alone. The potential for harm to individual interests as a result of unpreventable disclosures requires additional legal strategies to combat discrimination against persons with HIV infection.

The Interests at Stake

The physician–patient relationship

One of the most frequently cited reasons for protection against disclosure of personal medical information is the integrity of the relationship between patient and physician. Confidentiality has been viewed as the cornerstone of that relationship. The doctrine of patient confidentiality has its roots in early medical practice codes, such as the Hippocratic Oath:

> Whatever, in connection with my profession, or not in connection with it, I may see of the lives of men which ought not to be spoken abroad I will not divulge as reckoning that all should be kept secret.[2]

Confidentiality, in its traditional sense, characterizes a relationship between persons. A confidant is a person trusted with knowledge of one's private affairs; hence, to confide is to have confidence in or be trustful of another. A duty of confidentiality arises in the context of an expectation that information disclosed to another will be protected from unwanted disclosure to third parties. A breach of that duty occurs when someone under a duty to protect a person's interest in nondisclosure either deliberately discloses the information without the individual's consent or fails to take reasonable steps to protect that information.[3]

The physician's duty of confidentiality in modern society is not viewed as having quite the absolute character the language of traditional medical codes would suggest, however. A more modern statement of the duty of confidentiality is reflected in the American Medical Association's 1957 Code of Ethics:

> A physician may not reveal the confidences entrusted to him in the course of medical attendance, or the deficiencies he may observe in the character of patients, unless he is required to do so by law or unless it becomes necessary in order to protect the welfare of the individual or the community.[4]

Such statements by professional associations have greatly influenced both judicial decisions and legislative enactments. Accordingly, developments in the law reflect an increased awareness of the importance of a variety of competing societal and individual interests. Although the general expectation is that physicians will take appropriate steps to limit access by others to personal medical information, there is considerable controversy over what expectations are reasonable in light of the realities of modern health care delivery.

Mark Seigler has argued that confidentiality as patients and physicians have traditionally understood it no longer exists.[5] In the course of routine medical care, extensive personal and highly sensitive medical information is made available to a large number of persons who are directly or indirectly responsible for providing or supporting the delivery of health care. Confidentiality in the traditional sense is routinely compromised when persons other than the patient's primary providers of care have access to medical information and claim a legitimate need to know the contents of medical records based on their functions in the health-care system.

The issue of medical confidentiality is further complicated by the fact that threats to confidentiality can arise outside of settings associated with the traditional physician–patient relationship. Sensitive medical information is collected in a variety of institutional settings, including those related to military service, employment, insurance eligibility, law enforcement, day care, immigration, and school enrollment—many of which affect women and children with HIV infection. Thus it is appropriate to shift the focus away from the narrower concern with confidentiality in the physician–patient relationship toward the general problem of fashioning a legal policy for protection of confidential medical information in light of a variety of institutional practices.

At a minimum, an individual's interest in nondisclosure of confidential medical information includes the expectation that persons who receive such information will neither negligently nor deliberately disclose it to those without a legitimate need to know or without the individual's consent. However, it seems equally clear that there is a reasonable expectation—and hence a proper subject for legal protection—that anyone who has access to personal medical information should have a legal duty to protect against disclosures that are likely to result in foreseeable harm to the individual. Thus preservation of the relationship of trust between physicians and patients is but one of a number of interests that may be harmed and that reasonable persons would seek to protect by comprehensive confidentiality policies. The nature of these other interests will now be considered.

Privacy and confidentiality

Some of the interests at stake in medical confidentiality policies are often described under the conceptual heading of privacy. Court decisions, statutes, and legal commentators frequently speak of confidentiality as roughly synonymous with privacy. In many instances, an individual's interest in nondisclosure of information is treated as a member of a family of privacy interests.[6] Conceptual objections abound, and any attempt at a systematic reform of usage is beyond the scope of this chapter. For the purposes of this discussion, it is enough simply to describe the nature of these disputes and alert the reader to instances in which usage of these terms in the law is likely to be confusing.

In American jurisprudence, the concept of privacy has taken on a rather expansive meaning, incorporating a number of different interests that justify special legal protection. The earliest developments in the protection of privacy occurred in tort law. Influential scholars and jurists argued for legal recognition of a broad class of privacy interests, the violation of which would allow individuals to bring suit against others who are responsible for the resulting harms.[7] Privacy violations in tort law include unwanted intrusions in the realm of personal choice and decision, nonconsensual bodily intrusions, physical intrusions into a person's intimate circumstances and activities, and placing someone in a false light in the public eye.[8] The unauthorized disclosure of medical information has been viewed by many courts as an invasion of one or more of these privacy interests.

In addition to tort law developments, the U.S. Supreme Court, in a series of cases, has recognized constitutional rights of privacy that are relevant to the protection of confidential medical information. Judicial decisions protecting certain personal choices and activities from governmental interference or intrusion have been supplemented by a line of cases that extend limited protection to an individual's privacy interest in preventing disclosure of personal information.[9]

The concept of privacy as developed in both tort and constitutional law connotes some limitation on the *access* others may have to a person, but—as this discussion suggests—the interests protected from intrusion are various. Many commentators argue that the breadth and diversity of the interests subsumed under privacy make the concept vacuous and incapable of principled application.[10] One suggestion is that we should reserve the notion of privacy for unwanted disclosures of information.[11] Interference with certain kinds of individual decisions would be better characterized as interference with constitutional liberties of a different sort.[12] Others have argued that privacy is best understood in terms of limiting access to the person by prohibiting intrusion in certain personal activities and decisions.[13] In addition, some argue that interests in intimacy, secrecy, anonymity, and solitude are the core interests relevant to the concept of privacy.[14] General agreement on terminology appears unlikely, but it is clear that a variety of interests are potentially relevant to any policy designed to prevent disclosure of medical information, however those interests are denominated.

An expanded list of interests

Threats to interests that might be harmed by unwanted disclosure of information on HIV status can be subdivided into at least three kinds: (1) interference with the patient's ability to make important medical decisions; (2) damages to reputation, social standing, and social relationships; and (3) invidious forms of discrimination in the availability of important opportunities, such as employment, housing, and medical and social services.

The first category primarily reflects a concern with an individual's interest in autonomy. In some instances, a breach of confidentiality, or the fear of a breach of confidentiality, may constrain a person's conception of available or acceptable medical options. The impact of unwanted disclosure of medical information on medical decision making is perhaps most familiar in the context of abortion, where such disclosure to parents or spouses, for example, may effectively deter women from terminating their pregnancies.[15] In the context of HIV infection, the potential for unwanted disclosures could deter some individuals from seeking testing, counseling, and treatment.

The second category includes a person's "intangible" interest in maintaining a reputation and, in some instances, in maintaining anonymity. While the prospect of unwanted disclosure may not interfere with or change the outcome of an individual's decision to be tested, it may result in social stigma and an increased sense of isolation—a phenomenon well documented in the context of HIV infection.[16]

The third category reflects the potential for harm to a person's more tangible interests. Adverse consequences include the loss of such opportunities as employment, housing, and access to social services. Unlike the loss of reputation and companionship, these consequences may be preventable through anti-discrimination laws, even if the disclosure of medical information or the loss of social standing is not.

Approaches to legal protection

The diversity of interests, cited above, that justify the need for legal protection of confidential medical information, and the variety of threats to those interests, require a combination of legal approaches.

The first approach is a "pre-event" one and focuses on the prevention of disclosures. Pre-event strategies can be classified into two types. In one, strategies focus on the context in which harm is likely to occur. Their goal is to prevent harm by creating barriers to injury or changes in the environment to reduce the possibility of injury. Examples include legally mandated changes in the way confidential information is generated, maintained, stored, and transmitted. Because the aim is the prevention of disclosure, these strategies are particularly well suited to the protection of individual interests in autonomy, reputation, and anonymity.

The second type of pre-event strategy actually involves intervention after disclosure but is classified as a pre-event strategy because it is meant to deter future breaches of confidentiality.[17] Such strategies include tort remedies permitting individuals to recover monetary damages for injuries sustained from unauthorized disclosures. The success of these pre-event strategies depends on a number of factors relating to the efficacy of the proposed deterrent. Among these factors are the motivations for compliance, the probability of enforcement, the number of exceptions to mandated compliance, the likelihood of detection and apprehension of violators, and the scope of public awareness of widespread enforcement.[18]

The second approach to legal protection of individual interests in confidentiality, termed "postevent" strategies, aims to reduce the injuries or damages that otherwise may be a foreseeable consequence of disclosure or public identification of medical status. Postevent strategies arise from the recognition that not all disclosures or unwanted public identification of HIV status are avoidable. Among the possible postevent strategies are antidiscrimination provisions designed to limit such unwanted consequences of disclosure as the loss of important opportunities for employment and housing. Postevent strategies also may have a beneficial effect on the individual's social standing and reputation. The extension of civil rights protection sends a powerful symbolic message condemning the underlying attitudes that lead to loss of economic and social opportunities.

Both pre-event and postevent strategies are necessary components of an integrated public policy. Priority should be given to those measures that will most effectively reduce the harms consistent with other important social goals.[19]

Constitutional Protections

Before considering the specific strategies legislators and judges might adopt, it is important to review the constitutional parameters within which these options figure more generally.

In theory, recent developments in constitutional law provide protection against unwanted disclosure of confidential medical information. A group of constitutional privacy cases confers a measure of protection for what has become known as "informational privacy." In *Whalen* v. *Roe,* the original decision in this line of cases, the U.S. Supreme Court recognized that state-sanctioned disclosures of highly personal information may be an unconstitutional invasion of privacy.[20] The Court considered the claim that the maintenance by a state of a prescription drug registry specifically identifying patients prescribed certain opium-derivative drugs unconstitutionally interfered with the patient's right of privacy. It upheld a New York statute authorizing physician reporting and computerized collection of such highly sensitive and personal medical information. The *Whalen* Court was keenly aware of the opportunities for unwanted disclosure in the health-care delivery context: "disclosures of private medical information to doctors, to hospital personnel, to insurance companies, and to public health agencies are often an essential part of modern medical practice even when the disclosure may reflect unfavorably on the character of the patient."[21]

However, the Court appeared unsympathetic to the adverse effects of unwanted medical disclosures on an individual unless it could be shown that some other fundamental right or exercise of a constitutionally protected liberty was threatened. The Court acknowledged that the dissemination of information about such drug use may result in some stigmatization, which, in turn, may determine a patient's decision on whether to undertake treatment or may influence a physician's decision to prescribe treatment.[22] But the Court held that interests qualifying for special constitutional protection must be so important that the state could not interfere with those decision processes in the first place. For example, if unwanted disclosure of medical information significantly interferes with the exercise of another constitutionally protected right, such as the right to determine whether or not to terminate a pregnancy, then such disclosures may be found to be constitutionally impermissible.[23] However, in the *Whalen* case, no impermissible deprivation of liberty was involved inasmuch as the state could make the use of such drugs illegal.[24]

Although the Court in *Whalen* upheld the right of New York State to maintain the drug registry, it did acknowledge that disclosures of highly personal information may be an unconstitutional invasion of privacy. However, the constitutional protection of privacy interests offered by *Whalen* and subsequent cases is quite narrow. The principal limitation is that constitutional protection applies only against invasions of informational privacy attributable to governmental action. Protection against nongovernmental intrusions must be found in legislation or common law court decisions.

Moreover, the precedential significance of the informational strand of the privacy doctrine is uncertain and controversial for two reasons. First, the scope of the *Whalen* ruling is limited to the facts of that particular case as presented in the record.[25] The Court noted that when a state's procedures "evidence a proper concern with, and protection of, the individual's interest in privacy," and there is no specific showing that the procedures are ineffective, there is no basis for declaring a law unconstitutional.[26] The Court also acknowledged that the risks of unwanted disclosure, and the concomitant duty to protect information, typically are recognized and provided for in statutory schemes, although it offered no specific guidance for future courts to use in determining what safeguards would be constitutionally adequate.[27]

A second source of uncertainty in applying *Whalen* as a precedent for future cases concerns the degree of judicial scrutiny to be given to laws having adverse consequences for medical confidentiality. Privacy decisions preceding *Whalen* held that although no explicit right to privacy is to be found in any provision of the constitution, privacy is a "fundamental right"[28] derived from the Constitution by implication.[29] In theory, governmental regulation affecting a fundamental right requires a showing of a "compelling state interest" to justify state interference.[30] However, the *Whalen* Court showed little inclination to subject state-mandated programs involving unwanted disclosures of medical information to similarly stringent burdens of justification. Significantly, the Court did not adopt the strong language of the "strict scrutiny" test that it required in earlier privacy cases.[31] The Court spoke instead in terms of a less demanding standard requiring only that the statute be a "reasonable exercise of New York's broad police powers."[32]

Subsequent decisions on the issue of informational privacy similarly suggest a less demanding test for the judicial weighing of competing interests than was required in earlier privacy cases involving other rights.[33] Recent lower court opinions interpreting *Whalen* and later Supreme Court decisions concluded that the constitutional permissibility of state interference with informational privacy should be left to "a case by case method, balancing the individual rights to confidentiality against the government's interest in limited disclosure."[34]

We can, however, look to these subsequent cases for some indication of the factors to be considered in weighing individual interests in the privacy of personal information against state interests in collecting and maintaining that information. Among the most important are criteria announced in *United States* v. *Westinghouse Electric Corp.*:[35] (1) the adequacy of safeguards to prevent unauthorized disclosures;[36] (2) the degree of need for access; (3) whether there is an express statutory mandate, articulated policy, or other reasonable public policy militating toward access; and (4) the comprehensiveness and degree of detail contained in medical records (such as complete medical histories compared with the more limited information retained under the New York drug registry statute in *Whalen*).[37] Taken together, these guidelines suggest that the state-mandated medical information collection programs most likely to be found constitutional are ones in which there is an express statutory mandate, the need for the information is considerable, safeguards against disclosure are strong, and the information collected is not more comprehensive than would be required to comply with the legitimate statutory aim.

These factors should be viewed as rough guidelines for a court's analysis in future cases inasmuch as the relevance of each consideration may vary in particular circumstances. For example, the comprehensiveness or detail of the information collected does not automatically create a greater potential for important interests to be compromised by unwanted disclosure. At least one court has held that greater protection may be warranted in cases involving potential disclosure of "sensitive" medical information, such as psychological records, than for routine pulmonary function tests.[38] This rationale for greater protection of sensitive information arguably is applicable in the context of HIV information. The disclosure of someone's HIV test results may be more damaging than wholesale disclosure of other kinds of medical records whose total contents may not have equal potential for harm to the patient's interests.

Nonetheless, to the extent that the need for information is apparent, safeguards appear adequate, the information is not unduly comprehensive in nature, and an articulated governmental policy justifying collection is discernible, state-sanctioned interferences with informational privacy are not likely to be considered unconstitutional. Thus it appears that constitutional requirements will not offer much protection against unwanted disclosures of medical information, including disclosures pursuant to screening programs, health reporting requirements, notification of third parties at risk of infection, and the reporting of health information to insurers, law enforcement agencies, or others with a bona fide need to know the details of personal medical records.

Common Law and Statutory Protections

Most legal protections of confidentiality and informational privacy are found either in legislation or in judicially developed common law, rather than in constitutional law.[39] In the absence of applicable constitutional or statutory provisions, protection against unwanted disclosures of medical information must be found in common law remedies created by judges. However, common law protection is more limited than many people ordinarily assume, and many confidentiality statutes have not adequately expanded its scope.

Scope of application, exceptions, and impediments to enforcement

Common law and statutory protections frequently are limited in three important respects. First, most laws protecting against disclosure of medical information have fairly significant limitations on the *scope of application*. Such laws often apply to only specific persons, institutions, or contexts. Not everyone having access to personal medical information is under a legal duty to safeguard against disclosures, and no legal duties of confidentiality exist in many institutional settings where medical information is generated, collected, or received.

A second limitation appears in the form of *exceptions to the duty* to protect confidential information from disclosure. Even where the duty to protect medical information applies to designated persons in specific institutional settings, it may be overridden by other legal duties to specific persons or to society in general.

A third limitation is *unenforceability*. A variety of institutional and practical obstacles may make enforcement of legal rights to the maintenance of confidentiality difficult or impossible.

The physician–patient privilege

One of the most familiar forms of legal protection of confidentiality is the professional privilege, such as the physician–patient privilege. A privileged professional communication is defined as a communication to a professional that the professional is bound by special prohibitions not to disclose. Although physician–patient privilege laws differ somewhat from state to state, the general rule at present is that, under certain circumstances, physicians are not permitted to disclose any information that (1) was acquired in their professional capacity *and* (2) was necessary to the care and treatment of their patients.[40] Such information ordinarily includes information learned in the course of consultation, examination, observation, diagnosis, or treatment.[41]

Although the physician–patient privilege is one of the most frequently discussed forms of protection for confidential medical information, it has a very limited function. *The main limitation is that a professional privilege protects information conveyed in the course of the professional relationship from unwanted disclosure in judicial proceedings only.* Many of the contexts in which the patient's interests in confidentiality may be adversely affected arise outside the context of disclosure in legal proceedings. Thus the scope of the privilege's application is too narrow to shield against many breaches of confidentiality.

Moreover, there are numerous exceptions under which the privilege will be overridden in the judicial context. In cases in which the health status of the patient or the contents of the medical records are material issues in litigation, courts may order disclosure in the interest of justice or to secure the protection of other individual or societal interests. If, for example, the health status of a patient is an issue in a criminal trial in which the patient is a defendant, the physician cannot refuse to disclose that information, even though the patient does not authorize such disclosure. In cases where a physician is compelled to disclose confidential information in a court proceeding or is otherwise required by law to make such disclosures, the physician generally has no liability for disclosure.[42] In addition, the existence of the privilege ordinarily does not provide independent grounds for the physician or other health-care provider to refuse to disclose information in judicial proceedings. The privilege against disclosure can be invoked only by the patient in most jurisdictions, and it may be waived by his or her actions or express consent.[43]

Another important concern is that the physician–patient privilege is not as firmly entrenched in the law as many people think. Physician–patient privilege statutes currently exist in some form in the majority of states, but unlike the attorney–client privilege, they are not generally recognized as part of the common law in the United States.[44] This means that in jurisdictions where no statutory privilege exists, there is no special protection from disclosure in judicial proceedings apart from the general powers of the courts to determine the admissibility of evidence. For example, no physician–patient privilege is recognized either in federal common law or under the Federal Rules of Evidence, but federal judges have the authority to protect any information if doing so is reasonable in light of "reason and experience."[45] The scope of available protection is thus left to a case-by-case determination.

Limited application of medical privilege statutes

Even where medical privilege statutes exist, such laws frequently do not apply to health-care providers other than physicians.[46] However, some courts have extended privileges against disclosure to ancillary health-care and administrative personnel, especially when state medical practice acts and licensure requirements specifically prohibit such disclosures in other contexts.[47]

Even the limited protections afforded by professional privilege laws generally do not extend to the research context, as most states do not recognize a researcher–subject privilege. Researchers who testify as expert witnesses may be asked to disclose the data that support their conclusions and are subject to cross-examination regarding the methods of obtaining that data. As a consequence, the confidentiality promised to research subjects—who have no connection to a lawsuit—may be at risk if the data subpoenaed contain patient identifiers. Further, the relation between the patient and the pending litigation may be extremely remote. For example, sometimes researchers receive information about individuals with whom they have no personal investigator–subject relationship, as is the case when researchers receive confidential information from the treating physicians or medical records.

Courts may protect the confidentiality of medical subjects in judicial proceedings by requiring the deletion of personal identifiers from the data, although the burden of doing so may be onerous and the potential for error considerable.[48] Accordingly, several commentators have recommended statutes granting the absolute protection of medical research records from subpoena.[49] Similar protection already exists for records in alcohol or drug abuse research generated by the Department of Health and Human Services and its various institutes.[50] The federal Drug and Alcohol Abuse Act prohibits disclosure of the name, date of admission, and description of the medical condition of persons being treated for substance abuse.[51] The act affords strong protection in the drug and alcohol abuse treatment and research settings. Its rationale seems equally applicable to

HIV infection, where there is similar potential for social stigma and other adverse consequences of disclosure. In addition, there is considerable overlap between public health activities to control HIV infection and drug use.

General duties of nondisclosure

Legislatures and courts have held that certain persons may be under legal duties not to disclose medical information in contexts other than judicial proceedings. Legal duties of nondisclosure arising under professional privilege laws should not be confused with more general legal duties not to disclose confidential medical information, however. As indicated already, the confidentiality protections embodied in professional privilege laws apply to judicial proceedings only. Professional privilege laws and general duties of nondisclosure are independent, and the purposes of each (contrary to what most nonlawyers ordinarily might assume) are distinguishable.

The primary purpose of a professional privilege law is to restrict the information that may be introduced into evidence in a civil or criminal proceeding. *Professional privilege statutes may permit judges to exclude information from disclosure in a judicial proceeding, even in cases where there is no general legal duty not to disclose such information in other contexts.* For example, medical information may be excluded to ensure a fair trial or to ensure that the judicial process itself does not become a vehicle for the dissemination of personal information.

Moreover, laws designed to limit disclosures in judicial contexts do not automatically give rise to the existence of legal protections against disclosures in other contexts. Thus even the existence of a professional privilege statute offers no guarantee that individuals will have a privately enforceable remedy against those who disclose personal medical information.

The modern trend is toward an expansion of protection of confidential medical information in judicial and nonjudicial contexts alike. Many—but not all—jurisdictions now recognize a basis for the recovery of monetary damages against physicians for unauthorized disclosures of medical information, although the underlying legal theories may differ.[52] Some courts have established *tort* liability for injuries caused by unauthorized disclosures. These cases typically classify such torts as a "breach of a duty of confidentiality" or an "invasion of privacy." For example, in a 1973 Alabama case involving disclosure of medical information to a patient's employer, the court held that "unauthorized disclosure of intimate details of a patient's health may amount to unwarranted publicization of one's private affairs . . . such as to cause outrage, mental suffering, shame or humiliation to a person of ordinary sensibilities."[53] Other states have recognized a basis for damages for disclosure of information contained in a patient's medical records on the theory that the duty of confidentiality is an implied condition of the contract between physician and patient.[54]

General duties of confidentiality not extended to other health professionals and institutions

Some of the problems associated with the professional privilege laws applicable to judicial proceedings are found in laws governing medical confidentiality in nonjudicial contexts. For example, states holding physicians liable for breach of their general duties of confidentiality frequently do not extend legal liability to other health-care personnel, medical and behavioral researchers, or health-care institutions.[55] As a rule, judges have been more reluctant to hold other health professionals to a special duty of confidentiality comparable to that of physicians, even though the risk of harm from disclosure may be as great or greater.[56] That reluctance is due, at least in part, to viewing the rationale for a legally enforceable remedy as linked to the *special contractual relationship* between the physician and the patient, rather than to the potential for harm that persons would reasonably expect as a consequence of disclosure. Courts often have relied on the requirements embodied in medical codes of ethics, medical practice acts, and other statutes creating physician–patient privileges as providing the major justification for creation of private legal remedies. The result is a narrow focus on the contractual duties of the physician.

Tort theories that emphasize the potential for harmful consequences rather than the traditional contractual basis for enforcement of rights may expand the list of parties who might be liable for damages and the kinds of misconduct that might be held legally objectionable. Tort claims based on invasion of privacy may permit recovery against persons who cause harm, not only through improper disclosure but by improperly obtaining or using medical information, even when there is no contractual relationship, as there is between physician and patient.[57] The development of tort law remedies reflects a move away from viewing the rationale for a legal duty as primarily a function of the contractual arrangement between professional and patient. *The focus is shifted to the potential for harm* and the role anyone with access to medical records reasonably might be expected to play in its prevention.

The tort approach offers two advantages for the protection of confidentiality interests. First, the shift of emphasis from contractual obligation to reasonable societal expectations may make the law explicitly more sensitive to limitations of confidentiality inherent in many clinical and institutional settings. Second, the move away from contractual expectations better reflects the range of institutions and persons best positioned to protect interests in confidentiality—regardless of whether there is a contract between the parties.

Comprehensive statutes

The shift to remedies influenced by the rationale of tort law is evident in recent statutory confidentiality protections. Some states have enacted comprehensive medical confidentiality statutes that cover a range of health-care records in addition to those maintained by physicians. Medical records acts often permit recovery of damages for the unauthorized disclosure of the contents of medical records.[58] The provisions often apply to hospitals, outpatient and ambulatory surgical treatment centers, independent laboratories, and peer review committees, as well as others who have no direct contractual relationship with the patient. However, many of these statutes continue to reflect a piecemeal approach to medical confidentiality protection. For example, some jurisdictions have made the unauthorized disclosure of patient information by hospital and peer review committees a violation of criminal law, yet they do not recognize a legally enforceable duty of confidentiality that would permit individuals to recover monetary damages for unwanted disclosures of personal medical information.[59]

Recent federal legislation

Although most of the legal protections discussed so far have been implemented at the state level, significant efforts have been made in the area of federal legislation. An important example of federal statutory protection is the Privacy Act of 1974.[60] This extensive federal statutory attempt to ensure confidentiality of highly personal information has served as a model, or at least the starting point for discussion, for privacy legislation at the state level. The act protects information held by federal agencies from being disclosed to the public or to other governmental agencies, and it includes protection of information regarding medical history, financial, and other personal matters.[61]

The Privacy Act's protections are limited in a number of respects, however. First, the statute exempts a potentially large number of communications from its coverage by virtue of its "routine use exception."[62] Under this exception, agencies may communicate confidential information to a wide range of other governmental entities, including state and local agencies. Second, the protections against disclosure apply to only federal agencies and governmental contractors.[63] The requirements extend to some nongovernmental institutions, such as universities and contracting hospitals, but many institutions, such as private hospitals subject to extensive governmental regulation and involvement, are not covered. Third, the act protects information bearing individual names or personal identifiers (e.g., Social Security number, fingerprints, photographs), but not information about persons who, by further investigation and inferential means, are identifiable.[64] Fourth, although provision is made for both civil and criminal penalties for disclosures to those not entitled to the information, there are a number of practical impediments to enforcement. Aggrieved persons may file suit in federal district court for damages and may recover monetary damages and attorneys' fees for any actual harm proved to have resulted from the improper disclosure. However, the burden of proof—as well as the considerable burden of expense—rests on the aggrieved party to demonstrate that the disclosure was willful.[65]

Impediments to enforcement

There are significant impediments to patients who attempt to enforce their legal rights to medical confidentiality. The successful use of litigation to protect confidentiality remains relatively rare.[66] At least until recently, few cases have been brought against physicians, and according to one survey, as of 1974, there were no reported cases in the United States in which a physician or hospital had ever had to pay money damages for breach of confidentiality.[67] Whether this state of affairs is best explained by the relative infrequency of breaches of confidentiality or by widespread aversion or other impediments to successful litigation remains unclear.

Statutory provisions creating civil penalties usually contemplate individual enforcement through the institution of a civil lawsuit. Although the financial— and emotional—costs of individual enforcement may be burdensome, the statutory remedies frequently provide the successful plaintiff recovery of attorneys' fees, court costs, and, in some instances, statutorily defined minimum damages independent of the need to demonstrate actual financial loss. However, the difficulties may all too often be insurmountable. In some jurisdictions, no privately enforceable remedy for unauthorized disclosure is available unless there is an intent to harm.[68] Proof of intent is often extremely difficult to find. More significantly, by the very nature of the complaint, the matters are highly sensitive, and hence the further opening up of these matters to trial in a public judicial forum undermines one of the litigant's original objectives—minimizing unwanted public disclosure.

For all the reasons cited above, litigation is not likely to be a realistic or timely alternative for many persons, including those affected by HIV infection. Moreover, in many instances, reliance on private litigation to secure one's rights to confidentiality simply is misplaced. Individuals may be harmed by unauthorized disclosures of medical information even though they may never learn of the disclosures. For example, improper disclosures of medical information may prevent someone from being accepted for day care services, although the applicant (or the applicant's parents) may never know the reason for rejection or the source of the information.

Statutes allowing imposition of criminal penalties, by contrast, usually contemplate public prosecution. The burden of instituting legal proceedings falls on government prosecutors. The potential deterrent effects of the criminal law, as well as the ability to punish systematic violations of many persons' rights, are its chief merits. It offers the possibility for greater efficiency by eliminating the need for private individuals to pursue their own cases independently. However, the disadvantages include the higher standard of proof required in criminal proceedings, as well as the impediments to effective and timely prosecution created by the overburdened criminal justice system. Moreover, prosecutors may be reluctant to prosecute institutional or corporate violators when individual responsibility and accountability may be difficult to determine. The fact that potential criminal defendants may be powerful and respected members of the community may add to that reluctance.

Recommendations

Several factors discussed in this section raise doubts about the capacity of the legal system to protect confidential medical information from unwanted disclosure. Nonetheless, the creation, promotion, and enforcement of legal duties of confidentiality remain the primary legal vehicle for protecting confidentiality. Since no single enforcement mechanism is likely to be the best for every circumstance, a variety of options is needed. Civil penalties for individuals and institutions are appropriate in cases of negligent disclosures. Criminal penalties may be appropriate in some instances, especially where disclosures are intentional. Health-care licensure requirements are an important enforcement tool, particularly if the policies for maintaining confidentiality are provided for in established protocols and the economic disincentives for noncompliance are substantial.

In addition, the extension of duties of confidentiality to all persons having access to personal medical information is needed to ensure consistency across a wide range of institutional settings and among medical and ancillary personnel. Pediatric infection exemplifies the scope of the problem as it pertains to HIV. The sophisticated management of pediatric AIDS cases is likely to require the participation of a variety of medical and social service professions, as well as a constellation of institutions providing different levels of custodial, long-term, acute, and rehabilitative health-care services. Medical confidentiality laws should be carefully drafted to ensure that duties of confidentiality extend to all persons involved in health-care administration and direct patient care. Among those who should be covered are registered nurses, vocational nurses, physician's assistants, physicians, midwives, medical laboratory technicians, dentists, dental hygienists, custodians of medical records, unlicensed personnel with access to medical charts and records, administrators, educational pyschologists, counselors and social service workers, members of peer review and institutional ethics committees, program auditors, and licensure inspectors.

Other institutions that explicitly should be covered by a legal duty of confidentiality include nursing homes, psychiatric facilities, outpatient and ambulatory treatment centers, blood banks and plasma centers, private laboratories, rehabilitation and social service programs, independent data systems and pooled insurance company information networks, research institutes, universities, and employers and regulatory agencies with which information is shared. It seems archaic to think that only physicians, because of their special contractual relationship to their patients, should be held to stringent legal duties of confidentiality. Such legal duties should apply to anyone who (1) has access to personal information that renders individuals vulnerable to the harmful consequences of disclosure and (2) is in a position to take feasible steps to reduce the likelihood of such disclosure.

Even with excellent and comprehensive legal protections, many threats to the confidentiality of medical information remain and are endemic to the health-care delivery system. These threats are a function of the fact that in any modern medical, research, or public health setting, a large number of persons have access to information. Problems of this sort are addressed primarily by internal security procedures designed to restrict unauthorized or unnecessary access to information. An important aspect of any internal security system is the establishment of clear, widely understood confidentiality policies and procedures.[69] Health-care institutions need protocols for maintaining the security of manual and electronic records, and provision for periodic review of HIV confidentiality policies and procedures should be required.[70] Such policies should provide for lists of job titles, and the functions within those titles, authorized to have access to HIV information.[71] Equally important are employee training and compliance plans requiring initial and annual in-service training on legal prohibitions and mandating that only persons who have completed such training have access to HIV information.[72]

Exceptions to Legal Duties of Confidentiality

State laws prohibiting unauthorized disclosure of medical information contain a variety of exceptions, including ones that readily allow disclosures to government agencies, law enforcement officers, medical review committees, and persons who may be at risk of harm. These exceptions exacerbate the problem of controlling access in that the institution generating the information loses the ability to ensure that the information is protected from improper use once it is transferred. Legal protections designed to balance the needs for such disclosures and to limit their harmful consequences are few in number and of recent vintage. In some instances, additional restrictions on the release of information to others are needed.

The insurance industry

The relationship between the insurance industry and health-care institutions is a special source of concern. The exchange of information is routine and comprehensive, and the information is maintained in large, systematic computerized data banks, greatly increasing the possibility for breaches of confidentiality.[73] Numerous persons in the insurance industry without a bona fide need to know a patient's health status may learn of a diagnosis through the data banks, such as the ones maintained by the Medical Information Bureau.[74] The Medical Information Bureau is a central information exchange system that collects and makes available to its more than 800 member life insurance companies information about health or health risk activities.[75] Other consumer investigative firms collect information about life-styles to determine eligibility for insurance or employment. Access to such information is widely available to employers, insurance agents, and lending institutions that issue insurance policies in conjunction with retail credit agreements.[76] One means of combating abuse with regard to HIV reporting is to require changes in the way medical information is reported to data banks and medical information bureaus. For example, most computerized medical information reporting codes readily permit identification of a patient's diagnosis. Recent amendments to the New York Insurance Code require the use of more general reporting codes—that is, ones not designated solely for HIV-related test results—for reporting of HIV test results by medical information exchange centers.[77]

Requests for law enforcement personnel

Another frequent source of conflict between patient confidentiality and other public interests is the need for information by law enforcement personnel. For example, the Internal Revenue Service (IRS) has the authority to request patient-identifiable information in order to locate individuals, verify medical deductions, and verify physician-reported income figures. Although the Tax Reform Act of 1976 was meant to restrict the IRS's authority in information gathering and limit its disclosures to other governmental agencies, the authority remains quite broad.[78] Justice Department guidelines issued in 1983 give the Federal Bureau of Investigation similarly broad authority to investigate matters of domestic security and terrorism on the basis of a reasonable indication, including the oral statements of anonymous informers.[79]

State laws should make explicit the duties of health-care institutions to honor law enforcement requests only if certain safeguards have been implemented. For example, no information should be made available to law enforcement agencies unless authorized by the patient or on presentation of a subpoena or probable cause warrant. In addition, disclosures pursuant to a warrant or subpoena should be narrowly tailored to meet the requirements of the request while minimizing the danger of disclosure of material not explicitly requested or material that reveals personal information about other persons.

Reporting requirements

Efforts to maintain confidentiality of HIV information are confounded by the fact that the relevant information is reportable to other agencies and organizations, such as state and local public health departments or disease control centers. AIDS is currently reportable to the Center for Disease Control in every state.[80]

Every state requires reporting of communicable diseases to the state public health department, and all states include some provision for reporting of HIV infection. However, reporting laws differ in their specific requirements. States may require the reporting of only fully developed AIDS cases, patients with ARC, or all seropositive persons. The trend is toward reporting of all seropositive persons, regardless of whether the person has manifested any symptoms of illness.[81]

Reporting requirements also differ in the extent to which HIV information is linked to identifiable persons. There are a number of variations among state practices. Reports may be transmitted either anonymously or with patient identifiers. Nine states currently use confidential reporting systems that require that the individual's name or some other form of patient identifier be reported.[82] Although there has been much public debate about the need to identify asymptomatic HIV-infected individuals—for example, to facilitate prophylactic treatment with zidovudine (AZT)—most states use some system of anonymous reporting. Anonymous reporting requirements permit the transmission of useful epidemiologic data via a code. For example, California collects HIV information for epidemiologic surveillance purposes and for monitoring the prevalence of the disease.[83] Before the physician transfers information to the AIDS Registry, the names are converted to a Soundex code. The code consists of a letter representing the first letter of the last name followed by three digits that depend on the other letters of the last name. Use of such a code reduces the potential for duplication in reporting, but because different surnames may have the same Soundex code, persons having access to the Registry may not determine the identity of any individual.[84] Other states use a code consisting of the last five digits of the patient's social security number, which helps the state avoid duplication in prevalence estimates but does not permit the discovery of the identity of the person tested.[85]

Although some of the risks of breach of confidentiality may be lessened by the use of anonymous reporting mechanisms, some critics worry that epidemiologic data necessary for accurate assessment of prevalence may be sacrificed.[86] Some public health officials who are more confident of their prevalence estimates of adult AIDS cases have expressed concern about the reporting of pediatric AIDS cases.[87] An alternative designed to counteract deficiencies in prevalence information is to conduct independent seroprevalence studies. In some instances, the studies are conducted through "blind testing" programs. In some of these programs, blood left over from other procedures may be tested without the patient's knowledge or consent, and identifiers are removed from the blood samples so that neither the researcher nor the patient can learn the results for specific persons. Several studies of this sort have been conducted on newborn infants, and unless these alternatives prove inadequate or objectionable in some other respect, the importance of confidentiality warrants continued reliance on this approach.[88]

In addition, it has been argued that anonymous reporting frustrates contact tracing. Contact tracing has been one of the standard methods for control of sexually transmitted diseases.[89] Colorado, for example, requires the reporting of the names of HIV-infected persons, coupled with a systematic effort to obtain the names of other sexual and needle-sharing partners and, in turn, to contact those persons for testing, counseling, and interviewing to obtain additional names.[90] The American Medical Association (AMA) has defended the availability of anonymous testing and reporting as a means of encouraging voluntary testing, and it has strongly endorsed an active program of contact tracing by public health authorities.[91] Critics of anonymous testing have noted an inconsistency in the AMA's recommendations.[92] The complaint is that anonymous testing does not serve the goal of an active contact tracing program, which is to identify all infected persons through their sexual and needle-sharing partners and thereby interrupt the spread of disease.

Recent evidence suggests, however, that requiring physicians to report the names of persons testing positive for HIV infection tends to discourage people from being tested. For example, when Oregon modified its named reporting system to allow anonymous testing, the number of persons tested increased by 50 percent and the number of seropositive persons identified doubled.[93] A similar study in South Carolina concluded that implementation of mandatory reporting of HIV-positive results in that state reduced the number of homosexual men tested by 50 percent and decreased the number of seropositive persons identified by 43 percent.[94]

Without more convincing evidence either of epidemiologic necessity or of inability to protect third parties through alternative means, anonymous testing is a reasonable approach to balancing the need for confidentiality protection with the need to encourage people to seek testing and early treatment.

Notification requirements

In all states, AIDS also is what is known as a "notifiable" disease, meaning that, at least in certain instances, there is some procedure for notifying third parties who may have been exposed.[95] Notification programs differ from active contact tracing in three important respects. First, partner notification programs, unlike most active contact tracing programs, rely primarily on voluntary notification. Active contact tracing programs are designed to ascertain the names of as many HIV-exposed persons as possible by requiring persons who test positive to disclose the names of all their sexual and needle-sharing partners.

Second, notification programs do not depend on the development of extensive lists of the names of infected persons and profiles of their sexual and needle-sharing relationships. Active contact tracing programs employ investigators to locate and interview every person named by persons who test positive for HIV, and then, in turn, to attempt to ascertain the names of all their contacts so that they may be interviewed. The purpose of notification programs is less ambitious.

Their aim is not to identify every HIV-infected person, but to assist and encourage individuals to notify others of the potential exposure to infection.

Third, notification programs do not disclose to the notified party that a named individual is infected and has listed that person as a sexual or needle-sharing contact. Active contact tracing involves a personal interview in which the persons being notified learn the identity of other infected persons and, that such persons have already disclosed to an investigator highly personal information about their relationship. By contrast, notification programs are designed to provide persons at risk of infection with needed information without revealing the identity of the individual from whom the information was obtained.

Notification is achieved either by patient referral or by provider referral. In the latter case, the provider rather than the patient informs third parties of their potential exposure. Forty-eight states and the District of Columbia offer provider referral upon request of the patient, and Georgia and Nebraska authorize notification by health department personnel to specific types of partners, such as women of childbearing age.[96] Provider referral makes it easier to preserve the anonymity of persons tested while achieving the aim of warning others who are at risk (and who may be putting others at risk). Nonetheless, the potential for inferring the identity of the patient remains a real problem. This potential may be reduced further by a process in which the physician's duty to notify is discharged indirectly. By passing on the name of the persons to be notified to the public health department, the tracing of patients to specific physicians also can be avoided.

Duties to warn third parties at risk of harm

Recent developments in tort law create duties in marked conflict with the physician's duties of confidentiality. Some courts have held that physicians have a duty to warn third parties of dangers to their health and safety even if the discharge of this duty to warn is in conflict with other duties owed to their patients. Leading cases like California's famous *Tarasoff* decision involve mental health professionals' duties to warn potential victims of violence of the threats to their safety revealed in confidential therapeutic conversations.[97] Although no court has yet held a physician liable for damages for failure to warn third parties of the possible danger of exposure to HIV infection, the same duty-to-warn principle has a plausible application to the potential for AIDS transmission.[98] Indeed, various commentators have speculated on the possibility of having to choose between the risk of tort liability for failure to warn and the threat of criminal or tort liability for violation of confidentiality requirements.[99]

Several states recently have enacted stringent legislation to safeguard against the disclosure of HIV information.[100] However, even the strongest of these HIV confidentiality statutes contain important exceptions, including ones permitting disclosures for the protection of third parties at risk of infection.[101] Legislation in Rhode Island requires a "clear and present danger of transmission to third parties" *and* reason to believe that the patient "has not or will not warn" those in danger, "despite the physician's strong encouragement."[102] Similar confidentiality provisions in a Hawaii statute require a "good cause showing" before the confidentiality requirement may be overridden.[103] A Hawaii state judge held that the good cause requirement would not allow its strict confidentiality protections to be overridden unless there was a factual basis to support the health-care provider's belief that others were at risk of infection. The court held that rumor and unsubstantiated speculation are not enough to dispense with the presumption in favor of confidentiality.[104]

Amendments to California and New York AIDS confidentiality laws go one step further by providing legal protection for physicians who face such a dilemma. The New York law provides immunity from liability for physicians either for failing to warn third parties or for warning third parties at risk of infection. Immunity from physician liability to his or her patients is qualified, however. A physician may make such disclosures only when he or she believes that it is medically necessary, that there is a substantial risk of transmission, that the patient will not notify the individuals at risk, and, where possible or appropriate, without the name of the patient.[105] Similarly, the California law provides immunity from civil and criminal prosecution for disclosure of information to "persons reasonably believed to be a spouse, or to a person reasonably believed to be a sexual partner, or a person with whom the person has shared the use of hypodermic needles."[106] However, the requirements for receiving immunity are (1) that the physician must not disclose any identifying information to the third party and (2) that such notification can be undertaken only after discussing the test results with the patient, offering counseling, attempting to obtain voluntary consent for contact notification, and advising the patient of his or her intent to notify the contacts.[107]

Requirements of the sort developed in Hawaii, California, and New York appear to be reasonable attempts to balance the interests of patients in confidentiality with the competing societal and individual third-party interests in providing others with appropriate information about their own health risks. The presumption in favor of confidentiality should reinforce the public trust in the integrity of the physician–patient relationship, while the "bypass" mechanisms for third-party notification without patient identification appears to discharge competing duties to different segments of the public.

It should be noted that legislative efforts to criminalize the intentional or knowing transmission of HIV may undermine these efforts to induce patients to share information about their sexual contacts for fear of its use in potential criminal prosecution. Even if legislatures find merit in criminalizing such willful and knowing conduct, there may be good reason to exclude information supplied to physicians from use in those prosecutions.[108]

Research records

Medical records used in research pose additional problems. As noted already, most medical privilege laws do not provide adequate protection of research subjects' medical records in judicial proceedings. Similar problems exist in non-judicial contexts. Only a few state laws expressly protect against disclosure of personally identifiable research records containing sensitive medical information. A California statute provides for civil penalties for negligent disclosures as well as criminal penalties for willful breaches of patient confidentiality in the research context.[109] A New York statute specifically dealing with AIDS research further prohibits publication of data in such a way that the identities of the research subjects can be inferred.[110]

Matters may be complicated further when the research is federally funded, as is much of the current research on HIV infection. The Freedom of Information Act requires public access to documents held by governmental agencies unless such documents are covered by one of the act's exceptions.[111] In 1980, the Supreme Court held that medical records kept by federally funded medical school investigators were not "agency records" within the meaning of the statute.[112] Hence they would not be accessible under the provisions of the Freedom of Information Act. One court has extended the protection against Freedom of Information Act disclosure to a case in which a governmental agency received raw data, including individual medical records.[113] These rulings would seem to provide at least some protection for subjects involved in HIV research, but other issues remain unanswered. The need to clarify the scope of such protection for research records is especially important in the context of HIV infection. If recommendations for the development of a national AIDS data base and a federal agency–sponsored program of exchange of research information are implemented, researchers and research subjects should not be uncertain about the extent of protection from Freedom of Information requests.[114]

Patient authorization and notification requirements

The problem of numerous requests for medical information by other persons and institutions has spawned several proposals. One proposal is a requirement that a health-care institution notify its patients of all types of disclosure that may be made without authorization and renotify them whenever a new category of disclosure is created.[115] Some argue that the requirement to compile a statement of every possible external disclosure would be too burdensome for the institutions. A less burdensome requirement having a similar intended effect would be notification of each actual disclosure made. Still less burdensome would be a requirement of a record entry for each disclosure. In the case of HIV-related information, it may be argued that none of these proposals for after-the-fact notification offers the patient adequate protection. More timely safeguards may be preferable. Recent legislation in Rhode Island requires health-care institutions, in advance of any third-party disclosure of HIV- or AIDS-related information, to make a reasonable effort to inform the patient of the nature and purpose of the disclosure, the date of the disclosure, and the identity of the recipient of the information.[116] The effect of statutes of this sort would be to grant patients a veto against specific disclosures, although the scope of this veto might be limited by other requirements of public health information gathering, judicial, and law enforcement activities. Advance patient notification policies are aimed directly at preventing breaches of confidentiality, rather than relying on an enforcement mechanism to deter them. A likely consequence of such a requirement is that it will impress on patients and health-care personnel the seriousness of the duties of confidentiality and the adverse consequences resulting from the breach of those duties. For these reasons, the advance patient notification policy offers the best opportunity to limit the adverse consequences that may result from the number and variety of exceptions to duties of confidentiality.

The need for uniformity

The President's Commission on the Human Immunodeficiency Virus Epidemic (hereafter, the President's Commission) has recommended enactment of a national policy to replace the considerable variation among the state statutes with a uniform HIV confidentiality policy.[117] One important reason for national uniformity is that the flow of information itself is not restricted to the state jurisdiction in which it is generated. Information generated in New York, under one set of legal expectations of confidentiality, may end up in other states, for example, due to the need for research collaboration or insurance reimbursement. Without a uniform system of confidentiality rules that individuals may consider in deciding whether or not to be tested, it is difficult for them to give truly meaningful informed consent with respect to the risk of unwanted disclosure.

Why Confidentiality Protection Is Not Enough

Confidentiality procedures and personnel training, civil or criminal penalties for intentional or negligent disclosure, and restriction of access to sensitive information must play a central but not exclusive role in protecting the interests of patients. There are four major reasons why confidentiality protection alone may not be enough. Three of these reasons have been addressed in the previous sections: many of the persons who have access to medical information are under no clear legal duty to maintain confidentiality; there are substantial practical impediments to enforcement of the remedies afforded even by well-designed confidentiality protection statutes; and because there are numerous persons with a plausible claim for a need to know the contents of medical records and the results of HIV tests, there are myriad exceptions to duties of confidentiality. To these we can add a fourth: there are inherent institutional limits to preventing public identification of HIV status.

Inherent limits to preventing disclosures

The potential for public identification of persons with HIV infection exists in spite of any measures that might be taken to impede improper disclosures. No medical or research setting can guarantee complete anonymity to its patients. No health-care provider can ensure that the patient's health status or reason for seeking care will remain secret or undiscoverable by the general public through inferential means. Special hospital clinics or in-patient units, segregated prison health-care facilities, designated treatment centers, and other special counseling programs make anonymity impossible. Administrative procedures, such as the posting of hazardous bodily fluid warnings on patients' doors or charts, or the maintenance of dual hospital record-keeping systems to meet statutory demands for security of HIV test results, may make it apparent or readily inferable that particular persons are HIV-positive. A medical prescription for AZT or a laboratory request for confirmatory tests reveals the identity of persons infected with HIV just as surely as the disclosure of the contents of medical records. Consequently, there is significant potential for unwanted dissemination of personal information that has nothing to do with any direct breach of confidentiality. Indeed, one conclusion we might draw is that the overall goal of confidentiality policies should include a provision special systems designed to protect against disclosures do not, in fact, become counterproductive.

The practical limits to protection of confidentiality in clinical, research, and related medical settings suggest that still more protection is needed against harm to the underlying interests of the persons screened. A comprehensive approach should be aimed at reducing the adverse consequences of disclosure or public identification of HIV status. Thus any law designed for the protection of persons with HIV infection should be concerned with the potential for invidious discrimination on the basis of actual or perceived HIV infection or AIDS.

The rationale for antidiscrimination protection

Many have defended the need for legal protections against discrimination on the basis of HIV infection or AIDS on a variety of grounds. Some have cited the need for public health officials to secure the cooperation of infected individuals, and have argued that without such protections, many individuals will not seek testing or treatment or provide information about others who may be at risk of infection. Many "fear that they will be unable to retain their jobs and housing, and that they will be unable to obtain the medical and support services they need because of discrimination based upon a positive HIV antibody test."[118] Some public health officials who favor reporting requirements in which the names of

HIV-infected individuals are used endorse stronger antidiscrimination protections and are reluctant to institute such programs until stronger statutes are enacted.[119] Others emphasize the need for antidiscrimination protections either to plug the gaps where legal protections against breaches of confidentiality fail or to educate and encourage fundamental changes in behavior toward persons with HIV infection.[120] Another reason must be added to this list. Antidiscrimination statutes send a powerful symbolic message to all members of society: invidious discrimination and arbitrary treatment of persons on the basis of disability is like other forms of unacceptable discrimination. It is repugnant to the nation's commitment to equality under law and therefore ought to be rejected.

Proposals

The President's Commission recommended comprehensive state and federal legislation to prohibit discrimination against persons with disabilities or handicaps, with HIV infection included as a covered handicap.[121] In addition, the Commission recommended that antidiscrimination education programs should be made mandatory for health employees and that health-care professionals who have repeated and substantiated discrimination complaints against them should be subject to discipline.[122] Finally, the Commission noted that the availability of patient advocates in health-care institutions and expedited procedures for review of complaints may increase the efficacy of the antidiscrimination provisions.[123]

If, as many have argued, the success of public health objectives related to HIV testing depends on the ability to reassure people that adequate steps are being taken to protect confidentiality and prevent discrimination, then comprehensive federal legislation is necessary to provide uniform and thorough protection.[124] Just as this chapter has argued that it is unreasonable for prospective test subjects to rely on the confidentiality protections of a single state, it also argues that adequate protection against discrimination requires a national approach. The reason is apparent. The flow of medical information and the potential for economic loss and social harm do not end at state borders. Nor should prospective test subjects be expected to make informed decisions regarding the advisability of HIV testing given the uncertainties and vagaries of the current patchwork of state laws.

Existing state laws suffer from a number of deficiencies that a comprehensive federal antidiscrimination statute should address. First, there is a wide variation in the areas of activity covered by such laws. Among the areas covered in some states are employment, public accommodations, insurance, public services, housing, availability of financing and credit, and education.[125] Second, there need to be uniform and predictable definitions of the classes of persons who, on the basis of their disabilities, benefit from coverage. For example, the protections of a comprehensive statute should cover persons with AIDS, with asymptomatic

HIV infection, and those perceived as having a handicap.[126] Third, there need to be consistent definitions of the classes of persons excluded. For example, in some states and in current federal proposals, there are provisions to exclude from antidiscrimination protection in employment persons who are mentally handicapped (e.g., those with AIDS-related neurologic impairment), who work in food service industries, or who are alcohol or drug dependent.[127]

There are many additional considerations that might be addressed in a comprehensive federal statute. However, it is important that some legal framework be in place at the national level for the protection of persons with HIV infection. Two qualifications are necessary. First, the area of antidiscrimination law is complex, and it is unlikely that a single federal statute will offer needed protection in many important contexts. Consequently, a federal statute should be viewed as defining the minimum, rather than setting a limit on the protections the various states may see fit to provide. Second, it is important to remember that antidiscrimination statutes themselves suffer from some of the same inherent limitations that affect confidentiality protections. The enforcement of either requires litigation, which is always expensive and often of little immediate benefit to persons who are the victims of discrimination or breach of confidentiality.

Conclusion

Given the realities of clinical, research, and screening settings, the goals of maintaining confidentiality and anonymity can be realized, at best, only incompletely. A comprehensive legal strategy to protect the interests of HIV-infected persons must incorporate a three-tiered approach to protect against (1) unwanted disclosures, (2) unwanted identification of patients' HIV status through means other than disclosure, and (3) the potentially disastrous consequences of unwanted disclosure or identification of a patient's HIV status.

Many of the protections discussed in this chapter apply to all persons with HIV infection, not just pregnant women and newborns. However, consideration of pregnant women and newborns highlights two concerns that receive less attention in most discussions of the subject. First, the powerlessness and lack of resources of many poor and minority women and infants who may be affected by these policies illuminate the inherent limitations of relying on the legal system for their enforcement. Second, although poor and minority women and infants do not stand to lose many of the economic and social opportunities that other groups of HIV-infected persons may have, it is clear that the risk of loss of available social and medical services, and the social ostracism and loss of support of family and friends, can be as devastating as any other loss for others who are less disadvantaged. Their special vulnerability adds powerful arguments to the case for strong confidentiality and antidiscrimination protections.

Notes

1. See Chapter 5 of this volume.
2. Quoted in Ann H. Britton, "Rights to Privacy in Medical Records," *Journal of Legal Medicine* 3 (July–August 1975): 30.
3. Tom L. Beauchamp and James Childress, *Principles of Biomedical Ethics,* 3rd ed. (New York: Oxford University Press, 1989), 329.
4. *Principles of Medical Ethics,* pamphlet 1E-206-8400-1230:558-L:8/75: 10M (Chicago: American Medical Association, n.d.). In 1980, this statement was revised to hold simply that a physician "shall safeguard patient confidences within the constraints of the law" (Beauchamp and Childress, *Principles of Biomedical Ethics,* 330).
5. Mark Seigler, "Confidentiality in Medicine—A Decrepit Concept," *New England Journal of Medicine* 307 (1982): 1518–1521.
6. The definition of "privacy" changes according to the legal context. In constitutional and common law contexts, a more expansive definition often is found. See *Olmstead* v. *United States,* 277 U.S. 438, 478 (1928) (Brandeis, J., dissenting) ("The makers of our Constitution . . . sought to protect Americans in their beliefs, their thoughts, their emotions and their sensations. They conferred as against the government, the right to be let alone"). By contrast, statutory definitions of privacy generally are concerned with the individual's right to control personal information. See, for example, the federal Privacy Act of 1974, 5 U.S.C., sec. 552a (1982).
7. Louis D. Brandeis and Samuel D. Warren, "The Right to Privacy," *Harvard Law Review* 4 (1890): 193, 198. They argued that "the common law secures to each individual the right of determining, ordinarily, to what extent his thoughts, sentiments, and emotions shall be communicated to others."
8. William Prosser, "Privacy," *California Law Review* 48 (1960): 383–423. See also *3 Restatement (2d) of Torts,* sec. 652A(2) (1977) (the right of privacy is invaded by (1) unreasonable intrusion on the seclusion of another, (2) appropriation of the other's name or likeness, (3) unreasonable publicity given to the other's private life, or (4) publicity that unreasonably places the other in a false light before the public).
9. See also Chapter 7 of this volume.
10. The notion of access to a person is itself indeterminate, and the correlative notion of limiting access within certain "zones" or "spheres" of privacy is highly metaphorical. The metaphor has been stretched to cover various means of invasion and many conceptions of what is invaded. Invasions of privacy can be achieved through (1) intrusion into the body to discover its secrets, for example, by drawing blood, pumping someone's stomach to determine its contents, or administering drugs to cause one to speak the truth; (2) intrusion into one's physical space, as in entry into one's home or property; (3) direct or electronic observation of one's intimate activities; (4) listening to or electronic eavesdropping on one's intimate conversations; (5) intrusion into one's state of mind or mental processes, for example, by interfering with one's autonomy or decision-making capacity; or (6) intrusion into one's relationship with others when there is a reasonable expectation that the matters disclosed would not be made public.
11. W. A. Parent, "Privacy, Morality, and the Law," *Philosophy and Public Affairs* 12 (1983): 269–288.
12. See, for example, Sylvia Law, "Rethinking Sex and the Constitution," *University of*

Pennsylvania Law Review 132 (1984): 955. She argues that the result reached in *Roe v. Wade* protecting a woman's right to make decisions about abortion would be better supported on grounds of the requirements of the equal protection clause. She argues that what is constitutionally suspect about antiabortion laws is not so much their potential for interfering with privacy interests as their potential to cause great disadvantage to women, in some cases destroying their opportunity to lead lives routinely available to men.

13. See the discussion in Beauchamp and Childress, *Principles of Biomedical Ethics,* 319–20.

14. See Ruth Gavison, "Privacy and the Limits of Law," *Yale Law Journal* 89 (1980): 428.

15. This category of privacy interest is best described in terms of the decisional privacy interest discussed by Anita Allen in Chapter 7 of this volume. In instances such as the abortion decision, social opprobrium may be attached to one's choices, and one of the chief consequences of the unwanted disclosure of personal medical information may be the restriction of one's autonomy because of fear of such disclosure. The notion of decisional privacy is a broader one inasmuch as there are ways other than unwanted disclosure to interfere with one's choices, and not all disclosures interfere with one's autonomy. However, to the extent that disclosures do interfere with autonomous choice, then the privacy interest at stake is both decisional and informational.

16. *Report of the President's Commission on the Human Immunodeficiency Virus Epidemic* (Washington, D.C.: President's Commission, 1988), 119–120. See also Robert Blendon and Karen Donelan, "Discrimination Against People with AIDS," *New England Journal of Medicine,* 319 (1988): 1022–1026.

17. Classification of traditional tort remedies as pre-event strategies may seem counterintuitive to some. The notion of a remedy familiar to tort lawyers connotes a legal option designed to make whole an injured party. But in the context of contemporary injury prevention theories, tort law is increasingly viewed as having another, equally central purpose—to serve as a front-end approach to the regulation of human conduct. For a discussion of the role of tort law as a means of injury prevention, see Tom Christoffel, "The Role of Law in Reducing Injury," *Law, Medicine, and Health Care* 17 (1989): 7–16, and Stephen Teret and Michael Jacobs, "Prevention and Torts: The Role of Litigation in Injury Control," *Law, Medicine and Health Care* 17 (1989): 17–22.

18. L. S. Robertson, *Injuries: Causes, Control Strategies, and Public Policy,* (Lexington, Mass.: Lexington Books, 1983), 133.

19. For a discussion of the choice between pre-event and postevent strategies in injury prevention theory, see Christoffel, "Role of Law," 80.

20. *Whalen* v. *Roe,* 429 U.S. 589 (1977). For a more general discussion of the constitutional right to informational privacy, see Chapter 7 of this volume.

21. *Whalen* v. *Roe,* 429 U.S. 589, 602 (1977).

22. Ibid., 595, 602.

23. Although Supreme Court decisions recognize the important relation between an individual's privacy interest in nondisclosure of medical records and the ability to make constitutionally protected medical decisions regarding abortion, other societal interests may outweigh the privacy interest in medical records. See *Planned Parenthood of Central Missouri* v. *Danforth,* 428 U.S. 52, 80 (1976) ("recordkeeping and reporting requirements that are reasonably directed to the preservation of maternal

health and that properly respect a patient's confidentiality and privacy are permissible").

24. *Whalen* v. *Roe*, 429 U.S. 603–604 (1977).
25. Ibid., 601.
26. Ibid., 605.
27. Ibid., 605–606 ("We therefore need not, and do not, decide any question which might be presented by the unwarranted disclosure of accumulated private data—whether intentional or unintentional—or by any system that did not contain comparable security provisions").
28. *Roe* v. *Wade*, 410 U.S. 113, 152–153 (1973).
29. *Griswold* v. *Connecticut*, 381 U.S. 479, 484 (1965).
30. *Roe* v. *Wade*, 410 U.S. at 155.
31. But contrast Justice Brennan's concurring opinion, in *Whalen*, 607 ("broad dissemination would trigger strict scrutiny and need for showing compelling state interest"), with Justice Stewart's concurring opinion, in *Whalen*, 608 (denying the existence of any broad right of privacy that would warrant strict scrutiny of cases presenting the sole issue of an unwanted disclosure of personal information).
32. Ibid., 598. The standard of judicial scrutiny in the *Whalen* case looks like the ordinary rational basis test. The Court speaks in terms of a "rational legislative decision" (ibid., 597) and of a "vital" rather than a "compelling state interest" in "controlling the distribution of dangerous drugs" (ibid., 598).
33. *Detroit Edison Co.* v. *NLRB*, 440 U.S. 301, 313–317 (1979); *Nixon* v. *Administrator of General Services*, 433 U.S. 425, 457–458 (1977).
34. See *Woods* v. *White et al.*, 689 F. Supp. 874 (W.D. Wis. 1988).
35. *United States* v. *Westinghouse Electric Corp.*, 638 F.2d 570, 578 (3d Cir. 1980).
36. In *United States* v. *Westinghouse Electric Corp.*, 638 F.2d 570, 579, the Court cites *Detroit Edison* v. *NLRB* for this proposition.
37. *United States* v. *Westinghouse Electric Corp.*, 638 F.2d 570, 577, 578 (3d Cir. 1980). But compare the different formulation in *Detroit Edison* v. *NLRB*, 315 (there was no principle of NLRB policy that denial of access would disserve).
38. *United States* v. *Westinghouse Electric Corp.*, 579 (noted a difference between private and sensitive information). But compare *MacDonald* v. *Clinger*, 84 A.D.2d 482, 488, 446 N.Y.S.2d 801, 805 (1982).
39. See, for example, *Bishop* v. *United States*, 334 F. Supp. 415, 418 (S.D. Tex. 1971) ("The common law is generally described as those principles, usage and rules of action applicable to the government and security of persons and property which do not rest for their authority upon any express and positive declaration of the will of the legislature").
40. Arthur F. Southwick, *The Law of Hospital and Health Care Administration*, 2nd ed. (Ann Arbor, Mich.: Health Administration Press, 1988), 525.
41. However, courts have held that the physician–patient privilege does not apply to medical examinations that are not performed for the express purpose of rendering medical advice or care, at least when the patient lacks a reasonable expectation that the consultation will be confidential. See *Van Sickle* v. *McHugh*, 430 N.W.2d 799 (Mich. App. 1988).
42. See, for example, *Boyd* v. *Wynn*, 286 Ky. 173, 150 S.W.2d 648 (1941).
43. See *Tucson Medical Center* v. *Rowles*, 21 Ariz. App. 424, 429, (Ariz. Ct. App. 1974) (the patient must expressly waive the privilege in order to permit disclosure of

confidential information), and *Lanbdin* v. *Leopard*, 20 Ohio Misc. 189, 192 (Ct. Common Pleas 1968) (the plaintiff is deemed to have waived his privilege by bringing a personal injury action that puts his medical record at issue).

44. See Note, "Developments in the Law—Privileged Communications," *Harvard Law Review* 98 (1985): 1450.

45. See Federal Rules of Evidence, sec. 501, cited in *Deichman* v. *E.R. Squibb & Sons, Inc.*, 740 F.2d 556, 566 (7th Cir. 1984).

46. See "Physician–Patient Privilege as Extending to Patient's Medical or Hospital Records," in *American Law Reports*, 4th ed. (Rochester, N.Y.: Lawyers Co-operative, 1981), 10: 552.

47. See, for example, *Tucson Medical Center* v. *Rowles*, 21 Ariz. App. 424, 520 P.2d 518 (1974).

48. Angela Holder, "The Biomedical Researcher and Subpoenas: Judicial Protection of Confidential Medical Data," *American Journal of Law and Medicine* 12 (1986): 405.

49. Ibid.

50. 42 C.F.R., part 2a.

51. Ibid.

52. For examples of states that do not recognize a general legal duty of physician confidentiality, see *Collins* v. *Howard*, 156 F. Supp. 322 (S.D. Ga. 1957), and *Quarles* v. *Sutherland*, 215 Tenn. 651, 389 S.W.2d 249 (1965). However, Tennessee has a statute regulating public health department disclosures of confidential information on sexually transmitted diseases, including AIDS (Tennessee Code Annotated 68-10 [1988]). Georgia has recently enacted a statute that makes it a misdemeanor to disclose HIV information intentionally or knowingly (Code of Georgia Annotated, sec. 24-9-47 [1988]). It remains an open question whether Tennessee and Georgia would recognize a private right of action against persons who disclose HIV information. For an earlier case in which Tennessee courts held that enactment of a criminal confidentiality statute did not give rise to a private right to sue for breach of confidentiality, see note 59.

53. See *Horne* v. *Patton*, 287 So. 2d 824 (Ala. 1973). Unauthorized disclosures of medical information may be protected by the common law right of privacy associated with unreasonable publicity given another's private life if the matter publicized is of a kind that "(a) would be highly offensive to a reasonable person, and (b) is not of legitimate concern to the public" (*Restatement (2d) of Torts* 3, sec. 652D [1977]).

54. Some courts have incorporated both tort and contract theories of liability for disclosure of medical information. See, for example, *Hammonds* v. *Aetna Casualty & Surety Co.*, 243 F. Supp. 793 (N.D. Ohio 1965).

55. See Note, "Public Health Protection and the Privacy of Medical Records," *Harvard Civil Rights—Civil Liberties Law Review* 16 (1981): 265, 286–289.

56. Barry B. Boyer, "Computerized Medical Records and the Right to Privacy: The Emerging Federal Response," *Buffalo Law Review* 25 (1975): 37, 77. But see *Tucson Medical Center, Inc.* v. *Rowles*, 21 Ariz. App. 424, 520 P.2d 518 (1974).

57. See Note, "Public Health Protection and the Privacy of Medical Records."

58. For example, Maryland Health, General Annotated Code, sec. 4-301 (1982 & Supp. 1988).

59. For example, Tennessee recognizes no physician–patient privilege and no other duty of physician confidentiality, even though it makes it a misdemeanor for members of

a hospital peer review committee to disclose any matter pertaining to patients' medical conditions discussed in peer review meetings. See *Quarles* v. *Sutherland*, 215 Tenn. 651, 389 S.W.2d 249 (1965).

60. 5 U.S.C. 552.
61. 5 U.S.C. 552(a)(4).
62. 5 U.S.C. 552(b)(3) and (a)(7).
63. 5 U.S.C. 552(a).
64. 5 U.S.C. 552 a(4) and (a)(5).
65. 5 U.S.C. 552(a)(g)(4). See, for example, *Edison* v. *Dept. of the Army*, 672 F.2d 833 (C.A. Ga. 1982).
66. See Note, "Public Health Protection and the Privacy of Medical Records," 265, 286–289.
67. Alan F. Westin, *Computers, Health Records, and Citizen Rights* (Washington, D.C.: National Bureau of Standards, 1975), 26.
68. See *Simonsen* v. *Swenson*, 104 Neb. 224, 177 N.W. 831 (1920).
69. See Jo Anne Czecowski, *Privacy and Confidentiality of Health Care Information* (Chicago: American Hospital Publishing Company, 1984), 104–124.
70. New York Public Health Law, art. 27-F, and pt. 63, subch. G; General Laws of Rhode Island, sec. 23-6-18(a), and Proposed Rules and Regulations Pertaining to Counseling, Testing, Reporting and Confidentiality, R23-6-HIV-1, pt. V.
71. New York Public Health Law, art. 27-F, subch. G, Official Compilation of Codes, Rules, and Regulations of the State of New York (February 15, 1989).
72. See ibid. and General Laws of Rhode Island, sec. 23-6-18 (a)–(c) (1988).
73. Laurence Stern, "Medical Information Bureau: The Life Insurer's Databank," *Rutgers Journal of Computers and Law* 4 (1974): 1, 5–7.
74. The collection and sharing of medical information about their insureds by the Medical Information Bureau is a concern particularly identified in the report of the Privacy Protection Study Commission, *Personal Privacy in an Information Society* (Washington, D.C.: Government Printing Office, 1977), 159, 175.
75. American Council of Life Insurance, *Life Insurance Fact Book Update* (Washington, D.C., 1987), 56.
76. Davis W. Gregg and Vane B. Lucas, eds., *Life and Insurance Handbook* (Homewood, Ill.: Irwin, 1973), 1009. Equifax, formerly known as the Retail Credit Company, conducts more than 80 percent of the checks done on individuals for automobile, health, and life insurance companies (Czecowski, *Privacy and Confidentiality*). Activities of this sort are regulated by the Fair Credit Reporting Act, 15 U.S.C. 1681a–1681t (1982) (regulates persons or organizations that regularly collect and report on individuals for purposes of credit, insurance, or employment).
77. New York Insurance Law, sec. 321 (1989).
78. Privacy Protection Study Commission, *Personal Privacy in an Information Society*, 360.
79. For a general discussion of law enforcement exceptions, see Carol Cleaver, "Privacy Rights in Medical Records," *Fordham Urban Law Journal* 13 (1984–1985): 165, 196–210.
80. William Curran, Mary E. Clark, and Larry Gostin, "AIDS: Legal and Policy Implications of the Applications of Traditional Disease Control Measures," *Law, Medicine, and Health Care* 15 (1987): 27.
81. Forty-three states now require reporting of seropositive cases ("HIV Reporting in the States," *Intergovernmental AIDS Reports*, vol. 2, no. 5 [Washington, D.C.:

Intergovernmental Health Project, George Washington University, 1989]).

82. Ibid.

83. For example, California's registry has been in existence since March 1983 (K. Kizer, "California's Approach to AIDS," *AIDS and Public Policy Journal* 3 [1988]: 1–10). See also Illinois Annotated Statutes, ch. 111½, para. 7354 (Smith-Hurd 1988).

84. Kizer, "California's Approach to AIDS," 4.

85. Karen Rothenberg, "AIDS: Creating a Public Health Policy," *Maryland Law Review* 48 (1989): 176–177.

86. See Timothy J. Dondero, M. Pappaioanou, and James W. Curran, "Monitoring the Levels and Trends of HIV Infection: The Public Health Service's HIV Surveillance Program," *Public Health Reports* 103 (1988): 213–220.

87. Ibid.

88. Lloyd F. Novick, Donald Berns, Rachel Stricof et al., "HIV Seroprevalence in Newborns in New York State," *Journal of the American Medical Association* 261 (1989): 1745–1750. For a discussion of the ethical implications of such practices, see A. L. Alvins and Bernard Lo, "To Tell or Not to Tell: The Ethical Dilemmas of HIV Test Notification in Epidemiological Research," *American Journal of Public Health* 79 (1989): 1544–1548.

89. Curran et al., "AIDS," 27.

90. Colorado Revised Statutes, sec. 25-1402 (1987); 6 Colorado Administrative Code 1009-1, Regulation 2 (1988).

91. The AMA's position is contained in Report X of the AMA Board of Trustees (December 1989).

92. For criticisms of the AMA's position, see William E. Dannemeyer, Letter to Colleagues, February 15, 1989.

93. Laura J. Fehrs, David Fleming, Laurence Foster et al., "Trial of Anonymous versus Confidential Human Immunodeficiency Virus Testing," *Lancet* 2 (1988): 379–382. See also Bernard Lo, "Clinical Ethics and HIV-Related Illnesses: Issues in Treatment and Health Services Research," in *Conference Proceedings, New Perspectives on HIV-Related Illnesses: Progress in Health Services Research,* ed. William N. LeVee (Rockville, Md.: National Center for Health Services Research and Health Care Technology Assessment, Public Health Service, 1989), 173.

94. W. D. Johnson, F. S. Sy, and K. L. Jackson, "The Impact of Mandatory Reporting of HIV Seropositive Persons in South Carolina," Abstract 6020 *Programs and Abstracts of the Fourth International AIDS Conference, June 1988* (discussed in Lo, "Clinical Ethics," 173).

95. See Centers for Disease Control, "Partner Notification for Preventing Human Immunodeficiency Virus (HIV) Infection—Colorado, Idaho, South Carolina, Virginia," *Morbidity and Mortality Weekly Report* 37 (1988): 393–402.

96. Ibid.

97. *Tarasoff* v. *Regents of the University of California,* 17 Cal. 3d 425, 441, 131 Cal. Rptr. 14, 27, 551 P.2d 334, 347 (1976).

98. See *Simonsen* v. *Swenson,* 104 Neb. 244, 177 N.W. 831 (1920) (grants immunity from liability for breach of confidence when necessary to protect third parties against contagious diseases).

99. States that have passed strong AIDS confidentiality laws with criminal penalties for disclosure present the physician's dilemma most dramatically (Note, "Between a Rock and a Hard Place: AIDS and the Conflicting Duties of Preventing Disease

Transmission and Safeguarding Confidentiality," *Georgetown Law Review* 76 [1987]: 169, 197; Larry Gostin and William Curran, "AIDS Screening, Confidentiality, and the Duty to Warn," *American Journal of Public Health* 77 [1987]: 361–365).

100. Among the states with such legislation are California, Idaho, Illinois, Indiana, Kentucky, Massachusetts, and Texas (Rothenberg, "AIDS: Creating a Public Health Policy," 93, 174).

101. See, for example, California Health and Safety Code, sec. 199.21 (West 1988). The California statute prohibited disclosure of test results to any third party without written notification, but subsequent amendments contained in ch. 1216 (September 22, 1988) provided a number of exceptions to what briefly was a very strict requirement.

102. General Laws of Rhode Island, sec. 23-6-17(b) (v) (1988).

103. Hawaii Revised Statutes, sec. 325-101 (1988).

104. *Drug Addiction Services of Hawaii* v. *Doe,* Hawaii Cir. Ct. (1st Cir.), Civil No. 88-3838-12 (January 23, 1989). The court ruled that the rumor that an infected patient was engaging in sexual conduct and needle sharing, thereby putting others at risk of contracting the disease, did not meet that state's strict AIDS confidentiality requirement. The court held that no factual basis sufficient to satisfy the "good cause" requirement was presented. This conclusion was reached even though the physician may be liable in tort for failure to warn third parties and even though U.S. Department of Health and Human Services regulations permit disclosure of the identities of drug treatment program participants.

105. Laws of New York 9265-A, sec. 2782 (4) (1988).

106. Ch. 1216 (1988 Sessions Laws) amending California Health and Safety Code, sec. 199.25 (West 1988).

107. Ibid.

108. Indiana and Minnesota statutes specify that names and other information obtained in partner notification programs cannot be used against persons providing the information during proceedings to determine noncompliant behavior (*Laws Governing Confidentiality of HIV-Related Information,* 1: I-37).

109. California Health and Safety Code, sec. 199.37(a)–(d) (West 1985).

110. New York Public Health Law, sec. 2775–2779 (McKinney 1984).

111. 5 U.S.C. 552(b) (1982).

112. *Forsham* v. *Harris,* 445 U.S. 169 (1980).

113. *Public Citizen Health Research Group* v. *FDA,* 704 F.2d 1280 (9th Cir. 1983).

114. *Report of the President's Commission,* 37, 43–44.

115. Privacy Study Commission, *Personal Privacy in an Information Society,* 309.

116. General Laws of Rhode Island, sec. 23-6-20 (1988); Proposed Rules and Regulations Pertaining to Counseling, Testing, Reporting and Confidentiality, R23-6-HIV-1, pt. V.

117. *Report of the President's Commission,* 127.

118. Ibid., 119.

119. Intergovernmental Health Project, "HIV Reporting in the States."

120. Bernard Dickens, "Legal Limits of AIDS Confidentiality," *Journal of the American Medical Association* 259 (1989): 3449–3451; R. Roden, "Educating Through the Law: The Los Angeles AIDS Discrimination Ordinance," *UCLA Law Review* 33 (1986): 1410–1441.

121. *Report of the President's Commission,* 121–124.

122. Ibid., 126.
123. Ibid., 126, 124.
124. At the time of this writing, the Congress was considering the Americans with Disabilities Act of 1989, S. 933. That bill has been enacted as P.L. 101-336, Americans with Disabilities Act of 1990.
125. See Mona Rowe and Bethany Bridgham, *Executive Summary and Analysis: AIDS and Discrimination—A Review of State Laws that Affect HIV Infection—1983– 1988,* (Washington, D.C.: Intergovernmental Health Project, George Washington University, 1989), 1: I-5 to I-6.
126. Ibid., 1: I-17.
127. Ibid., 1: I-8; Americans with Disabilities Act of 1989, S. 933, sec. 512 (a) (2).

IV

ETHICAL AND SOCIAL ISSUES

10

Screening Newborns for HIV: Ethical and Legal Aspects

RUTH R. FADEN AND JUDITH AREEN

This chapter examines the ethical and legal context in which policies concerning the screening of newborns for evidence of HIV infection must be made.

The chapter is divided into three sections. The first part provides an overview of the legal context for HIV screening of newborns. Specific legal issues raised by both mandatory and parental consent programs are examined.

The second part presents a moral justification of parental consent requirements, as well as an analysis of the conditions under which it is morally permissible to override or bypass such requirements in medical and public health contexts.

In the third part, we argue for a policy of parental consent for HIV testing of newborns. Arguments for a policy of mandatory newborn screening are reviewed and refuted. One set of conditions under which a policy of mandatory screening would be morally acceptable is presented. We conclude by discussing conditions other than maternal consent required of a morally acceptable newborn screening program.

Legal Aspects of Screening Newborns for HIV

There is a well-established tradition in our nation of judicial deference to parental authority. As the U.S. Supreme Court has observed, "It is cardinal with us that the custody, care and nurture of the child reside first in the parents."[1] Nonetheless, the Court has also held that the government "is not without constitutional control over parental discretion in dealing with children when their physical or mental health is jeopardized."[2] Unfortunately, no bright line has been established to determine precisely when it is appropriate to act to protect the health of a child over the objection of his or her parent.

Generally, courts have refused to intervene when the risk to a child's health is not immediately life-threatening.[3] Legislatures, by contrast, have carved out a number of broad statutory exceptions to the common law requirement of parental consent. These legislated exceptions typically are not limited to life-or-death situations.[4] Mississippi law, for example, provides that parental consent is not needed for "any unemancipated minor of sufficient intelligence to understand and appreciate the consequences of the proposed surgical or medical treatment or procedures."[5]

Another well-recognized exception to the common law requirement of parental consent exists for public health measures. Thus the Supreme Court has specifically held that a parent may not reject compulsory vaccination for his or her child, even on religious grounds.[6] Most states have extended the public health exception by specifically authorizing the treatment of minors for venereal disease without parental consent.[7]

A third exception has been created by the legislatures of a majority of the states for routine screening of newborns for one or more treatable conditions, such as syphilis and phenylketonuria (PKU). Chapter 6 provides a thorough review of these state requirements. As noted in Chapter 3, most states require that all newborns be screened for PKU. Of these, a majority permit parents to refuse screening, but only on religious grounds. A growing number of states have extended mandatory screening to other metabolic disorders, including maple syrup urine disease, histidinemia, homocystinuria, hyperlysemia, tyrosinemia, and galactosemia.

Voluntary screening of newborns

Voluntary screening—that is, screening with the consent of the newborn's parent or guardian—should in most instances satisfy the requirements of the common law. It also is likely that screening programs that are "routine with notification and the right to refuse" (to use the language of Chapter 1) also will be viewed as voluntary by the courts and thus as acceptable. Any legal challenge to such programs is likely to turn on whether the proffered right of parents to refuse was meaningful (see Chapter 12).

To say that there are no legal barriers is not the same thing as asserting that voluntary newborn screening programs will not be controversial, however. As the history of screening for sickle cell disease demonstrates (see Chapter 3, a program that appears to single out a minority group unfairly for testing or that lacks adequate counseling services may become extremely controversial, even though it is legal.

Voluntary screening may also present difficult issues concerning parental consent. Under common law principles, one parent has authority to act as agent for the other in giving (or withholding) consent for medical procedures, as well as for other matters of their child's upbringing and education.[8] In almost all instances involving newborns, the deciding parent is likely to be the mother. Because HIV antibody testing of a newborn reveals the HIV status of the mother, a mother might refuse to consent to testing not for the sake of her child, but to conceal her own HIV status. The question thus arises of whether or not health-care professionals are legally obligated in such a circumstance to seek the consent of the father.

As noted in Chapters 5 and 14, HIV testing is not clearly or unambiguously in the best interests of newborns. As a result, in the absence of state legislation to the contrary, it is unlikely that courts would view health-care professionals as legally obligated to seek paternal consent if a mother refuses testing.

If in the future, or with regard to a specific infant, however, testing is clearly in the infant's best interests, it would be at least prudent to make reasonable efforts to reach the father in the event of the mother's refusal, at least if the parents of the child are or were married.[9] If the parents were never married, by contrast, the Supreme Court's decision in *Lehr* v. *Robertson*[10] indicates that the father should be contacted only if he has demonstrated a commitment to parenthood, thus according him the same legal status as a father married to the child's mother.

In *Lehr*, the Supreme Court emphasized that although the father lived with the mother prior to the child's birth and visited her in the hospital when the baby was born, his name did not appear on the birth certificate. Moreover, he did not live with the mother or the child after the child's birth, never provided them with any financial support, and never offered to marry the mother. The court concluded:

> When an unwed father demonstrates a full commitment to the responsibility of parenthood by "com[ing] forward to participate in the rearing of his child . . . his interest in personal contact with his child acquires substantial protection under the Due Process Clause. At that point it may be said that he acts as a father towards his children." But the mere existence of a biological link does not merit equivalent constitutional protection.[11]

If disagreement does arise between the mother and the father over testing, regardless of whether the father has been present throughout the postnatal period or has been contacted by the health-care providers, a determination must be made as to which parent's decision should be followed. The option of turning to the legal system to resolve the impasse may not be available, as most state courts have declined to resolve disputes between parents over childrearing.

In *People ex rel. Sission* v. *Sission*,[12] the most influential opinion on this matter, the parents could not agree on the appropriate education for their child. The New York Court of Appeals declined to become involved, yet acknowledged that action would be proper if the health of the child were at stake:

> The court cannot regulate by its processes the internal affairs of the home. Dispute between parents when it does not involve anything immoral or harmful to the welfare of the child is beyond the reach of the law. The vast majority of matters concerning the upbringing of children must be left to the conscience, patience, and self restraint of father and mother. No end of difficulties would arise should judges try to tell parents how to bring up their children. Only when moral, mental, and physical conditions are so bad as seriously to affect the health or morals of children should the courts be called upon to act.[13]

Sission suggests that courts might be willing to adjudicate a parental dispute over testing, at least if it can be shown that the outcome of testing could make a serious difference to the health of the child. Alternatively, a health-care provider might rely on the father's consent to testing if there were reason to believe that the mother's refusal was motivated by a desire to hide her HIV status, rather than being in the best interests of the child.

It is possible that a state concerned that mothers may refuse consent in order to hide their own HIV status, rather than for the sake of their children, may enact legislation that requires health-care providers to notify the fathers about screening. Such legislation may be unconstitutional, however, in light of the recent decision of the Supreme Court in *Hodgson* v. *Minnesota*,[14] which declared unconstitutional a Minnesota statute requiring minors to seek the consent of both parents prior to having an abortion. The Court held that

> the requirement that *both* parents be notified, whether or not both wish to be notified or have assumed responsibility for the upbringing of the child, does not reasonably further any legitimate state interests. The usual justification for a parental consent or notification provision is that it supports the minor's best interest. . . . To the extent that such an interest is legitimate, it would be fully served by a requirement that the minor notify one parent who can then seek the counsel of his or her mate or any other party, when such advice and support is deemed necessary.[15]

But because testing a newborn for HIV always reveals the HIV status of the mother, a mother's refusal of consent may not be made in her infant's best interests. Therefore, a state requirement that fathers be notified might be upheld in the courts. In *Hodgson,* the Supreme Court observed:

> In the ideal family setting, of course, notice to either parent would normally constitute notice to both. A statute requiring two-parent notification would not further any state interest in those instances. In many families, however, the parent notified . . . would not notify the other parent. In those cases the State has no legitimate interest in . . . presuming that the parent who has assumed parental duties is incompetent to make decisions regarding the health and welfare of the child.[16]

The apparent conflict between a mother's interest in hiding her HIV status and the needs of her child might be deemed sufficient justification for courts to uphold a state requirement of paternal notification for newborn screening, unlike abortions for minors.

Mandatory screening

In the present circumstances, in which we can neither cure AIDS nor block transmission of HIV infection to the newborn, it is doubtful that most courts would uphold a program of mandatory screening of newborns for evidence of HIV infection in the absence of legislative authorization. Of the three categories of exception to the common law requirement of parental consent described earlier, it is the third category, routine screening of newborns for syphilis, PKU, and other treatable conditions, that is most analogous to mandatory screening of infants for evidence of HIV infection. This category of exception is entirely statutory, however. Thus in the absence of authorizing legislation, the category provides no precedent for court approval of a mandatory HIV screening program.

The risk–benefit ratio of screening also is more problematic than in most situations in which courts have authorized medical procedures despite parental objections. The screening procedure is not intrusive or intrinsically risky. But there are risks for the infant who is found to be "HIV-positive" that do not apply to an infant with a treatable condition such as PKU. For example, as noted in Chapter 5, it may be extremely difficult to find a relative or foster family willing to care for an infant whose HIV test is positive.[17] Worse, the false-positive rate is about 70 percent. Predictably, therefore, a mandatory screening program will inaccurately label a large number of children, who, as a result, may suffer both unnecessary rejection by potential caretakers and the rigors of unnecessary treatment.

Although courts are more deferential to legislative than to private action, the problematic risk–benefit ratio discussed above with respect to hospital policies might well lead a court to strike down a state law that required mandatory HIV screening of newborns on the ground that it violates the constitutional rights of parents. As the Supreme Court stated in *Hodgson,* "the family has a privacy interest in the upbringing and education of children . . . which is protected by the Constitution against undue state interference."[18] The principle that the state may not interfere with certain family matters was well established even before *Hodgson.* In *Stanley* v. *Illinois,*[19] for example, an unmarried father challenged an Illinois statute that made his children wards of the state after the death of their mother. The statute denied the father the benefit of a hearing regarding his fitness as a parent. The Supreme Court held the statute unconstitutional on the ground that it denied the father his right to due process of law. *Wisconsin* v. *Yoder*[20] recognized the right of parents to make educational decisions for their children. In *Yoder,* the Supreme Court allowed Amish parents to educate their minor child at home despite the existence of a state law requiring children to attend public school.

In summary, programs of mandatory screening of newborns for HIV infection are probably illegal in the absence of authorizing legislation from the state. State legislation authorizing such screening may be held to violate the constitutional rights of parents because the risk–benefit ratio of newborn screening for HIV is more problematic than for other conditions for which newborns are screened routinely.

Moral Basis for Parental Authority: Justifications for Parental Consent Requirements

In this section, we turn to the moral issues involved in this policy decision. From this point on, we focus solely on the question of whether newborn screening programs, if they are to be conducted, should be mandatory or should require parental consent. Other moral and policy issues, such as whether a newborn screening program of any description is warranted and the proper population for such programs, are not directly considered (see Chapters 5 and 14).

As noted in Chapters 1 and 12, the primary function and justification of the obligation to obtain informed consent for medical interventions is respect for individual autonomy. Although informed consent requirements also serve to further the welfare of patients, they are primarily in place to recognize the authority that individuals possess over choices and actions that affect the course of their lives.

When one moves from first-person consent to parental consent, a different justificatory structure is required. Parental consent requirements defer to the authority of parents to make decisions for and about their children. What is the moral justification for deferring to parental authority and thus for parental consent requirements?

On one account, the move from first-person consent to parental consent requires only a shift in the relative priority of the principles of respect for autonomy and beneficence. According to this position, the primary (if not sole) justification and function of parental consent requirements is to protect the welfare of children. Although parental consent requirements do serve to protect parental self-interest and prerogatives, respecting the autonomy of parents is not the main purpose of such requirements. Rather, parental consent is defended as a mechanism for protecting the welfare of children on the theory that parents are their children's most conscientious advocates and have their children's best interest most accurately in focus. This analysis of the primary function of parental consent requirements reflects a well-entrenched view in the literature of biomedical ethics regarding third-party consent obligations for persons who have never been competent—that they are grounded in the principle of beneficence rather than the principle of autonomy.

This is not to say, however, that considerations other than the welfare of children have no place in analyzing parental consent requirements or the moral basis of parental authority. Although contemporary accounts of the moral basis of the parent–child relationship often make parental duties of beneficence central to their analysis,[21] it is generally acknowledged that parents have nonpaternalistic rights over their children as well. These nonpaternalistic prerogatives of parents have been interpreted to include the right to form one's child's values[22] and the right to make decisions that affect one's child for reasons other than the child's interest without interference by the state. This concept of parental autonomy is justified as a particular instance of basic negative rights, such as the right to privacy, that belong to every mature citizen in a free society.[23] Respect for parental autonomy has also been grounded in the recognition that there exists no objective way to best prepare children to become autonomous agents. As any

mode of socialization necessarily transmits certain values and prejudices, the presumption of the liberal state must be to respect parental autonomy as part of its general commitment to toleration of multiple conceptions of the good life.[24]

The analysis of parental consent requirements only in terms of abstract principles such as respect for parental autonomy and parental duties of beneficence fails, however, to capture what is perhaps at the core of a moral account of parenthood. Although parents clearly owe duties of beneficence to their children and can be viewed as having parental rights, these duties and rights do not solely or even largely characterize the relationship between parent and child, nor do they capture the more important human dimensions of what it means to be a parent. The relationship between parent and child is among the most intimate and intense human relations. At the root of this relationship are deep bonds of identification and love. Hume viewed the love that parents naturally feel for their children, and not a general principle of beneficence, to be the foundation of parental duties.[25] Arguably, the special love between parent and child also can create independent moral grounds for respecting both the privacy of the parent–child relationship and parental authority, although precisely why or how this love argues for special rights of privacy and authority has yet to be developed.

Ferdinand Schoeman has argued that because of the special nature of the parent–child relationship, parents are not constrained by a best-interest criterion when dealing with children, although the state may be.[26] It is surely the case that parents regularly, and appropriately, make decisions for a child that are not in any simple sense in the child's best interest. Sometimes these decisions come about in attempts to balance the interests of the child against the interests of other members of the family, as when familial income that in the past was used to send a child to private school is diverted to the support of an elderly grandparent. In other instances, a child's interest in avoiding pain may be overridden by a parent's decision to conform to religious or cultural practices, such as circumcision. Such decisions illustrate how parental decision making reflects the parent's interpretation of the goals and purposes of the family as an independent and intimate social unit, as well as the values and preferences of parents as individuals with personal histories.[27]

Appealing to the special characteristics of the parent–child relationship suggests that there is something importantly right about respecting parental authority, apart from the likelihood that abiding by parental judgment generally does serve to foster the welfare of children. However, it is not clear whether this or any other nonconsequentialist interpretation of the justification for parental authority, such as appeals to parental autonomy, result in substantively different criteria for supervention of parental authority than a consequentialist account, at least in medical settings.

Proponents of the child welfare justification tend to support respecting parental choice in many, if not most, instances. They point to procedural and empirical difficulties in making someone other than the parent responsible for determining what is in the child's best interest, the prospect that parents may reject or abandon children who receive medical intervention over parental objection, and the need to support the family unit in its societal functions in child rearing and socialization.

The most widely accepted criterion for supervention of parental decision making in medical contexts is severe, irreparable harm to the child. Some, such as Joseph Goldstein, hold that parental authority validly overrides the interests of children as judged by others in all cases of clinical decision making, unless the child's life is at stake.[28] Others have defended a broader interpretation of severe, irreparable harm—for example, an interpretation that would include irreversible (but preventable) mental retardation as well as death.[29] Ferdinand Schoeman has argued that parental decisions should not be overridden in clinical contexts unless it can be shown that "no responsible mode of thinking warrants such treatment of a child."[30] Presumably, this criterion permits considerations other than the interests of the child to be treated as legitimate. However, Schoeman also acknowledges that parents are not entitled to sacrifice their children's lives or welfare. As a practical matter, there may be no differences in outcome between his criterion and a "severe, irreparable harm" criterion.

It is also generally acknowledged that parental authority may be overridden by large-scale societal interests. In medical contexts, these societal interests generally relate to the public's health. Perhaps the most widely accepted and used justification is the control and prevention of communicable diseases. This societal interest has been employed to justify limiting parental control in such areas as compulsory childhood immunizations and venereal disease management, where children are permitted to authorize treatment without parental consent or even parental notification. Although the interests of the particular children affected by such policies may be well served by them, the primary justification for limiting parental control is not the prevention of irreparable harm to these children, but the prevention of harm to other persons through the spread of a communicable disease.

By contrast, some public health programs that constrain parental authority, such as compulsory neonatal screening for PKU, have been defended on the ground that they prevent severe, irreparable harm to the children of the parents whose control is being limited. As Robert Bennett has argued, such public health programs focus not on any individual child but on some defined disease or condition as it affects children as a class.[31] Decisions about the beneficial character of an intervention in a public health context are thus judgments that are applicable to children in general—without regard to individual differences. This position presupposes that there are cases in which it is possible to make an objective determination about what is in the interests of children as a class, an assumption that not all may be willing to grant.

Some public health programs that constrain parental control meet neither the societal interest in controlling communicable diseases nor the severe, irreparable harm criterion. They can be defended by arguing that the program serves a societal interest in efficiency in the promotion of child health, in an instance in which the limitations imposed are themselves incidental to important parental choices.[32] Current policies of compulsory neonatal screening for hypothyroidism and galactosemia, which piggyback on existing screening programs for PKU, are perhaps best justified by this combination of arguments.

Regardless of the justificatory structure, public health programs that constrain parental authority generally do so in contexts in which the state is already and inevitably involved. In addition, these programs typically do not address whether parental refusal should be overridden, but whether parental authorization should be solicited in the first place. Because the policy affects all children, and not a particular parent and child, it is arguable that the threat to the integrity of the parent–child relationship is less in public health contexts than in clinical medical care. The reverse also could be argued, however—that state supervention of the authority of all parents poses a greater threat to the institution of the family and the parent–child relationship than the occasional use of the powers of the state to override parental judgment in particular cases.

Implications for HIV Screening of Newborns

Although it is possible that some courts might uphold state legislation establishing a mandatory newborn screening program for evidence of HIV infection, currently there is inadequate justification for such a policy. We do not see mandatory HIV screening of newborns as satisfying any of the exceptions reviewed above for sidestepping parental authority in public health contexts. Specifically, as noted in Chapters 2 and 5, there is little evidence that society's interest in prevention and control of a communicable disease would be served by such a policy. Transmission of the infection from infants to others has rarely been demonstrated. In addition, transmission of the infection to the infant currently cannot be prevented.

There are also insufficient grounds for arguing that mandatory screening programs would prevent severe, irreparable harm to infants as a class. If HIV screening enabled health-care providers either to prevent transmission of the virus to infants or to cure the infection, a severe, irreparable harm case arguably could be made. As already noted, however, this is not possible at present.

Even a weaker "best-interest" standard cannot currently be satisfied. As discussed in Chapter 5, the social risks to newborns identified as "HIV-positive" are thought to be considerable but are not well documented. Newborns doubtless suffer to the extent that their mothers experience social or institutional discrimination. In addition, "HIV-positive" newborns face the risk of being abandoned by their mothers, difficulties with adoption and foster home placements, and difficulties in access to day care.

Assessing the interests of infants is complicated further by the need to distinguish infants who contract the infection from their mothers from those who do not. For the approximately 30 percent of infants who would be identified as being at increased risk because maternal antibodies are detected and who are infected, the prospects for medical benefits are significant and substantially outweigh the risks of associated medical and social harms. Currently available benefits include the prevention or delay of death due to prophylactic treatment for *Pneumocystis carinii* pneumonia (PCP) and the likelihood that intensive primary care and pediatric follow-up will result in a higher quality of life for a longer period of time. Zidovudine is now approved for use in children, and preliminary experience suggests that the drug delays the development of symptoms in children as well as adults, particularly with regard to cognitive and developmental impairments. In the future, Zidovudine administered beginning at birth (or even earlier) may be found to prevent transmission of the virus to the newborn in at least some cases (see Chapters 2 and 5).

For the approximately 70 percent of infants who would be identified as being at increased risk because maternal antibodies are detected but who turn out not to be infected, the harm–benefit calculus is less clear. Access to high-quality primary care is doubtless a benefit to such infants, but interventions such as prophylaxis for PCP are likely to place these infants at some risk, with no appreciable offsetting benefit. The risks associated with Zidovudine in the newborn are not fully established but are expected to vary with the dose and duration of the regimen.

At present, the efficacy of such technologies as blood cultures and polymerase chain reaction (PCR) in distinguishing truly infected from uninfected newborns prior to the administration of specific preventive drugs has not been established (see Chapter 2). Currently, it must be assumed that these two groups cannot be reliably distinguished at birth, and thus that judgments about the interests of newborns as a class must be made for all newborns of HIV-positive women taken together. For the composite group of at-risk newborns—as defined by the presence of maternal antibodies—HIV screening is by no means clearly in their interests.

Even if it could be established that the interests of infants, taken as a class, would be served efficiently by a program of mandatory screening—with, for example, efficiency achieved by adding HIV testing to the panel of tests performed on the sample of blood currently obtained from almost all newborns for PKU testing—HIV screening does not constitute an incidental limitation on important parental choices or an incidental intrusion on the privacy of the family unit. In the present social climate, the decision to risk being identified as HIV-positive must be regarded as an important life choice, whether made by an individual for herself or by a parent for her child.

Finally, there is one dimension to the HIV screening policy problem that is perhaps unique in the history of newborn screening (see Chapter 3). Currently and for the foreseeable future, programs of newborn screening are de facto programs testing for HIV infection in the mother, not the infant. This fact provides justification for a policy of *maternal* consent that is independent of any argument grounded in a moral account of obligations to respect parental authority. At present, maternal consent for HIV testing of the newborn functions as first-person consent, as well as parental consent (see Chapter 12). A policy of mandatory newborn screening must show not only why bypassing parental control is justified, but also why mandatory screening of adults without consent is justified. From this perspective, even programs having a policy of *parental* consent are morally problematic, as they admit the possibility that the HIV status of at least some women would be ascertained without their express consent.

Because of the constitutional issues raised earlier, however, we refrain from advocating the adoption of policies that, legislatively or otherwise, remove fathers altogether from *any* authorization role. We are also concerned that the wider interests of women in gender-neutral public policies, especially with regard to issues of parenting, might be undermined in the long run by the precedent of maternal-only policies for HIV screening of newborns. Because in almost all cases it is the mother whose consent will be solicited, we believe that a policy of parental consent with no obligation to approach both parents is, as a practical matter, an acceptable compromise. It must be admitted, however, that when an involved father insists on the testing of his newborn over the objection of the mother, or when health-care providers believe that testing is clearly in the best interests of a particular infant, such a policy could result in the de facto HIV testing of a woman against her will. In these circumstances, the policy we propose does not necessarily justify morally, or require legally, the overriding of the mother's preferences. Such (hopefully rare) situations would have to be assessed on a case-by-case basis. In the event that a mother's refusal is overridden, the most stringent procedures should be followed to minimize the harm that might arise if the mother's HIV status were to become known by anyone other than those who need to know in order to treat the child.

It should be emphasized that in arguing *against* a policy of mandatory newborn screening, we are not simultaneously arguing *for* the implementation of voluntary newborn screening programs. The question of whether a voluntary program is needed and appropriate entails a more complex analysis than we have engaged in here, including, prominently, the relationship between screening of pregnant women and screening of newborns (see Chapter 14). Our position is simply that there is no warrant for mandatory screening of newborns for HIV and that any screening or testing of newborns that is conducted should require parental consent.

Also, our conclusion that a policy of mandatory newborn screening is unjustifiable is restricted to the current situation. As the medical and social situations change, so could our analysis. For example, if (1) a test became available that could reliably and efficiently detect HIV infection in the newborn, and (2) it was established that the screening program prevented severe, irreparable harm to newborns as a class, *or* (3) it was established that the program in important respects efficiently promoted the best interests of newborns, and either constituted only a minor intrusion on parental decision making or was necessary to ensure that infants would not be denied this important furtherance of their interests, our position would likely change (see Chapter 14).

This new fact situation addresses objections to a mandatory policy grounded in respect for the autonomy of women to determine for themselves whether they wish their HIV status to be identified. The availability of testing technologies that can reliably detect HIV infection in newborns will not eliminate altogether the problem of revealing the HIV status of the mother. This problem will then be restricted, however, to the 30 percent of HIV-positive women who have transmitted the infection to their newborns. Thus only the women whose babies would benefit from testing would have their autonomy and privacy interests infringed.

As noted earlier, a showing of severe, irreparable harm could be substantiated if an intervention were to become available that either prevented transmission of the virus to the newborn or cured the infection in the newborn. If a "magic bullet" of this sort for infants were available, we would advocate not only that screening programs be mandatory but also that in any clinical instance in which a parent refuses such intervention for a particular infant, the parent's wishes be overridden. It is in part because we would not feel morally obligated to respect a parent's refusal of an intervention that would cure a child of HIV infection that we would argue for mandatory screening.

Earlier we argued that, for infants who are infected, the prospects for medical benefits are significant even today and outweigh the risks of associated medical and social harms. Thus if a testing technology could identify infants who are truly infected, it would be in the interest of these infants to be screened. We hesitate to call for mandatory HIV screening, however, even under this condition. We are not confident that the privacy and autonomy interests of women would be justifiably infringed by the benefits to newborns (as these medical benefits are still short of cure). In contrast to the position taken earlier, in a clinical situation, if a parent were to refuse the medical interventions currently available for the management of the HIV-infected child, we clearly would not feel morally justified in overriding the parent's refusal. If the social risks associated with being HIV-positive were to diminish, thereby reducing the centrality of the mother's privacy and autonomy interests, our position might shift, at least with regard to a screening policy.

From a public health perspective, we are not persuaded that a policy of mandatory screening would sufficiently improve the cost efficiency of the program. The education and counseling costs of a mandatory program would not be markedly less than those of a program with a parental consent requirement. The most expensive component of the counseling costs for an HIV screening program is posttest counseling, which mandatory programs would be obligated to provide. There is also little reason to suspect that a mandatory program, in the context of a clear net benefit to infants in being screened, would be more efficient because new mothers would otherwise refuse to permit their newborns to be tested for HIV. Although occasional maternal refusal does occur, anecdotal evidence suggests that the overwhelming majority of women are eager to authorize a medical intervention that stands to benefit their children, even when such intervention places the mother at risk of harm.

Here again, we draw a sharp distinction between a situation in which HIV infection in the newborn can be cured or prevented, where the prospect of even one missed baby is morally intolerable, and a situation in which infants can be benefited but not cured, where the obligation to respect parental authority and the privacy and autonomy of mothers is more difficult to dismiss. Even in the latter case, if it were demonstrated that sizable numbers of mothers refused to permit their infants to be tested, and that as a result significant numbers of babies infected with HIV failed to receive appropriate medical treatment, the balance would likely tip in favor of mandatory screening.

All that we have argued thus far presupposes that the interventions necessary to prevent irreparable harm or otherwise to secure the interests of infants would be provided to all infants identified by a neonatal screen as in need of them. No mandatory program of newborn screening for HIV infection could be considered morally acceptable unless that program provided to infants the benefits that justify the program's existence. Even with voluntary parental consent, screening programs that cannot guarantee all infected infants access to treatment (without undue burdens) are at best morally suspect; at the very least, parents must understand the nature of any limitations on or problems with access to treatment in deciding whether to consent to testing.

Agencies and institutions that conduct HIV neonatal screening programs also assume a duty to minimize the risks associated with the screening program. Central to this duty is taking all feasible steps to protect the confidentiality of HIV information, particularly in view of the interests of mothers as well as infants in this information (see Chapter 9). This duty also entails following all infants identified as having maternal antibodies at least until it is established which infants are indeed infected. Once this has been determined, medical and social service records should be corrected to verify either that the infant has been diagnosed as infected or that the infant is not infected. Alternatively, where state law permits, any reference to HIV seropositivity should be expunged from the medical and social service records of infants determined not to be infected.

Notes

1. *Prince* v. *Massachusetts,* 321 U.S. 158, 166 (1943).
2. *Parham* v. *J.R.,* 442 U.S. 584, 603 (1979).
3. See for example, *In re Phillip B.,* 92 Cal. App. 3d 8796, 156 Cal. Rptr. 48 (1979), *cert. denied sub nom; Bothman* v. *B.,* 445 U.S. 949 (1980); and *In re Seiferth,* 309 N.Y. 80, 127 N.E.2d 820 (1955). See generally 97 A.L.R.3d 421.
4. See generally Robert Bennett, "Allocation of Child Medical Care Decision-Making Authority: A Suggested Interest Analysis," *Virginia Law Review* 62 (1976): 285– 330.
5. Mississippi Code Annotated, sec. 41:41–43(h) (1989). Courts in many states have also recognized a mature minor exception to the requirement of parental consent. See, for example, *Cardwell* v. *Bechtal,* 724 S.W.2d 739 (Tenn. 1987) (adopting a mature minor exception for Tennessee). The exception is not relevant to the matter of newborn screening.
6. *Prince* v. *Massachusetts,* 321 U.S. 158, 166 (1943), citing *Jacobson* v. *Massachusetts,* 197 U.S. 11 (1905).
7 See, for example, California (civil) Code, sec. 34.7 (Deering 1980); Illinois Annotated Statutes, ch. III, para. 4504.4 (Smith-Hurd 1970); Pennsylvania Statutes Annotated, title 35, sec. 521.14a (Purdon 1971).
8. E. Spencer, *Law of Domestic Relations* (1911), 432; T. Reeve, *Law of Baron and Femme* (1816), 295; *Hodgson* v. *Minnesota,* 110 S. Ct. 2926 (1990).
9. For example, if a health-care professional thought that the interests of the infant in being tested were so great that she was willing to take legal action to override the mother's refusal, it would certainly be appropriate first to attempt to reach the father and seek his consent.
10. *Lehr* v. *Robertson,* 463 U.S. 248 (1983).
11. Ibid., 261.
12. *People ex rel. Sission* v. *Sission,* 271 N.Y. 285, 2 N.E.2d 660 (1936).
13. Ibid., 661.
14. *Hodgson* v. *Minnesota,* 110 S. Ct. 2926 (1990).
15. Ibid., 2945.
16. Ibid., 2945.
17. The policy implications are complicated by the fact that an infant whose screening test is negative may be easier to place.
18. *Hodgson* v. *Minnesota,* 100 S. Ct. at 2943.
19. *Stanley* v. *Illinois,* 405 U.S. 645 (1972).
20. *Wisconsin* v. *Yoder,* 406 U.S. 205 (1972).
21. See, for example, Jeffrey Blustein, *Parents and Children: The Ethics of the Family* (New York: Oxford University Press, 1982), and Amy Guttman, "Children, Paternalism and Education," *Philosophy and Public Affairs* 9 (1980): 338–358.
22. Charles Fried, *Right and Wrong* (Cambridge, Mass., Harvard University Press, 1978).

23. Blustein identifies two justifications for parental autonomy: as a special instance of the right to privacy (the parent's interest) and as necessary for the healthy growth and development of children (the child's interest). He argues that the child's interest in parental autonomy should be given greater moral weight than the parent's interest in any account of the moral basis of parenthood (*Parents and Children*, 5–12). Thus Blustein's ultimate appeal is to a conception of child welfare. Indeed, many justifications for parental autonomy, family privacy, and related notions intended to protect parental decision making from state intrusion have at their core the interests of children.

24. Guttman, "Children, Paternalism, and Education," 35.

25. David Hume, *A Treatise of Human Nature,* ed. L. A. Selby-Bigge (Oxford: Clarendon Press, 1975), book 3, pt. 2, sec. 1, as cited in Blustein, *Parents and Children,* 96.

26. Ferdinand Schoeman, "Parental Discretion and Children's Rights: Background and Implications of Medical Decision-Making," *Journal of Medicine and Philosophy* 10 (1985): 45–61.

27. To be sure, both of these examples can be made to fit a best interests interpretation. Taking the child out of private school may be an important experience in building the child's character, while failing to circumcise the child might alienate him from his family in ways that could be psychologically detrimental and might expose him to an increased risk of infection.

28. Joseph Goldstein, "Medical Care for the Child at Risk: On State Supervention of Parental Autonomy," *Yale Law Journal,* 86 (1977): 645–670.

29. Ruth R. Faden, Neil A. Holtzman, and A. Judith Chwalow, "Parental Rights, Child Welfare, and Public Health: The Case of PKU Screening, *American Journal of Public Health* 72 (1982): 1396–1400.

30. Schoeman, "Parental Discretion and Children's Rights," 58.

31. Bennett, "Allocation of Child Medical Care Decision-Making Authority."

32. Gerald Dworkin, "Autonomy and Behavior Control," *Hastings Center Report* 6 (1976): 25.

11

Ethical Issues in HIV Testing During Pregnancy

LEROY WALTERS

This chapter is divided into five sections. The first section outlines the pertinent empirical assumptions underlying the analysis. This section is necessary because some aspects of the ethical analysis may be contingent on a particular fact situation. The second section considers the major parties affected by HIV testing decisions made during pregnancy and examines the first of three central ethical questions surrounding prenatal HIV testing—the potential benefits and harms of testing. The third examines whether testing programs should be voluntary or mandatory. The fourth section analyzes who should be tested. The pregnant woman is clearly the primary focus of this section, but the fetus, the genetic father, health-care workers involved in the care of the pregnant woman, and society at large will also be considered. The final section comments on the social matrix of the prenatal testing question in the United States.

As this preview suggests, much of the ethical analysis that follows centers on the consequences of testing for various affected parties. Not all these parties are persons in the strict sense, and thus interests may need to be attributed to them. I have chosen this approach, rather than one that speaks immediately of rights or duties, because of my conviction that many of our rights and duties are based on the consequences of actions and policies. This approach may also help to avoid the controversies that frequently surround the notions of "fetal rights" and "obligations to the fetus." (For further background on the theoretical issues underlying this consequentialist approach, see the "Ethical Framework" section of Chapter 1 and especially the section on beneficence.)

The central conclusion in the ethical analysis that follows is that HIV testing in pregnancy should be handled in a manner similar to the manner in which prenatal diagnosis for fetal genetic conditions or anatomic abnormalities has been handled. The obvious differences between prenatal HIV testing and most other forms of prenatal testing performed until now are (1) that HIV infection is contagious and (2) that the pregnant woman is at risk of becoming ill (or more ill) if available treatments for HIV infection cannot be administered to her during pregnancy. However, the distinction between genetic conditions and communica-

274

ble diseases is not entirely clear-cut. Genetic conditions that are identifiable through testing can be conveyed to future generations through the germ line, either by the persons being tested or by members of their extended families. Further, the question of a pregnant woman's becoming ill or forgoing treatments potentially useful to her during pregnancy arises in other medical contexts, although not generally in contexts involving prenatal diagnosis. One thinks, for example, of pregnant women who discontinue antiseizure medications thought to be teratogenic.

Empirical Assumptions

The analysis in this chapter is based on a particular fact situation regarding HIV infection—a situation that prevails in 1990. (Evidence about this fact situation is found in Chapters 2, 4, and 5.) Empirical assumptions that are especially pertinent to the analysis are the following:

1. HIV antibody testing is reasonably sensitive and specific in adults, at least after the initial period of time before the production of antibodies.

2. The probability that an HIV-infected woman who becomes pregnant will produce an HIV-infected child is in the range of 25 to 35 percent in the United States.

3. There is no clear evidence to support the claim that pregnancy accelerates or retards the progression of HIV infection in the pregnant woman.

4. At least one treatment exists that delays the development of symptoms in asymptomatic HIV-infected adults and the progression to late ARC or AIDS in some infected adults who have early symptoms. It is not known whether the administration of this treatment to a pregnant woman would be harmful to the fetus.

5. No treatment exists that has been demonstrated to be beneficial to the fetus infected in utero.

6. The biological (genetic) father of a fetus can be determined with virtual certainty through the use of DNA-sequencing techniques.

7. Both the fetus and attendant health-care workers are exposed to maternal blood during the birth process.

8. It seems unlikely that a safe method for determining whether the fetus of an HIV-infected woman is itself infected will be available in the near future. (The concern is that any invasive technique used for prenatal diagnosis may itself expose the fetus to infection.)

9. The women and newborn infants who have been reported to the Centers for Disease Control as having clinical AIDS are disproportionately black

(women, 60.0 percent; infants, 57.7 percent) or Hispanic (women, 20.0 percent; infants, 26.2 percent). Intravenous drug use or sexual intercourse with one or more intravenous drug users is thought to be the mode of viral transmission in 51.6 and 19.7 percent of all AIDS cases involving women, respectively.[1] It seems likely that similar epidemiologic patterns are present in HIV-infected women and infants who have not yet progressed to clinical AIDS.

Parties Affected and Potential Benefits and Harms of Testing

The parties potentially affected by prenatal HIV testing policies include the pregnant woman herself, the fetus she is carrying, the genetic father of the fetus, health-care workers involved in the pregnant woman's care, and the general public.

The pregnant woman

This section presupposes that the principal decision maker regarding prenatal testing should be the pregnant woman herself. Some of the arguments for this presupposition are noted later in this section when the genetic father's interests and the mandatory or voluntary character of testing programs are discussed. The major argument for the presupposition, in my view, is that prenatal testing for HIV infection requires invading the privacy of an adolescent or adult woman— an action that generally requires either her consent or an extraordinarily powerful moral justification.

For the pregnant woman, the principal potential benefits of prenatal testing are medical. Timely knowledge of the fact that she is antibody-positive may facilitate her treatment with medication that has been demonstrated to delay the progression of HIV infection to more serious disease in patients with CD4 counts of less than 500.[2] In the future, more effective therapies may be developed. Further, some effects of HIV infection, for example, *Pneumocystis carinii* pneumonia, are amenable to prophylaxis or treatment if the woman's health provider knows that she has HIV infection.

There are also potential nonmedical benefits of testing for the pregnant woman. In a well-run testing program that includes counseling, she will receive information about risk factors and protective behaviors. Further, if she is antibody-negative, as the vast majority of those tested are, she will have the reassurance and peace of mind that accompany a negative test result (which is likely to be valid unless the onset of infection occurred quite recently).

The principal risks of HIV testing to the pregnant woman are social and psychological. If a woman decides to be tested, that fact alone suggests that she believes she has been exposed to infection. The decision to be tested itself may expose the woman to the loss of friends or to various forms of discrimination if the fact of her having been tested is disclosed to third parties. If the test results show that she is infected, she will face difficult decisions about to whom to disclose this finding. On a personal level, disclosure of positive test results to her husband or other sexual partner(s) or to friends may result in an irreparable breach—and, in some cases, in physical harm through battering. Socially, disclosure of her positive antibody status may result in a woman's exclusion from employment or housing opportunities or from health, life, or disability insurance. Clearly, public policies on confidentiality of HIV-related information and discrimination against HIV-infected people will have a major impact on an at-risk woman's risk–benefit calculus. (For more detailed discussion of the issues treated in this paragraph, see Chapters 5 and 9.)

There is one further potential consequence of testing for pregnant women that is more difficult to categorize: the harm or benefit of being confronted with an ethical decision about selective abortion. This decision is similar to the decision of any pregnant woman or expectant couple after prenatal diagnosis. However, at a time when the techniques of molecular biology are providing more and more precise information about the status of the fetus, HIV antibody testing will, for the foreseeable future, be able to provide only estimates of probability. At present, an antibody-positive pregnant woman cannot be told, "Your fetus is infected" or "Your fetus is not infected." She can be informed only that "the probability that your fetus is infected is in the range of 25 to 35 percent." Thus her situation is similar to that of women exposed to toxic chemicals, radiation, or other infectious agents, like the protozoan that causes toxoplasmosis or the rubella virus.

Is it ethically justifiable for an HIV-infected pregnant woman to terminate a pregnancy, given these odds? In the author's view, such a decision can be justified on several grounds. First, the pregnant woman may not wish to face the inevitable challenges of child rearing at the same time that she may be coping with the adverse effects of HIV infection on her own health. Giving up the child for adoption might be considered as an alternative, but if the child is infected, he or she will be difficult to place. Further, at the present time, an HIV-infected child can be offered only partially effective therapy, and faces the unpleasant prospect of repeated hospitalizations and almost certain death by the age of 10 at the latest. Finally, the pregnant woman may decide to terminate the current pregnancy in order to begin treatment for herself with the moderately effective therapy that currently exists. She may also entertain the hope that even if she herself is infected 5 years later, there may be a more effective therapy available for any child that she may then conceive and bear.

Is it ethically justifiable for an HIV-infected pregnant woman *not* to terminate a pregnancy, given the current odds? Again, in the author's view, the answer is yes. The pregnant woman may adhere to ethical principles that do not permit abortion—convictions that she cannot in good conscience violate. For example, she may believe that because of the fetus's right to life, abortion is morally wrong except when necessary to save the life of the pregnant woman. Further, the pregnant woman may consider that she is in a situation similar to that of expectant couples who know that they have a 25 percent risk of producing a child with a genetic or an anatomic defect and who nonetheless continue the pregnancy to term. Such couples are generally considered to be ethically at liberty *either* to terminate the pregnancy *or* to continue it. Alternatively, the pregnant woman may decide to carry the current pregnancy to term because she fears that she might be too ill in the future to become pregnant again. This decision could be defended by appeal to the woman's overall life plan, which, in all but the most extreme circumstances, may reasonably include bearing a child.

In short, *at the level of personal morality, either a decision for or a decision against selective abortion can be justified with strong and, in my view, convincing moral arguments.* Thus each HIV-infected pregnant woman will need to weigh the potential benefits and harms of termination and continuation in light of her deeply held beliefs and make her own decision. Thorough posttest counseling, as recommended in Chapter 13, should be helpful to the pregnant woman who confronts this important decision.

Better therapies for the treatment of HIV infection may be developed in the future. Such therapies would clearly have an impact on the risk assessment that must be conducted by the pregnant woman. If the future therapies are beneficial to the fetus as well as to the pregnant woman, they may help to tip the balance toward a decision to be tested and toward continuation of the pregnancy even if she tests positive. Several other scenarios are also possible. All the potential combinations of benefit and harm are presented in Table 11.1.

If combination 7 were factually the case, and a therapy existed that would help the pregnant woman but harm the fetus, she would have stronger reasons that at present to be tested and to terminate the pregnancy if she tested positive. (In fact, the pregnant woman who tested positive would be in a situation analogous to that of a pregnant woman who is discovered to have a cancerous uterus.) But if combination 1 or 2 were the factual situation, and a therapy existed that either helped or did not harm the pregnant woman but helped the fetus, she would have stronger reasons than at present to be both tested and treated while continuing the

TABLE 11.1.   Benefits and Harms of Therapy

	Effect on pregnant woman		
	Beneficial	Neutral	Harmful
Effect on fetus			
Beneficial	1	2	3
Neutral	4	5	6
Harmful	7	8	9

pregnancy to term. (In combination 2, her situation would be analogous in some respects to that of a pregnant woman discovered to have an Rh incompatibility with the fetus she is carrying and who is then faced with a decision about undergoing intrauterine exchange transfusions.)

Fact situation 3 would undoubtedly be the most agonizing for the pregnant woman—a situation in which a therapy existed that was beneficial to the fetus but harmful to her. (This situation was for a time *thought* to exist with intra-uterine surgery for fetal hydrocephalus or urinary tract obstructions.) While this fact situation might provide additional moral reasons for being tested, a positive test would present a pregnant woman with a difficult moral dilemma, particularly if the probable harm to herself were severe and irreversible. In my view, a pregnant woman's making such a major sacrifice on behalf of her fetus is best understood as an act of heroism that goes beyond any plausible construal of moral duties based on the principle of beneficence.

Not explicitly mentioned in the preceding paragraphs is the possibility that a mode of intervention will be developed that would combat HIV infection in the pregnant woman while at the same time *preventing* the transmission of the infection to the fetus. This fact situation would be a variation of combination 1. Whether this theoretical possibility is a real possibility depends on the time during gestation when perinatal transmission of infection usually occurs and on the usual interval between maternal and fetal infection. The notion of "therapy" in the foregoing analysis should be construed broadly enough to include interventions that would prevent fetal infection.

The fetus

In attempting to evaluate benefits and harms from the fetal standpoint, we who are persons must impute interests to a developing being that is not currently a person but that has the potential to become a person if certain conditions are fulfilled. Would a "prudent fetus," if such a being existed, want the pregnant woman who is carrying him or her to be tested for HIV infection? For the foreseeable future, the fetus would have no way of knowing whether he or she were destined to be infected with HIV. Rather, the fetus would only know that, in general, there is a 25 to 35 percent probability that he or she will be infected if delivered alive.

In the present circumstances, where no demonstrably beneficial treatment exists for the fetus, we are confronted with a straightforward comparison of the benefits and harms of existence (with or without the infection) and nonexistence. If the infant is delivered alive, there is a 65 to 75 percent probability that he or she will not be infected. However, if the infant is infected, he or she will face a short life beset with repeated hospitalizations. The alternative to these two pos-sibilities is never to exist outside the uterus, as would occur, for example, if the pregnant woman were tested, learned that she was positive, and decided to terminate the pregnancy. Most human adults prefer existence, even with serious disease, to nonexistence. Thus if the hypothetical prudent fetus were considering only his or her own interests and future, he or she might prefer that the pregnant woman *not* be tested—or at least that testing be deferred until the point in pregnancy where abortion is no longer an option—so that the question of selective abortion following the diagnosis of HIV infection would not even arise.

If, contrary to fact, the fetus were capable of reasoning, he or she might also consider the interests of the pregnant woman—a woman who is often called the "mother." At present, there is a therapy that delays progression of HIV infection in one subset of nonpregnant individuals—those who have T4 counts less than 500. If that therapy also proves to be beneficial to pregnant women and either benefits or does not harm fetuses (combinations 1 and 4 in Table 11.1), then the benefit–harm ratio would increase, as would the putative fetal inclination to accept prenatal testing for the sake of the pregnant woman who might one day be his or her social mother.

As noted above, future research may discover therapies that are beneficial to both the pregnant woman and the fetus (combination 1). Alternatively, treatments might become available that are most effective if administered to HIV-positive infants immediately after birth (see Chapters 2 and 5). In either case, the benefits of testing might seem clearly to outweigh the harms from the fetal standpoint. Indeed, prenatal diagnosis (of the pregnant woman's condition) and treatment (of both the pregnant woman and the fetus or the newborn infant) might become genuine alternatives to prenatal diagnosis and selective abortion.

The genetic father

The potential benefits and harms of prenatal HIV testing for the genetic father[3] of a fetus can be divided into two categories. There are, first, consequences that relate to his causal role as father. Second, his past (and often present and future) sexual partnership with the pregnant woman can also produce both benefits and harms for him.

The father as father

The biological (genetic) father is morally co-responsible for the fetus that is developing within the body of the pregnant woman. That is, he, or the members of the couple together, could have used a variety of contraceptive methods to ensure, with a high degree of probability, that no pregnancy would be initiated. Because the genetic father is morally and legally responsible for the care and welfare of the child after delivery, he also has a vital interest in the question of testing. If the woman with whom he has initiated a pregnancy (who may or may not be his wife) is HIV-positive during pregnancy and carries the pregnancy to term, he has a 25 to 35 percent chance of being co-responsible, with the mother, for the care of an HIV-infected child. At present, there are only partially effective treatments available for such a child (see Chapters 5 and 14). On the other hand, he has a 65 to 75 percent chance of being morally and legally responsible for a child who is not infected with HIV.

In most respects, the interests of the genetic father as father will parallel those of the pregnant woman, but there are at least four important differences. First, the father's interest in the welfare of the pregnant woman—the horizontal axis in Table 11.1—will be an altruistic rather than an egoistic concern. Second, it is the woman who carries the fetus and whose body will be minimally invaded during the testing procedure. Further, it is her medical record that will contain the test results if she is tested in the customary health-care setting; thus the woman faces the risk of tangible harms, such as the loss of health insurance, if test results are disclosed to third parties. Fourth, as a group, genetic fathers are much more prone to abandon genetic mothers and their joint children than are genetic mothers to abandon fathers and children—even without regard to the question of testing and the possibility of positive test results.

Given these circumstances, I conclude that the genetic father as father has a legitimate interest in being informed (and perhaps consulted) about the testing possibility for the pregnant woman, about her decision concerning testing, and about the test results if she decides to be tested. In addition, if the test results are positive, he has an interest in being informed (and perhaps consulted) about the abortion decision. However, this interest does not extend to being able to determine how the pregnant woman decides or to veto any decisions made by her. (Implicit in this conclusion is the argument that any male who assumes the risk of becoming a genetic father potentially bears the responsibilities of parenthood but loses control over all decisions regarding parenthood during the entire pregnancy.) Further, in specific circumstances, the genetic father's legitimate interest in being informed (and perhaps consulted) may be overridden by the woman's interest in self-protection.

The genetic father as sexual partner

The genetic father also has an interest in the pregnant woman's being tested because if she is infected with HIV, he may also be infected. If the pregnant woman is tested and determined (with appropriate confirmatory tests) to be antibody-positive, several explanations are possible. The genetic father may also be infected, in which case it may be difficult to determine the original direction of transmission. (The best available data suggest that male-to-female sexual transmission is more efficient than the reverse.) The genetic father may be uninfected, however, in which case he will want to take precautions in future sexual encounters to avoid becoming infected. Thus as sexual partner, the genetic father has an understandable interest in the pregnant woman's being tested, but this interest seems much less compelling than any of the interests discussed previously. In the era of the HIV epidemic, all prudent sexually active people will behave *as if* their sexual partners were in fact infected with HIV until they have clear and convincing evidence to the contrary.

Health-care workers involved in the care of the pregnant woman

For health-care workers, clear benefits and no significant risks would accrue from prenatal testing programs. Nurses, midwives, physicians, and others involved in prenatal care or labor and delivery would be able to take special precautions in their exposure to the blood or other body fluids of antibody-positive pregnant women. Perhaps the most important potential risk of testing would be the false sense of security that health-care workers might have if a particular pregnant woman had a negative antibody test despite recent exposure to HIV. Even this risk would be reduced if newer tests were able to detect the HIV antigen rather than the later-developing antibody to the virus.

Society at large

Society at large clearly has an interest in bringing the epidemic of HIV infection under control. It also has an interest in reducing or averting both the suffering and the expense caused by the perinatal transmission of HIV infection. Thus it can be argued that a program of prenatal testing for HIV infection, coupled with appropriate education and counseling, would prevent or at least mitigate some tangible medical and financial harms to society.

It is unlikely that a prenatal HIV testing program would *cause* harm to society, but if the costs of such a program were borne by the public, the question of cost effectiveness would surely arise. (See Chapter 14 for a more extensive discussion of various policy options that are currently being debated.) Even within the AIDS sector of public health budgets, programs of prenatal testing may not be the most prudent investment of limited resources. Particularly in low-prevalence areas, this investment may not be worth the cost. In Norway, for example, 115,600 pregnant women were tested for HIV antibody between September 1987 and December 1988. This large screening program discovered 4 new women who were HIV-positive and mistakenly identified 92 women as infected—all at a cost of 6 to 7 million Norwegian crowns (roughly $1 million.)[4]

Summary

Thus the question of benefits and harms in prenatal HIV testing cannot be answered without taking into account *whose* benefits and harms are being considered. Given the current state of technology, prenatal testing seems to be clearly beneficial to health-care workers, primarily beneficial to genetic fathers, and both beneficial and harmful to pregnant women and fetuses. For the general public, prenatal testing would prevent or reduce certain kinds of harm, but if prenatal testing programs took funds away from more cost-effective alternative programs, the use of testing to prevent those harms might not, on balance, be morally justifiable. Improved therapies could in the future enhance the benefit–harm ratio of testing for pregnant women and fetuses and, by implication, for society as well.

Should Testing Programs Be Voluntary or Mandatory?

In democratic societies, there should be a strong presumption in favor of voluntary programs unless and until overwhelming harm is demonstrated to be caused or allowed by such programs and no alternative to mandatory programs can prevent such harm. (See Chapters 7 and 8 for a discussion of relevant legal issues.) This presumption is in fact embodied in public health policies in the United States, where no screening programs are employed with the entire adult population. As noted in Chapter 6, programs aimed at detecting inborn errors of metabolism, conducted in the neonatal period, are mandatory in many states. Among adults, the closest approximations to universal screening are the mandatory testing for syphilis required by most U.S. jurisdictions during pregnancy (see Chapter 6) and mandatory testing for sexually transmitted diseases as a precondition for issuance of marriage license, currently required in 32 states and the District of Columbia.[5]

Any mandatory testing program directed exclusively at pregnant women would be ethically suspect because its burdens fall solely on one gender. Mandatory prenatal testing would also directly contradict the dominant model, carefully developed over several decades, in the human genetics field. There all testing of at-risk couples (often called "carrier screening") and all prenatal diagnosis are conducted on a strictly voluntary basis.[6]

The underlying ethical rationale for voluntary testing and screening programs is respect for the autonomy of adults and for the decisions that they make about their own health and the health of their progeny. The ethical principle of autonomy is so central in democratic societies (think, for example, of the Bill of Rights, appended to the U.S. Constitution) that it should be constrained or compromised for only the weightiest of reasons.

Implicit in the notion of "voluntary programs" is a genuine decision by the participants in such programs. Thus truly voluntary programs should, at a minimum, provide explicit notice and a clear opportunity for every individual to decline to participate. So-called routine programs that fail to provide such notice and such an opportunity are, on this view, in fact mandatory programs. (See Chapters 1 and 12 for more detailed discussion.)

Who Should Be Tested?

The first answer to this question, in light of the preceding section, is that only pregnant women who freely consent to be tested should be tested. Thus a more precise question for voluntary programs of prenatal HIV testing is, who should be *offered* testing?

There are two major approaches to answering this question, one based on general demographic variables and the other on individualized clinical decision making. Among the general variables that might be chosen as criteria for prenatal testing and screening programs are the prevalence of HIV infection in a geographic area, race or ethnic background, or participation in a treatment program for a particular disease or behavior (e.g., at a clinic for sexually transmitted diseases or a drug use treatment center). (In the last case, a person's appearance at a clinic or center would be considered a proxy for his or her having engaged in at-risk behavior.)

Any HIV testing program based on the general demographic variable of race or ethnic background would immediately be suspect on ethical grounds, for it would imply that every member of the targeted group is potentially infected with HIV, while members of other groups are not. Although HIV seroprevalence rates differ among white, black, and Hispanic women, the virus is widely dispersed among all three ethnic groups—even assuming that clear distinctions among the groups can be drawn. Thus the empirical situation for HIV infection is quite different from the situation with respect to genetic disorders like Tay-Sachs disease, sickle cell anemia, or thalassemia.

Testing programs targeted to pregnant women seeking treatment in particular health-related programs—for example, programs for sexually transmitted diseases (STDs) or drug use—would have a more rational foundation in the sense that they would be directed to women at substantially higher risk of HIV infection than the general population of women. Here, there is a judgment of prudence to be made, however. If knowledge that they would be offered HIV testing would deter a significant fraction of pregnant women (say, 10 percent) from seeking treatment for their health-related problems in relevant programs, then such targeted testing might prove to be counterproductive. This chilling effect could occur if women with possible STDs or with histories of drug use perceived themselves to be singled out for special screening.

A fairer and less discriminatory policy would seem to be one that offered testing to all pregnant women in a city or region where the seroprevalence rate for HIV infection had crossed a predetermined threshold. Even here there would be opportunities for the "gerrymandering" of testing programs—for example, if only the predominantly black wards of a city were selected for testing. This potential source of bias could be eliminated if there were agreement in advance that only integral units—such as cities, possibly metropolitan areas, counties, or states—would be employed as the basis for calculating seroprevalence rates and initiating testing programs.

The major alternative to a testing program targeted to high-prevalence areas would be a program in which testing (together with appropriate education and counseling) were offered to *all* pregnant women in the United States. Such a universal program would not distinguish between low- and high-prevalence areas. Thus one possible source of discrimination would be removed. My primary reservation about such a universal program is based on its probable lack of cost effectiveness. Direct comparisons with the Norwegian experience are not possible, especially because the testing was immediately done, not merely offered, in Norway. Nonetheless, the resources that would be expended in both offering testing and performing tests in low-prevalence areas could, in my view, be more prudently invested. Prime candidates for such alternative uses of resources would be vigorous programs of education for all men and women of reproductive age[7] and expanded treatment programs for intravenous drug users who desire to stop using drugs.[8]

Much less satisfactory than any of these relatively objective, population-based approaches would be any approach to testing that is based on individual clinical decision making. Clinical approaches would be likely to vary greatly from one clinician to another. They also have the disadvantage that they convey to the informed and sensitive patient that someone involved in her care suspects that *she in particular* is infected with HIV.

The preceding analysis does not consider whether a particular institution like a hospital should adopt a policy of routinely offering testing to all patients based on seroprevalence rates in its catchment area. If such a policy is publicly advertised, and if patients in the area have the possibility of seeking care in alternative settings that do not offer testing, the institutional policy may not be discriminatory. However, if patients have no realistic alternative, say, to securing care in a public hospital, they may then be confronted with a decision about testing that their more affluent and mobile neighbors can readily avoid.

The Social Matrix of the Prenatal Testing Question

As noted above, the perinatal transmission of HIV infection occurs with disproportionate frequency among black and Hispanic people in the United States. In 55.9 percent of AIDS cases involving black or Hispanic women, intravenous drug use by the woman is *acknowledged* as a risk factor. In an additional 21.8 percent of AIDS cases in this group, sexual intercourse with an intravenous drug user is *cited* as a risk factor.[9] For children who develop AIDS after prenatal infection, the corresponding figures are 43.0 percent for maternal drug use and 17.8 percent for drug use by the mother's sexual partner(s).[10] These figures are not cited to stigmatize particular ethnic groups. On the contrary, they are but one index of the long-term consequences of a pattern of discrimination and neglect by the white majority in the United States. Any policy on testing that ignores this history and this social matrix runs the risk of being perceived as yet another imposition of burdens on minorities by the dominant majority. Specifically, unless HIV testing (and associated education and counseling) is coupled with other social initiatives that aim to promote the welfare of the least well-off, they are unlikely to succeed.

The foregoing analysis did not discuss two of the most important public policy initiatives for *preventing* the spread of HIV infection among women in general and pregnant women in particular. The first initiative is a rational and consistent policy on intravenous drug use, in particular, the "treatment on demand" policy recommended by the President's Commission on the Human Immunodeficiency Virus Epidemic.[11] The second initiative is even more ambitious and expensive: to work vigorously toward the elimination of poverty, particularly in some of our major cities and especially among the most seriously affected segments of the black and Hispanic communities. It is the culture of abject poverty and loss of hope that makes intravenous drug use appear to be an attractive option.

As more effective therapies for ameliorating or even preventing the most serious consequences of HIV infection become available, the benefit–harm ratio for people considering whether to be tested for the infection will change (see Chapter 14). Further, if stronger and more reliable guarantees of confidentiality and nondiscrimination are instituted by society, more people—in this case, pregnant women—may accept the offer of testing or even volunteer to be tested. Indeed, one hopes for the day when the offer of prenatal HIV testing will be considered an opportunity rather than an imposition.

Notes

1. Centers for Disease Control (CDC), "HIV/AIDS Surveillance Report," May 1990, pp. 9–10.
2. Paul A. Volberding, Stephen W. Lagakos, Matthew A. Koch et al., "Zidovudine in Asymptomatic Human Immunodeficiency Virus Infection," *New England Journal of Medicine* 322 (1990): 941–949. See also Margaret A. Fischl, Douglas D. Richman, Nellie Hansen et al., "The Safety and Efficacy of Zidovudine (AZT) in the Treatment of Subjects with Mildly Symptomatic Human Immunodeficiency Virus Type I (HIV) Infection," *Annals of Internal Medicine* 112 (1990): 727–737.
3. This discussion assumes that the pregnancy was initiated through consensual sexual intercourse, not through rape.
4. M. Skogstad and S. Fossum, "HIV Screening of Pregnant Women and Women Seeking Abortion: A Preventive Measure against HIV?" *Tidsskrift for den Norske Laegeforening* 109 (1989): 3032–3034.
5. Paul D. Cleary, Michael J. Barry, Kenneth H. Mayer et al., "Compulsory Premarital Screening for the Human Immunodeficiency Virus: Technical and Public Health Considerations," *Journal of the American Medical Association* 258 (1987): 1757–1762. See also "Marriage Laws," in *World Almanac and Book of Facts: 1990* (New York: World Almanac, 1989), 824.
6. President's Commission for the Study of Ethical Problems in Medicine and Biomedical and Behavioral Research, *Screening and Counseling for Genetic Conditions* (Washington, D.C.: Government Printing Office, 1983), 47–59.

7. Harvey Fineberg, "Education to Prevent AIDS: Prospects and Obstacles," *Science* 239 (1988): 592–596.
8. *Report of the President's Commission on the Human Immunodeficiency Virus Epidemic* (Washington, D.C.: President's Commission, 1988), 93–104, 171.
9. CDC, "HIV/AIDS Surveillance Report," 10.
10. Ibid., 9.
11. *Report of the President's Commission,* 95.

12

Informed Consent in the Context of Prenatal HIV Screening

GAIL GELLER AND NANCY E. KASS

As discussed in Chapters 1, 10, and 11, many issues about the moral accept-ability of screening programs concern autonomy-related rights and obligations, such as the right of patients to refuse medical interventions and the obligation of providers to solicit informed consent prior to the implementation of such inter-ventions. In designing screening policies, the burden of moral justification rests on those who would compromise these autonomy-related rights.

Of the five approaches to HIV screening programs outlined in Chapter 1, the legal, ethical, and public health arguments raised thereafter support two options: routine screening with notification and completely voluntary screening. The former endorses utilization of an HIV antibody test by making it a standard part of medical care unless the patient expressly refuses it. The latter may or may not involve an endorsement of the procedure by the health-care provider, often includes a more extensive disclosure process, and leaves the choice of having the test completely up to the patient. Given our belief that informed consent is important in this type of physician–patient interaction, we believe completely voluntary programs are morally preferable to those that are routine with notifica-tion. However, the latter can be morally acceptable *because* they allow the patient the right to refuse and in this sense respect patient autonomy. With few exceptions, mandatory screening programs are morally unacceptable because they do not give patients a choice and therefore do *not* respect patient autonomy. Moreover, such a practice would set an inappropriate precedent for physician–patient interactions.

Both screening programs that are completely voluntary—which, as defined in Chapter 1, require patients to choose a test or intervention—and programs that are routine with notification are morally acceptable specifically because they allow patients the right to refuse. However, as will be discussed below, the degree to which they achieve valid informed consent varies substantially, leading us to recommend that, wherever possible, completely voluntary programs be the public policy choice for HIV screening of pregnant women. As a practical matter, it is more likely that valid informed consents and refusals will be obtained in programs that have explicit informed consent requirements.

The issues concerning informed consent in the context of neonatal HIV screening are comparable but not identical to those in the prenatal context. However, whereas it is considered acceptable for adults to refuse potentially beneficial treatments for themselves, there is more concern about a beneficial treatment being denied to a newborn who is never an autonomous decision maker. Moreover, in light of technologic advances affording newborns increased medical benefit, there may be greater reason for concern about the acceptability of completely voluntary HIV screening programs for newborns. Consequently, we can foresee a time when the autonomy-related rights of the mother may justifiably be overridden, at least to some degree, by claims of beneficence to the mother or to the newborn. Surrogate decision making for newborns is addressed more fully in Chapter 10. Our discussion in this chapter refers exclusively to informed consent for *prenatal* HIV screening programs.

There are some who believe that true informed consent, including the right to refuse testing, cannot be achieved in the context of prenatal HIV screening, particularly among disadvantaged women, who are among those at greatest risk for HIV. This belief leads to the conclusion that voluntary screening programs are not a viable public policy choice, at least in terms of achieving valid informed consent. The accuracy of this belief depends not only on the characteristics of the population, but also on the characteristics of the providers and the structure of the setting in which such screening would occur. Awareness of which characteristics compromise the informed consent process is relevant in establishing a public policy related to HIV screening in pregnant women. This chapter examines the substance and validity of the concerns raised in order to determine whether informed consent can be achieved at a sufficiently acceptable standard to justify advocating voluntary screening programs for pregnant women.

Moreover, it is important to consider to what one would be consenting in a voluntary screening program, for how this varies is relevant to the validity of the informed consent. When discussing the voluntariness of a screening program, one can refer to the testing alone or to the entire package of testing and subsequent events. In other words, screening programs potentially could exist in which testing per se was voluntary but all women who had a positive test result were denied prenatal care at that particular clinic, or were required to take Zidovudine (also known as retrovir or azidothymidine [AZT]) during the last trimester of their pregnancy, or were otherwise provided with a more limited range of options than women who either tested negative or opted not to be tested. This chapter considers primarily the degree to which testing itself should be voluntary, rather than discussing whether the availability of options, such as pregnancy continuation or termination, should be contingent on a woman's or newborn's antibody status.

This chapter is divided into five sections. The first section outlines the theoretical basis of informed consent. The second section examines literature on decision making and explores whether actual decision-making processes are consistent with the theoretical basis of informed consent. Included in this discussion is the theoretical work on normative decision making, as well as empirical studies of decision making among pregnant women specifically. The third section addresses the possible limitations to the informed consent process. The fourth describes ways in which the informed consent process can be facilitated. Finally, the chapter concludes with a discussion of the practical implications of the issues raised in the first three sections for guiding the solicitation of informed consent in HIV screening of pregnant women.

Informed Consent

There are many models and conceptions of informed consent,[1] including the theoretical models founded in legal and ethical principles and the practical models applied to research and clinical settings. One of the theoretical models on which we draw heavily defines informed consent as an autonomous action by a subject or a patient who, (1) with substantial understanding, (2) with substantial absence of control by others, and (3) with intentionality, (4) authorizes a professional to initiate a medical plan, a research involvement, or both.[2]

Substantial understanding

What does it mean for a woman to have a substantial understanding of the act of consenting to HIV testing? According to Faden and Beauchamp, the answer to this question is complex and is composed of several elements. First, there is an objective dimension to the woman's understanding of what she is authorizing. This objective dimension requires the woman to understand specific information that the health professional considers to be material in deciding to be tested for HIV, as well as the professional's recommendation, if there is one. Second, the woman must understand that by consenting to testing, she is giving the health professional permission to do something that the health professional otherwise would not have authority to do. In other words, she must understand that in consenting she is committing an act of permission giving in which control or authority is transferred from herself to the health professional.

Third, she must understand what she is authorizing. She not only must understand the information provided concerning the nature of HIV testing and the foreseeable consequences of consenting to or refusing testing, but also must attend to the information that she considers to be *material* to her decision to authorize testing. This element is entirely subjective. A material description is any description that is or would be viewed by the woman as worthy of consideration in deliberating about whether to agree to be tested.

In many cases, there is likely to be substantial overlap between what the woman and the health professional view as material, but the inclusion of both components is important to ensure a shared understanding between them and to provide the woman with a core of information based on which she can formulate her own concerns and questions.

Substantial noncontrol

In order to achieve a valid informed consent, a woman not only must have a substantial understanding of her consent decision, but also must act in the substantial absence of control by others. A pregnant woman's decision to consent to or refuse HIV testing often is made amid attempts by many others to influence her. Threats of physical harm, promises of approval and affection, economic incentives, reasoned argument, lies, and appeals to emotional weaknesses all may be employed. Unfortunately, there are no magic formulas for establishing the threshold that distinguishes influence compatible with substantial noncontrol from influence incompatible with informed consent.

Faden and Beauchamp have attacked this problem by dividing influence into three distinct categories: coercion, manipulation, and persuasion. Coercion always is controlling, and therefore is entirely incompatible with informed consent. Persuasion never is controlling, actually facilitates choice, and as such is wholly compatible with informed consent. Manipulation lies on a continuum from completely controlling to completely noncontrolling influence. Therefore, it is within the category of manipulation that the threshold problem for substantial noncontrol exists.

Coercion is said to occur if one party intentionally and successfully influences another "by presenting a credible threat of unwanted and avoidable harm so severe that the person is unable to resist acting to avoid it". In coercion, the will of someone else dominates, so that the coerced person's choice is not in any meaningful sense *her* choice but is effectively that of the other. Persuasion, by contrast, is "the intentional and successful attempt to induce a person, through appeals to reason, to freely accept—as his or her own—the beliefs, attitudes, values, intentions, or actions advocated by the persuader."[3] So understood, persuasion is never done in a clandestine manner, nor can persuasion ever involve appeal to reasons or arguments that the influence agent believes are false.

Nevertheless, some may view even this narrow interpretation of persuasion as incompatible with informed consent because persuasion assumes that the reasons presented ought to take precedence over the wishes of the consent giver. For example, it would be considered persuasion if a provider recommended an HIV antibody test to a woman who had disclosed that her previous sexual partner had used intravenous drugs. Although some would consider the provider's advocating testing to negate the validity of substantially autonomous informed consent, we consider such an approach to be compatible with informed consent, assuming that the woman is not being denied control of the situation and the provider is being candid about his or her own biases.

Manipulation falls between coercion and persuasion. It includes any intentional and successful influence of a person that noncoercively alters the actual choices available to the person or nonpersuasively alters the person's perceptions of those choices. Unlike coercion, manipulation may involve offers as well as threats. What distinguishes threats that are manipulative from those that are coercive is that the threat still is resistible, albeit not necessarily easily resistible. A key issue here is which, if any, threats or offers are compatible with the condition of substantial noncontrol, and thus with informed consent. Faden and Beauchamp propose the following guidelines. Any offer that is welcomed by the person from whom consent is being solicited, and any threat or unwelcome offer that can be *reasonably easily resisted* by the person, is acceptable.[4]

Manipulation also can occur with lying, withholding information, misleading exaggeration, appealing to emotional weaknesses, and framing how information is presented. All these strategies are clearly inconsistent with the concept of rational persuasion discussed above. It is unlikely that the successful use of any of these strategies ever would be compatible with informed consent. Such strategies necessarily involve keeping the person in ignorance; thus unlike the use of threats or offers, they do not admit of any resistibility test. In addition, there is generally no way to establish whether the information withheld or the false belief induced is material to the person's decision, and thus whether the manipulation compromises informed consent by compromising the condition of substantial understanding.

Manipulation can be subtle, as in deceptive presentation of information. A woman who is encouraged to be tested without being told that the names of those with positive results will be released to state public health authorities is the subject of manipulation due to deception. Alternatively, manipulation can be explicit. A woman who is told that she cannot receive prenatal care at any public health clinic if she does not agree to be tested is the subject of this more explicit type of manipulation. Because the threat of not receiving prenatal care is resistible, in that the woman can seek care elsewhere or decide that being tested is worse for her than foregoing prenatal care, we would define this situation as one of manipulation rather than coercion.

Decision Making

Thus far, we have discussed the components of a theory of valid informed consent. We now turn to the question of how people actually make decisions and whether their decision-making processes support these theoretical standards. Specifically, in this section we review the theoretical and practical literatures on decision making in an attempt to determine if rationality, as defined in those literatures, is a necessary additional condition for valid informed consent.

Decision theory

Decision theory is a field of interdisciplinary research whose goal is to understand how individuals and groups make or should make decisions. Among its contributors are economists, psychologists, social scientists, philosophers, and statisticians. Although the lines are not precise, it is customary to draw a distinction between normative and empirical decision theory. Normative decision theorists attempt to prescribe how decisions *ought* to be made according to assumptions about ideally rational agents. Empirical researchers, by contrast, conduct experiments to discover how people actually behave in decision-making contexts. The rich body of empirical research often indicates that individuals do not conform to the expectations of normative theory. Such inconsistencies have led some analysts to conclude that actual decision making often is irrational. Others have responded differently by suggesting that empirical research may lead us to rethink normative criteria for decision making. Such findings have led to vigorous debates about the nature of rationality itself. Increasingly, it appears that rationality is best understood relative to decisional contexts, and that the nature and extent to which rational agents ought to incorporate and give weight to information depends on differences in decisional contexts and personalities.[5]

Tversky and Kahneman, psychologists who have conducted extensive research in the field of decision making, propose that in making decisions people typically employ heuristics, or simplifying rules of thumb, that "while useful, sometimes lead to severe and systematic errors."[6] Understanding that people make decisions in this way is important for the clinical setting because providers must recognize and overcome a number of obstacles that "have [their roots in] . . . the idiosyncrasies of the human mind."[7]

One of the heuristics described by Tversky and Kahneman is representativeness. This says that people attempt to assess how much the characteristics of the person or situation with which they are confronted represent, or match, their *own* notions of what is associated with the factors relevant to their decision. For example, women who believe they are able to identify bisexual men by appearance or mannerisms would be likely to ignore statistical figures telling them that one in five men has had a previous relationship with a man, and instead make a decision about the likelihood of a prospective partner's being bisexual based on how representative he is of their stereotype. Even when women are provided with statistics about the actual prevalence of bisexuality in their community, if what they see does not represent bisexuality to them, they will draw their own conclusions, ignoring the statistical likelihood.

Another heuristic described by Tversky and Kahneman is availability, which says that people predict that a certain situation will have a certain result based on whether they have had experience with a similar situation and can recall the outcome. For example, an HIV-positive woman whose HIV-positive friend had a child who developed AIDS most likely would predict her own chances of having a child who would ultimately develop AIDS to be considerably higher than the true statistical probability (of about 30 percent) provided to her. Tversky and Kahneman would say that the woman is overweighting the likelihood of such an event based on availability. Further, it has been shown that continued preoccupation with a certain outcome increases its availability and hence its perceived likelihood.[8] Slovic has written that "any factor that makes a hazard unusually memorable or imaginable, such as a recent disaster, heavy media coverage, or a vivid film, could seriously distort perceptions of risk."[9]

Another influence on the perceived likelihood of events is the amount—in contrast to the type—of information given: the more information provided, the easier it is for people to envision the scenario and the more likely the scenario then seems. When asked to predict how many HIV-positive babies will be born in the United States this year, a woman probably would guess a lower number than if she were asked to predict how many HIV-positive babies will be born to women who live in an inner city with a known history of intravenous drug use. Logically, the second prediction should be smaller, since it is a subset of the first, but because it includes a greater detail, it is more available to subjects and consequently is awarded a higher likelihood.[10]

Nisbett et al. have examined the role of emotions in perceived likelihood assessments. They conclude that choice often is more a function of emotional interest than of factual information: "Some kinds of information that the scientist regards as highly pertinent and logically compelling are habitually ignored by people. Other kinds of information, logically much weaker, trigger strong inferences and action tendencies."[11]

Slovic also points out that strong beliefs held by people when they enter a decision-making situation are difficult to modify. People have a tendency to dismiss contradictory evidence as unreliable and to incorporate new evidence only when it is consistent with their preexisting beliefs.

In what is perhaps their classic work, Tversky and Kahneman discuss how people's choices differ depending on how the information they are given is framed. This is similar to what we call "formulation effects." People make choices differently depending on whether potential outcomes are framed as gains or as losses. People tend to be risk averse with gains and risk seeking with losses; that is, most people choose a sure gain over the chance of either a slightly higher gain or no gain at all, whereas most people choose the chance of either a large loss or no loss at all over a certain, but smaller, loss. Moreover, research has revealed that both physicians' and patients' preferences among therapies for lung cancer varied "markedly when their probable outcomes [were] described in terms of mortality or survival."[12] Similarly, it would be predicted that HIV-positive pregnant women told that their chance of having an infected baby was about 30 percent might make a pregnancy continuation decision differently from HIV-positive pregnant women told that it was more likely that their baby would be uninfected than infected. Such behavior violates the notion that preference among options should not depend on how those options are described.

Framing effects are not the only means by which probabilities of outcomes can be misconstrued. People also tend to overweight extreme probabilities,[13] no matter on which end of the spectrum they fall. For example, people perceive the difference between a 0 percent and a 5 percent chance of survival as much greater than the difference between a 30 percent and a 35 percent chance. Because differences in probabilities at either end of the spectrum are overweighted, long shots seem more likely to occur, and people go to greater lengths to avert an unlikely loss than is appropriate for the statistical chances. People interpret differences at either end of the spectrum as absolute, rather than relative, thereby making them *appear* more severe.

Salient to the issue of HIV, Fischoff has pointed out that when uncertainty surrounds the information available for a particular decision—that is, when the chances of a particular outcome are unknown—people have a tendency to underestimate the importance of the omitted information and overestimate what is known.[14] For example, an asymptomatic, HIV-positive woman offered an experimental drug meant to delay the onset of symptoms, who could be told only that the chance of her developing AIDS in the next 5 years ranged from 20 to 40 percent, would be likely to overweight the known factors relevant to the decision, such as the side effects and the cost of the drug, and overlook whether the amount of risk makes her an appropriate candidate for the drug treatment in the first place.

The decision-making literature cited thus far suggests that changing the characteristics of an encounter or a presentation can affect understanding, which, in turn, can alter one's perception of risk. This has led some investigators to conclude that such behavior is irrational. Research done with populations of pregnant women has described similar behaviors that would be considered irrational according to normative classifications of decision theory.

Studies of pregnant women

One basic assumption of the decision-making literature discussed above is that rational decision making involves the careful and, in certain instances, quantified weighing of alternatives and an exploration of the consequences of each. That individuals often do not make reproductive decisions in accordance with this rational scheme was verified by Pauker and Pauker.[15] They conducted research in which prospective parents were asked to assign values to various pregnancy outcomes, with the goal of facilitating parents' decision about whether to have amniocentesis. Pauker and Pauker attempted to incorporate these values into mathematical formulas to facilitate decision making. However, this quantitative approach proved inappropriate because considerable discrepancies arose between the decisions that parents ultimately made and the rational decisions predicted with use of the formulas. The authors concluded that since probabilities may not be useful as a basis for decision making, mathematical models may be inappropriate for prenatal decisions.

Another study, by Faden et al., examining pregnant women's attitudes toward the abortion of fetuses who would be born with disabling conditions, also suggested that probabilities can be misinterpreted. They found that a *certain* loss is overweighted relative to a highly likely, but still *uncertain,* loss. This bias was reflected in the sharp increase in the number of women saying that they would have an abortion when the probability of the fetus's being affected rose from 95 percent to 100 percent.[16]

Overweighting of extreme possibilities occurs not only in situations of potential risk, but in those of potential benefit as well. Johnston et al. demonstrated that women considering in vitro fertilization overweighted the chance of conception, in part due to their extreme desire to have a baby.[17]

Wertz et al. confirmed the limited use of probabilities by demonstrating that clients' prior beliefs about risk were more influential in their decision making than actual numeric risks provided by health professionals.[18] Frets et al. lend further support to this claim in a study of the reproductive decisions of 164 couples after genetic counseling. They found that "issues at stake *before* genetic counseling such as the desire to have children and the familiarity with the disorder seem to be more important in reproductive planning" than risk level or disease severity.[19] Beeson and Golbus confirmed these findings in a study of the decision-making process among 26 women at risk of having a child with an X-linked disorder.[20] They found that (1) parents usually make up their minds before counseling; (2) parents' most strongly held beliefs become operative when they do perceive a choice; (3) when they do consider alternatives, they do so in binary rather than probabilistic terms, (that is, they predict that an event either will or will not happen, not that there is a certain chance that it will happen); and (4) parents focus on their own coping potential in making such decisions: "the salient issues are not precise risks of occurrence of the disorder or risks of tests. They are more closely related to the meaning of life with a disabled child."[21] The severity of the risk of having a child with disabilities may be more important to people than the likelihood of its occurrence. The authors concluded that attempts to quantify risk and burden divert parents from efforts to examine their coping potential and therefore are an inappropriate approach to making decisions. Another study with pregnant women demonstrated that absolute numbers or probabilities are less meaningful than *relative* comparisons.[22]

Threats to rationality that stem from misunderstanding of probabilities are exacerbated when uncertainty exists. Various types of uncertainty have been defined. "Measurable uncertainty" or "risk" is that which may be represented by numerical probabilities, while "unmeasurable uncertainty" or "ambiguity" cannot. Risk refers to situations where the probabilities are known. Ambiguity refers to situations where they are not, due to either lack of information or uniqueness of the situation.[23]

Lippman-Hand and Fraser show that decisions about genetic screening are more ambiguous than risky.[24] Typically, ambiguity renders decision making more difficult for people than risk. In either case, people tend to compensate for unknowns by assuming that an event either will or will not happen. The typical response to an unknown is to imagine what a situation would be like and how others would react if a *certain* choice were made:

> [Parents'] predominant perception of their chances of having an affected child is bina-
> ry—it either will or will not happen, no matter the rate associated with it or the parents'
> excellent recall of this factual information . . . knowledge of their actual chances is in
> a sense irrelevant to the fact that something can happen—and uncertainty is docu-
> mented at that level.[25]

This process increases parents' feeling of confidence about what will happen, enabling them to reach a decision. The notion of responding with a (false) sense of certainty to an unknown risk or range of risks is relevant to the context of HIV screening, for the conditions under which a choice must be made are not of a definable risk.

Not only can inaccurate perceptions of risk compromise understanding, but inadequate disclosure can as well. A study of pregnant women considering newborn screening for phenylketonuria (PKU) demonstrated that whether the women received information about the screening accounted for more variation in the amount of knowledge they had than any other factor studied.[26] To the degree to which knowledge is necessary, albeit not sufficient, for understanding, receiving less information can lead to compromised understanding. The amount of knowledge people have before entering a screening program also affects the outcome. Moreover, certain medical conditions are better publicized and understood by the public than others, or they are better understood by the particular population targeted for the screening. In such instances, one could assume that the educational value of a disclosure statement decreases.

There also is evidence that the availability heuristic operates in reproductive decision making. Black investigated how parents of a retarded child cope with subsequent genetic risks under conditions involving different levels of uncertainty. She found that the more severe the retardation of the first child, the more likely the parents were to consider the risk of recurrence in their subsequent decisions about reproduction.[27]

The studies discussed in this section suggest that the meaning individuals attach to numeric risks is affected as much by interpretations of uncertainties, prior beliefs, and experience as by the numbers themselves. Moreover, what people consider to be important in making a decision may not be captured in statistical probabilities.

Compromises to Informed Consent

Compromises to achieving a valid informed consent in the context of HIV screening of pregnant women could occur in several ways: programs intentionally could be designed to undermine free choice, or there may be limitations in resources or "structural" problems (such as insufficient numbers of staff or inadequate space in which to see patients privately) that compromise the consent process.

Programs of routine screening with notification are less likely to respect patient autonomy than completely voluntary programs. The requirement of substantial understanding may be compromised, since although the notification part of a routine program requires that a woman be informed that she will be tested unless she expressly refuses, it does not necessarily impose extensive disclosure duties on providers, nor does it impose any obligation to assist patients in determining what information is material to them. How much information and the types of information provided automatically are a function of the priorities of those designing the program. The condition of substantial understanding is more likely to be satisfied when women initiate inquiries about information on their own and when women are familiar with the meaning and possible consequences of HIV testing prior to being notified about the screening policy.

Routine screening programs also are more likely to compromise voluntariness. Women may not appreciate that they really do have the option to refuse the test or the degree to which they may refuse the test without being subject to compromised medical care or the disdain of their medical practitioners. Even if women believe they have a meaningful right to refuse, making the test a standard procedure sends the message that there must be a good reason for doing so. At the very least, a policy of routine screening implies that the local medical staff believes that the benefits of screening outweigh the risks. If this indeed is what the staff believes, and if women, trusting the judgments of their health-care providers, elect to be tested, this does not necessarily undermine either the condition of substantial noncontrol or the condition of substantial understanding. If women falsely conclude, however, that because screening is routine, no or only minimal risks are involved, understanding is significantly compromised.

Even when no recommendation is explicitly made, just *offering* a test may be viewed by women as an endorsement and again may cause them to conclude naively that testing is necessarily risk free or in their interest. Therefore, in practice, even completely voluntary programs will not be problem free.

In a completely voluntary program, where explicit informed consent is a requirement for testing, there are no guarantees that the consent obtained is valid. Although voluntary programs are likely to provide patients with more information than routine screening with notification programs, the disclosures made still may be inadequate. Many voluntary programs may not provide women with the information appropriate for making such a decision, or they may fail to assist women to understand the information and to appreciate the issues that are material to them.

An obvious illustration here is when "adequate" disclosures are made in a language patients do not understand or through the use of terms and concepts that do not translate across cultural or ethnic lines. Health-care providers or counselors charged with soliciting consent may undermine the validity of the process either by failing to disclose to patients the information necessary to satisfy the condition of substantial understanding or by acting coercively or manipulatively. Providers may not disclose information because they believe there is no controversy concerning the appropriate decision or because of their own discomfort with an ambiguous situation. In some cases, they may be incapable or unwilling to bridge cultural, language, or educational barriers. In other instances, prejudices may underlie a failure on the part of providers to value or respect their patients. The greater the discrepancy between the backgrounds or values of providers and patients, the more likely this is to occur. Particularly where the gap is large, providers may act coercively or manipulatively because they do not trust their patients to make the "right" decision.

In some instances, it may be difficult for even the most well-intentioned health-care providers to help patients achieve an adequate level of understanding and personal meaning—for example, when patients are incompetent or do not have the cognitive ability or minimal understanding of the social and medical issues at stake to grasp whatever information was thought to be necessary for adequate understanding. In other instances, patients are disinclined to listen to or process the information; in effect, they elect not to participate in the informed consent process.

In still other situations, problems with the informed consent process are directly a function of resource or other system constraints. Examples of such limitations include a reimbursement structure demanding too many appointments in too short a time to allow for adequate interaction between patients and providers; no money for counselors, staff training, or translators; and overcrowded conditions that do not allow for privacy and thus make it difficult for patients to ask personal questions that may be relevant to the consent decision.

A Broader View of Informed Consent

Jay Katz, a psychiatrist, proposes that informed consent is a process of *shared* decision making, requiring conversation between patients and providers that exposes each of their unconscious motivations.[28] His views about what he calls "psychological autonomy" and informed consent have important implications for decision making between patients and providers. First, thought and action never can be brought fully under the domination of consciousness and rationality. Katz's definition of rationality, moreover, is distinctly different from Kahneman and Tversky's. In Katz's view, an examination of the provider's, as well as the patient's, rationality is in order:

> Conscious–unconscious refers to internal mental states, to the constant interplay of consciousness and unconsciousness on thought and feelings. The terms rational–irrational highlight . . . persons' . . . abilities to take reality into account and to give some account of the conflicts between their inner and outer worlds to themselves and others. . . . Thus, any evaluation of perceived "irrational" conduct must take into account that such a judgment may be based on differences in values, life style, and other personal matters between the two interacting parties.[29]

Second, since psychological grounds for interfering with patients' choices can be found readily and exploited for purposes of coercion,[30] patients' choices deserve to be honored in the absence of substantial evidence of incompetence. Katz argues that physicians must facilitate opportunities for reflection in order to prevent ill-considered rational and irrational influences on choice. Indeed, the obligations that Katz advocates are imposed on *both* parties. Of course, it is difficult to achieve a balance in communication between providers and patients because it is more typical for physicians to structure the interaction.

That physicians are likely to structure the interaction becomes particularly problematic given differences in physicians' communication styles, knowledge, and tendency to impart their own values. Roter et al. have demonstrated that physicians' nonverbal as well as verbal communication have an effect on patient satisfaction, recall, and impressions.[31]

With respect to knowledge, it has been demonstrated that physicians, too, have a tendency to employ the availability heuristic, which can result in an inaccurate presentation of risk. Marteau and Baum found that physicians working with adult patients who were experiencing complications related to their juvenile-onset diabetes were more likely to consider this disease risky than physicians working only with children with the condition who had not yet developed the inevitable complications.[32]

It also has been demonstrated that physicians' decision making is more a function of their "philosophic stance" than of the science of medicine.[33] Therefore, physicians must be made aware of their tendency to influence patients' decisions due to their particular communication style, their presentation of unrepresentative statistics, and their interjection of personal values.

Not only may physicians be unaware of their tendency to present unrepresentative statistics, but they also may be unconscious of their tendency to manipulate or coerce patients, thereby compromising patient autonomy. Furthermore, these practices are reinforced in medical school.[34] "Whether the power, the right and the authority [of physicians] have been given to [them] by the public or whether this 'extraordinary role' was imposed on and passively accepted by the public,"[35] its existence highlights a facet of humans' propensity toward irrationality, identified as their pervasive need to deny fallibility. That physicians project their irrationalities onto patients may prove to be one of the most pervasive and fateful countertransference reactions.[36]

Clearly, there are many influences that can impinge either appropriately or inappropriately on the decision-making process. From our moral perspective, the ultimate test of whether informed consent has been achieved is if the patient's decision is based on an adequate understanding of what is or would be material to her in light of her values and history, and not whether, in making her decision, a standard of "normative" rationality has been satisfied. Our justification for this conclusion arises out of the overriding value we place on respecting autonomy and self-determination. Although a prerequisite for any decision is a certain minimal core of understanding, we are willing to accept what others may view as a compromised level of understanding with regard to probabilities and statistical information as long as the patient's appreciation of this minimal core and what is additionally material to her is adequate. If, however, one did not give patient autonomy preeminence, perhaps due to a belief that one option clearly was superior and therefore was important for the patient to choose, a provider might spend more time on those aspects of understanding he or she considered to be material to the decision. It is through the decision-making process that salient issues and values are identified for both patient and provider so that patient understanding is maximized and provider control is minimized.

Implications

The question germane to HIV screening for pregnant women is, To what degree do limitations exist that prevent attainment of valid informed consent? To answer this question, one must determine not only what kinds of limitations may be present, but also the extent to which they interfere with substantial understanding and control.

Women at greatest risk for prenatal HIV infection typically have less formal education and are more disadvantaged economically than the prenatal population as a whole. They often do not enter prenatal care until the second or third trimester of pregnancy,[37] and some also use intravenous drugs or other addictive substances. Such characteristics make these women less likely than other women to understand medical information or numeric probabilities. They also may be more vulnerable than other women to controlling influences from medical authority figures, particularly as these authority figures are perceived as having control over their impending child's birth and care.

Some high-risk pregnant women are adolescents, for whom there is legal and moral controversy about the capacity to give consent and the role of parental consent or notification. Recent cases brought before the Supreme Court have argued against the competence of minors.[38] Opponents of this view argue that minority does not automatically render a person incompetent for all purposes. In many states, statutes exist permitting older children to validly authorize the administration of certain limited kinds of medical care (e.g., treatment for mental illness, substance abuse, venereal disease, pregnancy), or the common law may permit mature minors to validly consent to medical care.[39] Many believe that the decision-making capacity is specific to a particular decision and depends not on a person's status (such as age) or on the decision reached, but on the person's actual functioning in situations in which a decision about health care is to be made. While infants and young children are obvious examples of decision-making incapacity, this criterion need not necessarily be extended to older children. In fact, the claim is made that many older children can make at least some health-care decisions.[40] The approach to determining incapacity, particularly germane for children above a certain age (variously described as from 7 to the mid-teens), is the individual's actual functioning in decision-making situations.[41]

Culture, background, and maturity all can influence what a person considers to be material with respect to a consent decision. Specific to reproductive decisions, women vary widely with regard to how they value their own health and the health of their babies, their views about the acceptability of abortion, the importance of being a mother, and their trust in medical professionals and governmental authorities, to name but a few. Persons soliciting consent for HIV testing need to be mindful of this variation in values and concerns.

In a pilot study of knowledge and attitudes about HIV screening among pregnant women at demographically higher risk,[42] we found that women expressed overwhelming concern about the health of their babies, often at the sacrifice of their own health. They discussed their babies with an attitude almost of sanctity or reverence. This orientation contributed to many women's disdain for abortion as a reproductive option. We also found that women with less education were more likely to prefer some kind of mandatory screening program than women with more education. Although the relationship among preference for mandatory screening programs, orientation toward the sanctity of babies, and educational background needs further exploration, whether we would hear the same concerns and values from women of other backgrounds is unclear.

Not only is there heterogeneity in the population we are concerned about, but there is also variation in the practice patterns and attitudes of providers that affects the achievement of valid informed consent. Of concern in the context of screening for HIV is the likelihood of many providers to treat high-risk women paternalistically. In a survey of two pediatric residency programs in New York City, 65 percent of the respondents "agreed" or "strongly agreed" with the statement that "women should not have babies who will be at risk for [AIDS]." This contrasts with only a 25 percent comparable response when the risk was for Tay-Sachs disease, 15 percent when the risk was for cystic fibrosis, and 9 percent when the risk was for Down's syndrome.[43] Inevitably, a paternalistic approach to the informed consent process threatens the extent to which patients make their decisions voluntarily. This is especially worrisome with pregnant adolescents, who may be more susceptible to manipulation than older women.

There also is evidence that patients respond adversely to having control removed from them. Kathleen Nolan reports that families whose children were tested for HIV without their consent are much less likely to perceive subsequent services as positive and supportive and may be less willing to cooperate with treatment regimens.[44]

Pregnant women who are demographically at increased risk of infection, and therefore may have more at stake with respect to HIV testing, are more likely than other women to attend public clinics.[45] Public clinics, although a potential forum for group education, are more likely to be under resource constraints that can undermine informed consent than are private physicians. As noted earlier, resource constraints can compromise the ability to obtain valid informed consent due to lack of time, insufficient reimbursement, and/or inappropriate personnel. As Katz has proposed, reflection is necessary for a valid informed consent process. However, reflection requires dialogue, which takes time, and time is at a premium in any physician–patient encounter. Time is particularly precious in encounters involving higher-risk women.

In formulating practical recommendations to facilitate the achievement of informed consent as we have defined it, the morally *preferable* HIV screening program would include disclosure, counseling, and authorization components. The disclosure would convey information about the nature and risks of the procedure itself and about the benefits and risks to knowing, or having others know, the test results. These include possible changes in medical care and transmission rates or possible breach of confidentiality to employers, insurers, or significant others. In addition, the patient would be informed of her right to refuse the test. Counseling would include solicitation of what is material to the patient,[46] acknowledgment by the counselor of his or her own biases and values, and assistance to the patient in selecting the option that best matches the patient's priorities. Further detail of what ought to be included in the pre- and posttest counseling sessions are discussed in Chapter 13. Finally, the authorization would be a clear statement from the patient that she is *choosing* to be screened.

Of course, this triad of disclosure, counseling, and authorization is offered with the assumption that the patient is competent.[47] There is some controversy about whether adolescent patients or those using intravenous drugs or other mind-altering substances are competent to give valid informed consent. It must be remembered that competency is not necessarily an all-or-nothing phenomenon. Someone may be incompetent to perform certain tasks and competent to perform others, or may be incompetent at certain times (e.g., when actually high on drugs) and competent at others. Whether a woman is competent to authorize the performance of an HIV test must be determined based on her cognitive and emotional state at the time of counseling.

Given the constraints inherent in many clinical settings, the extent of disclosure and counseling will not be uniform. Therefore, a minimum set of standards for a morally *acceptable* informed consent process must be determined. The process of obtaining written informed consent is one means of achieving that minimum level *if* the consent statement includes both the disclosure and authorization components, the patient is allotted sufficient time to read the document, the document is at a reading level and in a language appropriate for the patient, and the practitioner asks if the patient has any questions and reiterates her right to refuse. An institutional policy that required written informed consent, with the above conditions, for every HIV test performed in that institution would satisfy what we consider a minimum standard. Certainly, provisions can be incorporated into an institutional policy, such as a laboratory's refusal to test any tube of blood unaccompanied by a signed consent form, that would maximize the likelihood of achieving this minimum level of informed consent.

One example of a voluntary screening program that would not necessarily satisfy the conditions of disclosure, counseling, and authorization would be a routine or an automatic one that allowed the patient the right to refuse. In such a program, it is unlikely that patients would be given the opportunity to ask questions or to have a meaningful discussion about the purposes and risks of the test, discussion that facilitates substantial understanding and noncontrol. Therefore, although a routine with notification program allows the patient the right to refuse, it typically does not satisfy the conditions for valid informed consent and, as such, may be morally acceptable but not morally preferable. A program that more regularly satisfies the conditions of informed consent is the morally preferable option.

We have argued that the ideal screening program would be *voluntary,* that understanding and voluntariness are the primary components of informed consent, and that decision making based on an adequate understanding of material information is more important than normative rationality. The degree to which screening programs consider understanding, voluntariness, and materiality depends on two criteria: (1) which standard of informed consent is used, and (2) the resources available to engage in reflection and conversation. When it is practical to meet only the requirements of what we have called a minimum standard for informed consent, there at least is the opportunity for the decision regarding HIV testing to reflect what might be called a *sufficient* level of autonomy. By contrast, the morally preferable standard for informed consent procedures that involved disclosure, counseling, and authorization maximizes the likelihood that the consent decision reflects a *substantial* level of autonomy. This substantial level generally requires reflection and conversation, which can occur only when resources are adequate. Reflection and conversation can facilitate substantial autonomy by exposing any irrational or unconscious values and motives of the provider and patient and by clarifying what is material to the patient.

Institutions must give a high enough priority to the informed consent process at least to establish a policy that would demand its attainment. They also should provide the resources required for meaningful provider–patient interaction, for example, by endorsing pretest counseling. Only then will most limitations to informed consent be moderated sufficiently for patients to be treated with appropriate respect.

Notes

1. Ruth R. Faden and Tom L. Beauchamp, *A History and Theory of Informed Consent* (New York: Oxford University Press, 1986), 237; Paul S. Appelbaum, Charles W. Lidz, and Alan Meisel, *Informed consent: Legal Theory and Clinical Practice* (New York: Oxford University Press, 1987).
2. Faden and Beauchamp, *History and Theory of Informed Consent,* 237.
3. Ibid., 261.
4. Ibid., 360.
5. Isaac Levi, *Hard Choices* (New York: Cambridge University Press, 1986), 83–107; Joseph Raz, *The Morality of Freedom* (New York: Oxford University Press, 1986), 321–363; James Griffin, *Well-Being: Its Meaning, Measurement and Moral Importance* (New York: Oxford University Press, 1986), 75–92.
6. Amos Tversky and Daniel Kahneman, "Judgment Under Uncertainty: Heuristics and Biases," in *Judgment Under Uncertainty: Heuristics and Biases,* ed. Daniel Kahneman, Paul Slovic, and Amos Tversky (New York: Cambridge University Press, 1982) 3.
7. Paul Slovic, "Informing and Educating the Public About Risk," *Risk Analysis* 6 (1986): 403.
8. Amos Tversky and Daniel Kahneman, "Availability: A Heuristic for Judging Frequency and Probability," in Kahneman et al., *Judgment Under Uncertainty,* 178.
9. Slovic, "Informing and Educating," 404.
10. See the discussion of extensional cues in Amos Tversky and Daniel Kahneman, "Extensional vs. Intuitive Reasoning: The Conjunction Fallacy in Probability Judgment," *Psychological Review* 90 (1983): 293–315.
11. Richard E. Nisbett, Eugene Borgida, Rick Crandall et al., "Popular Induction: Information Is Not Necessarily Informative," in Kahneman et al., *Judgment Under Uncertainty,* 116.
12. Tversky and Kahneman, "Judgment Under Uncertainty," 6.
13. Both this nonlinearity of how decisions are weighted and the framing effects discussed earlier violate what is known as the "principle of invariance."
14. Baruch Fischoff, "Cost–Benefit Analysis: An Uncertain Guide to Public Policy," *Annals of the New York Academy of Sciences* 2 (1981): 173–188.

15. Susan P. Pauker and Stephen G. Pauker, "Prenatal Diagnosis: A Directive Approach to Genetic Counseling Using Decision Analysis," *Yale Journal of Biology and Medicine* 50 (1977): 275–289.

16. Ruth R. Faden, Judith Chwalow, Kimberly Quaid et al., "Prenatal Screening and Pregnant Women's Attitudes Toward the Abortion of Defective Fetuses," *American Journal of Public Health* 77 (1987): 288–290.

17. Marie Johnston, Robert Shaw, and David Bird, "Test-Tube Baby Procedures: Stress and Judgements under Uncertainty," *Psychology and Health* 1 (1987): 25–38.

18. Dorothy C. Wertz, James R. Sorenson, and Timothy C. Heeren, "Clients' Interpretation of Risks Provided in Genetic Counseling," *American Journal of Human Genetics* 39 (1986): 253–264.

19. Petra G. Frets, Hugo J. Duivenvoorden, Frans Verhage et al., "Factors Influencing the Reproductive Decision After Genetic Counseling," *American Journal of Medical Genetics* 35 (1990): 496–502.

20. Diane Beeson and Mitchell S. Golbus, "Decision Making: Whether or Not to Have Prenatal Diagnosis and Abortion for X-Linked Conditions," *American Journal of Medical Genetics* 20 (1985): 107–114.

21. Ibid., 113.

22. Gary A. Chase, Ruth R. Faden, Neil A. Holtzman et al., "Assessment of Risk by Pregnant Women: Implications for Genetic Counseling and Education," *Social Biology* 33 (1986): 57–64.

23. Daniel Ellsberg, "Risk, Ambiguity and the Savage Axioms," *Quarterly Journal of Economics* 75 (1961): 643–699.

24. Abby Lippman-Hand and F. Clarke Fraser, "Genetic Counseling: Parents' Responses to Uncertainty," *Birth Defects* 15 (1979): 325–339.

25. Ibid., 332.

26. Neil A. Holtzman, Ruth R. Faden, Judith Chwalow et al., "Effect of Informed Parental Consent on Mothers' Knowledge of Newborn Screening," *Pediatrics* 72 (1983): 807–812.

27. Rita B. Black, "The Effects of Diagnostic Uncertainty and Available Options on Perceptions of Risk," *Birth Defects* 15 (1979): 341–354.

28. Jay Katz, *The Silent World of Doctor and Patient* (New York: Free Press, 1984), 111.

29. Ibid., 117.

30. Ibid., 113.

31. Debra L. Roter, Judith A. Hall, and Nancy R. Katz, "Relations Between Physicians' Behaviors and Analogue Patients' Satisfaction, Recall and Impressions," *Medical Care* 25 (1987): 437–451.

32. Theresa M. Marteau and J. D. Baum, "Doctors' Views on Diabetes," *Archives of Diseases in Children* 59 (1984): 566–570.

33. John P. Minogue and Nancy Jo Reedy, "Companioning Parents in Perinatal Decision Making," *Journal of Perinatal and Neonatal Nursing* 1 (1988): 25–35.

34. Katz, *Silent World of Doctor and Patient*, 225.

35. Ibid., 149.

36. Ibid., 150.

37. Institute of Medicine, National Academy of Sciences, *Preventing Low Birthweight* (Washington, D.C.: National Academy Press, 1985).

38. *Hodgson* v. *State of Minnesota* 110 S. Ct. 2926 (1990) and *Ohio* v. *Akron Center for Reproductive Health,* 110 S. Ct. 2972 (1990).

39. Appelbaum et al., *Informed Consent,* 83.

40. President's Commission for the Study of Ethical Problems in Medicine and Bio-medical and Behavioral Research, *Making Health Care Decisions: The Ethical and Legal Implications of Informed Consent in the Patient–Practitioner Relationship* (Washington, D.C.: Government Printing Office, 1982), 170.

41. Ibid., 55.

42. APHA presentation.

43. Betty Wolder Levin, Kathleen E. Powderly, and Jonathan Moreno, "Ethics and AIDS in the Neonatal Intensive Care Unit" (presented at the Meeting of the American Public Health Association, Chicago, October 26–29, 1989).

44. Kathleen Nolan, "Ethical Issues in Caring for Pregnant Women and Newborns at Risk for Human Immunodeficiency Virus Infection" *Seminars in Perinatology,* 13 (1989): 55–65.

45. IOM Report.

46. As mentioned earlier, it is consistent with the achievement of valid informed consent for the physician to make a recommendation when the patient considers this to be material. However, it remains important that the recommendation be acknowledged as the physician's own. What is more complicated is the situation involving a patient who does not merely ask the physician's opinion but actually wants the physician to be his or her decision maker, with the patient having no interest in hearing any other information or in discussing the options. It is our belief that in the context of HIV screening in pregnancy, where the social risks are substantial, a certain amount of disclosure *must* occur. Obviously, when a patient does not listen to or understand the disclosure, the physician should determine whether it is acceptable for the test to be performed.

47. For a fuller discussion of competence, see Faden and Beauchamp, *History and Theory of Informed Consent.*

13

Reproductive Decision Making in the Context of HIV: The Case for Nondirective Counseling

NANCY E. KASS

> Thou shalt conceive, and bear a son. Now therefore beware, I pray thee, and drink no wine nor strong drink, and eat not any unclean thing.
>
> *Judges 13:3–4*

For thousands of years, women have been counseled, instructed, persuaded, or forced to follow certain behaviors while pregnant, either for their own benefit or for the benefit of the fetus. Beliefs about how directive these interactions ought to be have changed over time. Consistent with a general trend in medical ethics in the United Sates during the past several decades toward increased respect for patient autonomy, the model of counseling most often endorsed in recent years advocates providing patients with complete information but allowing them to make their own decisions based on their own values and preferences. This emphasis on respect for patient autonomy has been particularly pronounced in the areas of genetic testing and reproductive decisions.

Counseling related to HIV disease, particularly with pregnant women or women considering pregnancy, seems to be challenging this trend. HIV disease is becoming increasingly prevalent among women, and pregnancy is one of the recognized routes of transmission of HIV. Consequently, many individuals and organizations have considered the counseling of women who are pregnant or of reproductive age as an opportunity to prevent transmission of HIV. However, inherent in this belief often is the assumption that it is appropriate not only to inform women of their risks but also to advise them to *avoid* the risk of transmitting the virus to their offspring by not reproducing. Thus the trend toward respecting patient autonomy, particularly with regard to reproductive decisions, may be threatened by a belief that patients should be advised that there is a "right" choice in the case of HIV. Whether this new trend indeed is appropriate remains the subject of much debate.

There are different situations in which HIV-related counseling with women of reproductive age might occur: counseling for women who are considering testing, counseling for seropositive women who may be considering pregnancy, and

308

counseling for seropositive women who already are pregnant. The latter two situations are the focus of this chapter, since they are the ones in which counseling related to a *reproductive decision* most likely would occur. It also should be noted at this point that the term "counselor," as used in this chapter, refers to whoever is counseling the woman. This person may indeed be someone whose full-time job is counseling patients regarding decision making and values clarification; however, the counselor may also be the woman's physician or another person designated by the health-care facility to interact with women concerning HIV and reproductive decision making.

In order to address these issues, this chapter considers the pattern of HIV disease in women, whether HIV disease is similar to other conditions that can be transmitted during pregnancy, the purposes of counseling, descriptions of different models of interacting with women of reproductive age, recommendations for HIV counseling put forth by leading figures and policy-making bodies, and arguments *against* being directive in counseling. The chapter concludes with a set of recommendations for the counseling session itself.

The Pattern of HIV Disease in Women

Chapter 2 provides a comprehensive discussion of the epidemiology of HIV infection in women. For our purposes, a few facts should be noted. Women now constitute approximately 10 percent of the AIDS cases thus far reported to the Centers for Disease Control (CDC).[1] Among those women, about 70 percent are of reproductive age. The number of women with AIDS who are *pregnant* is not known, however, nor is the number of pregnant women who are *infected* with HIV. Findings of seroprevalence surveys compiled by the CDC demonstrate a range of 0–1.7 percent HIV infection among prenatal patients and 0.4–2.3 percent infection in women tested at the time of delivery.[2] However, it is important to remember that seroprevalence studies typically have been conducted among inner-city populations, while the distribution of infection and disease varies tremendously across the country. In the Bronx, New York City, for example, among those aged 25–44 years, there is a seroprevalence rate of 5.4–12.5 percent among males and 1.4–3.3 percent among females,[3] and 1 in 80 births in New York City is to an HIV-infected woman.[4] Moreover, AIDS is not distributed randomly by ethnicity. AIDS is over 10 times higher in populations of African-American and Hispanic women than in populations of white women,[5] a fact relevant for counseling interactions.

Distinctions Among HIV Disease and Other Conditions

If indeed HIV counseling has taken on at least a somewhat different orientation from counseling for other perinatally transmitted diseases, it is relevant to consider the degree to which HIV disease is comparable to other conditions. Are any differences in counseling a function of relevant differences between HIV disease and other perinatally transmitted conditions? What is important to consider in addressing this question are the transmission rates, the severity of illness and the prognosis for the child, whether treatments are available, how prevalent the disorder is, whether the mother's own health is affected, and the population in which the condition is most prevalent. (See Chapter 3 for a more detailed analysis.)

With respect to transmission rates, it is predicted that if a woman is infected with HIV, there is a 30 percent chance that she will transmit the virus to her infant. This is contrasted with a 70–100 percent chance of vertical transmission for a woman with untreated syphilis,[6] a 70–90 percent chance of vertical transmission for a woman infected with hepatitis B virus,[7] and a 25 percent chance that a homozygous recessive condition will result from the coupling of two genetic carriers.

With respect to severity of illness, as described in Chapter 2, 75 percent of HIV-infected children will have symptoms by 2 years of age. Twenty-five percent of such children die within the first 2 years, 50 percent die within 70 months, and only 25 percent are alive by age 5. By comparison, 40 percent of the pregnancies of women with untreated syphilis result in fetal loss.[8] Among syphilis-infected children who survive, the effects range from very few symptoms to severe neurologic damage. For children with sickle cell disease, a genetic rather than an infectious condition, the prognosis also is variable. Children typically present after 6 months of age with symptoms such as failure to thrive, serious infections, and severe anemia.[9] Organs gradually are damaged as a result of the disease; thus persons with sickle cell disease typically have a shortened life expectancy. Children with cystic fibrosis now are thought to have a mean survival of 20 years, a dramatic change from even a few decades ago; for many, the disease remains fatal in childhood and early adult life. Classically, a child with cystic fibrosis presents with intestinal problems in the first year of life. Other obstructions of organ passages cause additional problems later in life due to an abnormal composition of the mucus. A child with Tay-Sachs disease has severe symptoms that almost without exception lead to death by age 5.

In terms of how treatable these conditions are, HIV rivals or exceeds most perinatally acquired or genetic disorders except Tay-Sachs disease in being unresponsive to medical intervention. Although certain therapies and monitoring are available for HIV that can briefly prolong life or improve a child's quality of life, no effective treatments exist and there is no cure (see Chapters 2 and 5).

As stated earlier, the prevalence of HIV among newborns is not known, but the existence of wide geographic variation in prevalence has been established. In one study in New York State, an overall seroprevalence rate of 0.66 percent was documented, with a rate of 2.2 percent seen in certain regions of New York City and a rate of 0.16 percent seen in upstate New York.[10] A similar variation was found in a study in Massachusetts, in which an overall seroprevalence rate of 0.21 percent was detected, but a difference of 0.1 to 0.8 percent was documented between rates in suburban and rural hospitals and rates in inner-city hospitals.[11] It must be remembered that only 30 percent of these newborns will remain truly infected, which means that prevalence rates can be expected to range roughly from 5 to 70 HIV-infected children per 10,000 births. By comparison, 1 in 12,000 to 15,000 children is born with phenylketonuria, 1 in 600 African-American children is born with sickle cell disease, and 1 in 2,000 white children is born with cystic fibrosis.[12]

HIV differs from other diseases transmitted through pregnancy in that it is virtually certain that the mother herself will become fatally ill from the infection. The time at which this may occur is not known; one study estimates the mean time from infection to AIDS to be 11 years.[13] Whether pregnancy reduces this interval is inconclusive at this time. What is important to consider is that ultimately it is unlikely that the woman will be available to raise and care for her child. Moreover, it may be recommended to her that she begin to undergo treatment herself. At present, the risks of medications such as zidovudine (formerly known as retrovir or azidothymidine [AZT]) on a developing fetus are not known. Protocols for treatment of seropositive pregnant women are changing rapidly. Although some clinicians are routinely treating seropositive pregnant women with zidovudine, others believe that pregnancy is a contraindication for prescribing it (see Chapter 4). At the present time, the vast majority of pregnant women who are being treated with zidovudine receive the drug as part of a research trial.

A difference between HIV disease and other diseases of pregnancy that cannot be ignored is the populations affected. As described above, HIV disease in pregnancy disproportionately affects disadvantaged African-American and Hispanic women, whereas the classic model of genetic screening and counseling, with the notable exception of sickle cell disease, involves white middle-class women. In terms of counseling, this is less of biologic than of sociologic importance. Cultural differences between health-care providers and patients may be greater in the context of HIV disease than in the context of many genetic diseases, and it may be less likely that women will be trusted by health-care providers to make reasonable decisions on their own.

Clearly, there have been many diseases that predated HIV in which women have faced the possibility of fetal harm and have had to make difficult reproductive decisions. Moreover, there have been and remain instances in which the chances of harm to the fetus are significantly greater than those for HIV. What distinguishes HIV from other conditions are the inevitability of the mother's becoming sick herself and the fact that the women at greatest risk are members of otherwise disadvantaged populations. As will be discussed below, these are not distinctions that justify a change in counseling practices that would render counseling for HIV to be different in orientation from the counseling models developed previously for reproductive decision making.

The Purpose of Counseling

The counseling of women concerning reproductive decisions has many purposes. One important function is providing a forum in which to convey information. In the context of HIV testing, for example, information provided in a counseling session with a pregnant woman who is being given her test results might include the meaning of a positive and a negative test, the known routes of transmission, and the estimated risk of perinatal HIV transmission. However, what distinguishes counseling from health education is the component of the counseling session that examines psychological issues. If there is a *decision* to be made, such as whether to terminate a pregnancy or whether to take a drug whose risks in pregnancy are unknown, it is crucial to sort out the counselee's values and feelings in regard to the decision. Even when there is *not* a decision to be made, a counseling session includes a psychological component. In the context of HIV testing, this may include determining and facilitating a patient's ability to tap her own support system and typical coping mechanisms.

The counseling session also provides a woman with a support system *at* her health-care setting, which, in turn, may provide her with another link with the health-care system. Arguably, a purpose of counseling can be to provide a patient with advice, either solicited or unsolicited. This last issue will receive further attention later in this chapter.

Types of Interaction for Reproductive Decision Making

Nondirective counseling

Perhaps the most influential model for reproductive decision making evolved out of the genetic counseling movement. This paradigm of nondirective counseling was described by Fraser to include helping individuals or families to (1) understand the medical facts, (2) understand the options for dealing with the risk of recurrence, (3) choose the course of action that seems appropriate to them in view of their risk and the family's goals, (4) act in accordance with that decision, and (5) make the best possible adjustment to the disorder in an affected family member.[14] What is clear from this description is that when a counselor and patient differ in opinion about what the patient should do, the role of the counselor is to assist the patient to achieve the outcome that the *patient* prefers.

Several professional organizations, including the National Academy of Sciences,[15] the Hastings Center,[16] and the President's Commission for the Study of Ethical Problems in Medicine and Biomedical and Behavioral Research,[17] have advocated a process of genetic counseling that allows individuals to make their own decisions. Ronald Bayer has noted that today the ethos of nondirective counseling for reproductive decision making retains its dominance both as a professional ideology and as a guiding principle for public agencies.[18]

However, nondirective counseling was not initially the dominant orientation of genetic counseling. Epstein writes that one of the original goals of genetic counseling was the prevention of genetic disorders; only later did an emphasis on communication and choice emerge.[19] According to Epstein, the rationale for the change in orientation from reducing the prevalence of a condition in the population to assisting parents to make choices based on their own values is an ethical one:

> Not all individuals at risk of transmitting a genetic disorder . . . are anxious to prevent its occurrence. While the prevention of genetic disease or defects might in many instances appear to be desirable to the counselor, it is by no means certain that the persons at risk will always be of the same opinion—the means of prevention may not be acceptable, or the family may only want information, not action. In situations such as this, it is generally felt that it is incumbent upon the counselor not to interpose his own personal opinions into the counseling situation. This feeling has been given expression in the notion that counseling should be non-directive.[20]

Kathleen Nolan further offers that "the imposition of unwanted advice by a paternalistic counselor may not only violate the ethical principles of autonomy and procreative freedom but may also paradoxically drive the counsellee into a defiant rejection of the counselor's position."[21]

Directive counseling

Advocates for directive counseling argue that the need to protect the fetus or the pregnant woman from harm or the need to protect the health or interests of the public (e.g., financial interests) outweighs whatever disrespect of autonomy might result from this approach. Often, practitioners do have a strong belief that a pregnant woman should do one thing rather than another. If the belief is strong enough, a practitioner may feel justified in urging her to act in a particular way.

There is no agreement as to whether a counselor's merely voicing an opinion compromises a patient's autonomy or whether actual manipulation or explicit coercion must occur before patient autonomy is threatened. Some believe that since the relationship between a counselor and a patient inevitably is unbalanced, any attempt at persuasion or advocacy is inherently coercive. If the counselor is also the woman's physician or is someone to whom she has entrusted her well-being, a woman may feel particularly compelled to act in accordance with his or her recommendation if it conflicts with her own. Others, however, argue that mere persuasion, even by a physician, does not threaten a patient's autonomy and, indeed, that it is the *responsibility* of a practitioner to voice an opinion.[22]

In any event, whenever a patient is urged to exercise one option over another, by definition, directive counseling is occurring. John Arras is one of many proponents of this position:

> It is time . . . to call into question the moral imperative of non-directive counseling . . . physicians are not obligated merely to accept the initial preferences of their patients, even if they are obligated to respect their final decisions. Indeed, it is perfectly consistent with the theory of informed consent and patient autonomy for physicians not merely to inform their patients, but also to vigorously advise them to accept a particular option.[23]

The public health or societal interests in this situation are in preventing the transmission of disease, either for the health of its members or when called on to financially support affected individuals. The debate concerning how much to respect individual rights when they cause societal burdens is not new, however. What must be given scrutiny is whether society is willing to sacrifice respect for individual autonomy in the context of HIV to a greater extent than in the context of genetic abnormalities, in which harm to the fetus and societal burden may be equally great.

Compelled intervention in pregnancy

In comparison with nondirective counseling, directive counseling has been interpreted by some to be disrespectful of the autonomy interests of women. However, further along the spectrum of threatening women's autonomy, albeit seen much less frequently, is compulsory physical intervention. As noted in Chapter 3, in most states pregnant women are legally compelled to be tested for syphilis, with limited or no right to refuse. Earlier in this century, many women presumed to be mentally incompetent were forcibly sterilized to prevent what was thought to be hereditary mental retardation. Currently, the central issue is compulsory intervention during pregnancy. Although a thorough treatment of this complex issue is beyond the scope of this chapter (see Chapters 8 and 14 for related discussions), a brief review is in order.

Kolder et al. have documented 21 cases in which court orders were sought by obstetricians to compel pregnant women to act or refrain from acting in a certain way against their will.[24] Orders were successfully obtained in 86 percent of these cases. Eighty-one percent of the women involved were African-American, Asian, or Hispanic, and 24 percent did not speak English as their primary language.

The same authors also reported that 46 percent of the heads of fellowship programs in maternal–fetal medicine thought that women who refused medical advice and thereby endangered the life of the fetus should be detained. Twenty-six percent advocated state surveillance of women in the third trimester who stay outside the hospital system. The authors cited a case of a 16-year-old girl from Wisconsin who was "held in secure detention for the sake of her fetus because she tended 'to be on the run' and to 'lack motivation or ability to seek prenatal care.' "[25]

Margery Shaw conducted a legal analysis of the rights of the fetus.[26] She concluded that the law, in general, does not recognize the fetus as a person. However, many courts have recognized a cause of action for the wrongful death of a viable fetus, and in cases in which a fetus is harmed during pregnancy and is born alive, all states recognize a cause of action.[27] Typically, cases of *preconception* negligence have been brought by mothers against their obstetricians, often citing that the physician failed to warn them of their risks or failed to conduct genetic tests and counseling before conception (see Chapter 8).[28] The first successful case of *prenatal* negligence was brought in 1946, and "the stage was set to allow children to sue their parents for prenatal harms."[29] According to Shaw, negligent exposure to noxious chemicals and drugs, refusal to accept genetic counseling and prenatal diagnosis, refusal to obtain therapy during pregnancy, or failure to provide a modified diet all could give rise to a cause of action.

In 1977, a California court held that the Penal Code prohibiting the endangering of a child did not include unborn children in the case of a woman addicted to heroin who gave birth to twin boys, both of whom were addicted. More recently, however, a Florida woman was convicted of child abuse for using cocaine while pregnant. Since then, at least six similar cases have been brought in Massachusetts, Florida, South Carolina, and Virginia.[30]

Policy Recommendations for HIV Counseling of Pregnant Women

Recommendations from organizations and professional bodies

Both governmental and private professional organizations have issued policy recommendations regarding HIV counseling of women of reproductive age. Perhaps two of the most influential organizations, the CDC and the American College of Obstetricians and Gynecologists, indeed are directive in their recommendations. The CDC urges that infected women "should be advised to consider delaying pregnancy until more is known about perinatal transmission of the virus."[31] The statement from the American College of Obstetricians and Gynecologists is even more forceful: "Women infected with HIV . . . should be strongly encouraged not to become pregnant. . . . Those who do become pregnant should be counseled again about the risks to themselves and their child and should be informed about the option of pregnancy termination."[32]

The American Public Health Association's policy statement regarding counseling and testing for perinatal transmission of AIDS is more in keeping with the nondirective approach. It recommends that all testing be voluntary, that the provision of information be "nonjudgmental and sensitive to cultural, parous, life-status and age factors," and that counseling and health care be available regardless of the decisions a woman makes.[33]

Recommendations from individual professionals

It is not only organizations that have urged practitioners to be directive when counseling women who are HIV-positive. Many professionals working in the field urge this approach as well.[34] John Arras's position, again, represents that of many: "Child-centered 'wrongful life' considerations, reflections on 'responsible parenthood,' and the social burdens of pediatric AIDS jointly justify directive counselling to the effect that HIV positive women should forego future childbearing."[35]

Levin et al. conducted a survey of ethical issues in the neonatal intensive care unit.[36] Her study sample included 247 neonatologists, neonatal fellows, pediatric residents, neonatal intensive care unit nurses, and ethics committee members in six New York City hospitals. She found that 65 percent of the respondents agreed with the statement that "women should not have babies who will be at risk for [AIDS]," whereas only 25 percent agreed when the risk was for Tay-Sachs disease and only 15 percent agreed when the risk was for cystic fibrosis.

Kathleen Nolan has suggested two reasons why the response to perinatal AIDS has been different from the response to other perinatal conditions. The first is that AIDS is viewed as more of a *public* health threat: "We did not and do not fear cystic fibrosis or children with it. Though they are sick, and they cost us tax dollars, they were no perceived threat to us or our loved ones. This is at the heart of distinguishing a genetic risk from a public health menace."[37]

The second reason offered by Nolan is that pediatric AIDS is primarily a disease of minorities, which "combines with the geographic maldistribution to make AIDS a more 'alien' disease."[38] The implication is that it is often easier to tell "others" what to do.

The strong feelings that some members of society hold about AIDS are only heightened in the context of perinatal AIDS, since children typically are viewed as the innocent victims of the epidemic. Arras believes that although autonomous risk taking for oneself might be considered acceptable, we as a society have a responsibility to step in to prevent harm to the innocent third party, the fetus, even if this means compromising the autonomy of the mother.[39]

Why Directive Counseling Is Inappropriate

All three approaches to interactions with women facing reproductive decisions—nondirective counseling, directive counseling, and compelling of certain behaviors—must be evaluated in terms of their medical and social implications for the mother and fetus, their threats to maternal autonomy, and their broader implications for women's position in society.

As described earlier, medical arguments for protecting the fetus from harm most typically are cited as justifications for any but nondirective counseling. It must be recognized that "protecting the fetus" can be used as the rationale in two, arguably opposite, types of scenarios: in one instance, such as in the Kolder article cited earlier, a woman might be compelled to undergo a procedure or adopt certain behaviors in order to *save* a fetus. The rationale is that if the mother did not undergo the procedure, the fetus likely would be harmed, and if the mother *did* undergo the procedure, the fetus likely would not be harmed or, at least, would be harmed to a lesser degree. In the second instance, by contrast, a woman would be compelled either to not become pregnant or to terminate a pregnancy in order to avoid the birth of a sick child. Although preventing harm is the rationale used in this instance as well, clearly the situations are not parallel. This circumstance is more akin to "wrongful life" cases, in which it is argued that there is a compelling interest in preventing the birth of an unhealthy child or a child with a terminal condition. It is from this second perspective that one might justify compelling or being directive regarding the reproductive decisions for a woman infected with HIV.

Also complicating much reproductive decision making is the fact that there is so much uncertainty surrounding medical decisions generally. Undeniably, conflicts between women and medical practitioners can arise in cases in which potential harm can be quantified or is known; however, it is more typical that the precise likelihood and degree of harm that will ensue are not certain. Kolder et al. reported that three of the women for whom court-ordered cesarean sections had been sought ultimately delivered vaginally and without problems. In the case of HIV, only 30 percent of the babies born to infected pregnant women will be infected. On which side either women individually or policy makers as a group should err given such uncertainties remains unresolved.

The social implications of the different approaches to reproductive decision making in the context of HIV deserve attention. If a particular style of counseling or interaction is unacceptable to a woman, this may alienate her from the health-care system. The women at greatest risk for HIV infection are most likely to be among those who already have a tenuous relationship with the health-care system, who may be getting inadequate care, or who may be experiencing barriers to access. Creating yet another impediment certainly is not prudent. Kathleen Nolan has stated that families whose children have been tested without their consent are much less likely to perceive subsequent services as positive and supportive and are less willing to cooperate with treatment regimens or to participate in clinical trials.[40] It is not unlikely that such a reaction similarly would result from doing other procedures without a woman's consent or, conceivably, from telling her that she *should* act in a certain way, such as not becoming pregnant.

Because childbearing carries different meanings in different cultures, there can be quite different social implications to directing a woman to postpone or terminate a pregnancy. Given that African-American and Hispanic women have been disproportionately affected by the HIV epidemic, such considerations are crucial to determining the most appropriate means of counseling.

> Latino and black cultures place great value on a woman's fertility. Having a child elevates the status of the woman in her family and her community. Yet our recommendations state that HIV-seropositive women should delay childbearing and imply that those who are already pregnant should strongly consider abortion. When counseling women in this manner, does the counselor even ask, "What would be the impact of this on your relationship with your partner?" It is not enough to make recommendations in a vacuum. We must understand what those recommendations may mean in the context of the woman's life.[41]

Susan Holman et al. similarly have described Hispanic women as defining themselves primarily through their role as mothers. Discouraging from having children a woman whose greatest source of fulfillment is motherhood has different implications than discouraging from childbearing a woman who finds greater fulfillment elsewhere.[42] Dazon Dixon, founder and executive director of Sisterlove: Women's AIDS Project, advises that not all women share the same sense of health and well-being and therefore will draw the line differently in deciding where to protect their health relative to other priorities.[43] This, too, must be considered when counseling because it may account for the varying impact on different women of the risks presented to them.

John Arras alternatively has stated that women respond to numeric risks differently because different cultures view risk itself differently. He suggests that the "majority culture," including the medical profession, considers a 25–35 percent risk unacceptable, whereas some members of "the poor, minority culture" consider it acceptable.[44] Frets and colleagues, however, report that the well-educated couples in their study of factors influencing reproductive decisions after genetic counseling similarly gave greatest importance to issues "at stake before counseling" in making their decisions and "tend to take high risks, even when the disease is perceived as severe and prenatal diagnosis is not available."[45]

Determining whether there truly is a different perception of "acceptable risk" in different populations, whether people attribute differing levels of importance to childbearing, or whether different people's ability to cope with a sick child varies, although providing an *explanation* for why conflicts occur, does not ultimately answer the question that must be resolved for interactions between providers and patients: Should the counselor, the medical community, or the larger society attempt to influence the reproductive decisions of HIV-positive women?

Finally, in evaluating the various approaches to counseling or in interacting with women making reproductive decisions, one must consider how each approach would affect women's role in society. More specifically, what would be the effect on women more broadly if reproductive freedom is tampered with?

There has been an evolving legal trend toward leaving reproductive decisions to the woman or couple alone.[46] Implicit in this trend is the notion that although certain individuals might exercise their reproductive choices in ways that others find inappropriate or offensive, it is ultimately the right of those individuals to exercise that choice; that is, the right to privacy outweighs other compelling interests (see Chapter 7).

There are two issues here. One is whether *anyone* has the right to make a decision against medical judgment; the other is whether women of reproductive age in general, or pregnant women in particular, have any less of this right because of the interest of the potential or existing fetus. In the context of HIV, for women of reproductive age who are not pregnant, this would arise in the case of forced or advised sterilization; for women who are pregnant, it would arise concerning forced or advised abortion and, presumably in the future, forced treatment during pregnancy thought to benefit the fetus. Let us assume that, in general, individuals are allowed to make autonomous choices in the context of medical care. That is, let us assume that when a patient wants to refuse surgery or wants to be taken off a ventilator, even if this is considered medically unwise, his or her wishes are granted. The question germane to this discussion, then, is whether women should similarly be allowed to have their wishes respected in making their reproductive decisions. Barbara Katz Rothman is a strong proponent of this view:

> Those arguing for the rights of pregnant women, as I am, are asking that no distinction be made between pregnant women and any other category of citizen. The American legal system permits people a great deal of freedom in what they can do with their own bodies, including the right to refuse any and all medical treatment they do not want. Pregnancy should not be used to change the status of the individual in regard to her own body. . . . We are in danger of creating of pregnant women a second class of citizen, without the basic legal rights of bodily integrity and self-determination.[47]

She argues that although a fetus *will* become a person, it is not yet a person. Rather, it is part of the pregnant woman, who is in danger of being viewed primarily as a "vessel" if the state is permitted to subsume "the interests and the civil rights of pregnant women to those of the fetus within them."[48]

Not respecting individual autonomy in *any* type of decision making, including reproductive decision making, jeopardizes respect for autonomy. However, the threat becomes more severe when only one class of individuals in society is singled out and constrained. Our society would consider it abhorrent to forbid other subgroups in the population from making their own decisions about medical care. For example, if restricting the choices of Asian-American men was suggested in response to a particular medical condition that affected only that group, it probably would be considered unacceptable because of the broader social implications of such a policy.

Limiting or, at best, strongly influencing the choices of only pregnant women or of only women of reproductive age is similarly troublesome. When creating policies, it is important to consider not only what their content will be but also how the policies, in turn, will affect the society. Establishing a policy of dictating women's choices creates a message that women are a means to some end in which society has determined it has an important interest. Moreover, it conveys to women that they cannot be trusted to make their own decisions and that someone other than themselves knows what is best for them or their children.

Of course, the flip side of this argument is that when people are allowed to make their own decisions, sometimes they will make what others consider to be the wrong decision, and harms will result. Indeed, there may be individual instances in which such is the case or most of us would regard it to be so. However, having as a policy a counseling strategy that overrides or seeks to override a woman's decision results in harms in the larger picture in terms of threats to personal autonomy and threats to the status of women in particular. Such a policy, therefore, cannot be considered acceptable.

In the context of HIV, this issue is heightened by the fact that the class of people potentially being singled out is not merely women but minority women. Given this, one must ask to what extent racism and eugenics issues are present in the current discussions. If some people believe that these women should not be having babies or more babies anyway, HIV poses the perfect excuse for legitimately encouraging them not to do so. It is important to recognize that few campaigns have been implemented that discourage pregnancy among women at risk for having children with cystic fibrosis, for example, as there have for HIV, although cystic fibrosis is more prevalent than HIV.

Another question often asked, given both that many women at risk for HIV are using illicit drugs and that there simply are differences in background between these women and the majority of providers, is whether patients at risk can be trusted to make "responsible" decisions. There are two responses to this concern. The first pertains to whether "responsible" can be defined;[49] that is, *is* there unarguably a blanket "right" decision or a "right" process for decision making? The distinction must be drawn between a right decision in *any* circumstance and a right decision for a particular woman in her own circumstances. These issues are given fuller attention in Chapter 12.

The second response allows that, in certain situations, there may be a definably responsible choice, at least in terms of what a majority of either professionals or lay people would express as a balance of benefit over harm. At the same time, it considers the consequences of not allowing individuals to make the decision that others would deem inappropriate. Except in the most extreme cases, the danger of interceding to take decision-making authority away from women in general or from minority women in particular is greater than the danger of "bad" decision making. As stated previously, this is not to say that, in certain cases, decisions that produce what some consider to be harms will not be made. It is to say that a policy of not allowing autonomous decision making, particularly to one class of society, cannot be considered acceptable.

The Counseling Session Itself

As stated earlier, there are different situations in which HIV-related counseling occurs with women of reproductive age. Although the content of the counseling session varies depending on the situation, it always involves conveying specific information and determining the woman's values, including, if appropriate, helping her to reach a decision and providing support. Specific content that should be included in a counseling session with a seropositive woman of reproductive age who may be considering pregnancy and with a seropositive woman who is pregnant will be discussed below.

Counseling of seropositive women considering pregnancy

The counseling of any seropositive woman will vary, depending on whether the counseling session includes informing the woman of her serostatus—that is, if this counseling constitutes her *posttest* session (in contrast to her coming for a visit knowing that she is HIV-positive). If the session is serving as her posttest session, of primary importance is getting a sense of how the woman is reacting to the news that she is HIV-positive: Is she surprised? Does she seem to understand? What is her emotional reaction? There should be some discussion of who else she thinks she might tell about her antibody status and what she thinks their reaction might be. It is important to help a woman who intends to inform others of her status to articulate a plan for doing so. It also may be helpful to have literature available for the woman who learns that she is seropositive. In part this is because much of the information conveyed in person may not be retained and also because those whom she tells may want information, and this is a means by which she can provide it. If the counseling session is when the woman first receives her antibody test results, it may be appropriate to schedule a second visit to discuss the other issues, particularly if it is believed that the woman would return. Again, upon hearing about a positive HIV antibody test result, many people do not retain information provided to them, and they may not be in the best state of mind to consider other important decisions.

In any event, whenever counseling involves a woman who is seropositive, is of reproductive age, and indicates that she is considering pregnancy, it first should include information about what being seropositive means. It should be made clear that a positive test result indicates infection with the AIDS virus but does not necessarily mean that she has the disease; more specific tests of her immune status can determine the likelihood of her becoming sick in the near future. She should be informed that the evidence on whether pregnancy speeds up the onset of disease is inconclusive at this time. She should be advised that treatment is available and recommended for seropositive people whose immune status is declining, but that treatment only *slows* the progression of the disease; at present, there is no cure for AIDS. Moreover, such treatment currently is not available to most pregnant women; it typically is available to pregnant women only as part of a research protocol or to pregnant women who have experienced symptoms related to the infection. Women also should be informed that the availability of treatment and access to follow-up services vary by locality and by ability to pay. The likelihood that she would be able to obtain HIV-specific treatments in her community, both currently and were she to become pregnant, should be explored.

A woman who is seropositive should avoid sexual and needle contact that could transmit the virus to others; moreover, she should inform previous and current needle-sharing and sexual partners of her serostatus and of their possible exposure to the AIDS virus.

If she does become pregnant, there is a 30 percent chance that the virus will be transmitted to the baby. A baby born to a woman known to be HIV-positive should be monitored more closely by health-care providers than usual because of the chance that the baby is infected with the AIDS virus. The woman should know that it may not be until her baby is 1.5 years old that doctors will know for certain whether the baby is infected. If the baby *is* infected, it is not known exactly when or in what way the baby will become sick, but at this point most children truly infected with the AIDS virus seem not to live beyond several years of age. The woman also should be informed of what treatment services will be available in her area for a sick newborn. (See Chapter 8 for a discussion of how much and what types of disclosure are legally mandated.)

Given that this woman is considering pregnancy, what should be stressed is the chance that she will transmit the virus to the baby if she becomes pregnant, current knowledge about likely scenarios for a baby born infected, and her own options for treatment and prognosis. She should be told why the use of zidovudine and other treatments for HIV infection in pregnancy is controversial, whether such treatments would be available in her geographic locality were she to become pregnant, and that this situation may change in the near future.

There should be discussions of who will care for her baby if and when she becomes sick, and what having a baby means to her. This last discussion will be valuable in helping her determine whether becoming pregnant is appropriate and whether her reasons for wanting to be pregnant outweigh the harms associated with being seropositive and pregnant. Asking a woman why she might want to be pregnant and why she might not, particularly given her positive serostatus, may be the most revealing part of a counseling session. It can inform the counselor if the woman has any *misinformation,* help the counselor to emphasize those pieces of information that seem particularly relevant to the woman's decision, and allow the counselor to help the woman sort out her values as they relate to the decision.

Counseling of women who are seropositive and pregnant

The content of a counseling session with a woman who is seropositive and pregnant also will vary depending on whether the counseling constitutes her *posttest* session; it also will vary depending on whether she is at a point in her pregnancy when termination is an option.

If the session is her posttest session, the discussions described in the previous section concerning learning of a positive serostatus should be initiated with this woman as well. The meaning of being HIV-positive should also be discussed. Because she already is pregnant, the information provided should emphasize perinatal transmission rates, current knowledge about the likely scenarios for an infected baby, and her own prognosis and options for treatment. Again, there should be discussion of who will care for her baby if and when she becomes sick and what having a baby means to her.

If the woman is both early enough in her pregnancy and open to the option, termination should be discussed. She should be asked why *she* would consider termination and why she would *not* as a means of determining whether the counselor can clarify facts that would facilitate her decision. For example, if a woman says that she wants to terminate the pregnancy because all seropositive women transmit the virus to their babies, she can be told that this is not true. But if the woman says that she wants to terminate the pregnancy because she could not cope with the death of a young child, she can be told that the death of a child is a possibility.

It also may be appropriate, particularly if the counseling is occurring relatively late in the pregnancy, to have a discussion about future reproductive decisions: How many children does the woman think she wants? What type of birth control does she think she might use? How does being HIV-positive and potentially becoming sick affect these decisions?

Conclusion

In both situations discussed here concerning reproductive decision making in the context of HIV, the question remains: Is it appropriate to include in the counseling session any information about professional recommendations, to the degree that a professional consensus exists? On the one hand, professionals do have experience, both with the facts and, presumably, with women in comparable situations. On the other hand, professionals not only have their own values, which may differ from those of individual women, but, as stated earlier, are not in a balanced relationship with their patients and consequently may wield more influence than perhaps is appropriate.

It is my position that it is not appropriate to voice a professional opinion as part of the information automatically provided. This is not to say that information cannot be provided in a balanced form. For example, it may be appropriate to say, "Some professionals have been discouraging seropositive women from becoming pregnant, at least until we know more about possible treatments for infected children, because of the chance that the child will be born infected with the virus and virtual certainty that if that happens, the child will die. At the same time, however, other professionals recognize that there is a greater chance that the child will not be infected than that it will be infected, and also that many women want to have a child even if there *is* a real chance that the child will become sick and die."

If a woman specifically asks for a recommendation or for the professional consensus regarding her situation, then it is appropriate to provide her with this information. In conveying a professional opinion, one should reiterate what *reasoning* supports that opinion, which will better enable the woman to decide if it applies to her own situation. In other words, if the professional opinion is that seropositive women should not become pregnant because there is a 30 percent chance that they will transmit the virus to their baby and that is an unacceptably high transmission rate, the woman herself can decide if 30 percent is unacceptably high.

To reiterate, in all situations, the key to an effective counseling session is to learn from the woman why she favors one or the other option (such as why she wants to become pregnant or why she thinks it does not make sense for her to become pregnant) and to combine that knowledge with the relevant factual information in order to reach a decision.

HIV disease brings to reproductive decision making a threat to autonomy and privacy, which have emerged as two of our most cherished, albeit tenuous, values. It poses a threat by virtue of the fact that when a woman, herself with a fatal illness, becomes pregnant and can transmit a fatal virus to her newborn, the issues that arise are extremely difficult and extremely emotional. Illness, perhaps particularly illness among children, can make interests that conflict with autonomy seem uniquely compelling. Indeed, it is only because autonomous reproductive decision making is so crucial for the preservation of respect for a class of human beings that, in the end, it must be given precedence. It is for this reason that nondirective counseling must be advocated when reproductive decisions are being made in the context of HIV.

Notes

1. Centers for Disease Control (CDC), "HIV/AIDS Surveillance Report," November 1989, pp. 1–16.
2. "Human Immunodeficiency Infection in the United States: A Review of Current Knowledge," *Morbidity and Mortality Weekly Report* 36 (Suppl. S-6) (1987): 1–48.
3. Ernest Drucker and Sten H. Vermund, "Estimating Population Prevalence of Human Immunodeficiency Virus Infection in Urban Areas with High Rates of Intravenous Drug Use: A Model of the Bronx in 1988," *American Journal of Epidemiology* 130 (1989): 133–142.
4. Sheldon H. Landesman, Howard L. Minkoff, and Anne Willoughby, "HIV Disease in Reproductive Age Women: A Problem of the Present," *Journal of the American Medical Association* 261 (1989): 1326–1327.

5. "Acquired Immunodeficiency Syndrome (AIDS) Among Blacks and Hispanics—United States," *Morbidity and Mortality Weekly Report* 35 (1986): 656–658.

6. Evan Welling Thomas, *Syphilis* (New York: Macmillan, 1949).

7. "Prevention of Perinatal Transmission of Hepatitis B Virus: Prenatal Screening of All Pregnant Women for Hepatitis B Surface Antigen," *Morbidity and Mortality Weekly Report* 37 (1988): 22.

8. Robert G. Petersdorf, Raymond D. Adams, Eugene Braunwald et al., *Harrison's Principles of Internal Medicine,* 10th ed. (New York: McGraw-Hill, 1983).

9. Ibid.

10. Lloyd F. Novick, Donald Berns, Rachel Stricof et al., "HIV Seroprevalence in Newborns in New York State," *Journal of the American Medical Association* 261 (1989): 1745–1750.

11. Rodney Hoff, Victor P. Berardi, Barbara J. Weiblen et al., "Seroprevalence of Human Immunodeficiency Virus Among Childbearing Women: Estimating by Testing Samples of Blood from Newborns," *New England Journal of Medicine* 318 (1988): 525–530.

12. Ibid.

13. Alvaro Muñoz, Mei-Cheng Wang, Sue Bass et al., "Acquired Immunodeficiency Syndrome (AIDS)-Free Time After Human Immunodeficiency Virus Type 1 (HIV-1) Seroconversion in Homosexual Men," *American Journal of Epidemiology* 130 (1989): 530–539.

14. F. Clarke Fraser, "Genetic Counseling," *American Journal of Human Genetics* 26 (1974): 636–659.

15. National Academy of Sciences, Committee for the Study of Inborn Errors of Metabolism, *Genetic Screening: Programs, Principles and Research* (Washington, D.C.: National Academy Press, 1975).

16. Institute of Society, Ethics and the Life Sciences, Research Group on Ethical, Social and Legal Issues in Genetic Counseling and Genetic Engineering, "Ethical and Social Issues in Screening for Genetic Disease," *New England Journal of Medicine* 286 (1972): 1129–1132.

17. President's Commission for the Study of Ethical Problems in Medicine and Biomedical and Behavioral Research, *Screening and Counseling for Genetic Conditions* (Washington, D.C.: Government Printing Office, 1983).

18. Ronald Bayer, "AIDS and the Future of Reproductive Freedom," *Milbank Quarterly* 68 (Suppl. 2) (1990): 179–204.

19. Charles J. Epstein, "Genetic counseling: Present Status and Future Prospects," in *Early Diagnosis and Prevention of Genetic Diseases,* ed. L. N. Went, Chr. Vermeij-Keers, and A. G. J. M. van der Linden (Leiden: Leiden University Press, 1975), 110–128.

20. Ibid., 115.

21. Kathleen Nolan, "Ethical Issues in Caring for Pregnant Women and Newborns at Risk for Human Immunodeficiency Virus Infection," *Seminars in Perinatology* 13 (1989): 63.

22. For further discussion, see Ruth R. Faden and Tom L. Beauchamp, *A History and Theory of Informed Consent* (New York: Oxford University Press, 1986), 337–373.

23. John Arras, "HIV Infection and Reproductive Decisions: An Ethical Analysis" (presented at the Vth International Conference on AIDS, Montreal, June 1989).

24. Veronika E. B. Kolder, Janet Gallagher, and Michael T. Parsons, "Court-Ordered Obstetrical Interventions," *New England Journal of Medicine* 316 (1987): 1192–1196.

25. Ibid.
26. Margery Shaw, "Conditional Prospective Rights of the Fetus," *Journal of Legal Medicine* 5 (1984): 63–116.
27. Ibid.
28. The law requires physicians to disclose information about therapeutic procedures and to obtain consent prior to the procedure. There is no legal requirement that the patient *understand* what has been disclosed. Chapter 8 provides an extended discussion of the legal implications of failure to test or to counsel pregnant women.
29. Shaw, "Conditional Prospective Rights of the Fetus," 95.
30. "Delivery Room Arrests," *Off Our Backs* 20 (April 1990): 8.
31. CDC, "Recommendations for Assisting in the Prevention of Perinatal Transmission of HTLV-III/LAV and Acquired Immunodeficiency Syndrome," *Morbidity and Mortality Weekly Report* 34 (1985): 721–731.
32. American College of Obstetricians and Gynecologists, *Prevention of Human Immune Deficiency Virus Infection and Acquired Immune Deficiency Syndrome*, ACOG Committee Statement, no. 53 (Washington, D.C.: American College of Obstetricians and Gynecologists, 1987), 1–4.
33. American Public Health Association, "APHA Policy Statement #8814," *American Journal of Public Health* 79 (1989): 359–360.
34. Donald Francis and James C. Chin, "The Prevention of Acquired Immunodeficiency Syndrome in the United States: An Objective Strategy for Medicine, Public Health, Business, and the Community," *Journal of the American Medical Association* 257 (1987): 1357–1366; Howard L. Minkoff and Richard H. Schwarz, "AIDS: Time for Obstetricians to Get Involved," *Obstetrics and Gynecology* 68 (1986): 267–268; Moses Grossman, "Human Immunodeficiency Virus Infection in Children: Public Health and Public Policy Issues," *Pediatric Infectious Disease Journal* 6 (1987): 113–116.
35. Arras, "HIV Infection and Reproductive Decisions."
36. Betty Wolder Levin, Kathleen E. Powderly, and Jonathan Moreno, "Ethics and AIDS in the Neonatal Intensive Care Unit" (presented at the meeting of the American Public Health Association, Chicago, October 26–29, 1989).
37. Nolan, "Ethical Issues in Caring for Pregnant Women and Newborns," 60.
38. Ibid., 61.
39. Arras, "HIV Infection and Reproductive Decisions."
40. Nolan, "Ethical Issues in Caring for Pregnant Women and Newborns," 57.
41. Janet L. Mitchell, "Women, AIDS, and Public Policy," *AIDS and Public Policy Journal* 3 (1988): 50–52.
42. Susan Holman, Marise Berthaud, Ann Sunderland et al., "Women Infected with Human Immunodeficiency Virus: Counseling and Testing During Pregnancy," *Seminars in Perinatology* 13 (1989): 7–15.
43. Dazon Dixon, comments at the National Academy of Sciences, Institute of Medicine, Conference on Prenatal and Neonatal HIV Screening, Washington, D.C., May 14–15, 1990.
44. Arras, "HIV Infection and Reproductive Decisions."
45. Petra G. Frets, Hugo J. Duivenvoorden, Frans Verhage et al., "Factors Influencing the Reproductive Decision After Genetic Counseling," *American Journal of Medical Genetics* 35 (1990): 496–502, 501.
46. See *Griswold v. Connecticut,* 381 U.S. 479 (1965); *Eisenstadt v. Baird,* 405 U.S. 438 (1972); *Roe v. Wade,* 410 U.S. 113 (1973); *Planned Parenthood of Missouri v.*

Danforth, 428 U.S. 52 (1976); *City of Akron* v. *Akron Center for Reproductive Health,* 462 U.S. 416 (1983).

47. Barbara Katz Rothman, *Recreating Motherhood: Ideology and Technology in a Patriarchal Society* (New York: Norton, 1989), 159–160, 164.

48. Ibid, 164.

49. This is meant to be a normative, rather than an epistemic, question.

V

CONCLUSION

14

HIV Infection, Pregnant Women, and Newborns: A Policy Proposal for Information and Testing

RUTH R. FADEN, GAIL GELLER, MADISON POWERS,
KATHERINE ACUFF, ANITA ALLEN, JUDITH AREEN,
NANCY HUTTON, TIMOTHY JOHNSON, NANCY KASS,
PATRICIA KING, JOHN MODLIN, JOHN REPKE, ALFRED SAAH,
LEROY WALTERS, AND LAWRENCE S. WISSOW

Should pregnant women or newborns be screened for HIV and, if so, under what conditions? To date, no national professional association or committee has called for the mandatory screening of either pregnant women or newborns, although arguments favoring mandatory policies have appeared in the literature.[1] Numerous national groups have advocated offering testing either to all pregnant women or to all high-risk pregnant women.[2] In addition, some organizations and commentators have called for directive counseling to discourage HIV-infected women from either becoming pregnant or bearing children.[3]

In this volume we have analyzed the numerous moral, legal, and policy issues raised by the prospect of screening and testing pregnant women and newborns for evidence of HIV infection. We have examined historical precedents for screening, as well as the current medical and public health contexts. In this chapter, we put forward a policy proposal for pregnant women and newborns based on the analyses and arguments presented in earlier chapters.

Specifically, this chapter presents a detailed 10-point program of policy recommendations for both pregnant women and newborns, and develops its rationale through the examination of potential objections and criticisms. We conclude with a discussion of how our recommendations should change with advances in diagnostic technologies and medical management.

Policy Recommendations

We advocate a policy of informing all pregnant women and new mothers about the epidemic of HIV infection and the availability of HIV testing. Although screening of either pregnant women or newborns is not the central focus of our policy, because we defend a consent requirement for testing, our position can be interpreted as a policy of voluntary screening. In our view, a policy of mandatory screening either for pregnant women or for newborns is not justified in the current fact situation on traditional public health criteria or other grounds. Moreover, we reject implementation of counseling and screening policies that interfere with women's reproductive freedom or result in the stigmatization of vulnerable social groups. Our specific policy recommendations are as follows.

1. All pregnant women and new mothers should be informed about HIV infection and the availability of HIV testing for themselves and their newborns. Pregnant women should be informed when they register for prenatal care.* Topics to be addressed are presented in Tables 14.1 and 14.2.

2. The information to be presented to pregnant women and new mothers may be provided through printed or audiovisual materials. However, in communities with a significant degree of HIV infection or drug use, a personal discussion is of particular importance and should be conducted. Whatever method is selected, the information disclosed should cover the same topics and content (Tables 14.1 and 14.2) and should be presented in a manner and language that is meaningful and understandable to the women served.

3. The information conveyed under recommendations 1 and 2 may not substitute for either pretest or posttest counseling. All women who express an interest in HIV testing for themselves or their newborns should receive personal pretest counseling; those tested should receive personal posttest counseling.

4. Both prenatal testing and newborn testing are to be voluntary, with a requirement of informed consent or parental consent, respectively. Consent for testing should be solicited only after pretest counseling.

5. The involvement of state and local health departments is essential to the successful implementation of this policy. Health departments should assume responsibility for developing and updating the educational materials referred to above, ensuring the availability of materials in several languages, providing protocols and training for pretest and posttest counseling, and developing evaluation mechanisms to ensure the proper conduct of the program.†

6. Health departments also should establish standards for laboratory procedures, including a requirement that all positive tests be confirmed on an inde-

*Ideally, all women should be informed about the HIV epidemic and HIV testing in advance of pregnancy as part of preconception care. In addition, it may shortly be advisable, either because an intrapartum intervention becomes available or it becomes desirable to manage third-trimester, HIV-positive women differently, to discuss HIV testing again late in pregnancy.

†State governments may seek regulatory or legislative means to mandate the obligation of providers of prenatal and newborn care to inform pregnant women and new mothers about the HIV epidemic and the availability of HIV testing. Alternatively, jurisdictions may choose not to mandate these obligations by regulation or legislation unless professional mechanisms for guiding professional conduct fail, over a reasonable period of time, to ensure adoption of the practice.

TABLE 14.1.   Informing Pregnant Women About HIV Infection and the Availability of HIV Testing: Topics to Be Addressed

Risk factors associated with HIV infection

Personal behaviors that protect against contracting or transmitting the infection

Relationship between HIV infection in pregnancy and prospects for the fetus/newborn

Relationship between HIV testing of the pregnant woman and HIV testing of her newborn

Risks and potential benefits of testing for both mother and baby (including limits on confidentiality, associated social risks, available antidiscrimination protections, pregnancy termination, medical benefits of early clinical intervention in HIV infection, and any constraints or obstacles to access to abortion or medical services for HIV-infected women and children)

Prevalence of HIV infection in the local community and impact on test results (where appropriate)

Availability of anonymous or alternative testing sites

Reassurance that testing is voluntary, in particular that the woman's decision about testing will not affect access to or quality of her prenatal care

Acknowledgment of the detail and complexity of the information presented; that personal pretest counseling is conducted with women interested in HIV testing before they have to make a final decision

TABLE 14.2.   Informing New Mothers about HIV Infection and the Availability of HIV Testing: Topics to Be Addressed

Risk factors associated with HIV infection

Personal behaviors that protect against contracting or transmitting the infection

Limits of the technology of HIV testing in newborns (e.g., that the test in newborns identifies maternal infection, not newborn infection, and the likely maternal–fetal transmission rate)

Testing of newborns necessarily reveals the HIV status of the mother

If the mother was tested in pregnancy, testing the newborn generally does not provide any additional information

Risks and potential benefits to both mother and baby of the baby's being tested (including limits on confidentiality, associated social risks, available antidiscrimination protections, medical benefits of early intervention in HIV infection, and any constraints or obstacles to access to medical services for HIV-infected women and children)

Prevalence of HIV infection in the local community and impact on test results (where appropriate)

Availability of anonymous or alternative testing sites

Reassurance that testing is voluntary, in particular that the mother's decision about testing will not affect the care the baby receives during this hospitalization

Acknowledgment of the detail and complexity of the information presented; that personal pretest counseling is conducted with women interested in HIV testing before they have to make a final decision pendently drawn second blood specimen prior to communicating the results to the pregnant woman or new mother.

7. Every effort should be made to secure specialized medical interventions for the management of HIV infection, appropriate social services and supports, and intensive primary care and abortion services (where requested by pregnant women) for all women and infants identified as HIV-positive as a result of prenatal or newborn testing. All women should be informed of any difficulties in obtaining these interventions or services for themselves or their newborns. Specific obstacles to treatment or services should be discussed during pretest counseling with any woman interested in HIV testing for herself or her newborn.

8. Once it is established whether infants born to mothers who are HIV-positive are infected with HIV, any medical or other records that include information about serostatus should be corrected to verify either that the infant has been diagnosed as infected or that it has been established that the infant is not infected.

9. To ensure the implementation of recommendation 7, regional networks of referral services for HIV-positive women and their infants should be established. This network should have the capacity both to assist health-care providers with the medical management and counseling of HIV-positive women and their infants and to offer supportive social services directly to pregnant women and new mothers.

10. All women should be informed of limits on confidentiality, associated social risks, available antidiscrimination protections, and available anonymous testing services (see Tables 14.1 and 14.2). The personal implications of these issues should be a discussed during pretest counseling with women interested in HIV testing for themselves or their newborns. In addition, existing laws should be strengthened to ensure that duties of confidentiality are extended to anyone in the health-care delivery system who has access to HIV information, and exceptions to such duties based on a third party's need to know should include procedural safeguards. Antidiscrimination protections should also be extended to persons with HIV infection to combat the harmful consequences associated with unavoidable disclosures or with public identification of HIV status. The variation among state confidentiality and antidiscrimination policies should be replaced by a uniform policy (which is applicable regardless of the state in which HIV information is generated, stored, or transmitted).

Major Objections to Policy Recommendations

Our position is subject to several powerful criticisms or objections, both from those who favor an aggressive screening policy and from those who have serious reservations about the propriety of any type of maternal or neonatal screening or testing.

Why pregnant women?

Why do we need a public policy on HIV screening of pregnant women? The justification for our policy proposals reflects the importance of four goals: (1) to advance the national campaign to educate the public about HIV disease and how it can be prevented; (2) to enhance the current and future reproductive choices of women; (3) to identify women and newborns who can benefit from medical advances in the clinical management of HIV infection; and (4) to allow proper obstetric management of women infected with HIV. Goal 1 is intended to contribute to the long-term public health objective of controlling the HIV epidemic through education and voluntary modification of behavioral risk factors. Goals 3 and 4 are intended to advance the public health interest in reducing morbidity and improving the quality of life for persons with HIV infection by therapeutic advances in early clinical intervention. Thus goals 1, 3, and 4 contribute, in either the short term or the long term, to the reduction of morbidity and mortality and thus are justifiable on public health grounds. By contrast, goal 2 does not appeal to either short-term or long-term public health benefits for its foundation but rather looks to the interest of women in reproductive freedom for its justification.

With the exception of goal 4, the goals of our policy are not specific to pregnant women. Goals 2 and 3 apply to all sexually active women and goal 1 to all persons. Nonetheless, we have focused on pregnant women in this volume for several reasons. First, the issue of vertical transmission has put pregnant women into the policy spotlight. In the near future, interventions may be available to reduce the rate of vertical transmission or to treat the fetus. We were motivated to head off policy directives that view pregnant women as mere vessels or vectors of disease by developing policies respectful of the rights and interests of pregnant women. Second, we believe that primary medical care is a desirable setting for educating individuals about HIV disease and availability of HIV testing. The medical benefits to HIV-positive persons of such interventions as zidovudine (also called AZT) treatment and *Pneumocystis carinii* pneumonia (PCP) prophylaxis provide partial justification for testing. Testing in the context of primary care facilitates referral for proper medical management of HIV infection and thus makes it more likely that these medical benefits will be realized. For many women, pregnancy is the only time when they have access to more or less comprehensive primary care services. Among women who do not receive prenatal care—which often is the situation for women who are at particular risk for HIV disease—the postpartum hospital stay frequently is the only opportunity afforded health-care providers to discuss HIV infection and attempt referral to appropriate medical services.

At the same time, we recognize that HIV disease in women and children is a disease of families, and that the needs and interests of fathers and other men also must be addressed. For this reason, we advocate that providers of primary care inform all their sexually active patients—male and female—about the HIV epidemic and the availability of HIV testing. We also hope that this policy will be embedded in an overall strategy of community interventions intended both to alter popular beliefs and practices concerning safer sex and to attack problems of poverty and powerlessness as they relate to drug use or dependence.

Why require informed consent?

It is often argued that when the benefits of testing far outweigh the risks, it is appropriate for clinicians to screen patients without express informed consent. Currently, it is common practice in obstetrics to order numerous screening tests without informing the patient or obtaining informed consent (see Chapters 4 and 6). Why should testing for evidence of HIV infection be treated differently? It is our view that conventional obstetric practice with regard to *all* testing should be modified. Testing in pregnancy should be used as an opportunity to educate patients about prenatal care and the impact of maternal behavior on fetal outcomes, and should be conducted with at least the affirmation of the patient.

There are, however, important respects in which HIV testing differs from testing for other conditions. Unlike most routine screening tests in pregnancy, HIV testing identifies a potentially fatal illness. Perhaps most centrally, HIV testing raises special issues of privacy, reproductive choice, and social risk that are not applicable to most other screening tests ordered in pregnancy, with the exception of toxicologic screening. Unlike, for example, prenatal testing for Rh factor, it cannot be argued that testing is so clearly in the best interests of pregnant women that proceeding based on clinical judgment without informed consent is justified.

We have heard it argued that women and children who are HIV-positive, unlike gay men, are less subject to social risks because they are less likely to have jobs, housing, and employment that may be lost if information about their HIV status becomes widely known. This position mistakenly assumes either that poor and minority women may have nothing left to lose or that what they have to lose is somehow less valuable than what others have at stake. Although the nature and extent of the harms experienced by HIV-positive women have not been documented, anecdotal evidence suggests that poor women of color risk the devastation of their personal and family relationships, the loss of social and medical services, the loss of control of their own medical decisions, and even the loss of their children.[4] These are significant losses for anyone; for women who have little else in the way of financial resources to lose, the potential for loss is greater still. At very worst, they risk the loss of everything they have.

Because the harm–benefit ratio of HIV testing varies markedly from person to person and because the issues are so complex, we advocate not only a requirement of informed consent for testing but also that consent be solicited only after individual and personal pretest counseling (see Chapter 12). Moreover, we believe there are close links between a policy of informed consent and the goal of educating women about HIV disease and how it can be prevented. For example, the content of a pretest counseling session should be viewed as integrally related to the counseling objectives pursued in the posttest counseling session. To underscore a point that was made in Chapter 13, many people do not retain information presented during the posttest session, either because of the shock of a positive result or because of the perceived irrelevance of the information with a negative result.

A requirement of informed consent entails more than adequate disclosure and pretest counseling at the time consent is solicited. We are particularly suspicious of policies that would give priority in access to drug rehabilitation, housing, or other needed social services to women who agree to be tested and who test positive. Although well intentioned, such policies undermine the ability of disadvantaged women to decide voluntarily whether they wish to be tested. Such policies are, in effect, what elsewhere in this volume we have called "conditionally mandatory policies." Because of their propensity to structure a woman's options in a profoundly influential way, they constitute morally objectionable interferences with her autonomy and her ability to make decisions for the welfare of herself and her family.

Our advocacy of a requirement of informed consent also reflects the position that there is currently no public health justification for mandatory screening of pregnant women. Although the state clearly has a legitimate interest in reducing the rate of transmission of HIV infection, it is not clear how mandatory screening in general, let alone mandatory screening of pregnant women, relates to this interest. With regard to horizontal transmission, prevention is largely a function of voluntary changes in the behaviors of individuals; there is no evidence or reason to believe that mandatory screening alters behavior more effectively than voluntary programs of education, counseling, and the offer of testing. While it is certainly the case that obstetric workers are at risk of occupational transmission of HIV infection, they probably are at no greater risk than those working in other surgical specialties or in emergency rooms (see Chapter 4). The decision of whether screening sufficiently reduces the risk of occupational transmission over a policy of universal precautions to warrant the attendant invasion of privacy and social risks must be made for all patients, not just pregnant women. Thus even if it were established that mandatory screening effectively reduced HIV transmission rates, additional arguments would be needed to justify a policy of mandatory screening of pregnant women. At the very least, it would have to be established that there were good, defensible reasons for singling out pregnant women and that no other measure or policy more respectful of the autonomy and privacy interests of women was as effective.

We specifically did not include prevention of vertical transmission among the goals of our policy. The goal of reducing vertical transmission is ethically problematic, either for policies designed to prevent future pregnancies or for policies aimed at terminating current pregnancies.

Achieving the public health goal of reducing vertical transmission through the promotion of abortion is morally unacceptable, even if it is argued that an HIV-infected woman's personal decision to terminate a pregnancy is morally permissible. The question of whether to terminate a pregnancy is among the most private and significant of life's choices. This decision should clearly be made by the HIV-positive woman, in consultation with her family if she chooses, but certainly without interference by the state and without unsolicited advice or other undue influence from health professionals.

Promoting abortion to achieve public health goals also is imprudent and (we believe) inappropriate public policy for a society deeply divided about the morality of abortion.

Apart from the implications of our society's divisive abortion debate, we have serious reservations about the use of abortion as a means of achieving the public health goal of prevention. Preventing the birth of a child who would have an illness or a disability is morally different from preventing illness or disability in persons already living. Two morally relevant differences merit greater attention.

First, a public health perspective that saw the two as equivalent—a case averted is a case averted—focuses too narrowly on the moral importance of health outcomes to the exclusion of the relevance of the means to their achievement. Ronald Bayer, for example, argues that while it may be rational for an HIV-infected woman to bear a child when she knows that there is an approximately 70 percent chance that the infant will not be infected, it may not be rational from a social point of view to treat the woman's decision as one in which society must remain neutral.[5] He concludes that from the social or public health perspective, the fiscal and human costs associated with pediatric AIDS provide strong argument for a policy that urges infected women not to become pregnant. However, an argument that proceeds *solely from an appeal to overall social outcomes* is in danger of proving too much. Although the conclusion Bayer draws is limited, exclusive attention to comparative health outcomes—which Bayer takes to be the central tenet of any public health perspective—can be used equally well to argue for policies prohibiting infected women from becoming pregnant or for compelling abortion, policies that Bayer does not appear to endorse. Thus an appeal to overall social consequences, without more, forces us to judge alternative public policies on only one dimension—aggregate public health benefits—and is therefore indifferent to variations in the means to their production.

A second objection to treating the prevention of the birth of a child who would have an illness or a disability as morally equivalent to preventing illness or disability in persons already living involves a morally unacceptable view of the social worth of such persons.[6] A public policy aimed at discouraging persons with inheritable disabilities or illnesses from having children embodies highly objectionable social affirmations of individual inequality. First, it denies that such persons have an equal right to participate in a highly valued aspect of the human experience—the begetting and raising of children. Second, it says to disabled and ill persons generally that the lives of some are not worth living, and hence that these persons are not entitled to a share of the social resources necessary for human flourishing. Third, it conveys the message that persons with a disability or an illness are to be understood as only an economic and social drain on society and never as a source of enrichment for the lives of others.

Some of these concerns cause us to have moral reservations about a public policy of reducing vertical transmission by attempting to influence HIV-positive pregnant women to delay or forgo future childbearing. Although the issue of abortion is removed, the importance of protecting reproductive choice from state interference remains, as do concerns about the propriety of preventing disease by preventing the birth of people who would have the disease. Although we recognize the importance of social interests in preventing vertical transmission and the tragic lives of many infants who have AIDS, on balance we are not persuaded that these interests override the opposing interest of women, minorities, and persons with disabilities in restricting state involvement in matters of reproductive choice.[7]

What about legal precedents for mandatory prenatal screening?

There are ample legal precedents for mandatory screening (see Chapter 6). However, as noted in Chapter 3, there are numerous relevant differences between screening for HIV infection and screening for other conditions. Indeed, potential legal objections to mandatory prenatal HIV screening policies far exceed any argument from precedent and reinforce our conclusion that testing should be voluntary and require informed consent. In advance of definitive court decisions, the legal status of nonvoluntary screening programs for pregnant women, whether conducted according to private-sector policies or public laws, remains uncertain. Nevertheless, it is clear that women's constitutional rights impose significant constraints on the nonconsensual HIV testing of pregnant women.[8] Chief among those constraints are, first, general constitutional liberties limiting the government's power to impose public health measures and, second, specific constitutional rights to privacy and equal protection of the law (see Chapter 7).

Individual liberty is not absolute in the face of a legitimate public health objective, but neither is the power of government to act for the public good. Measures that limit individual liberty to protect the public good must have at least a minimally rational relationship to the achievement of legitimate state interests. Under this standard, any action of the government (including legislation or administrative regulation) is presumed constitutionally valid if it has a reasonable relationship to a legitimate state interest, and it must not be arbitrary, capricious, or otherwise unreasonably oppressive.[9] In some instances, governmental action may be subjected to a stricter standard of judicial scrutiny. In matters involving fundamental rights, privacy interests, or bodily integrity, courts may require authorities to demonstrate both a compelling state interest overriding fundamental rights and adoption of the least restrictive means of furthering that interest.

Government has a legitimate and, indeed, compelling interest in controlling the spread of HIV infection, but it is less clear whether a nonvoluntary screening policy is a lawful means for furthering that interest. If, as we and many public health experts have argued, mandatory screening programs for pregnant women are of little utility in combating the spread of HIV infection, such programs may fail to meet the legal requirements for a minimally rational public policy. Moreover, mandatory screening programs may impinge on fundamental rights of privacy and would have to pass the more demanding strict scrutiny test. It is arguable that such a program would be an unconstitutional interference with bodily integrity and with a woman's right of privacy, which encompasses a woman's decision about whether to terminate a pregnancy.

Mandatory screening of pregnant women faces additional constitutional hurdles from the equal protection clause of the Fourteenth Amendment. The equal protection clause requires that governmental initiatives treat similarly situated persons equally in the distribution of socioeconomic and political benefits and burdens.[10] For government—or for private institutions with governmental functions or close ties to government—to single out pregnant women from the population at large for mandatory HIV screening raises a question of discriminatory unequal treatment. Obviously, targeted policies that further singled-out subsets of pregnant women for mandatory screening would be particularly suspect. (However, as the discussion in Chapter 7 indicates, the degree of constitutional protection available under prevailing trends in the development of the equal protection doctrine may not be as strong as we suggest here.)[11]

A general policy of mandatory screening of all pregnant women–with its potential for stigma, privacy invasion, and discrimination—also may conflict with the Fourth Amendment's guarantee that persons are protected against unreasonable searches and seizures.[12] To meet the requirements of the Fourth Amendment, it is not enough that a population pose a theoretical risk to others; the government is required to show that its testing policy makes more than a minimal contribution to the reduction of hazard.[13]

In addition to the specific privacy protection of the Fourth Amendment, the U.S. Supreme Court has recognized a general fundamental right of privacy, which includes "freedom to care for one's health and person."[14] This right has been declared broad enough to protect against a variety of governmental interferences with a woman's decision about whether to terminate a pregnancy. Although both the scope of and the future judicial attitude toward the constitutional privacy doctrine are matters of speculation, the fundamental right of privacy currently limits the extent to which screening programs may interfere with a woman's reproductive choices.

Moreover, state statutes or state constitutions may lend further support to privacy rights by regulating the ability to conduct HIV testing, to utilize the results of tests, or to reveal test results. Both private and governmental actors who impose nonvoluntary prenatal HIV testing risk civil liability to pregnant women for battery and negligence due to lack of informed consent; for invasion of privacy, defamation, breach of confidentiality, and infliction of emotional distress if confidentiality is violated; and additional common law liability when coercive testing is the proximate cause of loss of employment or interference with contractual relations (see Chapter 8).

Without a more persuasive demonstration that screening is a necessary element of an efficacious governmental policy and that prenatal screening is the least restrictive means to its achievement, these weighty constitutional interests of women stand as significant obstacles to lawful implementation of such programs. Even less firmly established constitutional objections to singling out either pregnant women or pregnant women who fall within certain high-risk or high-prevalence categories should discourage policymakers from implementing targeted screening policies. Health-care providers who wish to avoid exposure to costly civil liabilities and infringement of women's constitutional rights have good reason to refrain from all forms of nonvoluntary prenatal HIV testing.

Why require parental consent?

Turning from prenatal to neonatal screening, there again is no clinical or public health justification for a mandatory policy (see Chapters 5 and 10). Newborns and their mothers are a family unit; when HIV-infected mothers experience social or institutional discrimination, their infants suffer as well. "HIV-positive" newborns—70 percent of whom are not infected—face the further risk of being abandoned by their mothers, difficulties with adoption and foster home placements, and difficulties in access to day care.

At present, the expected benefits to newborns from HIV testing do not clearly outweigh these risks or the privacy and autonomy interests of their mothers. Although there are little scientific data on this point, we are persuaded that for the approximately 30 percent of infants who are infected, the prospects for medical benefits are significant and would be enhanced by early identification of at-risk status. Currently available benefits include the prevention or delay of death attributable to prophylactic treatment for PCP and the prospect that antiviral treatment may lengthen life and improve quality of life, particularly with regard to cognitive development (see Chapter 5). For the infants of HIV-infected women who turn out not to be infected, however, the benefit–harm calculus may well tip in the opposite direction. For both groups of infants, access to adequate medical care is by no means guaranteed. Where the interests of infants are so difficult to discern and evaluate, there is no justification for substituting the judgment of the state or the health professional for that of the parent.

Moreover, public policy should not reflect a presumption that women will not act responsibly to protect and promote the best interests of their children. It is our position that in the overwhelming majority of cases, pregnant women and new mothers share an identity of interests with their fetuses and newborns. We specifically reject a conflict or adversarial framing of the maternal–newborn relationship. There is anecdotal evidence that, in almost all cases, pregnant women and new mothers can be counted on to authorize interventions for themselves or their newborns when these interventions are clearly in the interests of their babies. We believe a *public health policy* for screening and testing of pregnant women and newborns should be guided by this reality, and not by the exceptional circumstance where the identity of interests between mother and infant breaks down.

In the preceding paragraph, we referred specifically to mothers and the identity of interests they share with their offspring. In almost all cases, it indeed is the mother who is available to be approached about newborn testing and whose consent will be solicited. A further set of questions concerns the weight that should be given to the interests of fathers and the need for or adequacy of paternal consent, in contrast to maternal consent. Currently and for the foreseeable future, programs of newborn screening are de facto programs testing for HIV infection in the mother, not the infant. This fact provides justification for a policy of *maternal* consent that is independent of any argument grounded in a moral account of obligations to respect parental authority. At present, maternal consent for HIV testing of the newborn functions as first-person consent, as well as parental consent. A policy of mandatory newborn screening must show not only why bypassing parental control is justified, but also why mandatory screening of adults without consent is justified. From this perspective, even programs having a policy of *parental* consent are morally problematic, as they admit of the possibility that the HIV status of at least some women would be ascertained without their express consent.

Because of the constitutional issues discussed in Chapter 10, however, we refrain from advocating the adoption of policies that legislatively or otherwise remove fathers altogether from *any* authorization role. Also, we are concerned that the wider interests of women in gender-neutral public policies, especially with regard to issues of parenting, might be undermined in the long run by the precedent of maternal-only policies for HIV testing of newborns. Because in almost all cases it is the mother whose consent will be solicited, we believe that a policy of parental consent with no obligation to approach both parents is, as a practical matter, an acceptable compromise. It must be admitted, however, that rarely—when an involved father insists on the testing of his newborn over the objection of the mother or when health-care providers believe that testing is clearly in the best interests of a particular infant—such a policy could result in the de facto HIV testing of a woman against her will. Even in these circumstances, the policy we propose does not necessarily justify morally, or require legally, the overriding of the mother's preferences. Such (hopefully rare) situations would have to be assessed on a case-by-case basis.

But services are not available

From a public health standpoint, no screening program, even if voluntary, is justified unless it provides tangible benefits. Currently, many women infected with HIV have no meaningful access to either general medical care or specific interventions for the management of HIV disease such as antiviral medications or prophylaxis for *Pneumocystis carinii* pneumonia. Gaps in eligibility for Medicaid, constraints on Medicaid coverage and reimbursement levels, and the absence of specialized medical services are significant problems. Also, it is increasingly being argued that HIV-positive pregnant women are being denied access to abortion services, treatment for HIV infection, and involvement in clinical trials.[15] Problems of access to services occur as well for newborns, and access to adequate social services for both mothers and babies, especially drug treatment and family support services, are also woefully inadequate.

Why, then, recommend that health providers inform women about the availability of HIV testing if there is no guarantee of treatment? We believe that to do otherwise is to compound the moral problem of unjust access and de facto rationing of treatments, with the further moral wrong of deceiving or misleading those for whom such treatments are difficult to secure. Women need to know that adults and children infected with HIV can benefit from medical intervention. They also need to know about obstacles they might face in attempting to secure these benefits for themselves or their children.

Is not a "targeted" program more appropriate?

As discussed in Chapter 2, HIV infection in women and children is a highly focal epidemic. It occurs disproportionately in poor women and children of color living in the inner cities of a few metropolitan areas. Would it not be more appropriate to target information and screening resources where there is the highest concentration of infection?

We reject a targeted policy for several reasons. Basing the offering of testing to pregnant women on an assessment of individual risk factors has been shown to be inefficient for both hepatitis and HIV infection.[16] As a result, targeting must be based on proxies for individual risk such as sociodemographic criteria. Targeting by sociodemographic criteria is, however, invidiously discriminatory on its face. Unlike certain genetic conditions, there is no biologic basis for targeting HIV programs by ethnicity. Although our program calls for only informing women about the HIV epidemic and the availability of testing, and although all testing is to be voluntary, targeting this program to only poor women of color would send the false and dangerous message that, among women, only persons of this ethnic and class description are at risk for HIV infection. Moreover, it labels all such women—the overwhelming majority of whom are not and never will be infected—as sources of contagion. That groups identified as "carrying the virus" for AIDS suffer discrimination, social prejudice, and hardship has been well documented with regard to gay men. Poor women and children of color already suffer these burdens disproportionately. Thus to add the stigma of AIDS contagion to poor women of color is to further harm a group of persons who already are unfairly disadvantaged.

Targeting based on community prevalence rates, rather than on sociodemographic criteria, also is morally problematic. Substantial efficiency is not likely to occur unless high-prevalence areas are narrowly defined. The more narrow this definition, the greater the potential that community prevalence rates will become merely thinly veiled proxies for ethnicity and poverty. Targeting by prevalence rates would also place an inappropriate burden on women in low-prevalence areas who have risk factors for HIV infection and for whom testing may be of benefit. Absent a policy such as the one we propose, these women may be unaware either of being at increased risk or of how to obtain testing. Certain women, such as migrant workers, might be particularly ill served.

There are also public health arguments against targeting. As noted previously, targeting may serve to create or reinforce in women outside the targeted group the dangerous view that they are invulnerable to HIV. Targeting thus could undermine the public health objective of universal adoption of safer sex and drug use practices. In addition, informing women about the HIV epidemic is of value in all areas of the country. There is some reason to suspect that the current epidemiologic pattern of HIV infection among women and children may be shifting.[17] An informed public is our best defense against today's low-prevalence community becoming tomorrow's newest area of outbreak. Of particular concern are communities with significant drug use problems but as yet no significant HIV infection.

It might be argued that in rejecting targeting, we have failed to understand what justice requires in the case of poor and minority women. Specifically, in this instance, justice may require not equal treatment but the provision of greater benefits to the worst-off members of society. Targeting, because it is more efficient, would presumably provide greater benefits to the women in the program. In order for this claim to be sustained, however, it would first have to be established that the benefits to poor women of color of a targeted program outweigh the harms of stigma and labeling discussed earlier. Given our nation's unfortunate history with regard to the treatment of minorities, women, and the poor, it is not surprising that some read in a policy of targeting not a desire to do good but an agenda of genocide.

Perhaps the two best arguments in favor of targeting are the problems of nondiagnostic or falsely positive results associated with testing in low-prevalence areas and the attendant costs incurred by an expanded program. In low-prevalence areas, more test results will be falsely positive.[18] As a practical matter, the false-positive issue can be accommodated by requiring a confirmatory test on a separate blood sample before disclosing the results to patients. Nondiagnostic results also should not pose significant problems. Nondiagnostic results have been found not to be associated with HIV infection in a large group of blood donors from a region of the country with a very low prevalence of HIV infection.[19] It appears that nondiagnostic results, in the absence of known risk behaviors, are not associated with HIV-1 infection in such communities. Because the ambiguity surrounding nondiagnostic results may cause women some lingering anxiety, women living in low-prevalence communities should be informed about this problem in advance of testing.

The cost issue is more complex. Embedded in our policy are at least three distinct "cost centers," each of which has different implications from the perspective of allocation of resources and related issues of comparative justice. The first set of costs are those required by our position that all pregnant women and new mothers should be informed about the HIV epidemic, the specific issues related to perinatal transmission, and the availability of HIV antibody testing for themselves and their infants. Let us call these the "education costs." Second, there are the costs associated with counseling and testing; all women who express an interest in testing are to receive personal pretest counseling, and all women who are tested are to receive personal posttest counseling. Finally, there are the costs entailed by our position that all women who test HIV-positive and all infants of mothers found to be HIV-positive should receive appropriate medical and social services. Let us call this third set of costs the "treatment costs."

We view both the education costs and the treatment costs of our policy as unproblematic. Assuming that most health-care providers elect to discharge their education obligations under this policy through the use of educational materials, the costs of informing women can be estimated at between $1 and $4 per woman. Assuming that there are approximately 3.6 million pregnant women each year, the annual national cost for this component of our policy would range from $3.6 to $14 million. We view this (comparatively) small expenditure as justifiable, even given the uncertainties associated with the likelihood and magnitude of the benefits to be derived from this kind of education.

By contrast, the costs of providing medical and social services to the women and infants found to be HIV-positive will be substantial.[20] By finding new cases of HIV infection earlier than they would otherwise come to the attention of medical and social services professionals, our policy certainly will increase the overall national expenditure for caring for people with HIV infection. Early identification of HIV infection is not likely to be cost saving to the health-care system because of the new financial burden of prophylactic treatment. In the case of infected women and infants, most of whom are not in the work force, there are few offsetting reductions in disability or sick days to put against the increased costs of prophylactic treatment.

Because many women and infants who are HIV-positive are economically disadvantaged and cannot afford to pay for medical and social services, our policy will add especially to the costs borne by federal and state sources.[21] Although the issue of what medical services should be provided to the poor remains unresolved, we are hard pressed to imagine how any defensible package claiming to provide a "decent" or an "adequate" level of health care to the poor would fail to include medically necessary treatment for HIV-infected women and their children. In our view, it is morally unconscionable to argue against our policy on the ground that, because it will identify persons in need of services they ought to receive, the policy is too costly. Although the discussion thus far has focused on medical services, our position applies as well to needed social services.

By contrast, it is with regard to the costs of counseling and testing that our policy indeed is vulnerable to criticism on allocation grounds. These costs can be only roughly approximated. Key unknowns include the percentage of pregnant women who will elect to be tested and whether the level of interest in testing will differ by community prevalence rates.[22]

One intent of our recommendations specific to education (Tables 14.1 and 14.2) and pretest counseling is to provide women with sufficient information to make their own judgments about whether HIV testing is in their best interests. It is likely that often, although by no means always, women will agree with many medical and public health professionals that testing is prudent in the face of known or uncertain risk factors and otherwise largely unnecessary. The empirical evidence is mixed with regard to the level of interest in HIV testing among pregnant women who have risk factors or who live in communities with a higher prevalence of HIV infection. Some studies suggest that the majority of women who are geographically or behaviorally at increased risk do, indeed, volunteer for testing. No data are available as to how likely women who do not have personal risk factors or who live in low-prevalence communities are to elect to be tested.[23]

Table 14.3 presents rough estimates of the costs of the prenatal counseling and testing component of our policy. Depending on the rate of testing of women with and without risk factors, these costs range from a low of approximately $20 million to a high of $67 million. The upper bound for costs is most sensitive to the proportion of women without risk factors who elect to be tested; if this proportion were to increase, costs would escalate. Similarly, the lower bound for costs is most sensitive to the proportion of women with risk factors who elect to

TABLE 14.3.   Costs of Counseling and Treating[a]

		"At risk" women[b] (N = 720,000)		
		Percentage electing to be tested		
"Other" women[c] (N = 2,880,000)		40	60	90
Percentage electing to be tested	5	$19,844,000	$26,756,000	$37,124,000
	15	31,884,000	38,796,000	49,164,000
	30	49,944,000	56,856,000	67,223,000

Note: This table does not include the costs of counseling new mothers and testing newborns.

[a]Costs of counseling and testing for HIV-negative women estimated at $43; costs of counseling, testing, and retesting for positive women estimated at $100.

[b]Assumes that (1) 20 percent of pregnant women have a risk factor for HIV infection, and (2) a seroprevalence rate of 5 percent among women with risk factors.

[c]Assumes a seroprevalence rate of .05 percent among women without risk factors.

be tested; if this proportion were to decrease, costs would be reduced. To place these cost estimates in some context, the president's budget request for fiscal year 1991 for total federal spending on HIV information, education, and preventive services is $565 million, much of which is earmarked for counseling and testing.[24] In fiscal year 1989, $64.9 million in state-only funds was spent on HIV education and information and an additional $46.3 million on testing and counseling.[25]

The cost of the screening program could be reduced by restricting the offering of testing to pregnant women and new mothers residing in high-prevalence areas, where, presumably, more women with risk factors reside. Substantial cost savings are not likely to occur, however, unless high-prevalence areas are narrowly defined. As noted earlier, the more narrow this definition, the greater the potential for social divisiveness and invidious targeting.

It cannot be denied that the cost of the policy we are proposing is substantial. Moreover, it must be assumed that this policy will not pay for itself. If such a program should go forward, it is not because it is cost saving but because it is beneficial and right to do so.

Underlying the question of whether our policy represents a good use of funds are seemingly intractable macroallocation issues concerning how best to distribute limited resources. How even to frame the question is problematic. Should we be comparing the worthiness of implementing our policy with the worthiness of implementing other HIV-related interventions that are currently unfunded or underfunded? Alternatively, is the relevant comparison unfunded or underfunded interventions that could improve the prospects for pregnant women and newborns in areas other than HIV disease? Or should we be arguing that the baseline assumption of limited resources that underlies such comparisons is itself ethically unacceptable, and that the proper response is a redirection of societal resources from other social institutions and from personal accumulation of wealth to increased health and welfare services?

At a programmatic level, how the costs of our policy would be financed affects how the allocation and justice issues should be framed. If, for example, the costs of our policy are to be paid primarily by federal and state funds that are currently earmarked for the financing of HIV education and testing, this suggests a different kind of comparative analysis from the scenario in which the costs are borne primarily by a combination of third-party payers. Alternatively, if the costs of our proposed policy are to be financed primarily through new appropriations targeted specifically for this purpose, the relevance of questions of justness in allocation is less clear.

We cannot presume to suggest to every jurisdiction in the nation how resources ought to be allocated. The hierarchy of unmet needs varies widely across the country, as does the political backdrop against which allocation decisions must be made. We recognize that some states may choose to concentrate their resources on other interventions, and that such allocation decisions may be just and right. What would be unjust, based on the arguments presented above, is for any state to structure programs in such a way as to explicitly or implicitly target poor women or children of color. In most instances, we believe the prudent course will be the creation of statewide programs in which all women are informed about the HIV epidemic and the availability of testing. As noted in recommendation 3, the intensity of the educational effort—for example, whether this information is communicated by printed material or personal discussion—properly may vary by the significance of HIV infection and drug use in local communities.

Are confidentiality and antidiscrimination protections sufficient?

Some might argue that we should not advocate even informing women about HIV testing until uniformly applicable protections for confidential HIV medical information and effective laws to deter and compensate for discrimination on the basis of HIV infection are in place. Because we are not optimistic about the speedy enactment of all such legal protections, we have refrained from making our policy recommendations conditional on the existence of a full complement of laws and protections. At minimum, however, we have insisted that women be informed of limits on confidentiality, associated social risks, available antidiscrimination protections (or the absence thereof), and the availability of anonymous testing services.

We do wish to underscore the priority we place on our confidentiality and antidiscrimination recommendation (10). As noted in Chapter 8, confidentiality protections alone are inadequate for two reasons. First, the financial and emotional costs of litigation constitute substantial impediments to enforcement, individuals often suffer the effects of disclosures of which they are unaware, and litigation is not likely to be a realistic or timely alternative for poor women or for parents of HIV-infected infants who are at risk of immediate economic and social discrimination. Second, not all disclosures of medical information are avoidable, and not all instances of public discovery of a person's HIV status are a result of a breach of a duty of confidentiality. No health-care or social service institution can guarantee absolute anonymity, nor should individuals be forced to rely on self-imposed secrecy to protect themselves against discriminatory and unfair treatment.

Uniformity of confidentiality and antidiscrimination policies serves an important function in the process of obtaining informed consent to testing. The flow of medical information is not restricted to the state in which it is generated. HIV information obtained in one state under one set of legal expectations may end up in other states—for example, due to the need for research collaboration or for insurance reimbursement. In the absence of uniform policies of confidentiality and antidiscrimination, counselors and decision makers lack a dependable basis for an informed assessment of the nature and extent of the social risks involved.

It should be emphasized that the implementation of the confidentiality and antidiscrimination policies discussed in recommendation 10 should not be viewed as an acceptable substitute for a requirement of informed consent. Although the lack of such protections, when coupled with nonvoluntary screening requirements, increases the potential for harmful consequences and makes such programs especially odious, we conclude that even with legal protections in place, the social risks remain considerable and the case for individual decision making retains its moral importance.

The perspective of women in the community

The Women's Action Committee of the AIDS Coalition to Unleash Power has criticized researchers and policymakers for proposing and implementing HIV screening of women of reproductive age without consulting women from the affected communities and their advocates.[26] It is admittedly often difficult, but always prudent and appropriate, to involve those affected by proposed policies in the formation of those policies. In developing our policy recommendations, we discussed HIV testing in group sessions with poor African-American and white women receiving prenatal care at the Hopkins Hospital Obstetrical Clinic; in addition, several of us interviewed more than 50 clinic patients about their opinions regarding HIV testing. Although these exchanges with clinic patients were not in themselves determinative of our policy recommendations, learning about the experiences, opinions, and policy preferences of these women—who are among those likely to be most affected by the policy—significantly advanced our understanding of the policy problems. We also discussed policy options with advocates for African-American and Hispanic women, as well as representatives of state and city health departments. We did not meet with disadvantaged Hispanic women or with women who are not demographically at increased risk of HIV infection.

Looking Toward the Future

Our policy recommendations depend critically on numerous assumptions about the state of current testing technology and the availability and nature of effective medical interventions. In the future, some of these assumptions are likely to change in ways that might materially affect our policy position. First, we consider the impact of changes in neonatal testing and intervention; second, we consider the issues raised by new developments in prenatal testing and intervention.

Neonatal developments

One change in the situation of newborns would involve a substantial and established improvement in the medical interventions available to newborns with no change in the current testing technology. Most plausibly, the intervention would be administered only after it is established that an infant is HIV-infected, either by a diagnostic test not suitable for population screening or by the development of an HIV-related condition. Neonatal testing would identify a high-risk group for diagnostic and clinical follow-up and thus would permit the intervention to be employed at the earliest possible point. It is also possible, however, that interventions would have to be administered to all newborns found to be HIV-positive before it is possible to distinguish which infants are truly infected.

As in the current situation, the prospect of medical benefit to affected infants would have to be weighed against the risk of medical harm to unaffected infants, the risk of social harm to all infants and new mothers, and the invasion of maternal privacy that follows from newborn testing being de facto testing of all new mothers. If the benefits to infected newborns were substantial enough—at the extreme, offering a reasonable prospect of cure—more aggressive public health policies, including, for example, a policy of routine screening with notification of a parental right to refuse, would be morally permissible, provided that access to the treatment intervention was guaranteed and adequate antidiscrimination and confidentiality policies were in place.

A reliable neonatal test that would distinguish between infected and uninfected infants would greatly change the shape of the issues. Even if no new medical interventions were available, the new situation would be one in which both classes of infants stand to benefit by testing. Those infants who are actually infected could take advantage of the medical benefits already available, and those infants who are not infected would be freed from the potential stigmatization associated with being born of an HIV-positive mother (if the mother's status is publicly known). In addition, testing would now be specific to the infant, not derivative from biologic information about the mother. HIV status would be revealed for only a minority of HIV-infected mothers. For these reasons, the affront to maternal privacy posed by a mandatory newborn testing policy would be substantially reduced.

The potential for medical benefit already available for infants whose HIV status is identified early, together with the benefit noninfected infants stand to receive and the fact that one is now testing infants and not mothers (through their infants), makes it reasonable and morally acceptable to consider stronger public health measures, but only under certain conditions. For example, a policy of routine screening with notification of a parental right to refuse might be morally acceptable if access to the medical and social services that justify this more aggressive public health approach were guaranteed. The case for routine screening with the right of parental refusal would be stronger still if the policy was coupled with adequate confidentiality and antidiscrimination protections.

A more straightforward situation would be one involving developments in both newborn testing technology and medical interventions. If, for example, a highly effective and easily administered treatment or cure, with little risk, becomes available, then the prospect of not identifying infants who would benefit would become morally intolerable. In such a case, a policy of mandatory newborn screening would be morally acceptable and perhaps morally preferable, provided that access to the intervention was guaranteed. (Under such circumstances, it would also be morally appropriate to override parental refusal of the intervention.) However, less dramatic improvements in available medical interventions or the development of interventions posing significant risks or involving painful or otherwise difficult administration would recommend a more cautious approach to fully substituting the judgments of public health authorities for those of parents. If a significant number of risks and benefits (to be weighed according to the particular values and ends of parents) remained, we would advocate a policy of routine testing of newborns with parental notification and parental right of refusal, coupled with a requirement of parental consent for treatment.

It is important to recognize that the development of a highly reliable newborn test still may require careful medical monitoring of infants who test negative at birth and are born to HIV-infected mothers. This is because infants infected through intrapartum transmission may test negative at birth.

Medical interventions and prenatal testing

Advances in medical interventions present more complicated issues for prenatal screening than for neonatal screening. The least controversial case is one in which a method of prenatal diagnosis of fetal HIV infection is established as safe and reliable, but there is no method of either preventing maternal–fetal transmission or treating the fetus. This situation makes HIV testing akin to maternal serum alphafetoprotein testing, where an initial blood test is the first step in a diagnostic chain involving invasive follow-up procedures, such as amniocen-

CONCLUSION

tesis, and leading to a decision about abortion or continuation of the pregnancy. On the basis of these facts, there is no justification for any shift in the policy outlined for the current situation.

Another set of cases involves the development of a medical intervention that can substantially benefit the pregnant woman infected with HIV. The impact of the intervention on the fetus could range from a net risk of substantial harm to a net prospect of substantial benefit. If the impact of the intervention on the fetus was unknown or if there were known or suspected appreciable risks to the fetus, any change in the policies we recommend for the current situation would be inappropriate. Indeed, in many respects this *is* the current situation. Both zidovudine therapy and prophylaxis for PCP are arguably of benefit to some HIV-infected pregnant women; the impact on the fetus is unknown.

If, in the future, the best available medical evidence suggested that the risk to the fetus from an intervention that benefits the HIV-positive pregnant woman is minimal (we will address cases where the fetus stands to benefit shortly), a move to a more aggressive screening policy might be appropriate. Certainly, it would be proper to implement a voluntary prenatal screening program involving an explicit medical recommendation to undergo testing and (if HIV-positive) to consent to the intervention, but, again, only if access to the intervention was guaranteed.

A more complicated set of issues emerges with the prospect of medical interventions that can benefit the fetus or newborn but that must be administered either prenatally or immediately after birth. These cases raise the difficult and controversial issue of whether a pregnant woman should ever be compelled to undergo a medical procedure or otherwise have her privacy invaded or her liberty restricted in order to benefit or prevent harm to her fetus or newborn. Under ideal circumstances, in which parents were treated equally without regard to gender, we can imagine situations where it would be morally acceptable to compel a parent or prospective parent to undergo a medical procedure so as to benefit his or her child. A major reason why we are opposed to any policy that identifies pregnancy as a state in which autonomy or privacy rights can be suspended on grounds of fetal protection is precisely that the current background situation is not just—because our society is characterized by widespread gender discrimination and because women in general, and mothers in particular, remain vulnerable to exploitation and mistreatment.

With regard to future scenarios as well as the current situation, we reject an adversarial framing of the issue. There is no reason to expect that adhering to a policy of respecting the right of pregnant women to refuse medical interventions will result in substantial harm to fetuses or newborns. Although there are no empirical data specifically on this point, it is our firm impression, based on clinical experience and conversations with pregnant women, that in almost all instances, pregnant women are eager to accept medical interventions that can improve the prospects for their babies. It is this reality that should guide public policy.

Still, a reminder of how issues of so-called maternal–fetal conflict have been dealt with in recent legal cases illustrates what is at stake in the debate over what policies are morally acceptable. With one significant exception, the judicial trend (as noted in published opinions) has been to support interventions framed in terms of fetal benefit over the objections of pregnant women, with little regard for other factors that weighed in the womens' decisions.[27] Critics of this trend (we believe, correctly) claim that these decisions reflect a public policy in which pregnant women are unique in the extent to which their decisions regarding their medical treatment are not respected.[28] These critics conclude that such a policy treats women as mere vessels for the unborn and thereby fails to show equal respect for their status as autonomous agents.

A public policy that treats the medical decisions of pregnant women differently must be judged against a background in which those singled out for different treatment already lack equality of conditions that enable them to exercise autonomous control over their own lives. Such differential treatment reinforces and entrenches forms of powerlessness and social subordination that undermine women's opportunities for meaningful exercise of their capacity for autonomy. These policies have the power to shape and distort the life prospects of women whose decisional capacities are circumscribed. For these reasons, much more of moral significance is at stake than the initial description of maternal–fetal conflict reveals. Because it ultimately may involve the coercive apparatus of the state for its enforcement, a defensible public policy for maternal screening must be sensitive to a larger constellation of moral considerations than we might deem relevant if all that were at issue were medical judgments presented in a particular clinical case.

This is not to say, however, that there should be no modifications in our policy based on advances in medical interventions for fetuses or newborns. What we find objectionable is a policy of compelling a pregnant woman to be tested or to receive an intervention beneficial to her fetus over her express objection. We can conceive of numerous situations, however, in which a more aggressive public health policy with regard to the conduct of screening would be morally appropriate.

Consider, for example, a very positive scenario in which the intervention would prevent HIV transmission to all or most of the fetuses or newborns who would otherwise be affected, is of therapeutic benefit to pregnant women, and does not place uninfected fetuses or newborns at any appreciable risk. In this fact situation, it would be morally imperative to implement a prenatal screening program involving an explicit medical recommendation to undergo testing and accept treatment (if one is HIV-positive). Although this is perhaps the strongest case for a policy of mandatory prenatal screening, for the reasons cited above we

354 CONCLUSION

view a policy of routine prenatal testing, with prior notification and the right to refuse, as morally preferable. And even here, using legal or other coercion to compel a pregnant woman to be tested or (in the case of a prenatal intervention) to be treated over an express refusal would be morally objectionable. Also, as with screening programs generally, moving from a voluntary to a routine screening policy would be acceptable only if access to the intervention were guaranteed. The justification for the policy would be stronger still if adequate anti-discrimination and confidentiality protections were in place.

One special case not yet addressed is the instance in which an intervention is available that can cure a pregnant woman of her HIV infection. At worst, the intervention would pose only minimal risk to the fetus; at best, it would simultaneously cure the infection in the affected fetus as well as in the pregnant woman. The key issue here is whether infected persons should be compelled to receive curative treatment against their will. In this instance, it seems to us that a woman's being pregnant is irrelevant to how this question should be answered. Following the model used for other communicable diseases, where there is a safe, effective cure and an individual poses a reasonable threat of contagion to others, it is morally justified to compel the individual to receive treatment in order to prevent significant harm to others. It is not likely, however, that compelling the pregnant woman to be treated would be necessary to prevent significant harm to the fetus or newborn. Presumably, an intervention capable of curing the infection in a fetus would work equally well in a newborn. Indeed, from the perspective of the interests of the newborn, it is likely that the best time to administer such a treatment is after birth in order to avoid even a minimal risk of teratogenic or other negative effects. At least at present, there is no reason to suspect that there would be any irreversible sequelae of consequence from the period of untreated infectivity in utero.

Conclusion

In the face of the complex issues and uncertainties that surround HIV infection and diagnosis in pregnant women and infants, any policy proposal is likely to be controversial and in some respects unsatisfactory. We have presented the 10 core elements of a policy that we believe represents the best compromise among competing interests and social goals. In addition, we have discussed some of the desiderata that would be relevant for revising these recommendations.

We do not expect our policy recommendations to have any immediate or isolated effect on HIV transmission rates. It is unrealistic to expect any program of information about HIV infection and the availability of testing by itself to affect transmission rates, let alone a program directed at women, given the history of inequality of power and the legacy of sexual subordination that all too often still characterize relations between men and women in our society. We do believe, however, that educational programs can make a difference. With regard to smoking, it has been established that while individual educational efforts were largely ineffective, the cumulative impact of multiple educational efforts in what amounted to a sustained national antismoking campaign dramatically altered cultural values and reduced the prevalence of smoking.[29] Hopefully, over time, our nation will have a similar experience with HIV infection.

Nevertheless, a comprehensive policy response to controlling the HIV epidemic requires a broader focus than we have adopted here. HIV disease in women and children is a disease of families and, as noted above, is intimately connected to relations between men and women. Any comprehensive policy must address the needs and interests of men as well as those of women and must address the root of the problem of HIV infection in women—drug dependence and the poverty and social isolation that make the use of drugs attractive. Without adequate drug rehabilitation services, and without social policies and programs that can empower both disadvantaged women and men to break the cycle of poverty that links them to drug use, policies of public information and the availability of HIV testing cannot be expected to affect significantly the pace of the HIV epidemic.

Notes

Excerpts from this chapter appear as Working Group on HIV Testing of Pregnant Women and Newborns, "HIV Infection, Pregnant Women, and Newborns," *Journal of the American Medical Association* 264 (1990): 2416–2420.

1. K. Krasinski, W. Borkowsky, D. Bebenroth et al., "Failure of Voluntary Testing for HIV to Identify Infected Parturient Women in a High Risk Population," *New England Journal of Medicine* 318 (1988): 185; Mark Gevisser, "Women and Children First," *Village Voice,* October 31, 1989, p. 18.
2. *Guidelines for Perinatal Care,* 2nd ed. (1988); American College of Obstetricians and Gynecologists, *Human Immune Deficiency Virus Infections,* ACOG Technical Bulletin, no. 123 (Washington, D.C.: American College of Obstetricians and Gynecologists, December 1988); Secretary's Work Group on Pediatric HIV Infection and Disease, Final Report, Department of Health and Human Services, November 18, 1988; American Academy of Pediatrics Task Force on Pediatric AIDS, "Perinatal Human Immunodeficiency Virus Infection," *Pediatrics* 82 (1988): 941–944; U.S. Public Health Service, *Caring for Our Future: The Content of Prenatal Care,* A Report of the Public Health Service Expert Panel on the Content of Prenatal Care (Washington, D.C.: Public Health Service, 1989).
3. R. Bayer, "Perinatal Transmission of HIV Infection: The Ethics of Prevention," in *AIDS and the Health Care System,* ed. L. O. Gostin (New Haven, Conn.: Yale University Press, 1990), 62–73; American College of Obstetricians and Gynecologists, *Prevention of Human Immune Deficiency Virus Infection and Acquired Immune Deficiency Syndrome,* ACOG Committee Statement, no. 53 (Wash-

ington, D.C.: American College of Obstetricians and Gynecologists, 1987), 1–4; Centers for Disease Control, "Recommendations for Assisting in the Prevention of Perinatal Transmission of HTLV-III/LAV and Acquired Immunodeficiency Syndrome," *Morbidity and Mortality Weekly Report* 34 (1985): 721–731.

4. Nan D. Hunter, *Report of the American Civil Liberties Union AIDS Project* (New York: New York American Civil Liberties Union, 1990).

5. Bayer, "Perinatal Transmission of HIV Infection."

6. Adrienne Asch, "Reproductive Technology and Disability," in *Reproductive Laws for the 1990's,* ed. Sherrill Cohen and Nadine Taub (Clifton, N.J.: Humana Press, 1989), 69–107.

7. K. E. Warner, "Cigarette Smoking in the 1970's: The Impact of the Antismoking Campaign on Consumption," *Science* 211 (1981): 729–731.

8. See references to discussions of the constitutionality of HIV testing and related practices in note 6, Chapter 7 of this volume.

9. See Laurence H. Tribe, *American Constitutional Law* (Mineola, N.Y.: Foundation Press, 1988), 1439–1450.

10. The equal protection clause of the Fourteenth Amendment provides in part that "no state shall make or enforce any law which shall . . . deny to any person within its jurisdiction the equal protection of the laws."

11. See Chapter 7 of this volume, where Anita Allen concludes that equal protection objections may be the most difficult constitutional challenges to sustain, despite the powerfully persuasive arguments for invoking the equal protection doctrine as a bar to targeted screening practices. She notes, first, that while the focus on testing during pregnancy is necessarily on women, courts have not been persuaded that discrimination on the basis of pregnancy is equivalent to discrimination on the basis of gender. A second problem is that while prenatal HIV testing may have a disproportionate impact on disadvantaged racial minorities, no violation of the equal protection clause will be found unless there is proof of discriminatory intent motivating the targeted program as well.

12. The Fourth Amendment provides for a "right of the people to be secure in their persons . . . against unreasonable searches and seizures."

13. The reasonableness of a privacy intrusion under the Fourth amendment is judged by balancing "the nature and quality of the intrusion on the individual's fourth amendment interest . . . against the importance of the governmental interest alleged to justify the intrusion" (*O'Connor* v. *Ortega,* 480 U.S. 709, 719 [1966]).

14. *Thornburgh* v. *American College of Obstetrics and Gynecology,* 476 U.S. 747 (1986).

15. See, for example, Public Health Consortium for New York City, "The Undeclared Women's Health Crisis in New York City," May 10, 1980.

16. P. R. Summers, M. J. Biswas, J. G. Pastorek, et al., "The Pregnant Hepatitis B Carrier: Evidence Favoring Comprehensive Antepartum Screening," *Obstetrics and Gynecology* 69 (1987): 701–704; Marguerite Barbacci, Gina A. Dallabetta, John Repke et al., "HIV Screening in an Inner City Pre-Natal Population" presented at the 29th Annual Meeting of the Interscience Conference on Antimicrobial Agents and Chemotherapy, Los Angeles, October 24, 1988.

17. Personal communication, Tim Dondero, HIV Seroepidemiology Branch, Centers for Disease Control (May 1990).

18. See, for example, M. J. Barry, A. G. Mulley, and D. E. Singer, "Screening for HTLV-III Antibodies: The Relation Between Prevalence and Positive Predictive Val-

ue and Its Social Consequences" (letter), *Journal of the American Medical Association* 253 (1985): 3395, and J. R. Carlson, M. L. Bryant, S. H. Hinrichs et al., "AIDS Serology Testing in Low and High-Risk Groups," *Journal of the American Medical Association* 253 (1985): 3405–3408.

19. J. B. Jackson, K. L. McDonald, J. Cadwell et al., "Absence of HIV Infection in Blood Donors with Indeterminate Western Blot Tests for Antibody to HIV-1," *New England Journal of Medicine* 322 (1990): 217–222.

20. The cost of medical (not social) services necessary to care for patients who are HIV-positive is increasing as we develop prophylactic treatments for asymptomatic individuals. A two-phase model has been proposed to estimate the medical costs of caring for HIV-positive individuals. The annual pretreatment costs (including monitoring through periodic clinical and laboratory exams but not including pharmacologic intervention) are estimated to be $854 per person. The annual treatment costs, which include AZT and PCP prophylaxis, are estimated to be $9,637 per person. The average total costs for in-patient care from the time of AIDS diagnosis until death range from about $50,000 to $150,000. The U.S. Public Health Service has estimated that the direct cost of care for the 174,000 AIDS patients projected to be alive in 1991 will be $8 billion to $16 billion in that year alone.

21. Lower-income women of childbearing age are less likely to have either private or public insurance than is the population as a whole. Thirty-one percent of women aged 15–44 with family incomes below 185 percent of the poverty level have no health insurance. This compares with the general level of uninsurance of 12.9 percent in the U.S. population. These women are more likely to have Medicaid. Twenty-nine percent of women of childbearing age with family incomes less than 185 percent of the poverty level are covered by Medicaid, compared with 8.7 percent of the general population with such coverage. Recent changes in federal law (the 1988 Omnibus Budget Reconciliation Act) permit states to cover pregnant women and infants with family incomes of up to 185 percent of the federal poverty level, and 1989 changes *mandate the coverage of pregnant women and infants with incomes up to 133 percent of the poverty level.* These women are also much less likely to have private health insurance (40 percent compared with 75 percent of the general population). Unless there is a major reform in the financing of care associated with HIV disease (as proposed by the Institute of Medicine), our current system of health-care financing will be called on to bear the burden. The changes that have already been implemented in the financing of care associated with HIV disease apply only to people who have private health insurance (i.e., Consolidated Omnibus Reconciliation Act [COBRA] coverage has been expanded from 18 to 29 months, at which time people who are ill can qualify for Medicare disability coverage. Some states are offering to pay the COBRA premiums for those who cannot afford them). Therefore, to the extent that pregnant women who are HIV-positive are neither sick nor covered by private health insurance, such changes do not apply to them.

For the 29 percent of low-income women who have or are eligible for Medicaid, this system is likely to assume the financing of HIV-related services during their pregnancies. For those who are among the 31 million persons who are uninsured, alternative strategies are currently being proposed. Maryland has already adopted the expanded SOBRA option for pregnant women, infants, and children up to age 2. Risk pools have been authorized in 21 states, are operational in 16 of these, and have been proposed in 15 others as a way to provide health insurance for those who are uninsurable because of a preexisting condition (e.g., included would be patients who are

seropositive) and f.. the low-income uninsured. In addition, the prevention component of Medicaid (Early Periodic Screening Detention and Treatment Program
[EPSDT]) has been expanded to allow physicians to do more routine screens. Moreover, if the need for a service is identified during EPSDT screening, Medicaid is
required to pay for it.

Consideration also is being given to the development of financing mechanisms for
poor children *regardless* of whether their parents are insured. Some options include
state-sponsored pools for children from lower-income families or state-supported
comprehensive pediatric clinics.

22. Most studies to date of the direct health-care costs associated with HIV disease have
focused on the costs arising from care in and out of the hospital *for patients with
AIDS*. One study that tried to estimate direct health-care costs for HIV-positive
individuals *excluded* the cost of the initial HIV antibody test and associated counseling precisely because it is difficult to estimate the number of individuals, whether
infected with HIV or not, who will appear for testing. The National Center for Health
Statistics estimates that about 4 million persons have had the HIV antibody test
voluntarily, the vast majority of those tested being in the 18–49 age group. The
proportion of these persons who were women is unknown.

23. Who will pay the costs of testing and counseling is also difficult to specify and
depends, to some degree, on where the test is performed. In states that have prospective, all-payer reimbursement systems, HIV laboratory tests done in hospital clinics
currently go through hospital payment systems and all payers are required to pay. If
testing is done at Title V clinics (for family planning, sexually transmitted diseases)
or at counseling and test sites, all costs, including those of counseling, are picked up
by the state AIDS dollars (full costs of counseling may not now be reimbursed). If
private physicians use state laboratories, the laboratory costs are picked up by state
AIDS dollars. The big unresolved issue is who will pay the cost of counseling in
private physicians' offices. We can establish a partnership of public health and private
sectors, perhaps have state counselors, or look to the maternal serum alpha-fetoprotein model for guidance. However, the majority of women who are at risk for HIV
disease are likely to receive their care in hospital clinics, not private offices.

24. Estimates have been prepared by the ASMB, Department of Health and Human
Services, and Office of Management and Budget.

25. Intergovernmental Health Policy Project, August 1989.

26. Margaret McCarthy, "Calls for HIV Antibody Testing in Women of Reproductive
Age Ignore the Realities of Women's Lives" (unpublished paper) Women's Action
Committee of the AIDS Coalition to Unleash Power, May 1990.

27. For discussion of and citations to cases involving judicial reluctance to respect the
medical decisions of pregnant women, see Alan Meisel, *The Right to Die* (New York:
Wiley, 1989), 110 ff. But see *In re A.C.*——F.2d——(D.C. Cir. April 26, 1990) (en
banc), which held that a pregnant woman has a right to bodily integrity that almost
always outweighs the right of the fetus.

28. See Mary Sue Henifin, Ruth Hubbard, and Judy Norsigian, "Prenatal Screening," in
Cohen and Taub, eds., *Reproductive Laws for the 1990's*, 155–184.

29. Warner, "Cigarette Smoking in the 1970's."

INDEX

Abandoned children, 106, 113–115, 266–267, 281, 341
Abbott Laboratories, 32
Abortion, 70, 72, 74, 77–80, 131, 169–172, 177–181, 189, 192, 194, 198, 209, 211–213, 218, 225, 249, 262, 277–278, 280–281, 286, 296, 302, 306, 318–319, 333–334, 338–339, 343, 352
Abrams, E. J., 55
Access to care, 111–113, 115, 129, 172–175, 178, 333–335, 341–343, 350–352, 354
Acuff, Katherine, 59, 121, 331
Acyclovir, 56
Adams, Raymond D., 325
Adenopathy, 44–45
Adolescents, 55, 276, 302–303
Advisory Committee on Immunization Practices (ACIP), 57, 76–77, 92–93, 133
Africa, 76
African-Americans, 31, 67–68, 70, 78, 84, 87, 89, 96, 106, 129, 132, 180, 195, 208, 309, 311, 314, 317, 325, 349
Agatisa, Patricia, 87
AIDS-related complex (ARC), 39, 44, 115, 166, 172, 188, 191, 194, 239, 275
Akron v. *Akron Center for Reproductive Health,* 306, 327
Alabama, 123, 134–135, 163, 232
Alaska, 24, 93, 135
Alcohol, 51, 101, 103, 106, 170, 175–176, 231, 247
Alferd, Rose, 157
Allan, J. S., 52
Allen, Anita, 166, 249, 331, 356
Allocation of resources, 67, 89, 170–171, 272–273, 345–348
Alpha-fetoprotein (AFP) screening, 73–75, 89, 91–92, 100–101, 123–124, 126–127, 129, 132, 137, 144, 148, 159, 162–163, 170–171, 358
Althouse, Nancy, 149
Altman, Lawrence K., 195
Alvins, A. L., 253

American Academy of Pediatrics (AAP), 65, 85, 89, 128, 133–134, 164
American College of Obstetrics and Gynecology (ACOG), 73–74, 79, 91–92, 128, 130–131, 133–134, 164–165, 355
American Medical Association (AMA), 240, 253
American Public Health Association (APHA), 307, 326
Amish, 263
Amniocentesis, 73, 75, 80, 90–91, 95, 101, 122, 132, 169, 204, 296, 306
Anderson, James, 88
Anderson v. *Strong Memorial Hospital,* 187, 191
Andrews, Lori B., 24, 81, 88, 207, 214, 216
Anencephaly, 72, 91
Annas, George, 84–85, 88, 90–92, 215–217
Antidiscrimination, 221–222, 225–226, 245–247, 333–334, 348–351, 354
Antismoking campaigns, 355–358
Anyane-Yeboa, K., 90
Appelbaum, Paul, 305–306
Areen, Judith, 259, 331
Arevelo, Jose A., 92
Arizona, 24, 88, 124–125, 135–136, 163
Arkansas, 136, 163
Arras, John, 314, 316, 318, 325–326
Asch, Adrienne, 220, 356
Asheld, Barbara, 93
Asian-American, 319
Atkins, Patricia S., 189
Authorizations, 5–6, 10, 85, 125–128, 136, 144, 149, 152, 154, 163, 179–180, 243, 262, 267, 269, 303–305, 342
Autonomy, 4–6, 13, 16–23, 26, 167, 172, 177–180, 183, 188, 200, 206, 210, 225–226, 248–249, 264–265, 270–273, 283, 289–291, 298, 300–301, 304–305, 308, 313–314, 316, 319–320, 324, 337, 341, 352–353. *See also* Freedom; Liberty; Self-determination
Aviles v. *United States,* 183, 191–192, 195

360INDEX

Axnick, N., 82
Azidothymidine. *See* Zidovudine
Azzolino v. Dingfelder, 219–220

Babies. *See* Children; Infants
Bacteremia, 46
Baez v. Rapping, 194
Bagarazzi, M. L., 117
Bailin, Gloria, 90
Balis, F. M., 58
Baltimore, 30–31, 39, 50, 71, 106, 132
Bapat, V., 138
Barbacci, Marguerite, 117, 356
Barin, F., 52
Barlow, M. A., 57
Barry, Michael J., 51, 356
Bartling v. Superior Court of Los Angeles,
  193, 197
Bass, Sue, 325
Bathhouses, 168
Baum, J. D., 300, 306
Bayer, Ronald, 24, 189, 196, 313, 325, 338,
  355–356
BCG vaccine, 48
Beasley, R. Palmer, 92
Beauchamp, Tom L., 24–25, 216, 248–249,
  290–292, 305, 307, 325
Beck, Lewis White, 26
Beeson, Diane, 296, 306
Behets, F., 55
Belair v. Carter, 198
Belman, Anita L., 56
Bender, Daniel R., 163
Beneficence, 13–19, 21–23, 264–265, 269,
  274, 279, 289
Bennett v. Norban, 199
Bennett, Robert, 266, 272–273
Berardi, Victor P., 53, 117, 325
Berman v. Allan, 220
Berns, Donald, 253, 325
Bernstein, Larry, 195
Bernstein, V., 117
Berthaud, Marise, 326
Bessman, Samuel J., 86
Beutler, Ernest, 88
Bias, 67, 174, 284, 292, 296, 303, 305
Bickle, H., 85
Biggar, Robert J., 51
Biotinidase deficiency (BD), 124–125, 132,
  135–139, 142, 147, 150, 155, 160, 162
Bird, David, 306
Biron, Karen, 56
Bisexual, 53, 101, 188, 293
Bishop v. United States, 250
Biswas, Manoj K., 92, 356
Black, Rita B., 306
Blanche, Stephanie, 54–55, 117
Blendon, Robert, 249
Bloodbanks, 183, 191, 236–238
Blumberg, R. S., 52

Blustein, Jeffrey, 272–273
Boggs, Dane R., 88
Boland, M., 117
Bolling v. Sharpe, 194
Bolton, A. E., 91
Borgida, Eugene, 305
Borkowsky, W., 55
Borucki v. Ryan, 198
Bothman, V. B., 272
Bouhasin, J., 118
Bowman, James E., 93
Boyd v. Wynn, 251
Boyer, Barry B., 251
Brain, 46, 53, 71, 86, 159
Brandeis, Louis D., 248
Brandt, Allan, 24, 81–83
Brandt, B. L., 51
Braunwald, Eugene, 325
Breastfeeding, 6, 41, 54, 217
Brennan, William J., 250
Brewer, A. Frank, 83
Bridgham, Bethany, 255
Britton, Ann H., 248
Broadway Books v. Gene Roberts, 193
Brock, D. J. H., 91
Broder, Samuel, 57
Brody, Howard, 210, 219
Broliden, P. A., 55
Brookmeyer, Ron, 51
Brown, Audrey K., 87
Brown, Louise, 158
Brown, W. J., 82
Bryant, Martin L., 51, 357
Bubonic plague, 168, 192
Buck v. Bell, 25, 193, 197
Buck, Billy E., 56–57
Buffalo, 251
Burke, M. D., 51
Burris, Scott, 24, 195
Butz, Arlene, 118

Cadwell, J., 357
Callahan, Daniel, 21, 26
Calvelli, Theresa A., 54
Cambridge, 26, 34, 82, 91, 272, 305
Candidiasis, 43–44, 118
Cao, A., 90
Capron, Alexander Morgan, 206, 213, 216,
  219–220
Carcassi, V., 90
Cardwell v. Bechtal, 272
Carlson, James, R., 51, 357
Carter, Thomas P., 85–86, 91
Casper, Gerhard, 24
Centers for Disease Control (CDC), 29–30,
  42–43, 45, 50–53, 55–57, 63, 83, 101,
  134, 152, 188–189, 194–195, 275, 309,
  315
Central America, 67
Central nervous system (CNS), 44–46, 60, 64